CONTENTS

KAGETO A

A Note from the Author

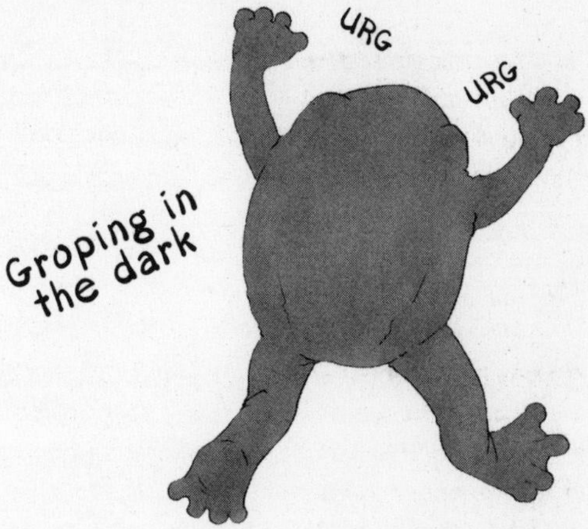
URG
URG
Groping in the dark

Lately, I've been pretty busy. I guess I'm not good at time management. But I think what causes it the most is my personality...I don't plan ahead. (laugh)

Segami

Honorifics Explained

Throughout the Del Rey Manga books, you will find Japanese honorifics left intact in the translations. For those not familiar with how the Japanese use honorifics and, more important, how they differ from American honorifics, we present this brief overview.

Politeness has always been a critical facet of Japanese culture. Ever since the feudal era, when Japan was a highly stratified society, use of honorifics—which can be defined as polite speech that indicates relationship or status—has played an essential role in the Japanese language. When addressing someone in Japanese, an honorific usually takes the form of a suffix attached to one's name (example: "Asuna-san"), or as a title at the end of one's name or in place of the name itself (example: "Negi-sensei," or simply "Sensei!").

Honorifics can be expressions of respect or endearment. In the context of manga and anime, honorifics give insight into the nature of the relationship between characters. Many English translations leave out these important honorifics, and therefore distort the feel of the original Japanese. Because Japanese honorifics contain nuances that English honorifics lack, it is our policy at Del Rey not to translate them. Here, instead, is a guide to some of the honorifics you may encounter in Del Rey Manga.

-san: This is the most common honorific and is equivalent to Mr., Miss, Ms., or Mrs. It is the all-purpose honorific and can be used in any situation where politeness is required.

-sama: This is one level higher than "-san." It is used to confer great respect.

-dono: This comes from the word "tono," which means "lord." It is an even higher level than "-sama" and confers utmost respect.

-kun: This suffix is used at the end of boys' names to express familiarity or endearment. It is also sometimes used by men amongst friends, or when addressing someone younger or of a lower station.

-chan: This is used to express endearment, mostly toward girls. It is also used for little boys, pets, and even among lovers. It gives a sense of childish cuteness.

Bozu: This is an informal way to refer to a boy, similar to the English terms "kid" or "squirt."

Sempai/
Senpai: This title suggests that the addressee is one's senior in a group or organization. It is most often used in a school setting, where under-classmen refer to their upperclassmen as "sempai." It can also be used in the workplace, such as when a newer employee addresses an employee who has seniority in the company.

Kohai: This is the opposite of "sempai" and is used toward under-classmen in school or newcomers in the workplace. It connotes that the addressee is of a lower station.

Sensei: Literally meaning "one who has come before," this title is used for teachers, doctors, or masters of any profession or art.

[blank]: This is usually forgotten in these lists, but it is perhaps the most significant difference between Japanese and English. The lack of honorific means that the speaker has permission to address the person in a very intimate way. Usually, only family, spouses, or very close friends have this kind of permission. Known as yobisute, it can be gratifying when someone who has earned the intimacy starts to call one by one's name without an honorific. But when that intimacy hasn't been earned, it can be very insulting.

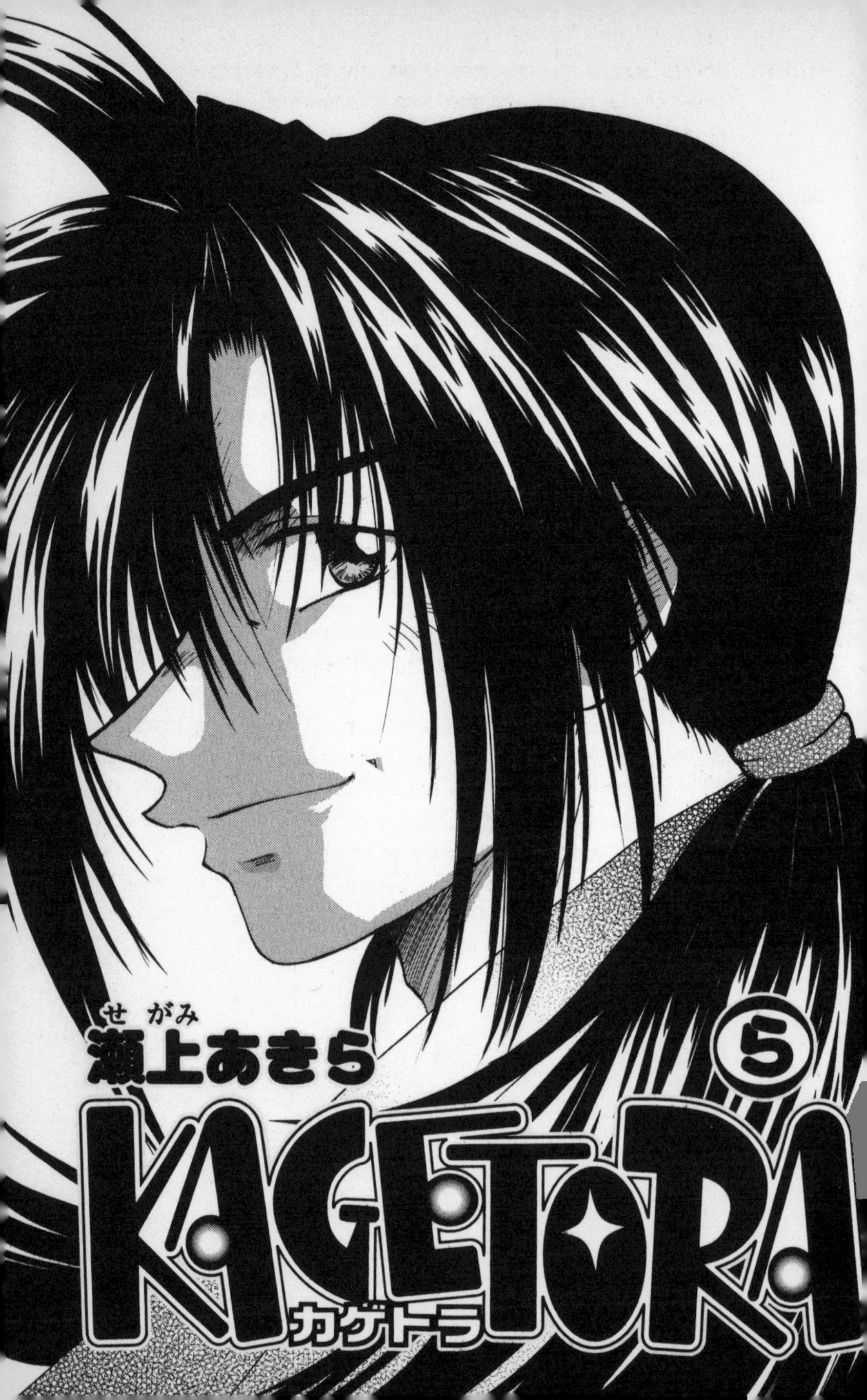
せがみ
瀬上あきら
5
KAGETORA
カゲトラ

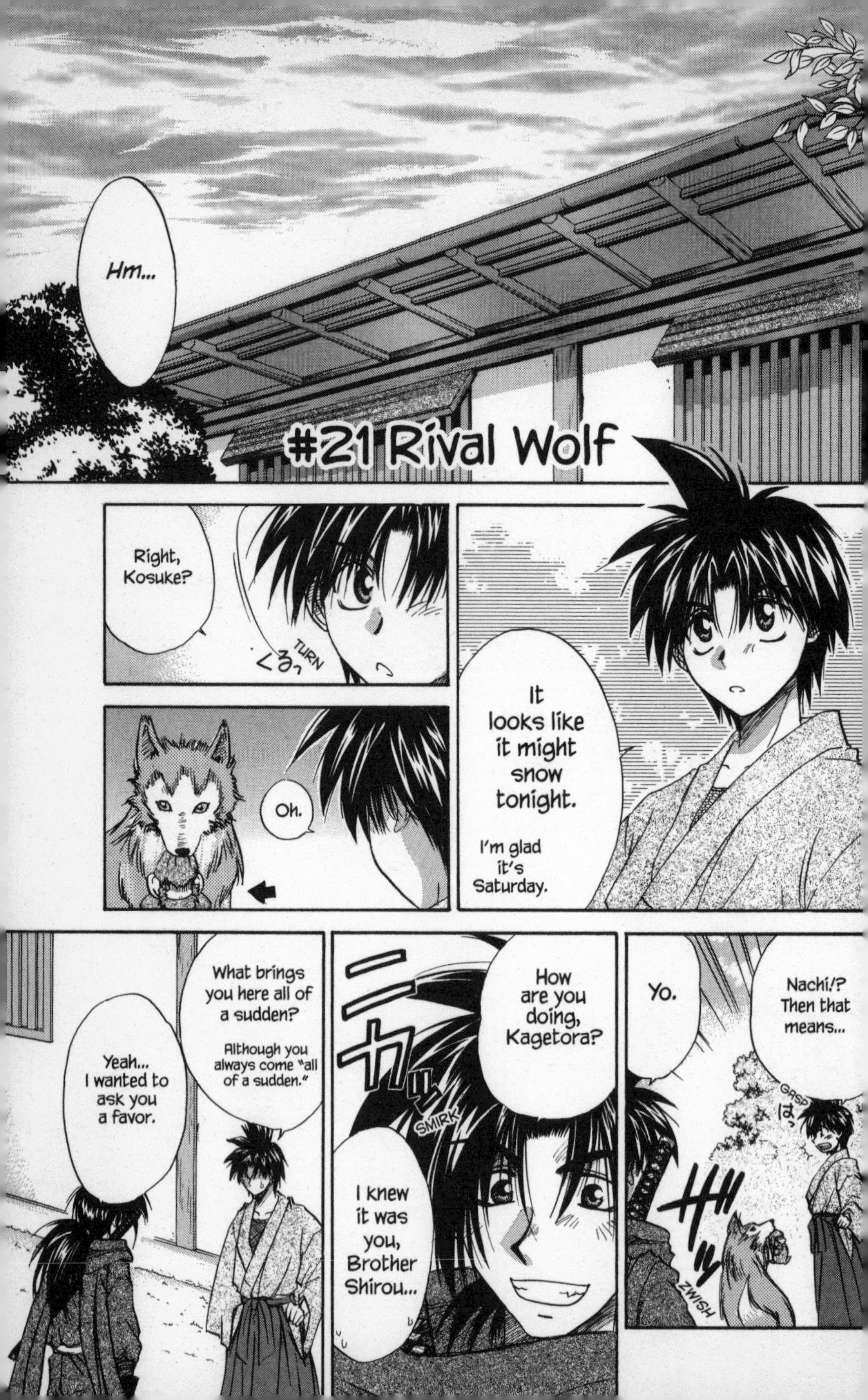
Hm...
#21 Rival Wolf
It looks like it might snow tonight.
I'm glad it's Saturday.
Right, Kosuke?
TURN
Oh.
Nachi!? Then that means...
Yo.
GASP
ZWISH
How are you doing, Kagetora?
SMIRK
I knew it was you, Brother Shirou...
What brings you here all of a sudden?
Although you always come "all of a sudden."
Yeah... I wanted to ask you a favor.

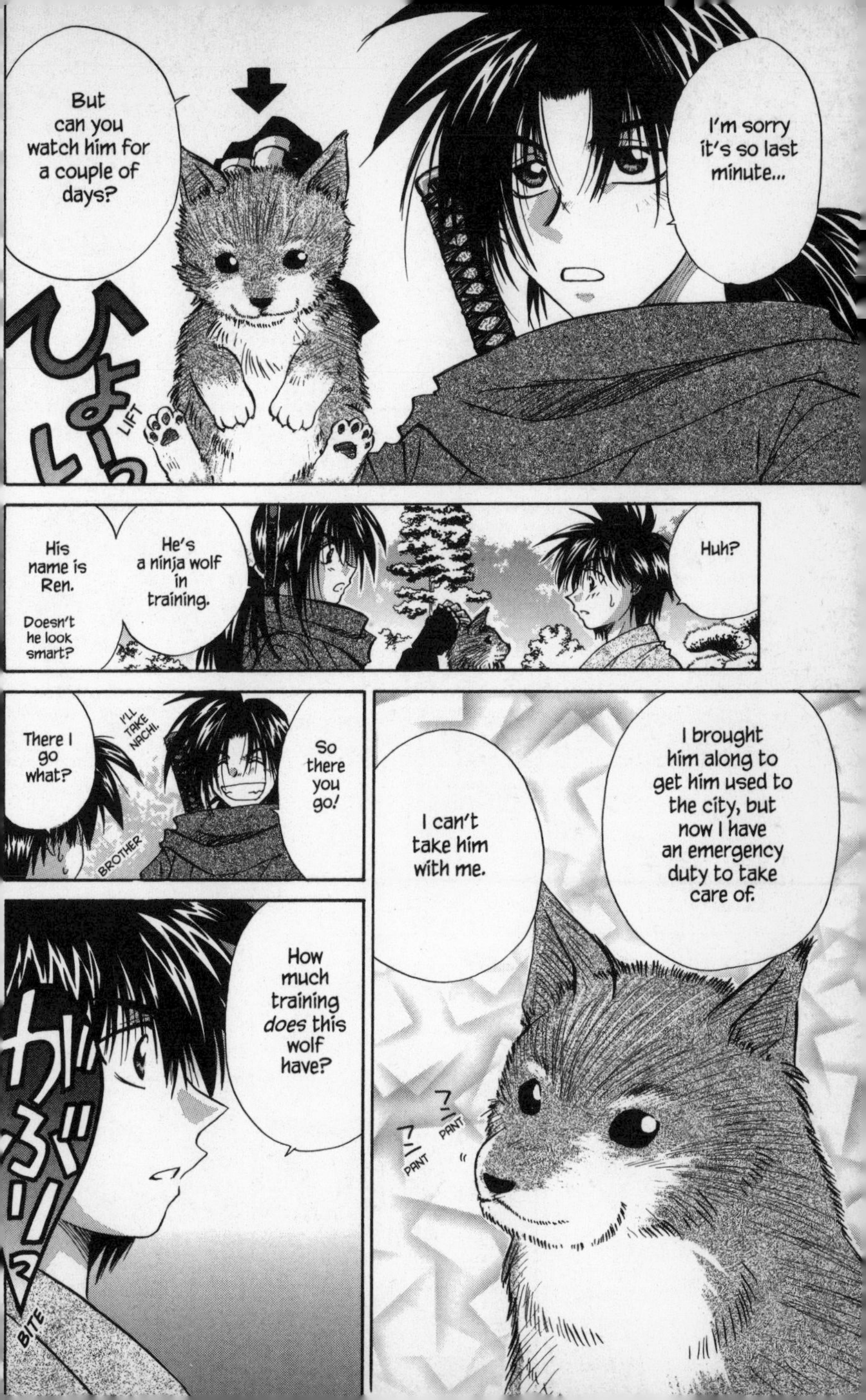

I'm sorry it's so last minute...
But can you watch him for a couple of days?
LIFT
Huh?
He's a ninja wolf in training.
His name is Ren.
Doesn't he look smart?
I brought him along to get him used to the city, but now I have an emergency duty to take care of.
I can't take him with me.
PANT
PANT
So there you go!
I'LL TAKE NACHI.
BROTHER
There I go what?
How much training *does* this wolf have?
BITE

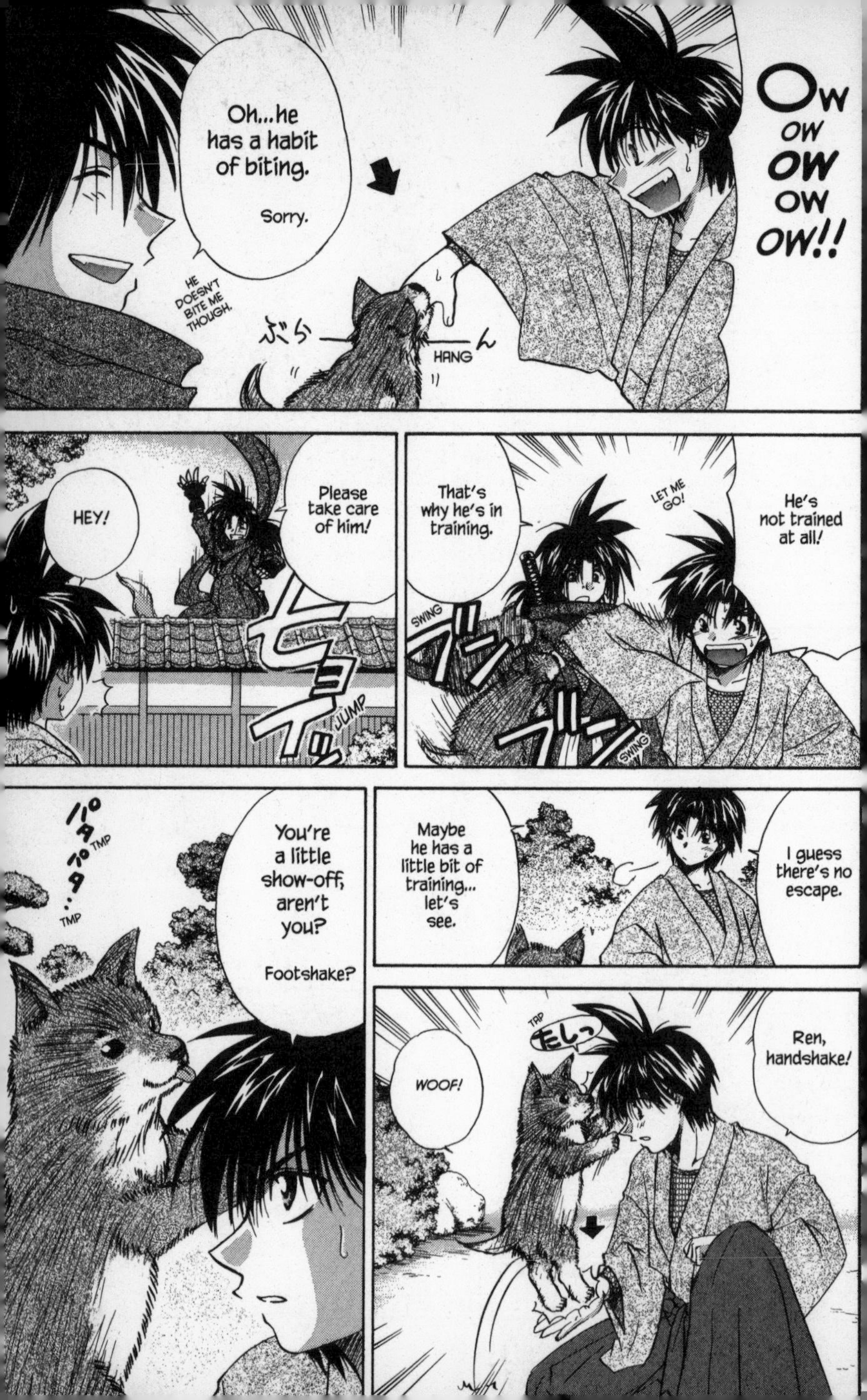
Ow ow OW ow OW!!
Oh...he has a habit of biting.
Sorry.
HE DOESN'T BITE ME THOUGH.
ぶら ん
HANG
He's not trained at all!
LET ME GO!
That's why he's in training.
SWING
SWING
Please take care of him!
HEY!
JUMP
I guess there's no escape.
Maybe he has a little bit of training... let's see.
Ren, handshake!
TRP
WOOF!
You're a little show-off, aren't you?
Footshake?
パタパタ..
TMP
TMP

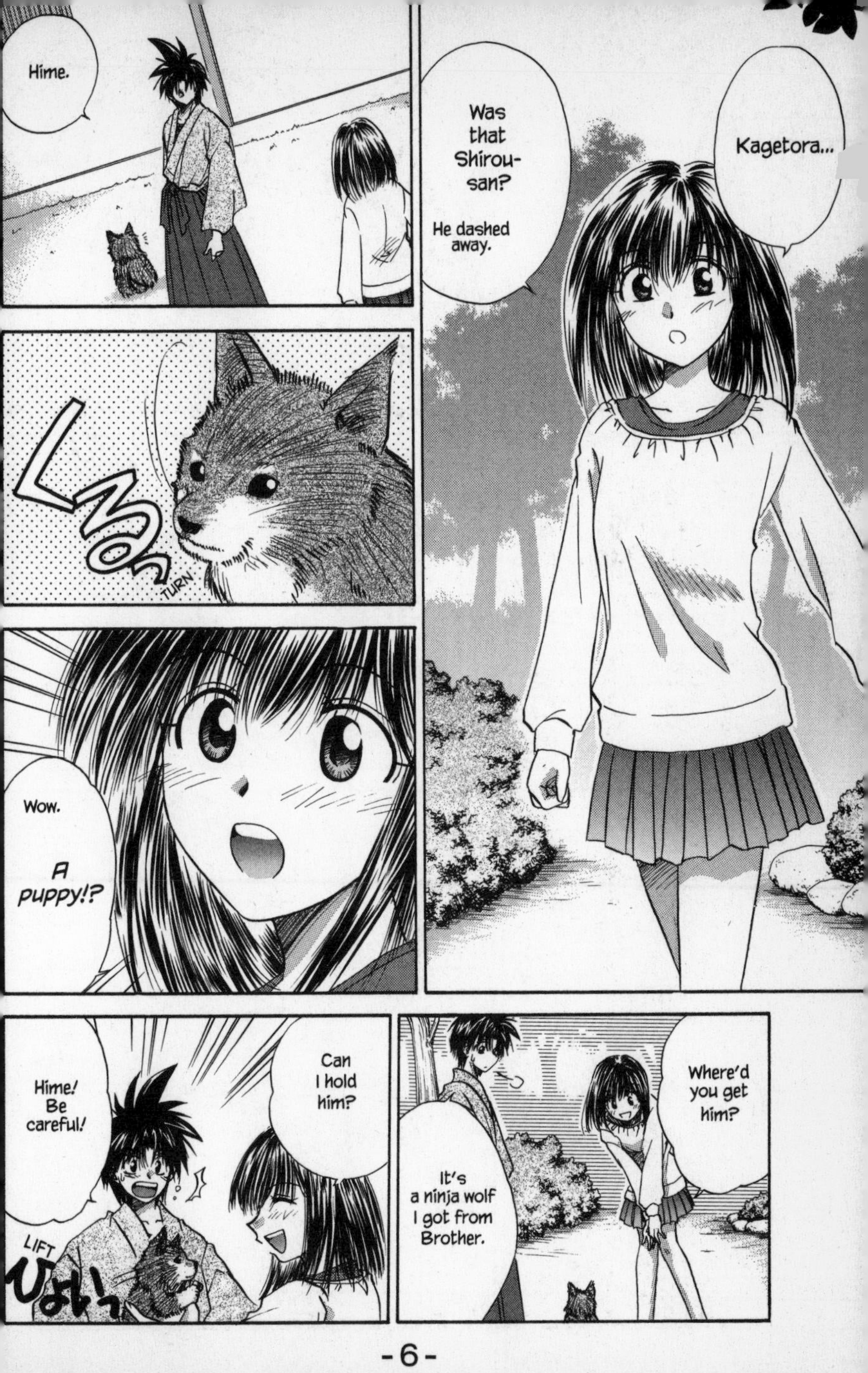
Kagetora...
Was that Shirou-san?
He dashed away.
Hime.
TURN
Wow.
A puppy!?
Where'd you get him?
It's a ninja wolf I got from Brother.
Can I hold him?
Hime! Be careful!
LIFT

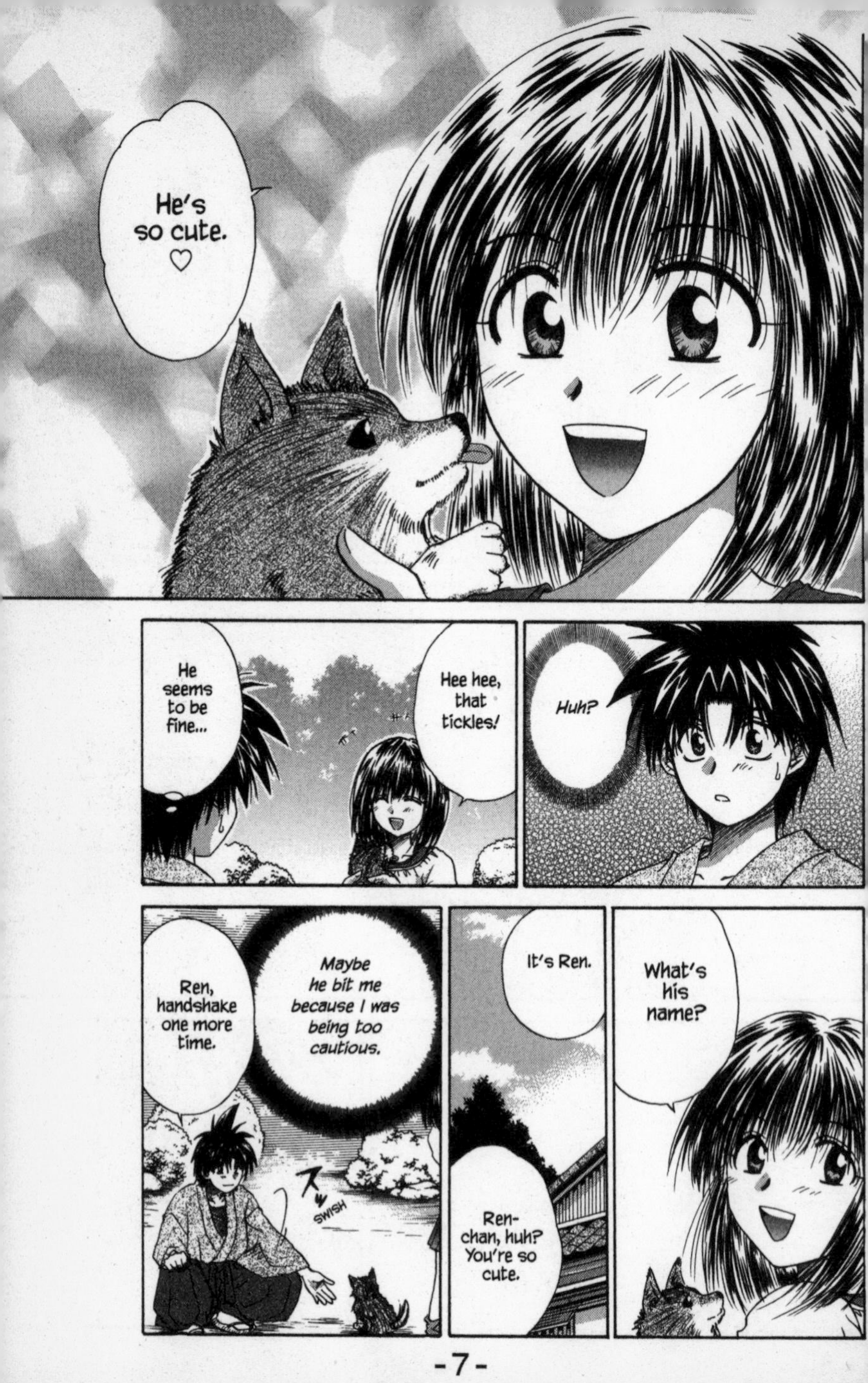
He's so cute. ♡
Huh?
Hee hee, that tickles!
He seems to be fine...
What's his name?
It's Ren.
Ren-chan, huh? You're so cute.
Maybe he bit me because I was being too cautious.
Ren, handshake one more time.
SWISH

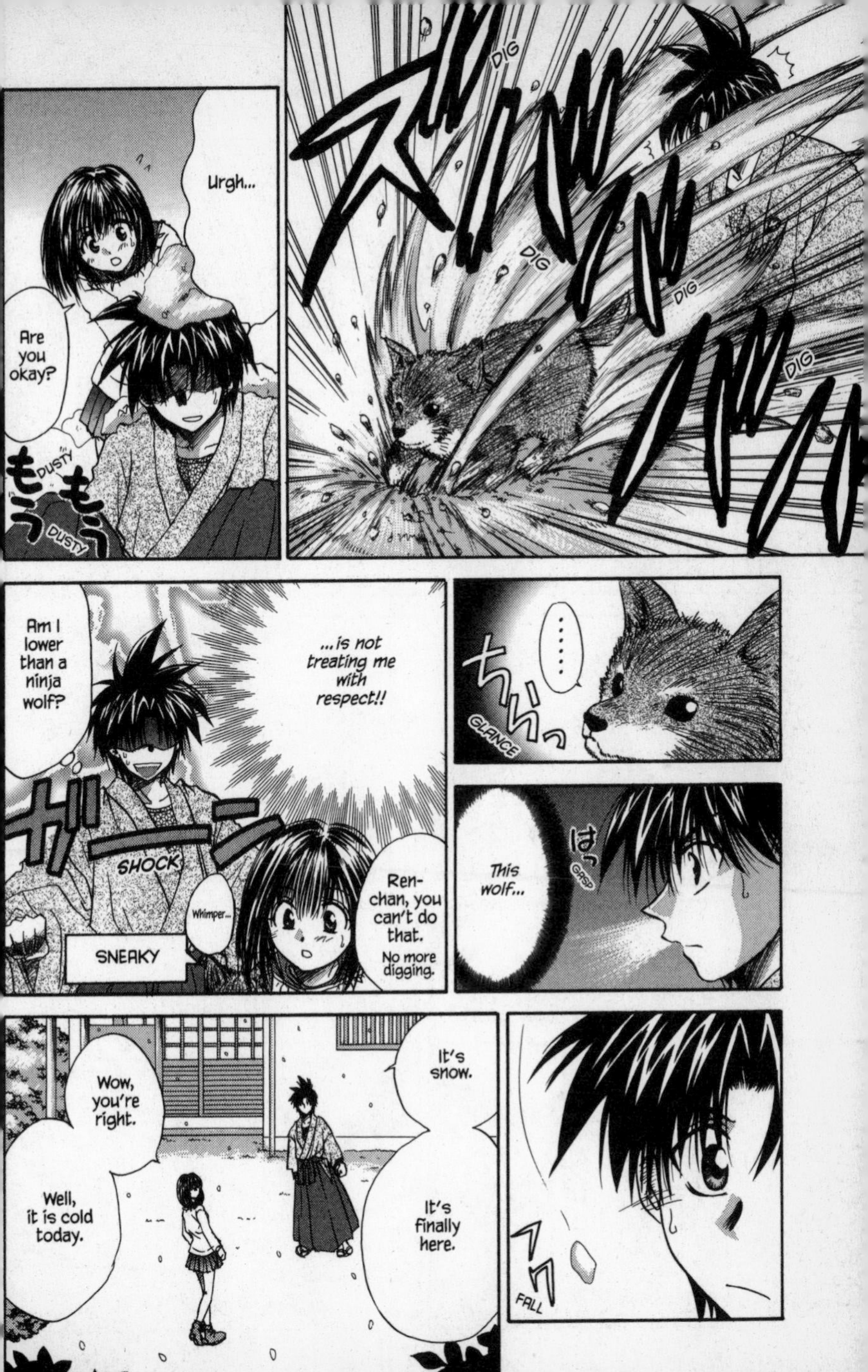
DIG
DIG
DIG
DIG
Urgh...
Are you okay?
DUSTY
DUSTY
......
GLANCE
This wolf...
GASP
...is not treating me with respect!!
Am I lower than a ninja wolf?
SHOCK
Whimper...
SNEAKY
Ren-chan, you can't do that.
No more digging.
FALL
It's snow.
Wow, you're right.
It's finally here.
Well, it is cold today.

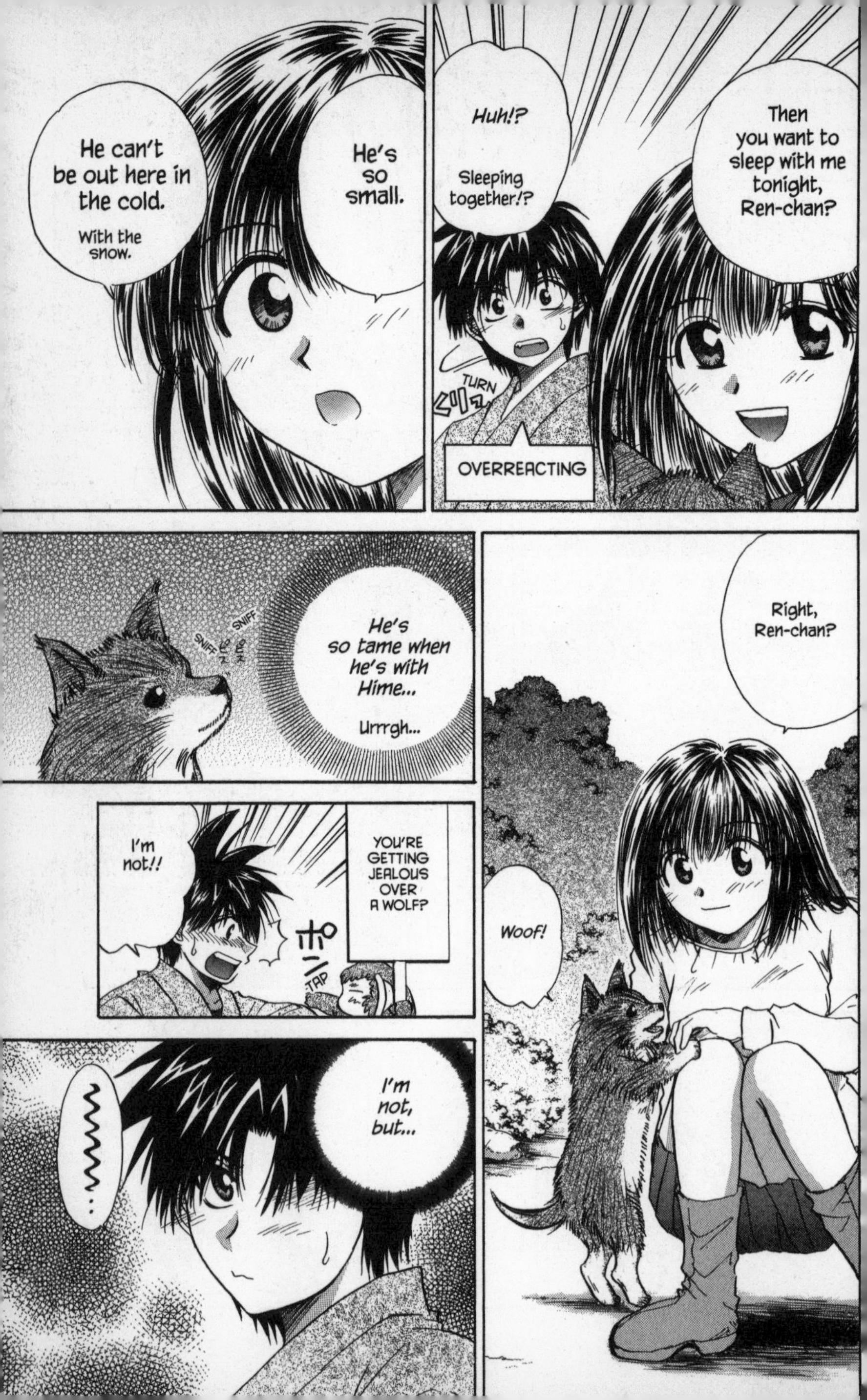
Then you want to sleep with me tonight, Ren-chan?
Huh!?
Sleeping together!?
TURN
OVERREACTING
He's so small.
He can't be out here in the cold.
With the snow.
Right, Ren-chan?
Woof!
He's so tame when he's with Hime...
Urrrgh...
SNIFF
SNIFF
YOU'RE GETTING JEALOUS OVER A WOLF?
I'm not!!
TAP
I'm not, but...
......

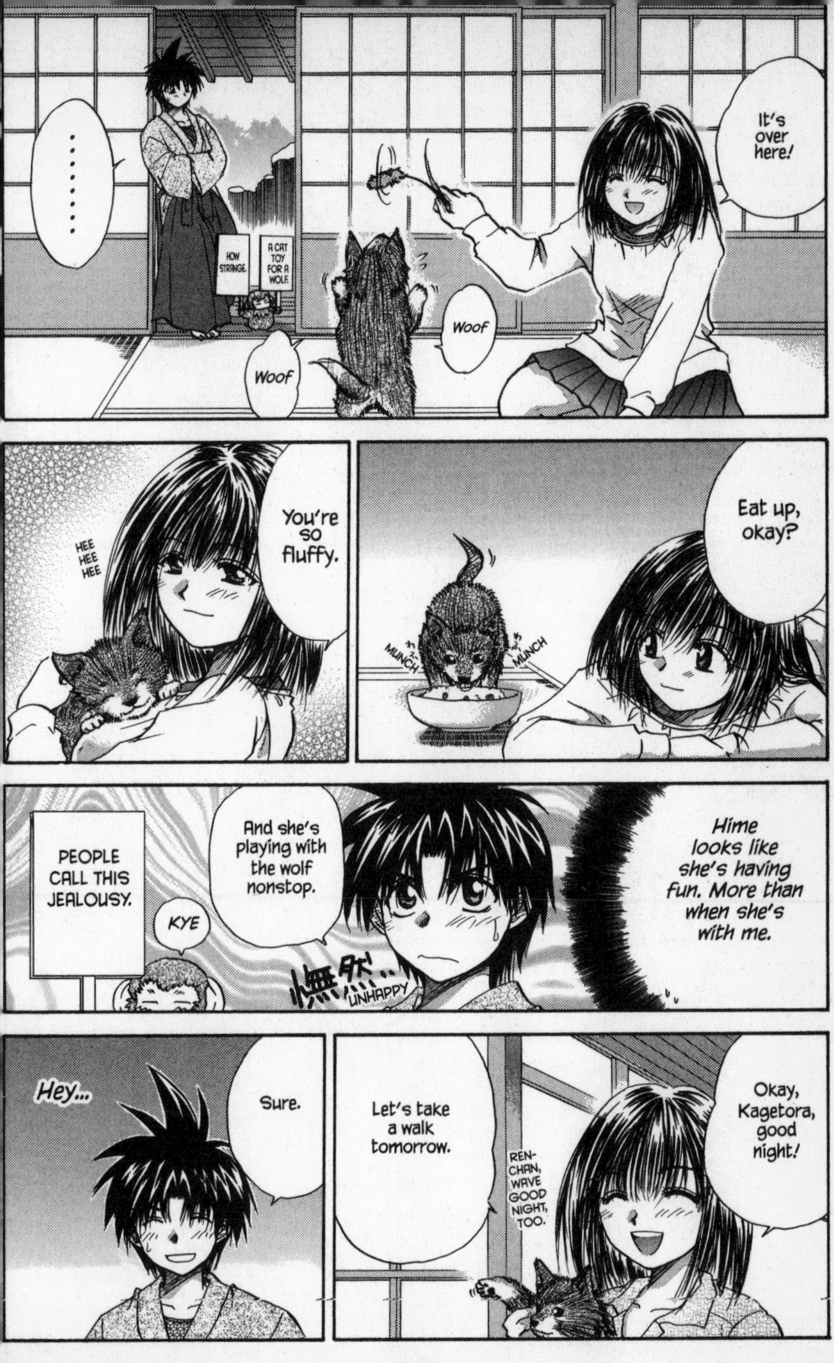
It's over here!
Woof
A CAT TOY FOR A WOLF.
HOW STRANGE.
Woof
....
Eat up, okay?
MUNCH
MUNCH
You're so fluffy.
HEE HEE HEE
Hime looks like she's having fun. More than when she's with me.
憮然..
UNHAPPY
And she's playing with the wolf nonstop.
KYE
PEOPLE CALL THIS JEALOUSY.
Okay, Kagetora, good night!
REN-CHAN, WAVE GOOD NIGHT, TOO.
Let's take a walk tomorrow.
Sure.
Hey...

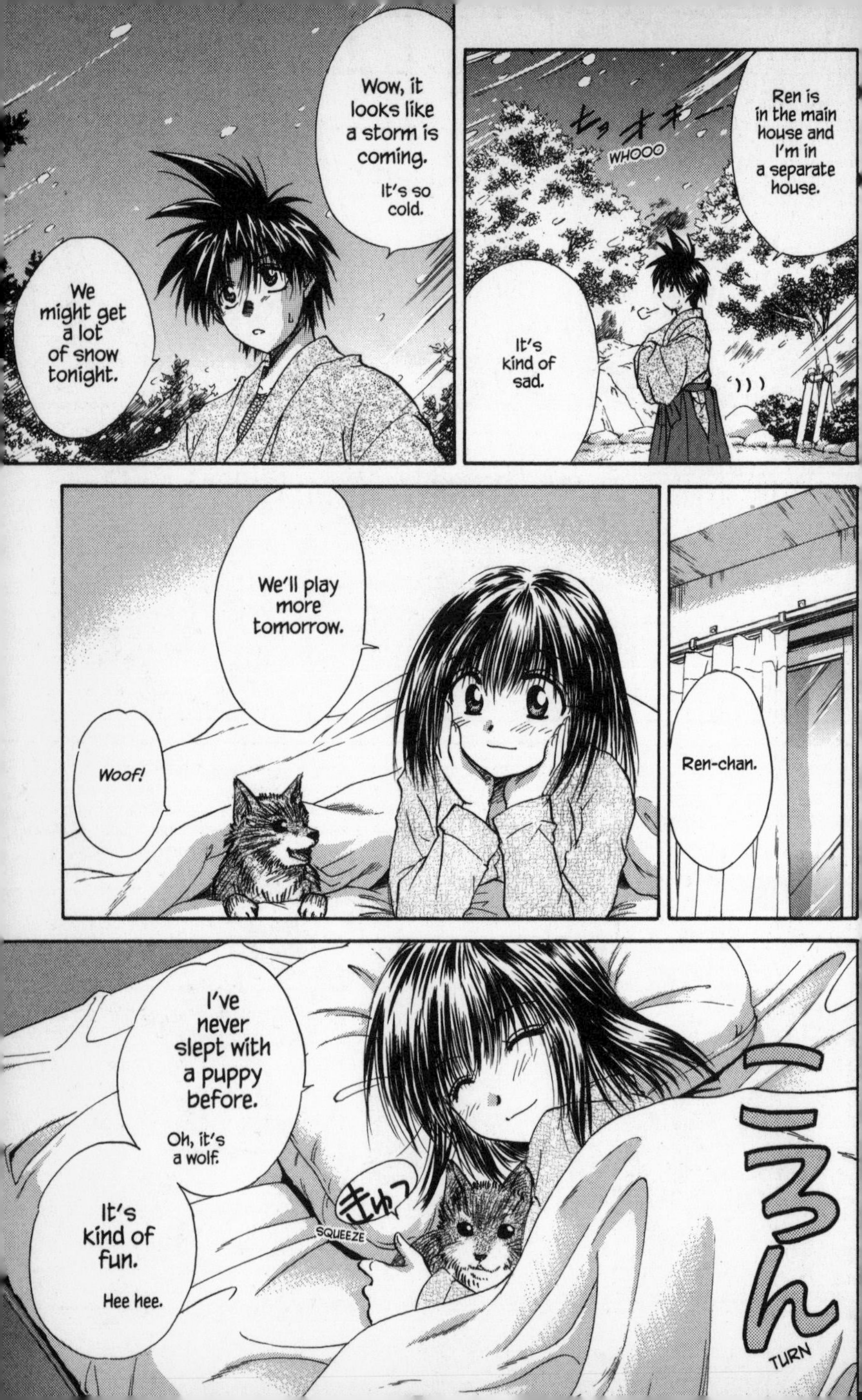
Ren is in the main house and I'm in a separate house.
WHOOO
It's kind of sad.
Wow, it looks like a storm is coming.
It's so cold.
We might get a lot of snow tonight.
Ren-chan.
We'll play more tomorrow.
Woof!
ころん
TURN
I've never slept with a puppy before.
Oh, it's a wolf.
きゅっ
SQUEEZE
It's kind of fun.
Hee hee.

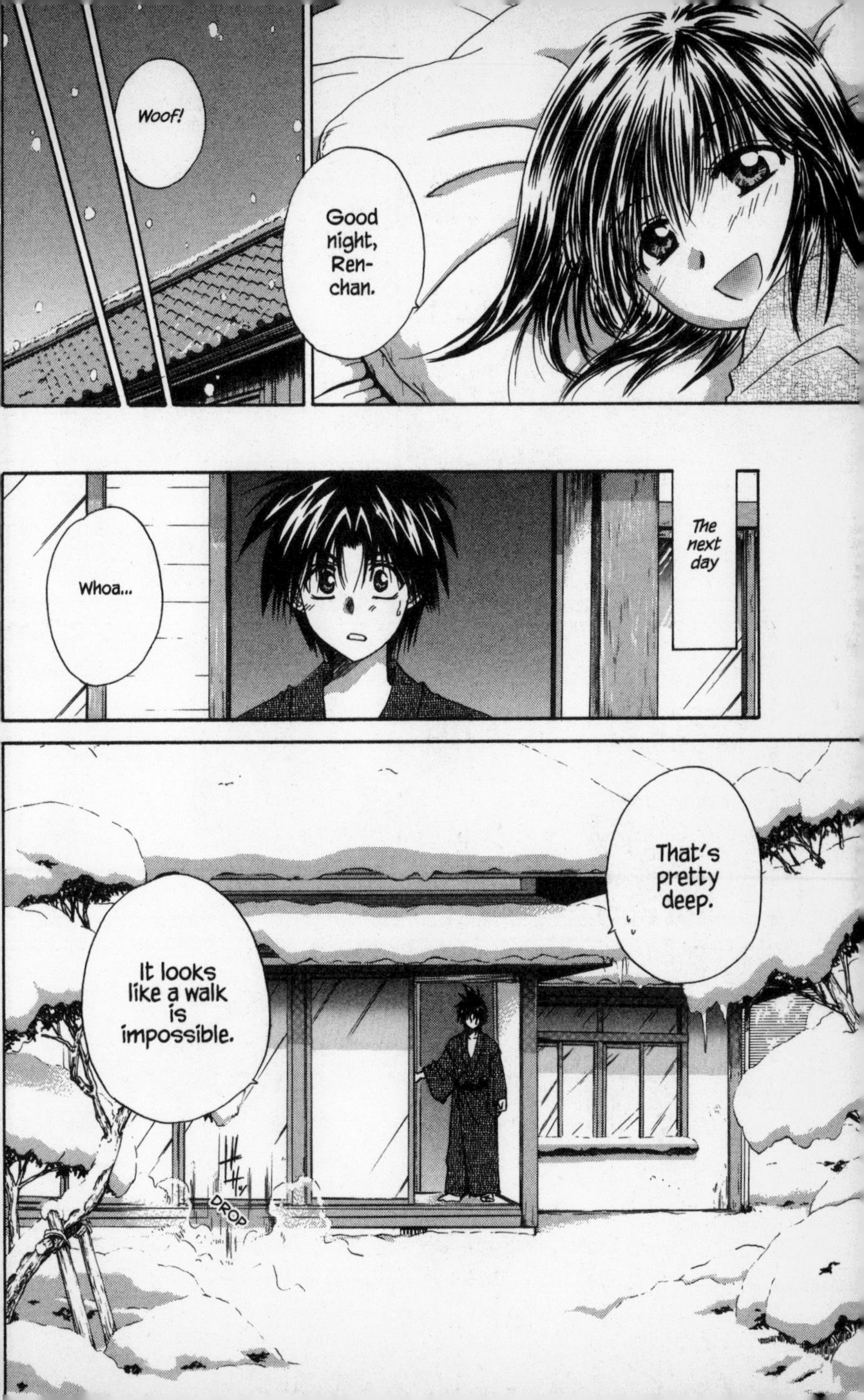
Good night, Ren-chan.
Woof!
The next day
Whoa...
That's pretty deep.
It looks like a walk is impossible.
DROP

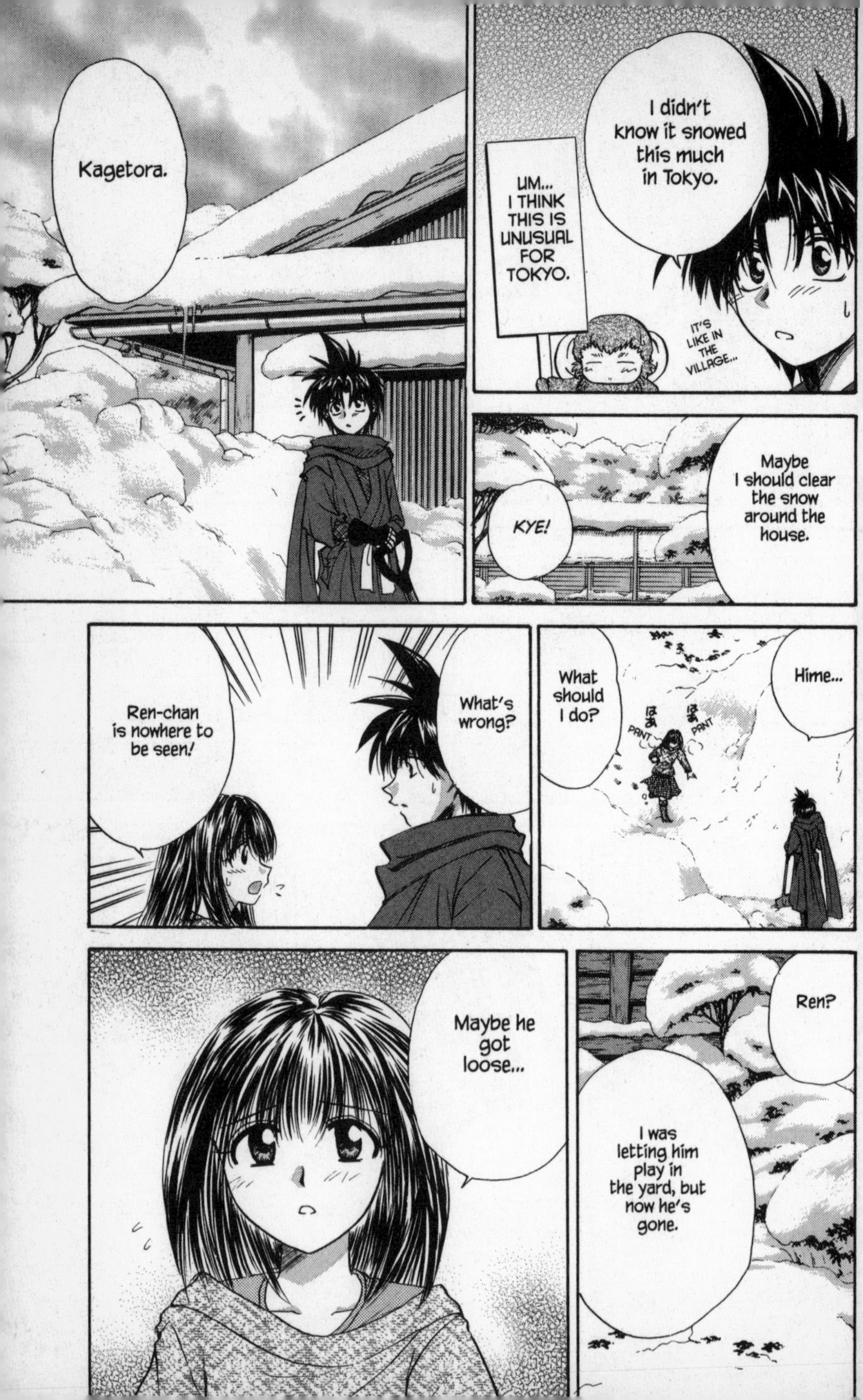
I didn't know it snowed this much in Tokyo.
UM... I THINK THIS IS UNUSUAL FOR TOKYO.
IT'S LIKE IN THE VILLAGE...
Maybe I should clear the snow around the house.
KYE!
Kagetora.
Hime...
はあ PANT
はあ PANT
What should I do?
What's wrong?
Ren-chan is nowhere to be seen!
Ren?
I was letting him play in the yard, but now he's gone.
Maybe he got loose...

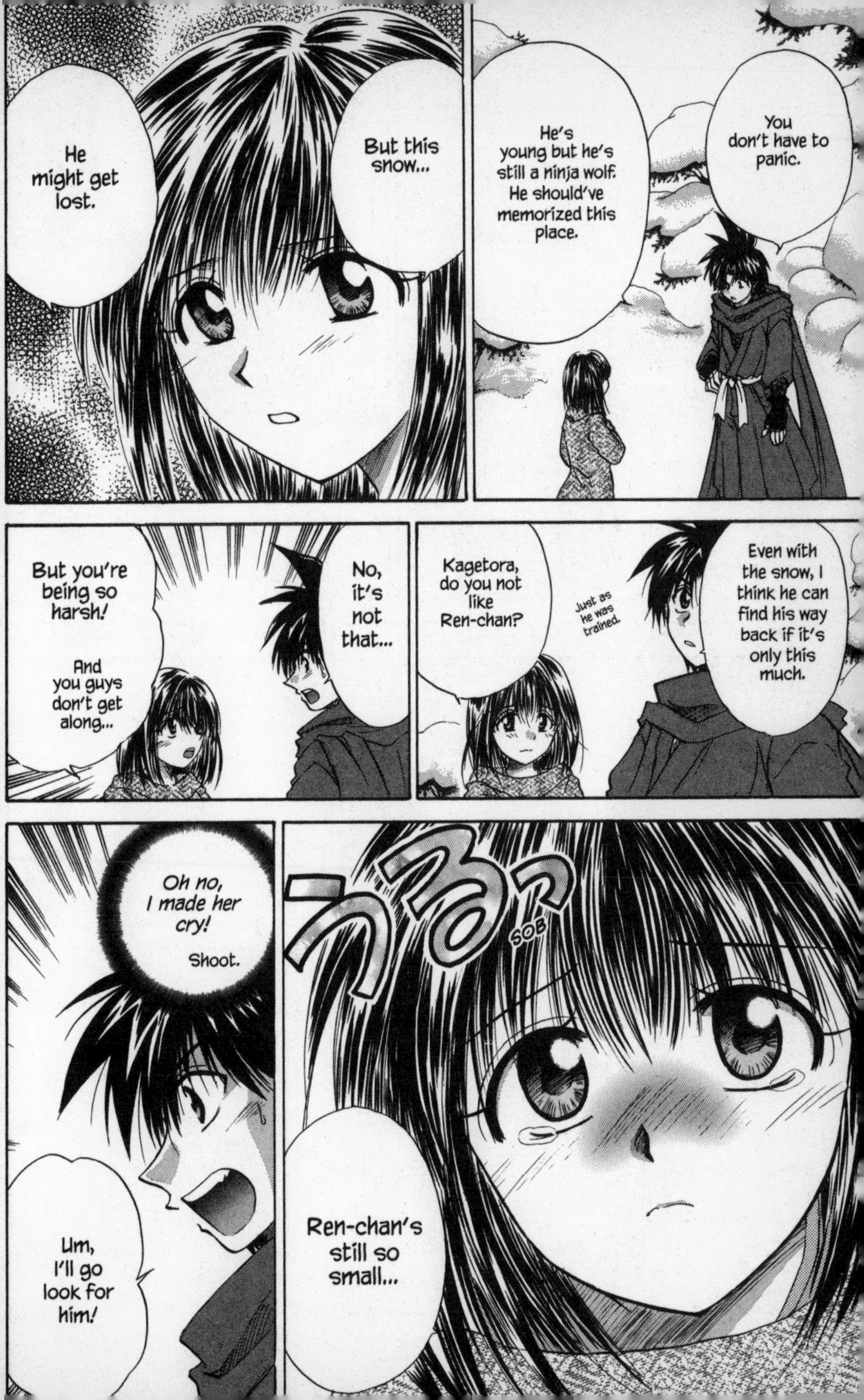
You don't have to panic.
He's young but he's still a ninja wolf. He should've memorized this place.
But this snow...
He might get lost.
Even with the snow, I think he can find his way back if it's only this much.
Just as he was trained.
Kagetora, do you not like Ren-chan?
No, it's not that...
But you're being so harsh!
And you guys don't get along...
うるっ
SOB
Ren-chan's still so small...
Oh no, I made her cry!
Shoot.
Um, I'll go look for him!

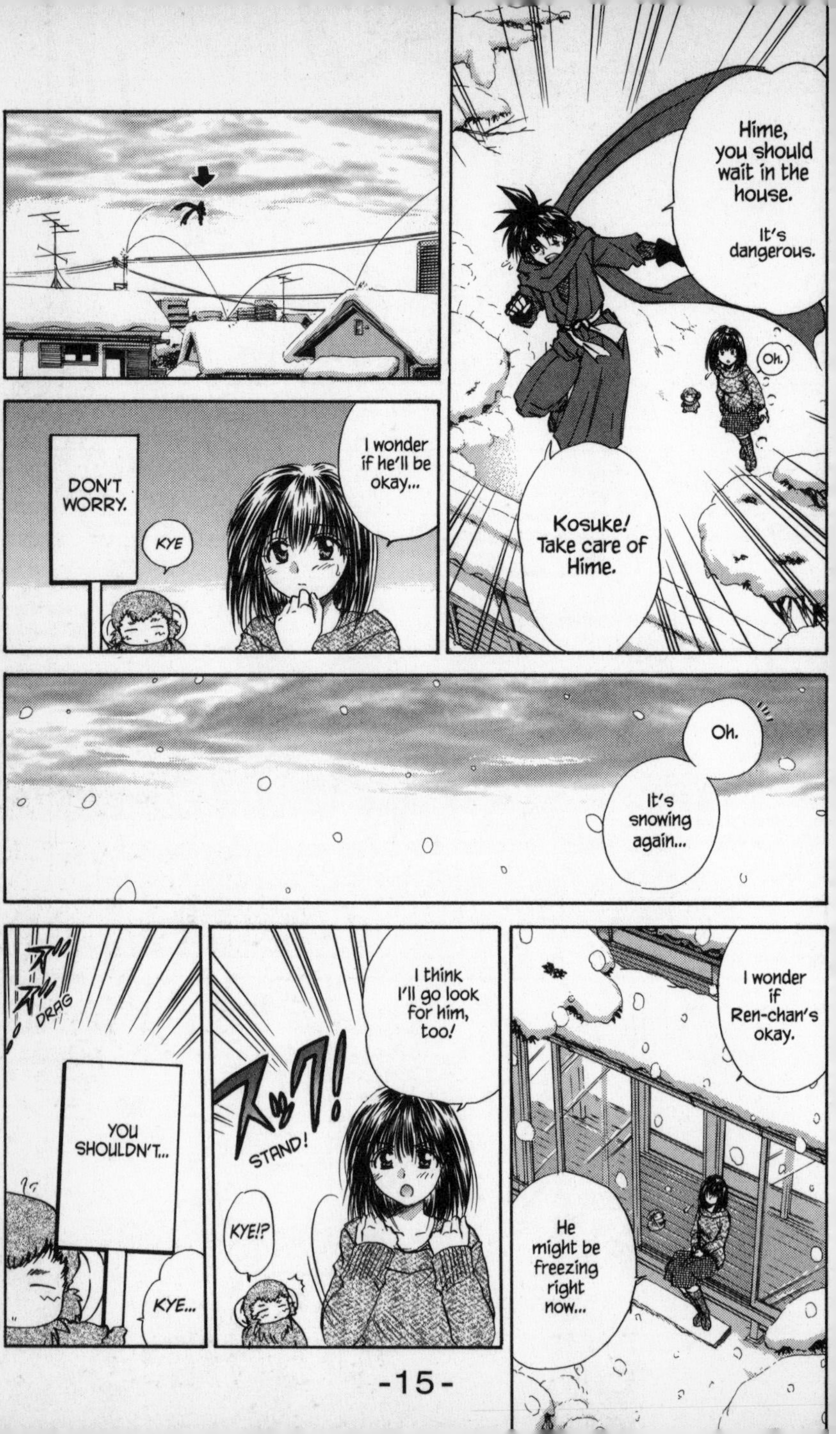

Hime, you should wait in the house.
It's dangerous.
Oh.
Kosuke! Take care of Hime.
I wonder if he'll be okay...
KYE
DON'T WORRY.
Oh.
It's snowing again...
I wonder if Ren-chan's okay.
He might be freezing right now...
I think I'll go look for him, too!
STAND!
KYE!?
DRAG
YOU SHOULDN'T...
KYE...

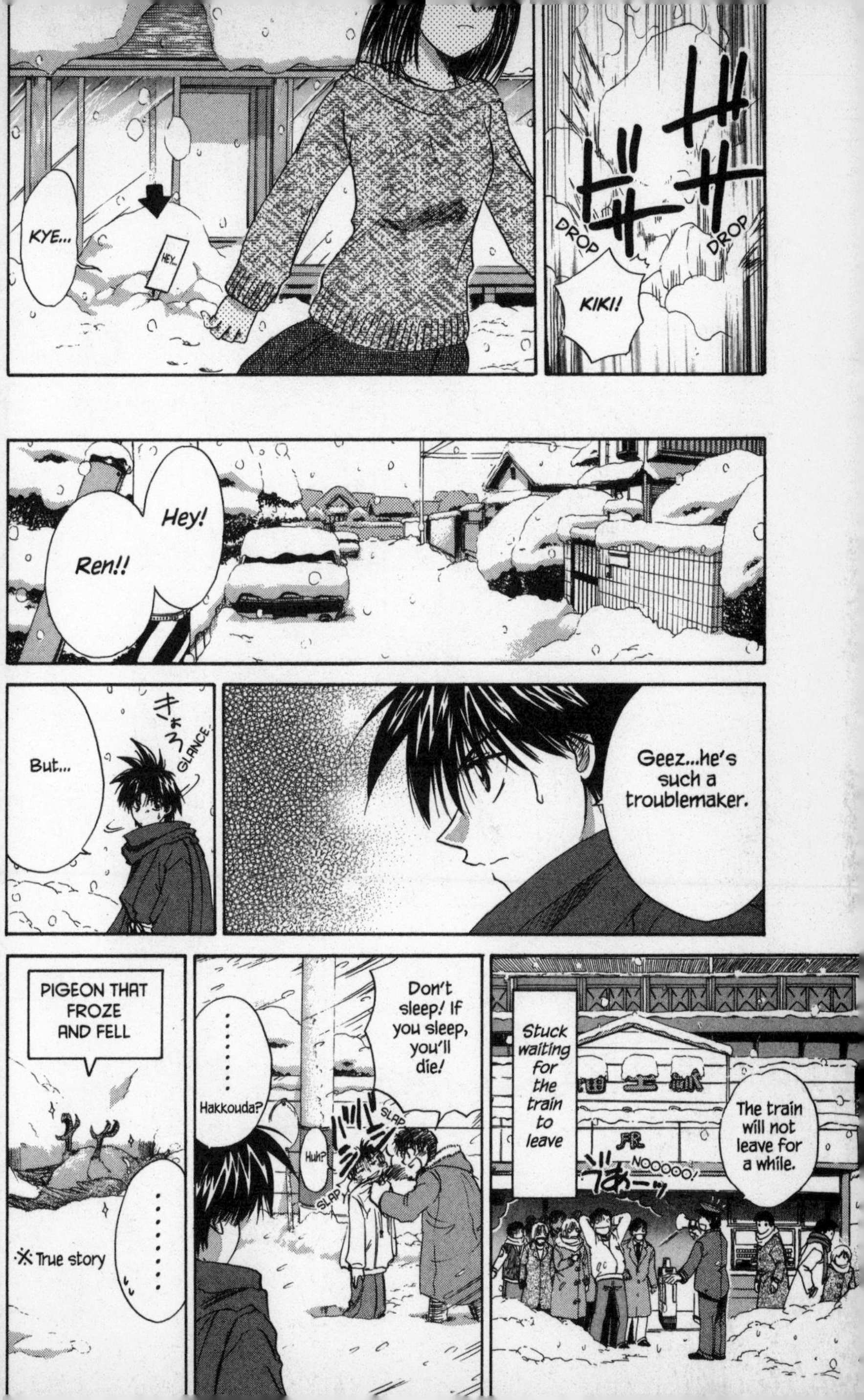
DROP
DROP
KIKI!
KYE...
HEY.
Hey!
Ren!!
Geez...he's such a troublemaker.
But...
きょろ
GLANCE
Stuck waiting for the train to leave
The train will not leave for a while.
うあーッ
NOOOOO!
Don't sleep! If you sleep, you'll die!
SLAP
SLAP
Huh?
......
Hakkouda?
......
PIGEON THAT FROZE AND FELL
※True story

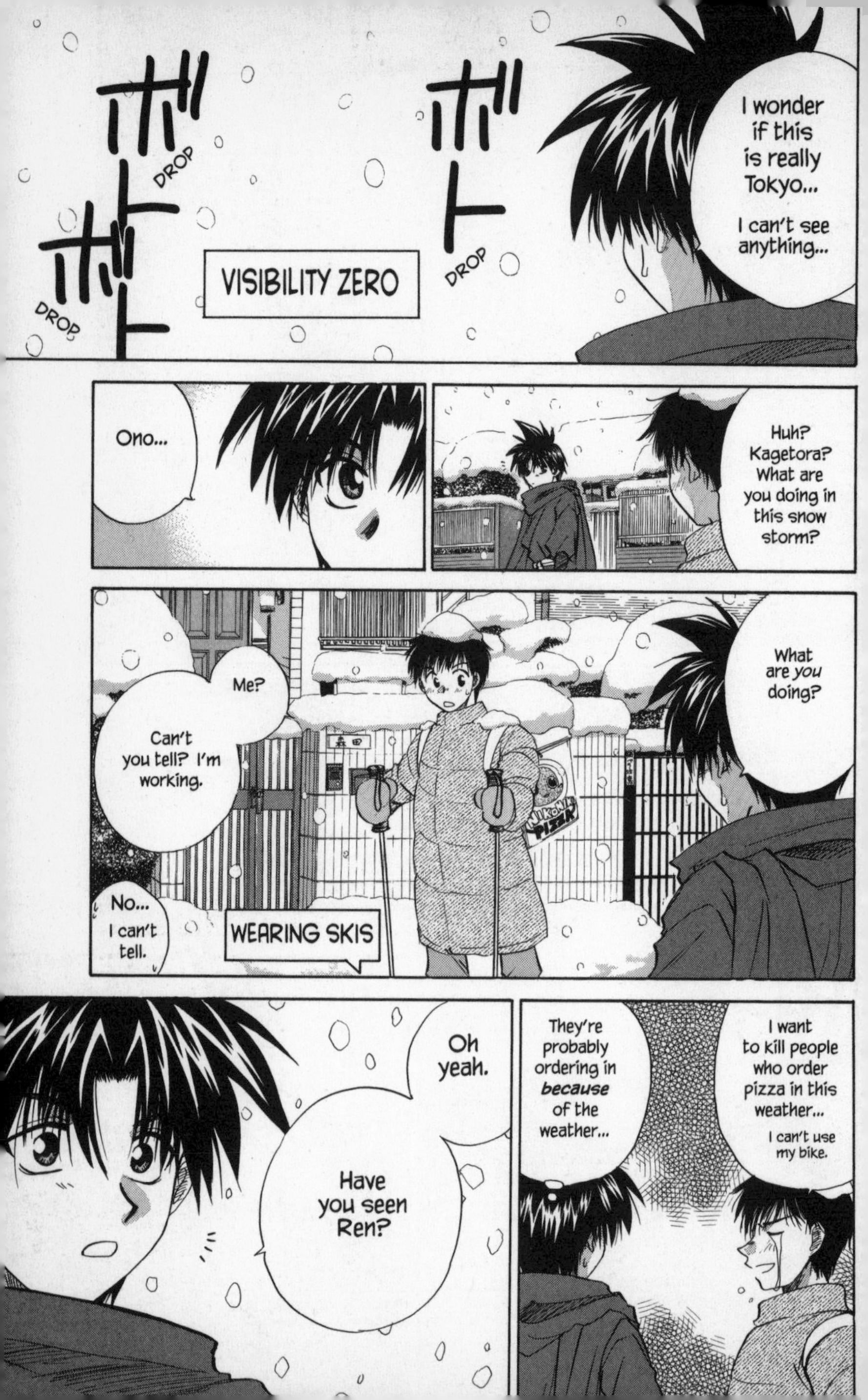

I wonder if this is really Tokyo...
I can't see anything...
ボト
DROP
VISIBILITY ZERO
ボトボト
DROP
DROP
Huh? Kagetora? What are you doing in this snow storm?
Ono...
What are *you* doing?
Me?
Can't you tell? I'm working.
No... I can't tell.
WEARING SKIS
I want to kill people who order pizza in this weather...
I can't use my bike.
They're probably ordering in ***because*** of the weather...
Oh yeah.
Have you seen Ren?

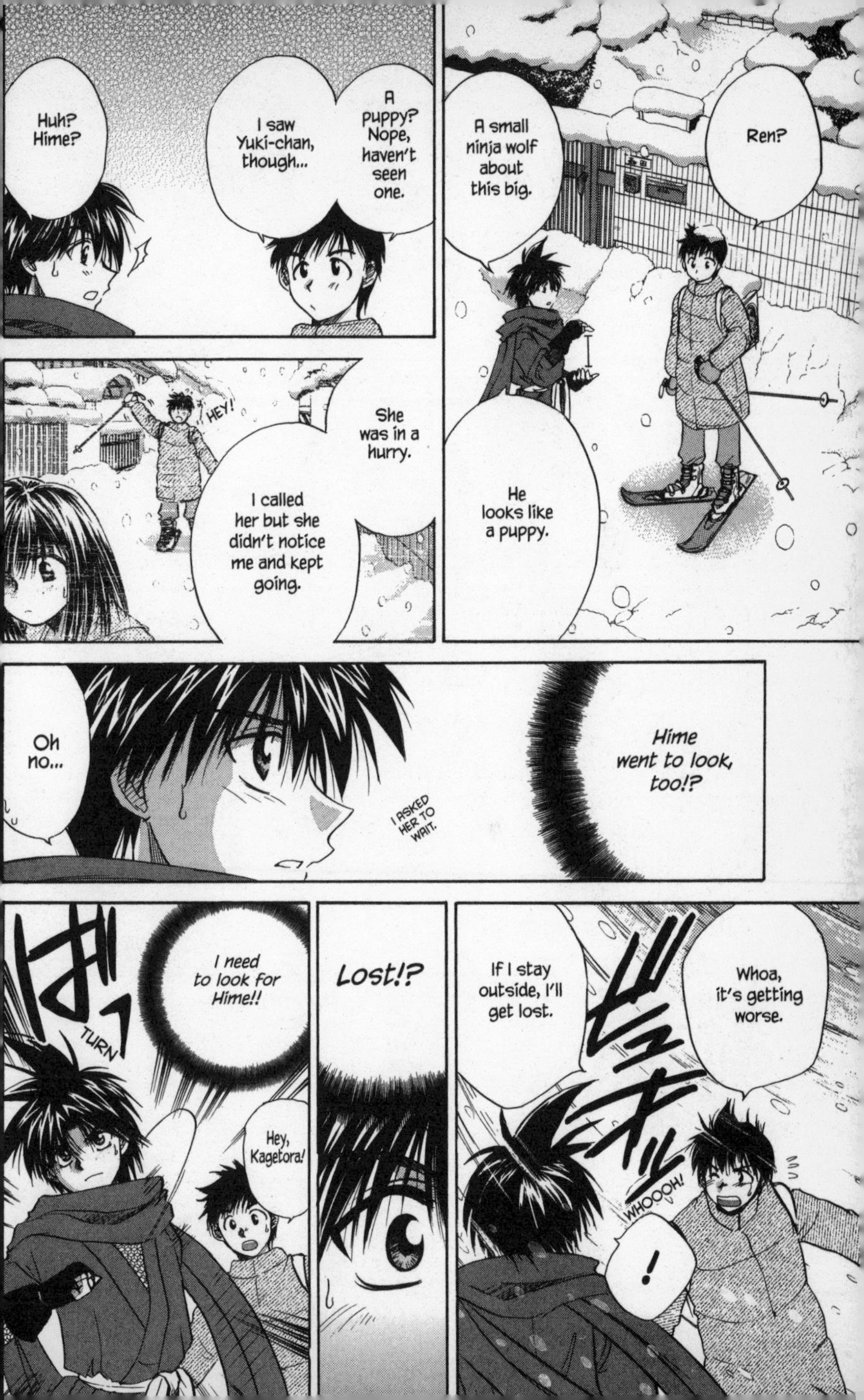
Ren?
A small ninja wolf about this big.
He looks like a puppy.
A puppy? Nope, haven't seen one.
I saw Yuki-chan, though...
Huh? Hime?
She was in a hurry.
I called her but she didn't notice me and kept going.
HEY!
Hime went to look, too!?
I ASKED HER TO WAIT.
Oh no...
Whoa, it's getting worse.
If I stay outside, I'll get lost.
ビュオッ
WHOOOH!
!
Lost!?
I need to look for Hime!!
ぱっ
TURN
Hey, Kagetora!

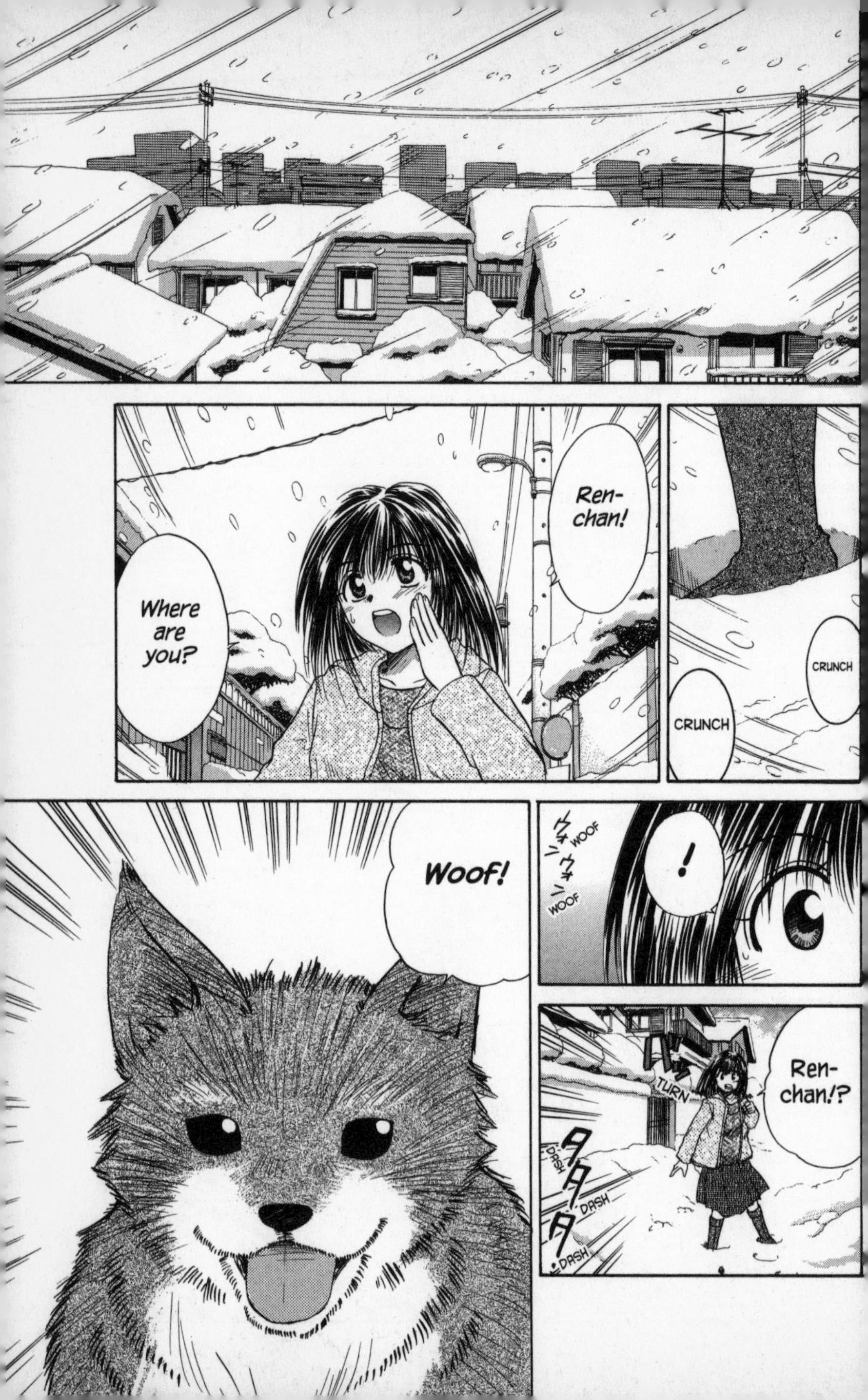
CRUNCH
CRUNCH
Ren-chan!
Where are you?
!
WOOF
WOOF
Ren-chan!?
TURN
DASH
DASH
DASH
Woof!

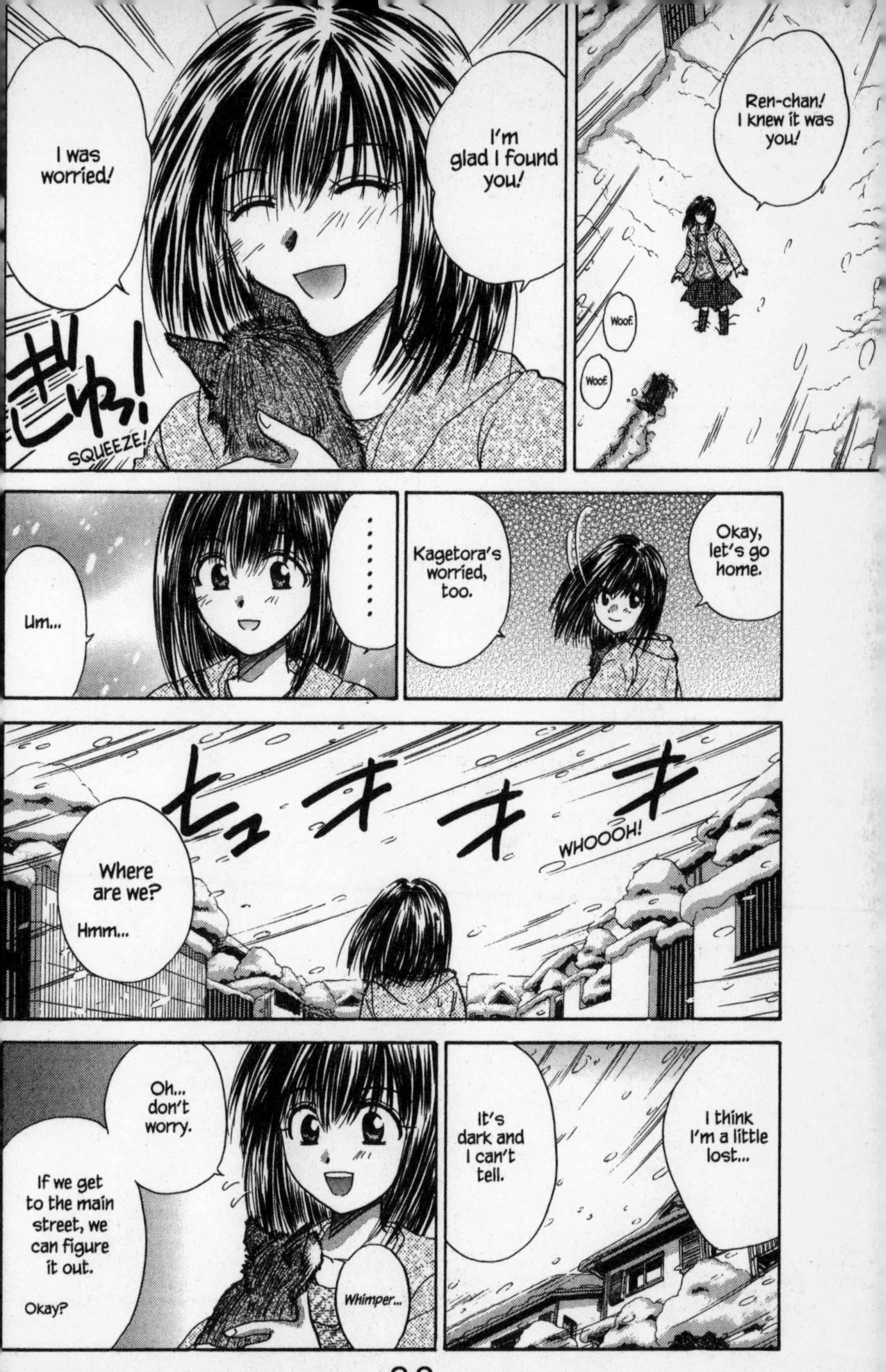
Ren-chan! I knew it was you!
Woof.
Woof.
I'm glad I found you!
I was worried!
SQUEEZE!
Okay, let's go home.
Kagetora's worried, too.
......
Um...
ヒュオオオ
WHOOOH!
Where are we?
Hmm...
I think I'm a little lost...
It's dark and I can't tell.
Oh... don't worry.
If we get to the main street, we can figure it out.
Okay?
Whimper...

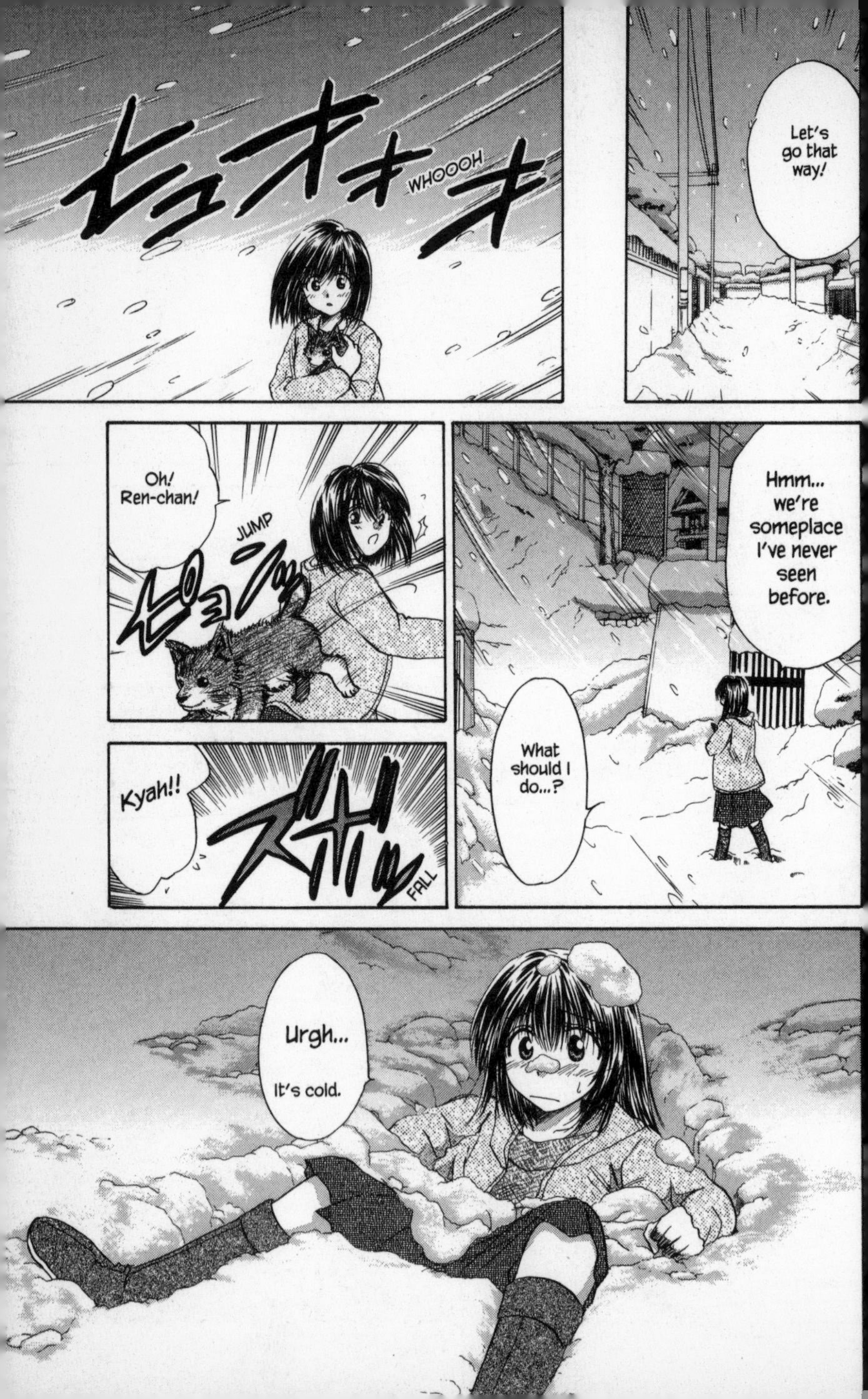
Let's go that way!
WHOOOH
Hmm... we're someplace I've never seen before.
What should I do...?
Oh! Ren-chan!
JUMP
Kyah!!
FALL
Urgh...
It's cold.

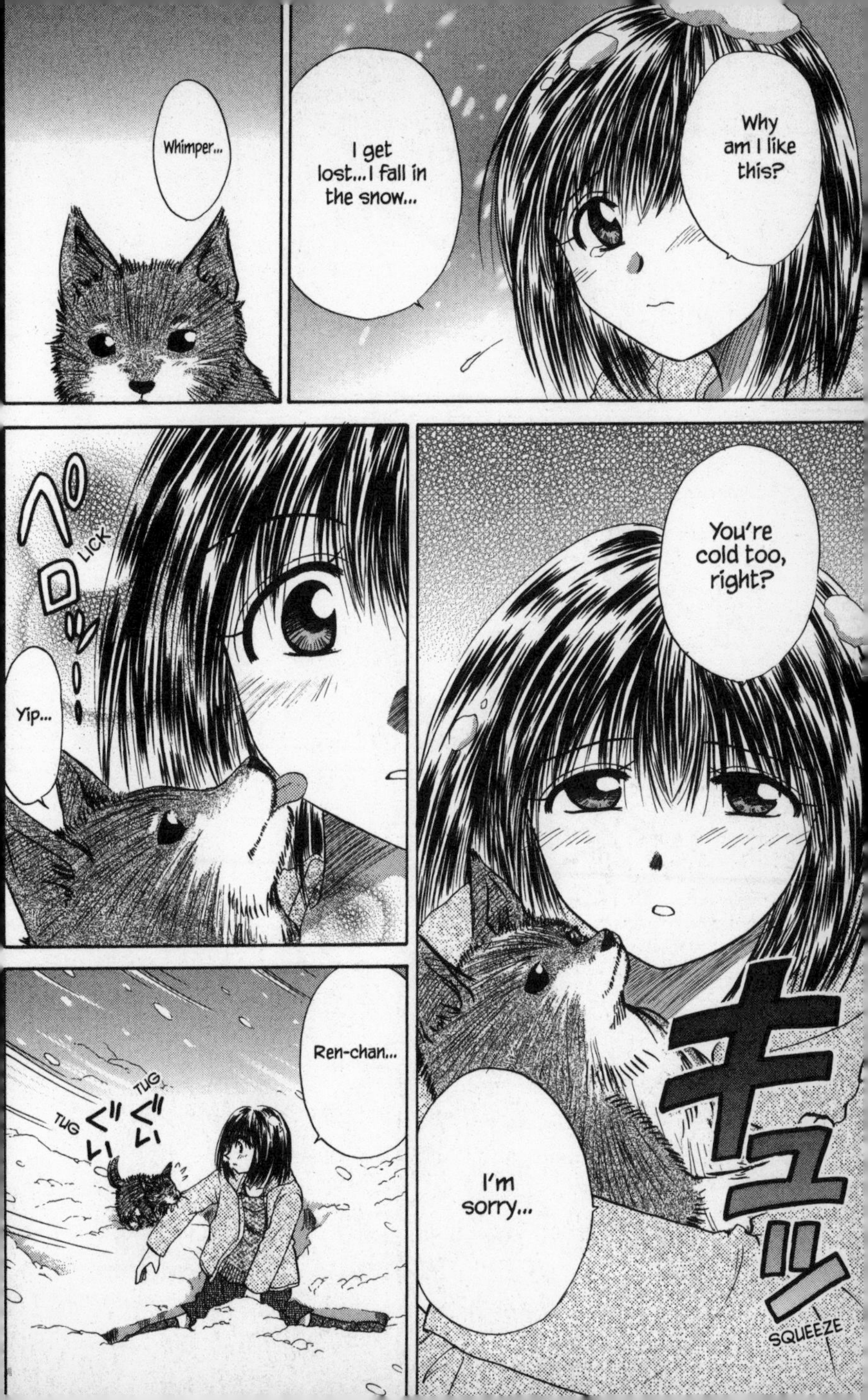
Why am I like this?
I get lost...I fall in the snow...
Whimper...
You're cold too, right?
キュッ
SQUEEZE
I'm sorry...
ペロッ
LICK
Yip...
Ren-chan...
ぐい ぐい
TUG
TUG

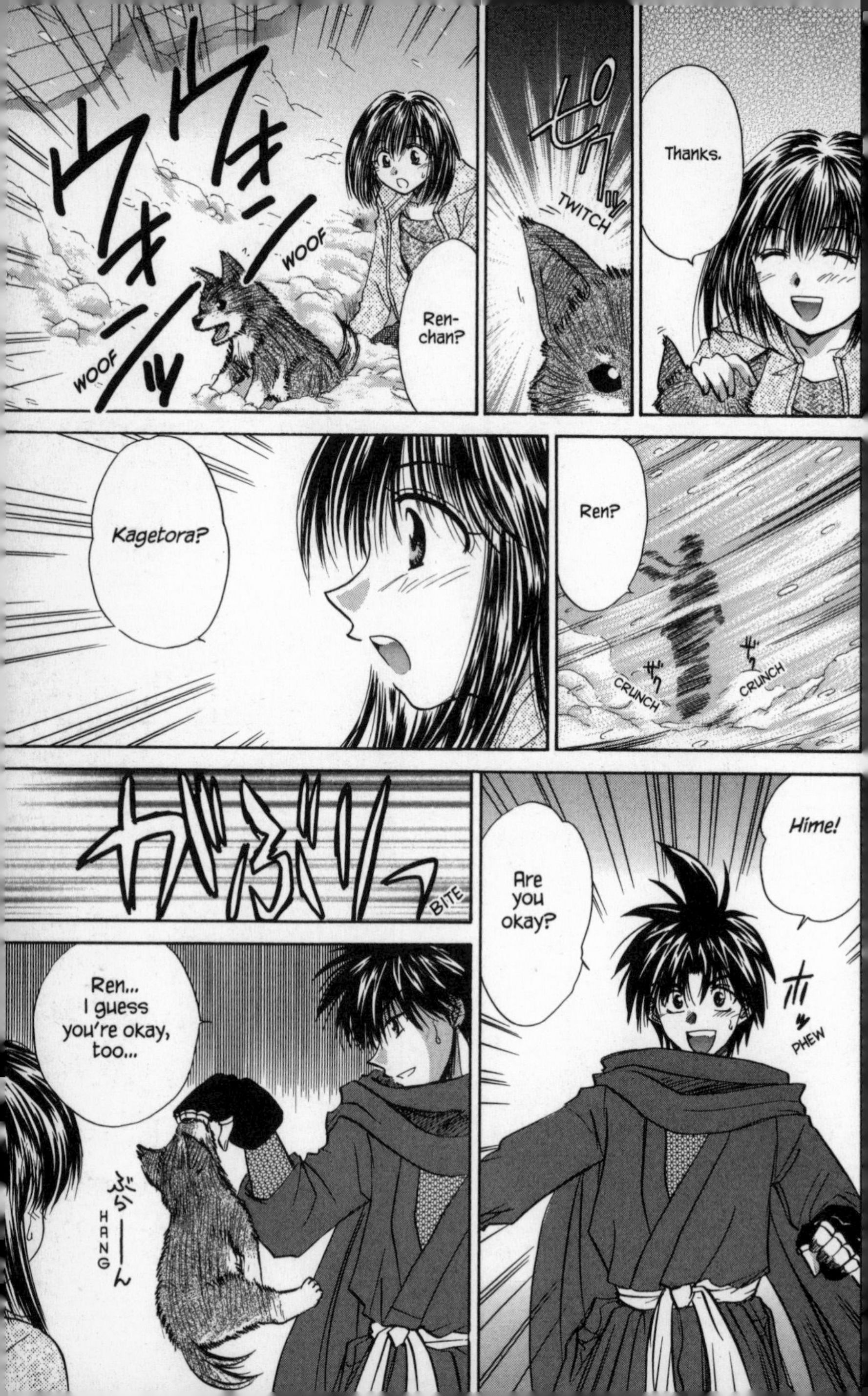
Thanks.
ピクッ
TWITCH
ウォンウォンッ
WOOF
WOOF
Ren-chan?
Ren?
CRUNCH
CRUNCH
Kagetora?
Hime!
Are you okay?
ホッ
PHEW
がぶりっ
BITE
Ren... I guess you're okay, too...
ぶら〜ん
HANG

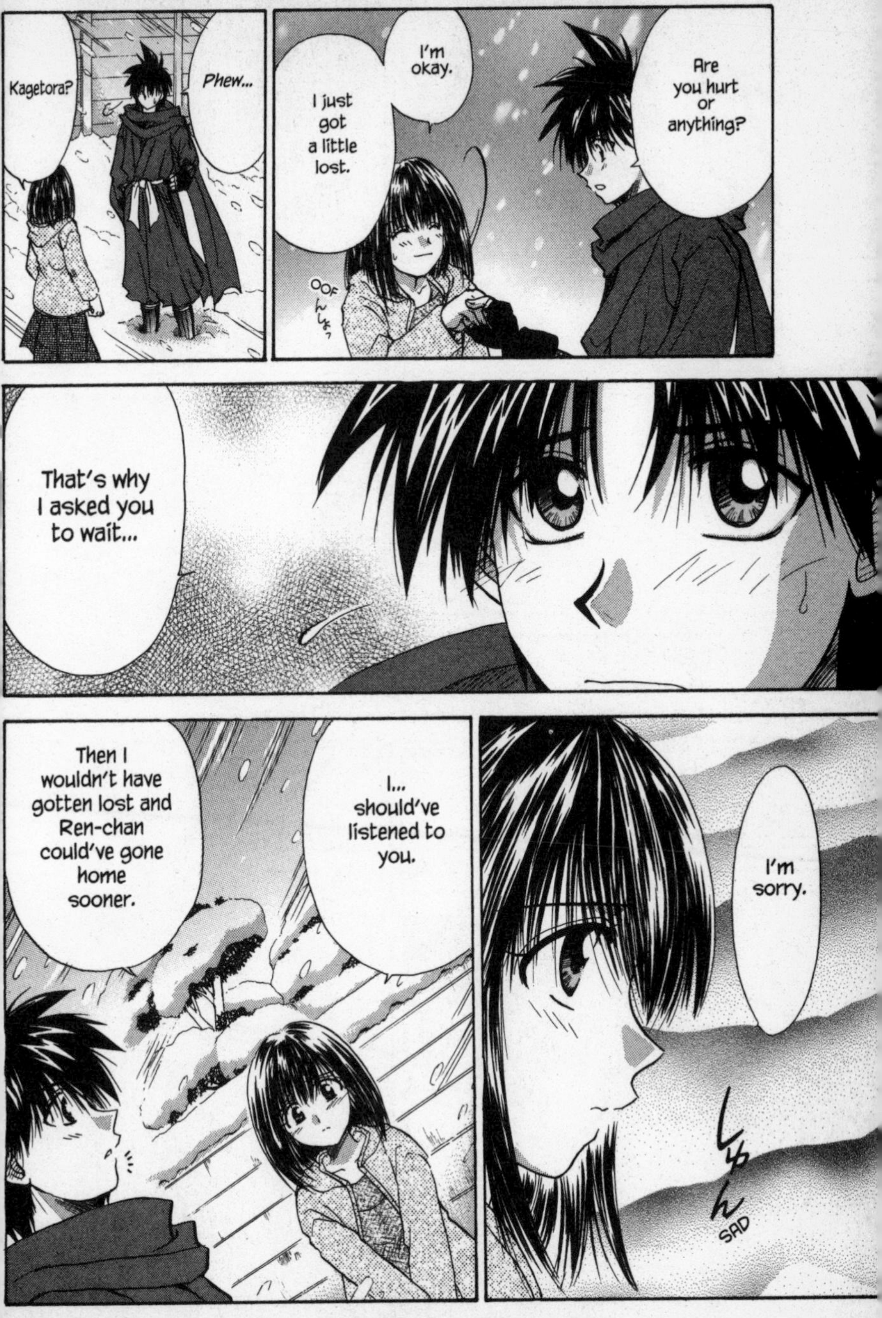
Are you hurt or anything?
I'm okay.
I just got a little lost.
OOF
んしょっ
Phew...
Kagetora?
That's why I asked you to wait...
I'm sorry.
しゅん
SAD
I... should've listened to you.
Then I wouldn't have gotten lost and Ren-chan could've gone home sooner.

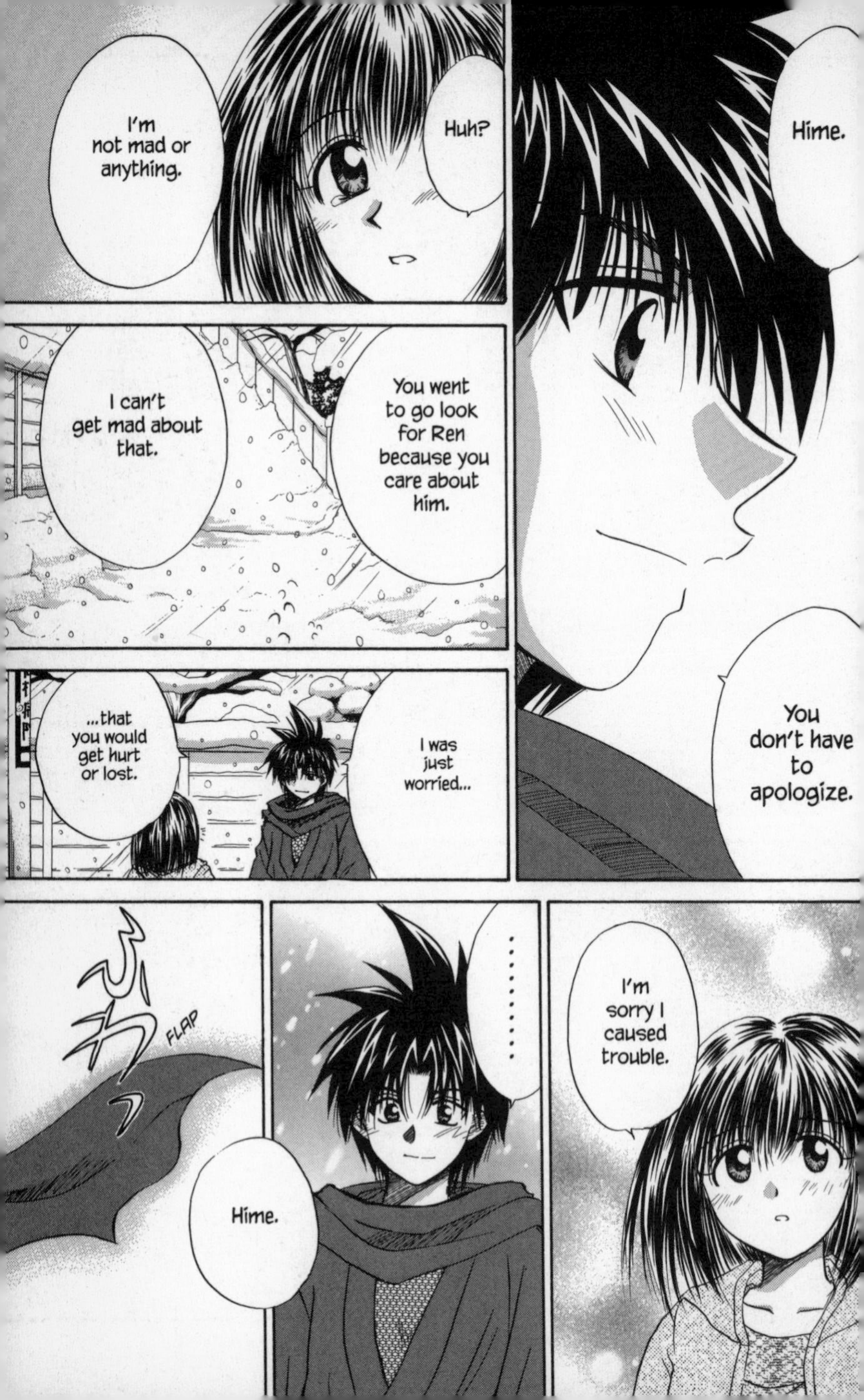
Hime.
You don't have to apologize.
Huh?
I'm not mad or anything.
You went to go look for Ren because you care about him.
I can't get mad about that.
I was just worried...
...that you would get hurt or lost.
I'm sorry I caused trouble.
......
Hime.
FLAP

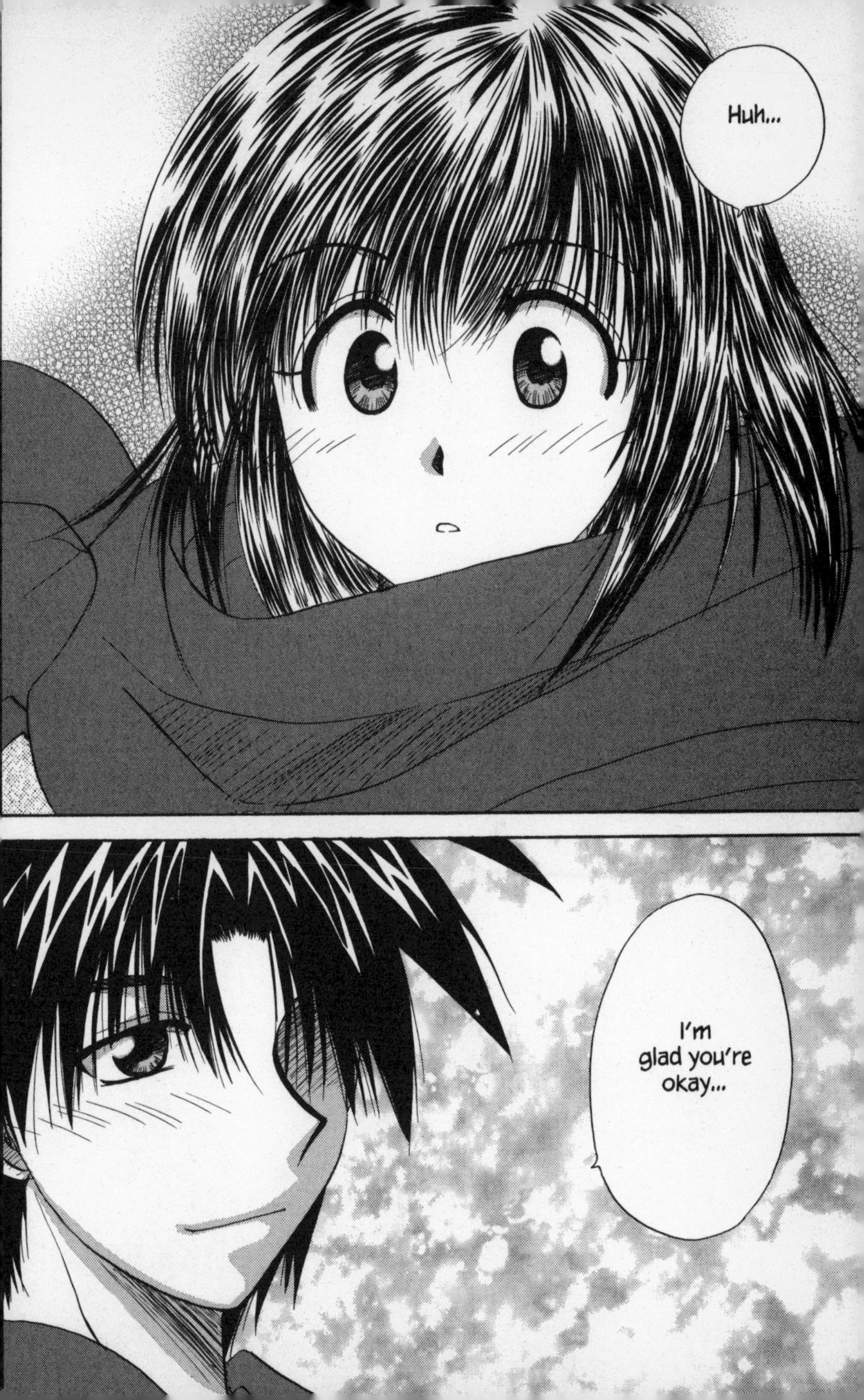
Huh...
I'm glad you're okay...

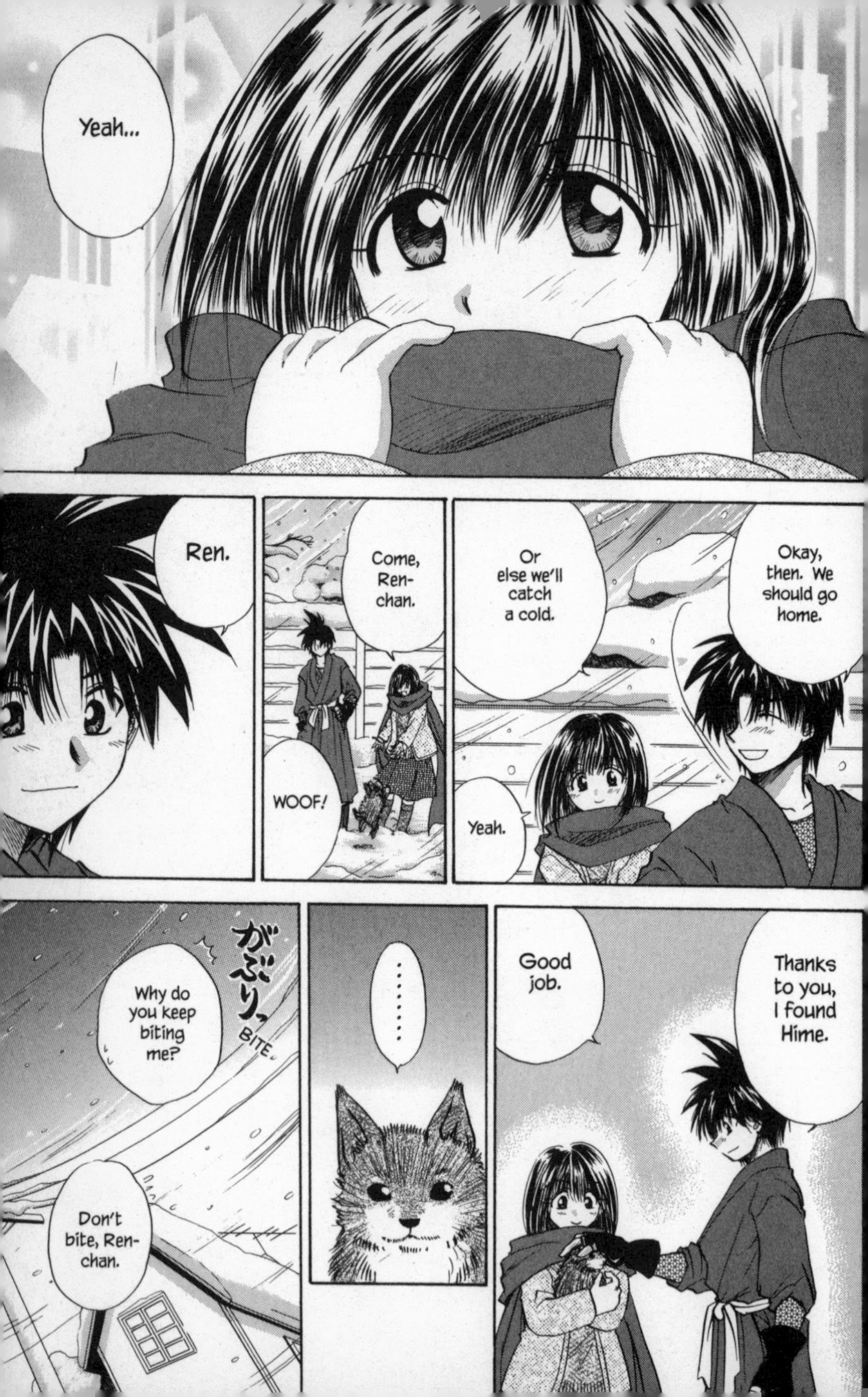
Yeah...
Okay, then. We should go home.
Or else we'll catch a cold.
Yeah.
Come, Ren-chan.
WOOF!
Ren.
Thanks to you, I found Hime.
Good job.
....
がぶりっ
BITE
Why do you keep biting me?
Don't bite, Ren-chan.

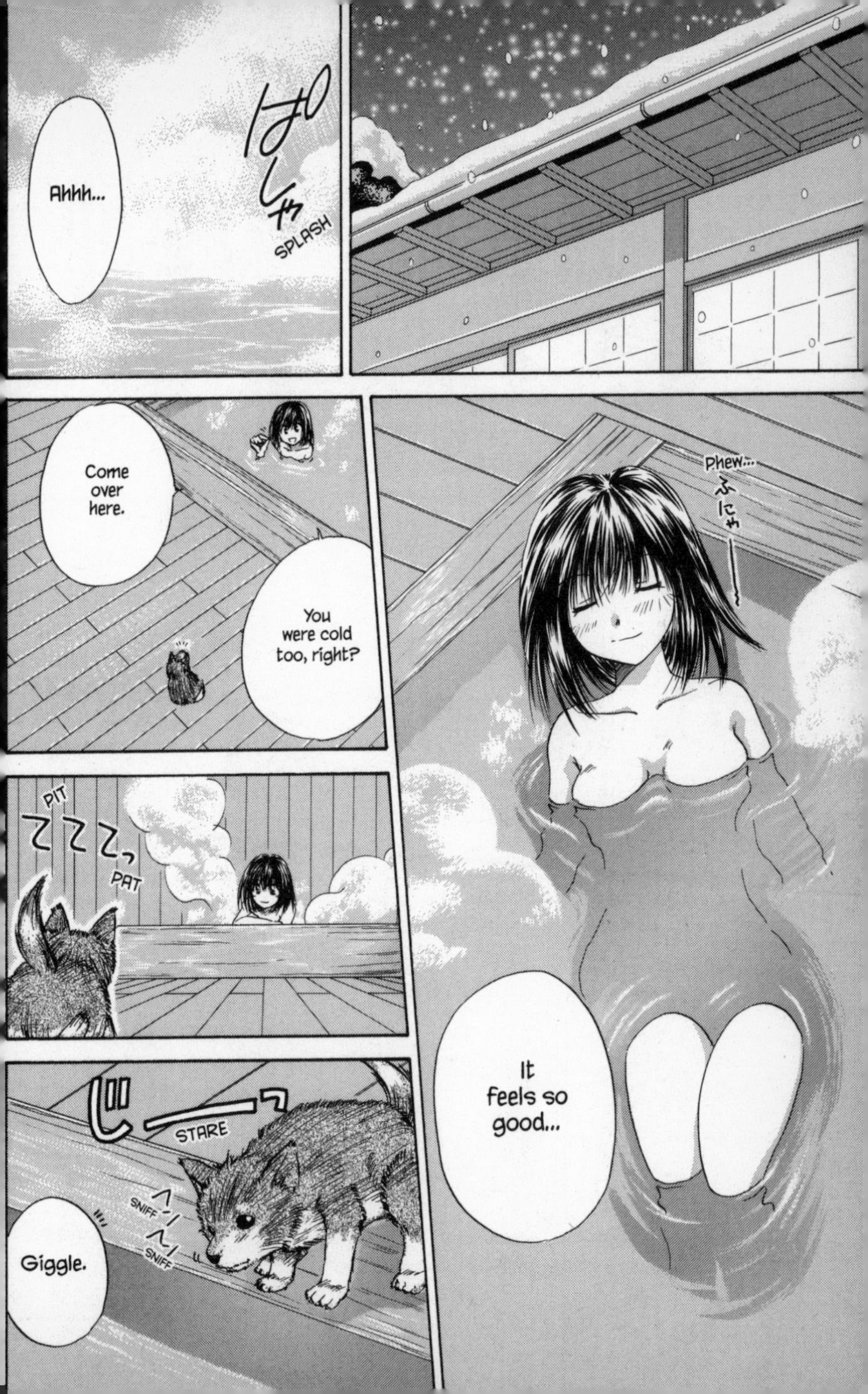
ぱしゃ
SPLASH
Ahhh...
Phew...
ふにゃ〜
It feels so good...
Come over here.
You were cold too, right?
てててっ
PIT
PAT
じーっ
STARE
へ/へ/
SNIFF
SNIFF
Giggle.

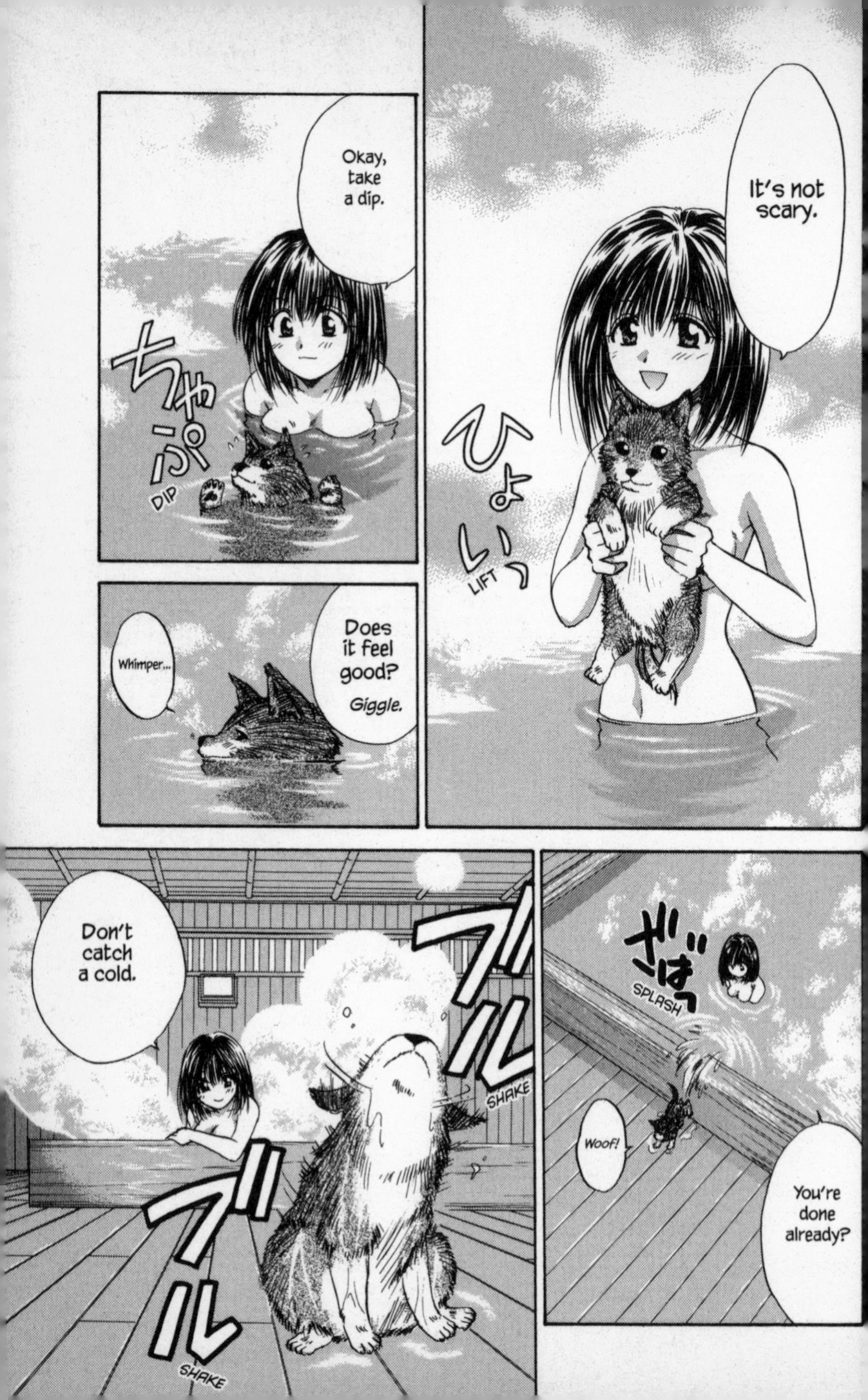
It's not scary.
LIFT
Okay, take a dip.
DIP
Does it feel good?
Giggle.
Whimper...
SPLASH
You're done already?
Woof!
SHAKE
Don't catch a cold.
SHAKE

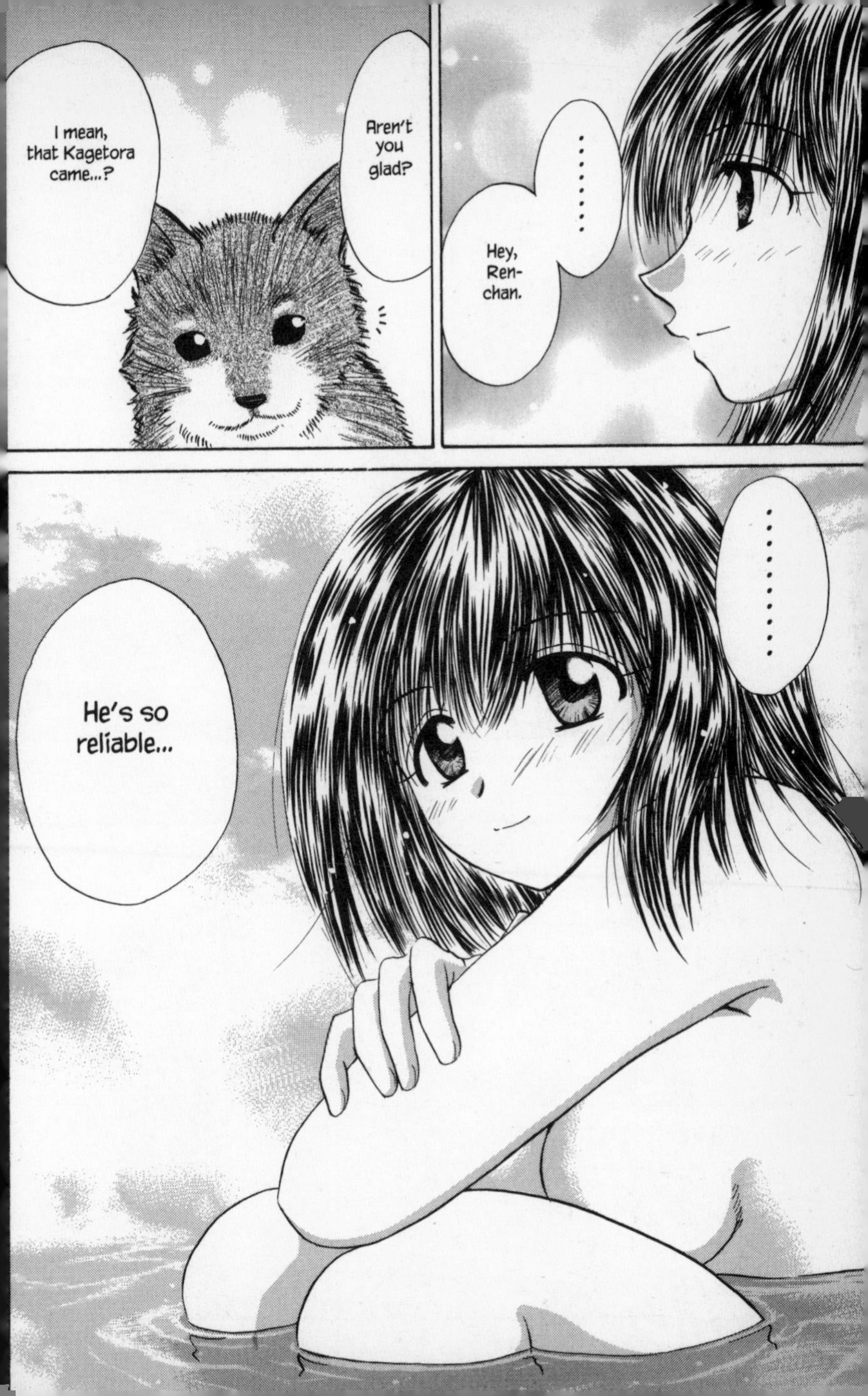
……
Hey, Ren-chan.
Aren't you glad?
I mean, that Kagetora came...?
……
He's so reliable...

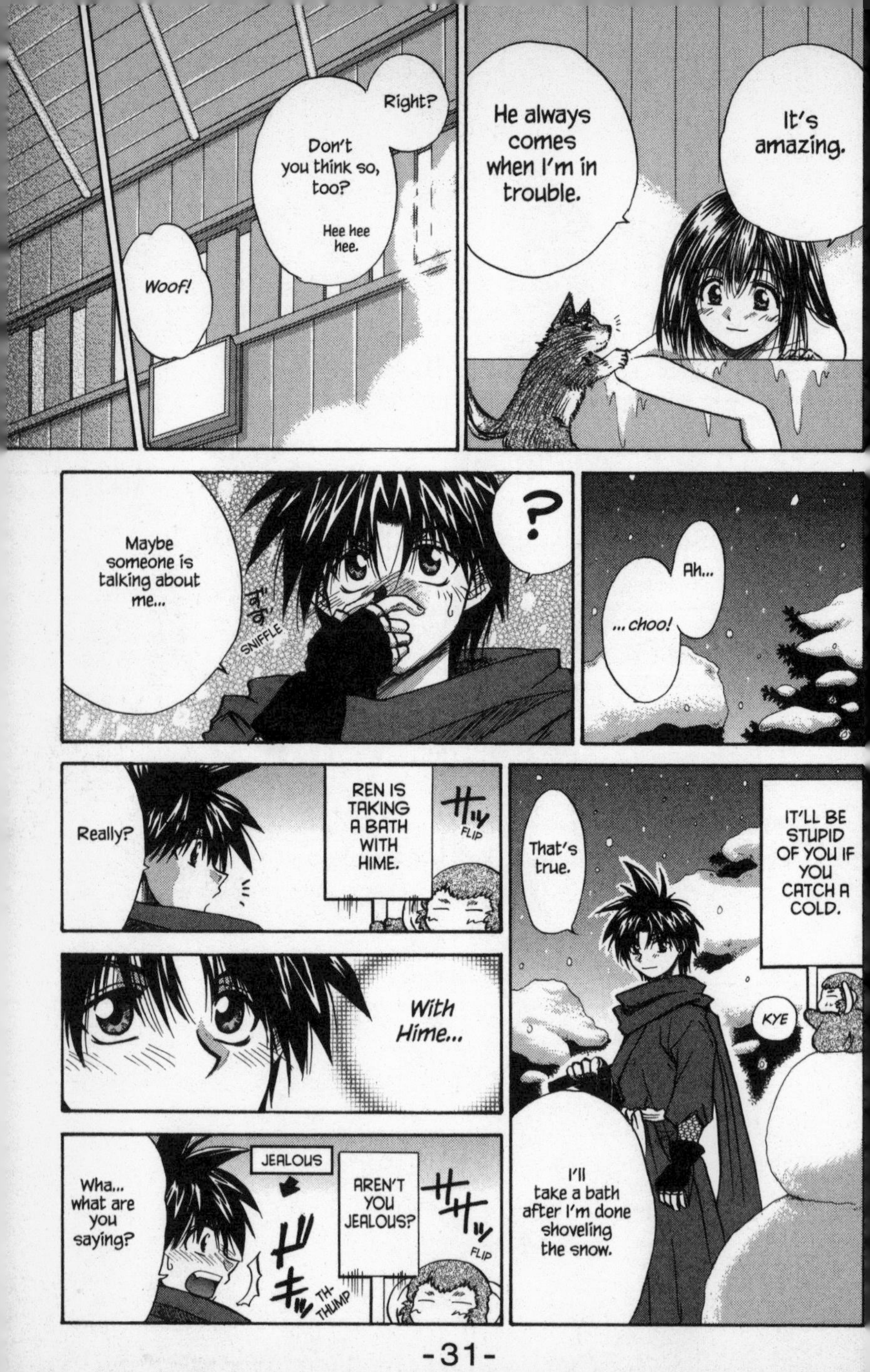
It's amazing.
He always comes when I'm in trouble.
Right?
Don't you think so, too?
Hee hee hee.
Woof!
Ah...
...choo!
?
Maybe someone is talking about me...
SNIFFLE
IT'LL BE STUPID OF YOU IF YOU CATCH A COLD.
That's true.
KYE
I'll take a bath after I'm done shoveling the snow.
REN IS TAKING A BATH WITH HIME.
FLIP
Really?
With Hime...
AREN'T YOU JEALOUS?
FLIP
JEALOUS
Wha... what are you saying?
TH-THUMP

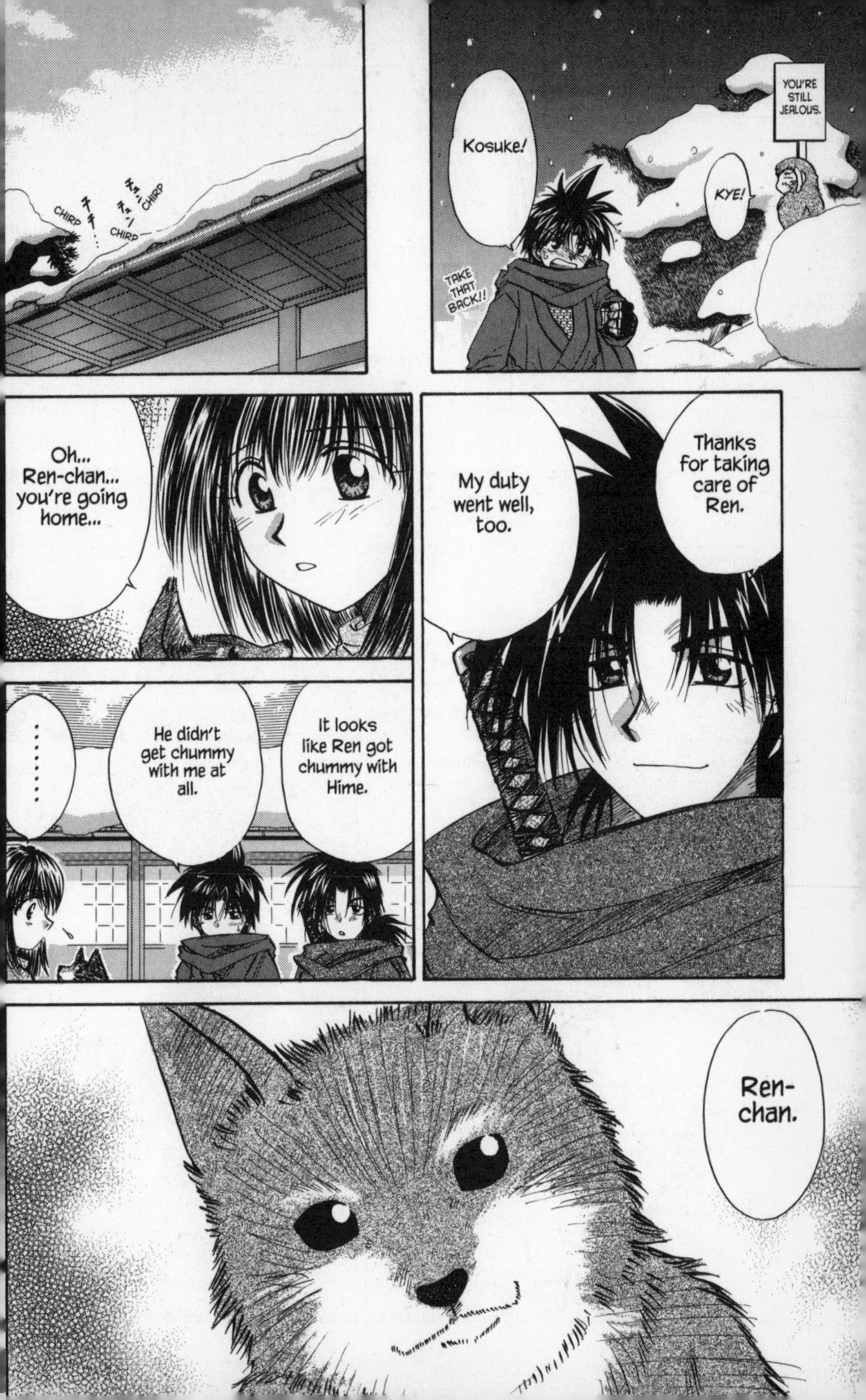
YOU'RE STILL JEALOUS.
KYE!
Kosuke!
TAKE THAT BACK!!
CHIRP
CHIRP
Thanks for taking care of Ren.
My duty went well, too.
Oh... Ren-chan... you're going home...
It looks like Ren got chummy with Hime.
He didn't get chummy with me at all.
......
Ren-chan.

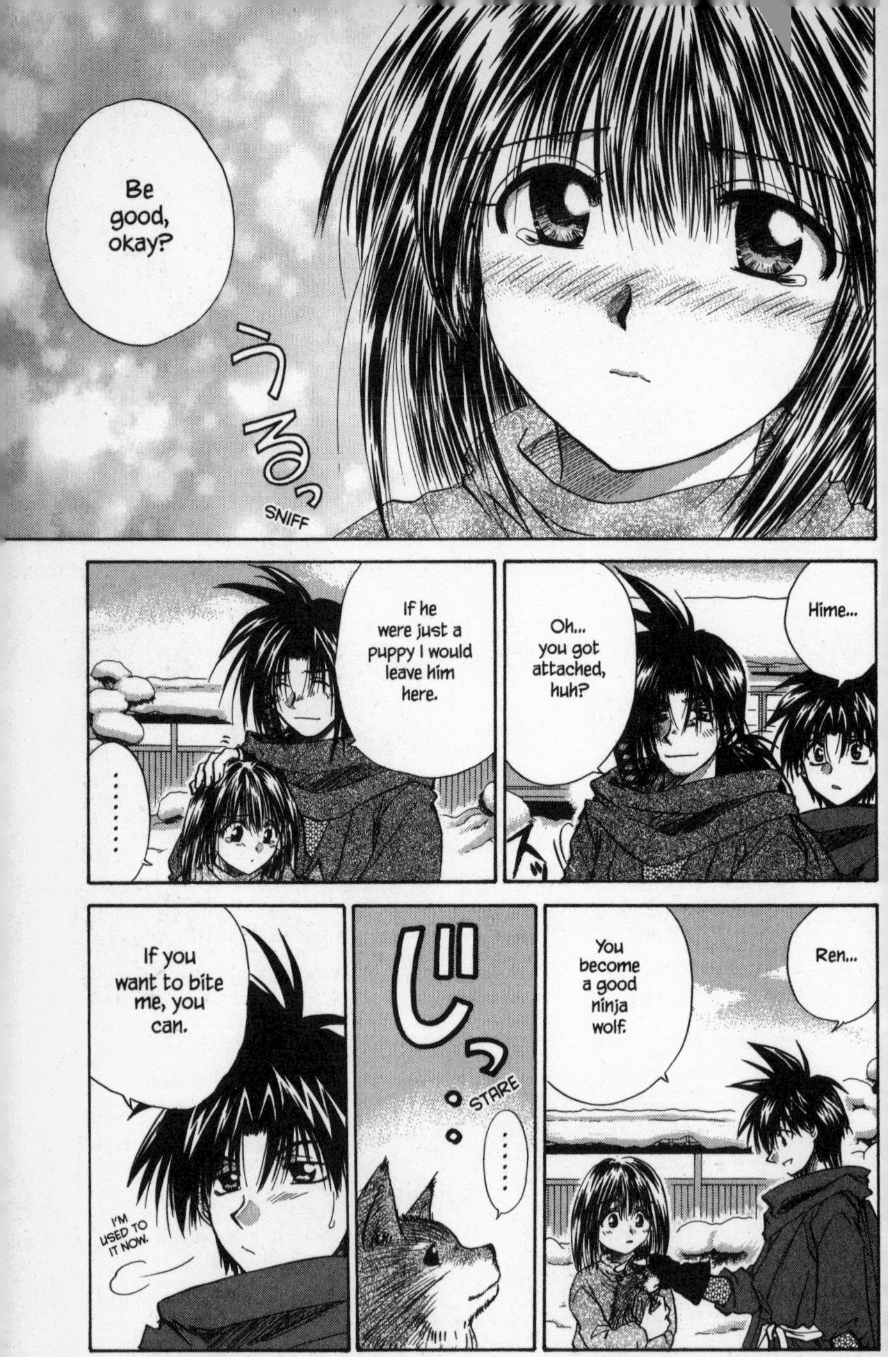

Be good, okay?
うるっ
SNIFF
Hime...
Oh... you got attached, huh?
If he were just a puppy I would leave him here.
......
Ren...
You become a good ninja wolf.
じっ
STARE
......
If you want to bite me, you can.
I'M USED TO IT NOW.

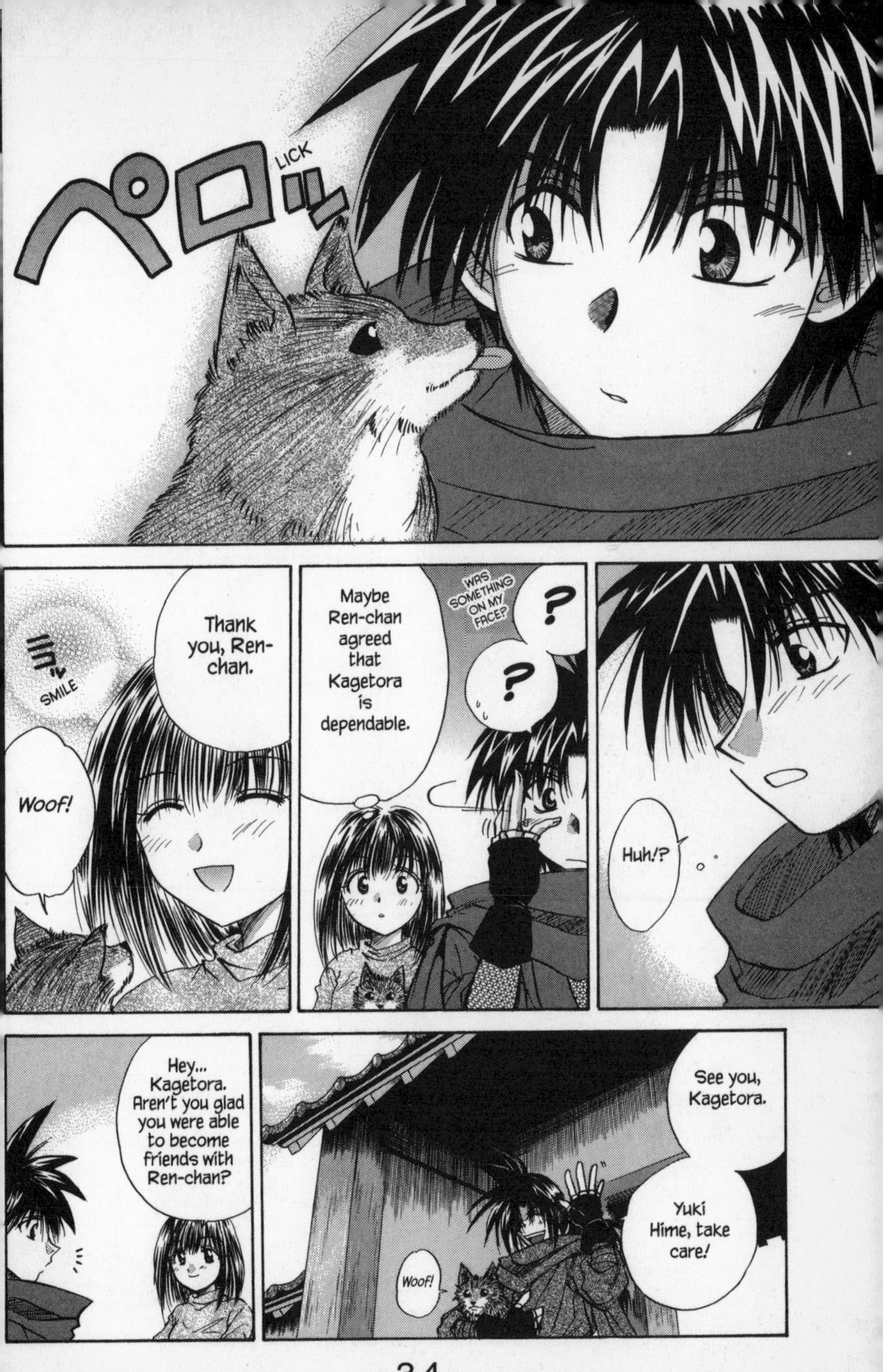

ペロッ
LICK
Huh!?
WAS SOMETHING ON MY FACE?
?
?
Maybe Ren-chan agreed that Kagetora is dependable.
Thank you, Ren-chan.
ニコッ
SMILE
Woof!
See you, Kagetora.
Yuki Hime, take care!
Woof!
Hey... Kagetora. Aren't you glad you were able to become friends with Ren-chan?

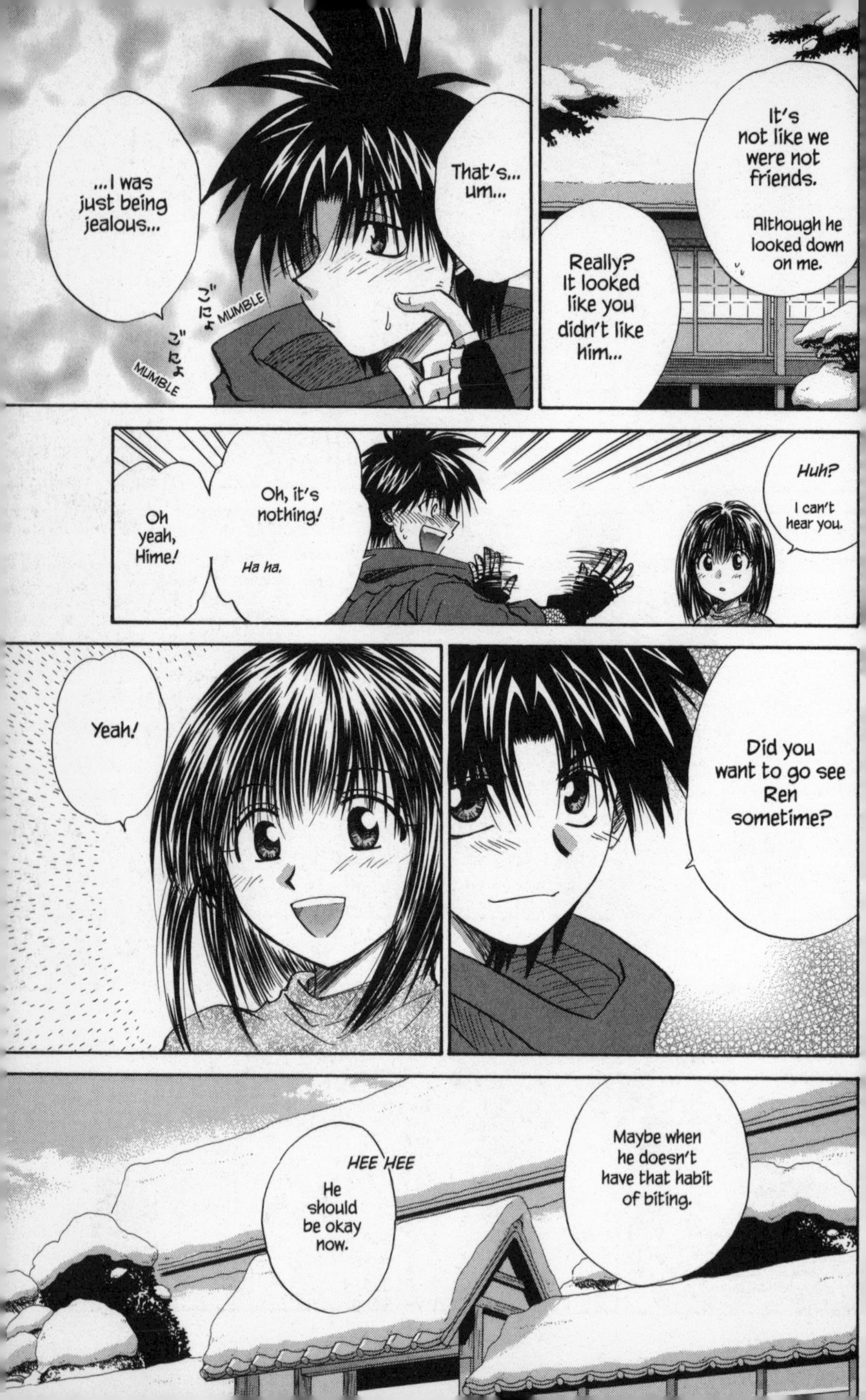
It's not like we were not friends.
Although he looked down on me.
Really? It looked like you didn't like him...
That's... um...
...I was just being jealous...
ごにょ MUMBLE
ごにょ MUMBLE
Huh?
I can't hear you.
Oh, it's nothing!
Ha ha.
Oh yeah, Hime!
Did you want to go see Ren sometime?
Yeah!
Maybe when he doesn't have that habit of biting.
HEE HEE
He should be okay now.

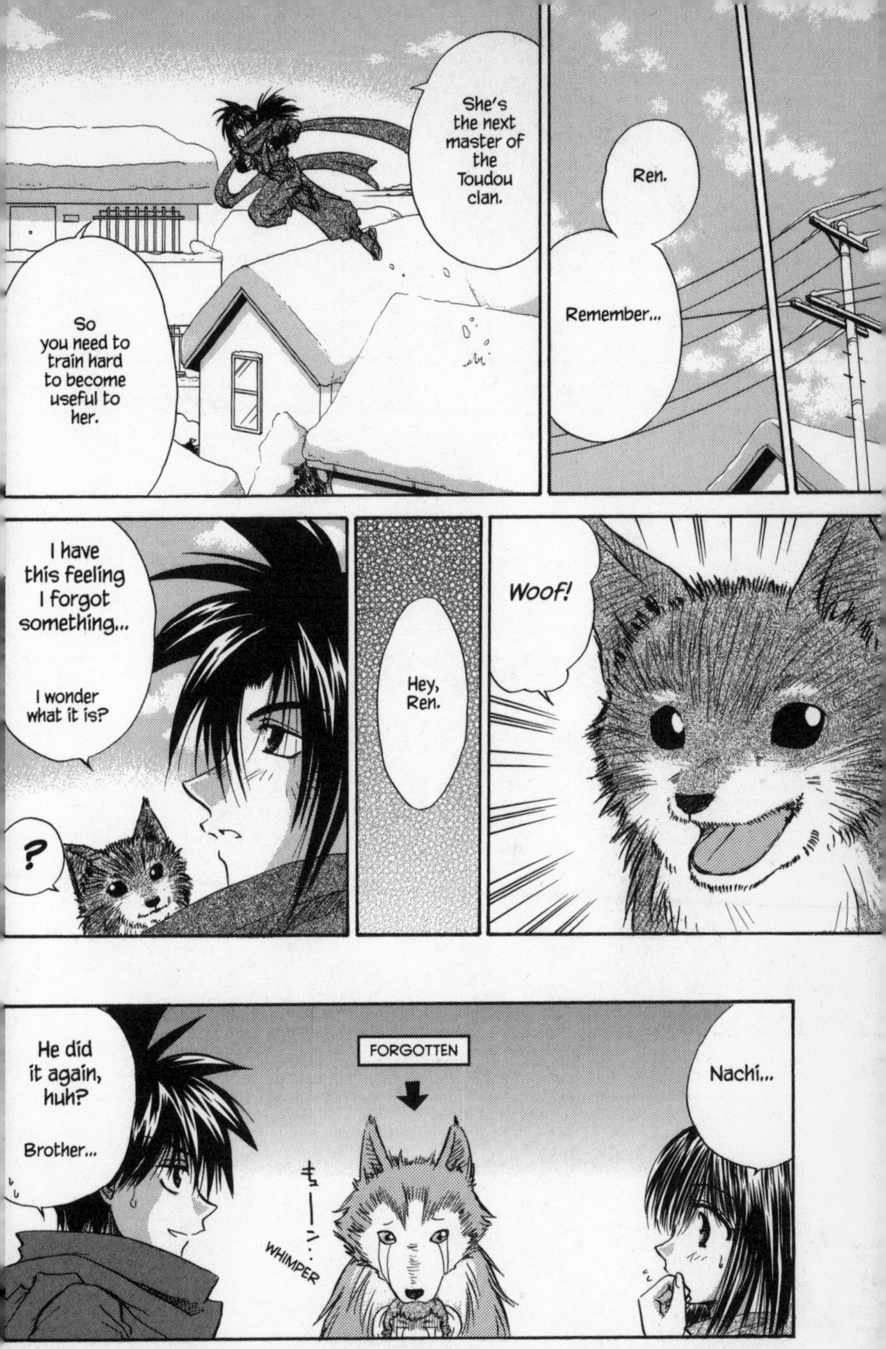
Ren.
Remember...
She's the next master of the Toudou clan.
So you need to train hard to become useful to her.
Woof!
Hey, Ren.
I have this feeling I forgot something...
I wonder what it is?
?
Nachi...
FORGOTTEN
WHIMPER
He did it again, huh?
Brother...

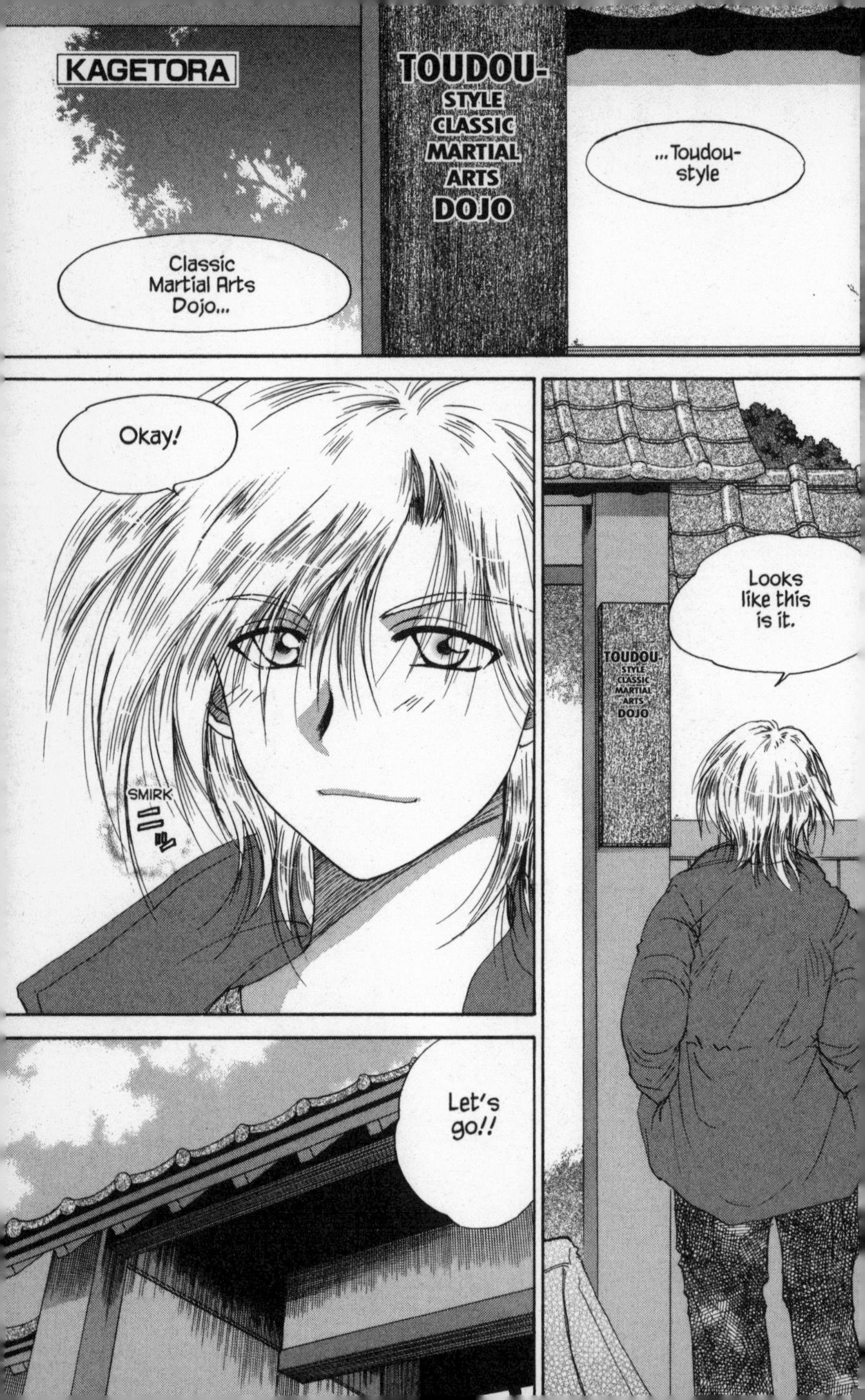
...Toudou-style
TOUDOU-STYLE CLASSIC MARTIAL ARTS DOJO
Classic Martial Arts Dojo...
TOUDOU-STYLE CLASSIC MARTIAL ARTS DOJO
Looks like this is it.
Okay!
SMIRK
Let's go!!

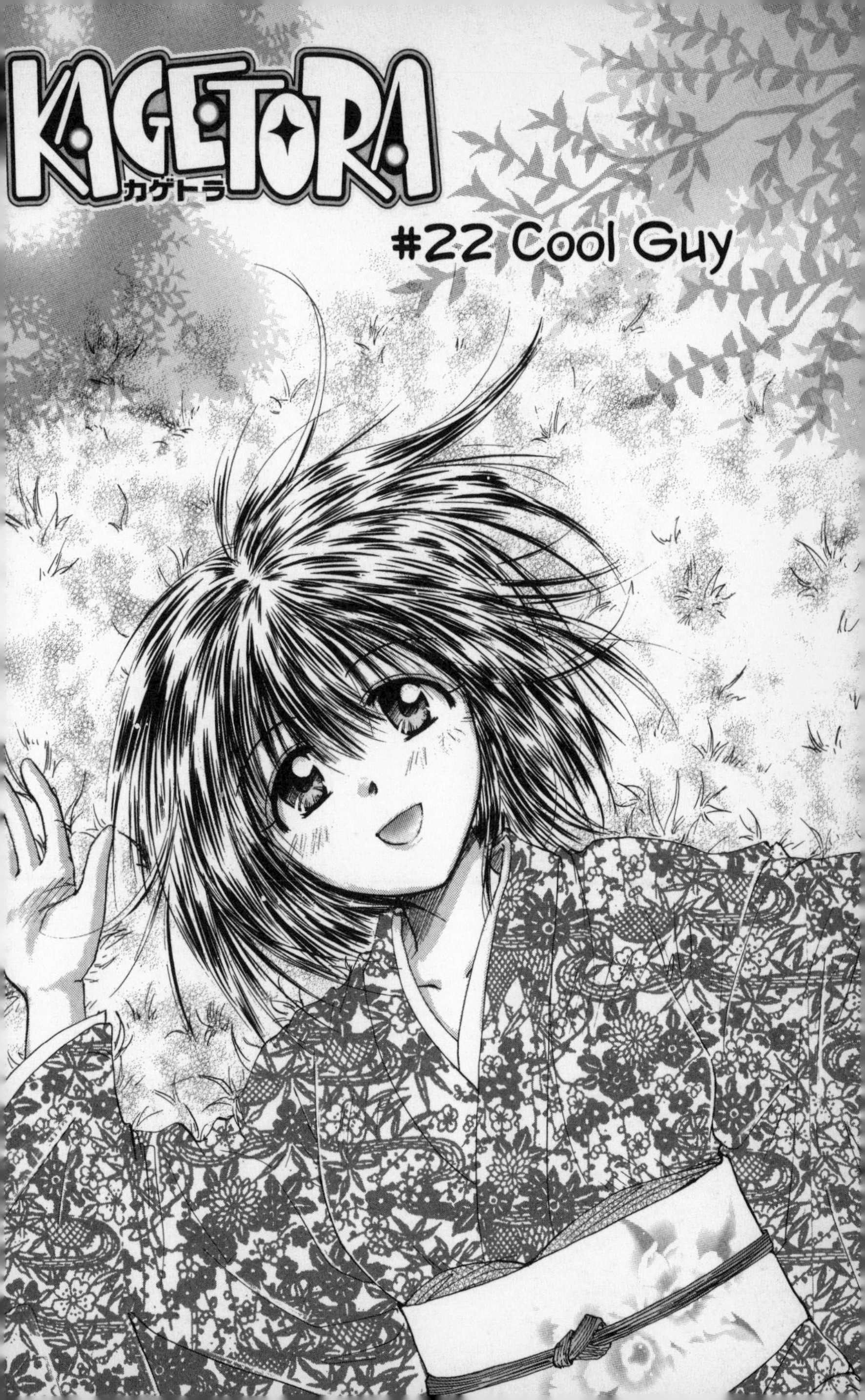
KAGETORA
カゲトラ
#22 Cool Guy

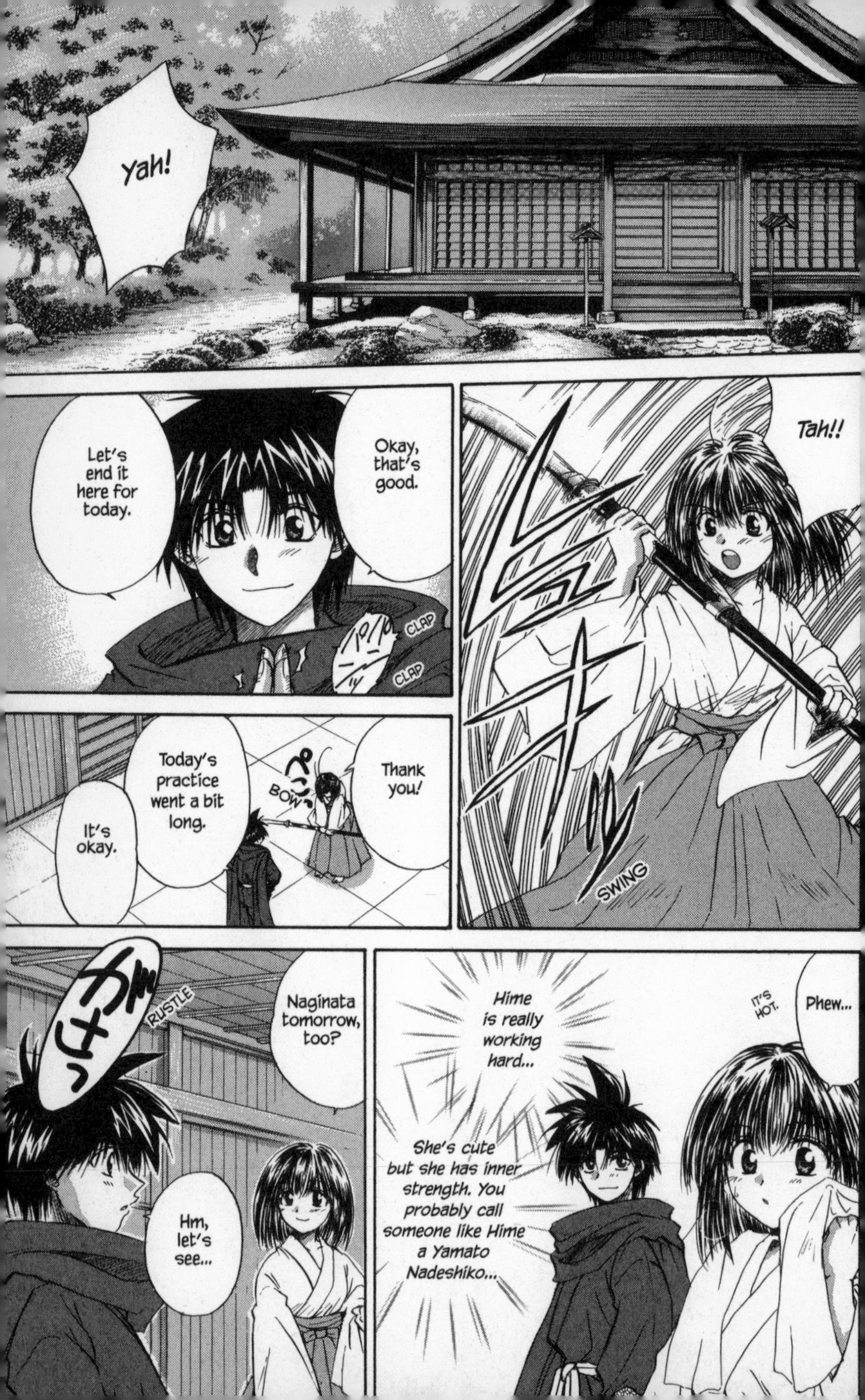
Yah!
Tah!!
SWING
Okay, that's good.
Let's end it here for today.
CLAP
CLAP
Thank you!
BOW
Today's practice went a bit long.
It's okay.
Phew...
IT'S HOT.
Hime is really working hard...
She's cute but she has inner strength. You probably call someone like Hime a Yamato Nadeshiko...
Naginata tomorrow, too?
RUSTLE
Hm, let's see...

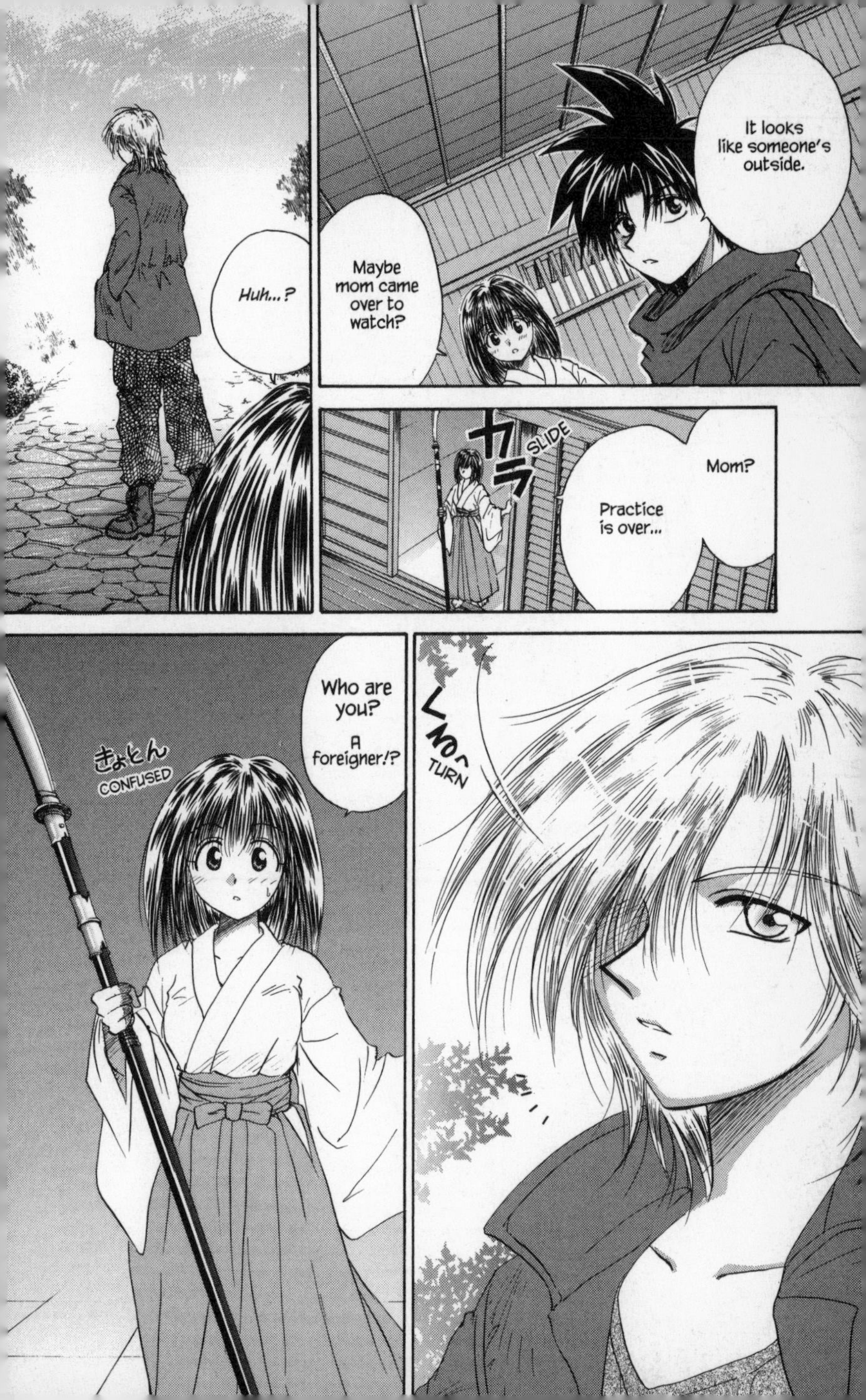
It looks like someone's outside.
Maybe mom came over to watch?
カラ SLIDE
Mom?
Practice is over...
Huh...?
TURN
Who are you?
A foreigner!?
きょとん CONFUSED

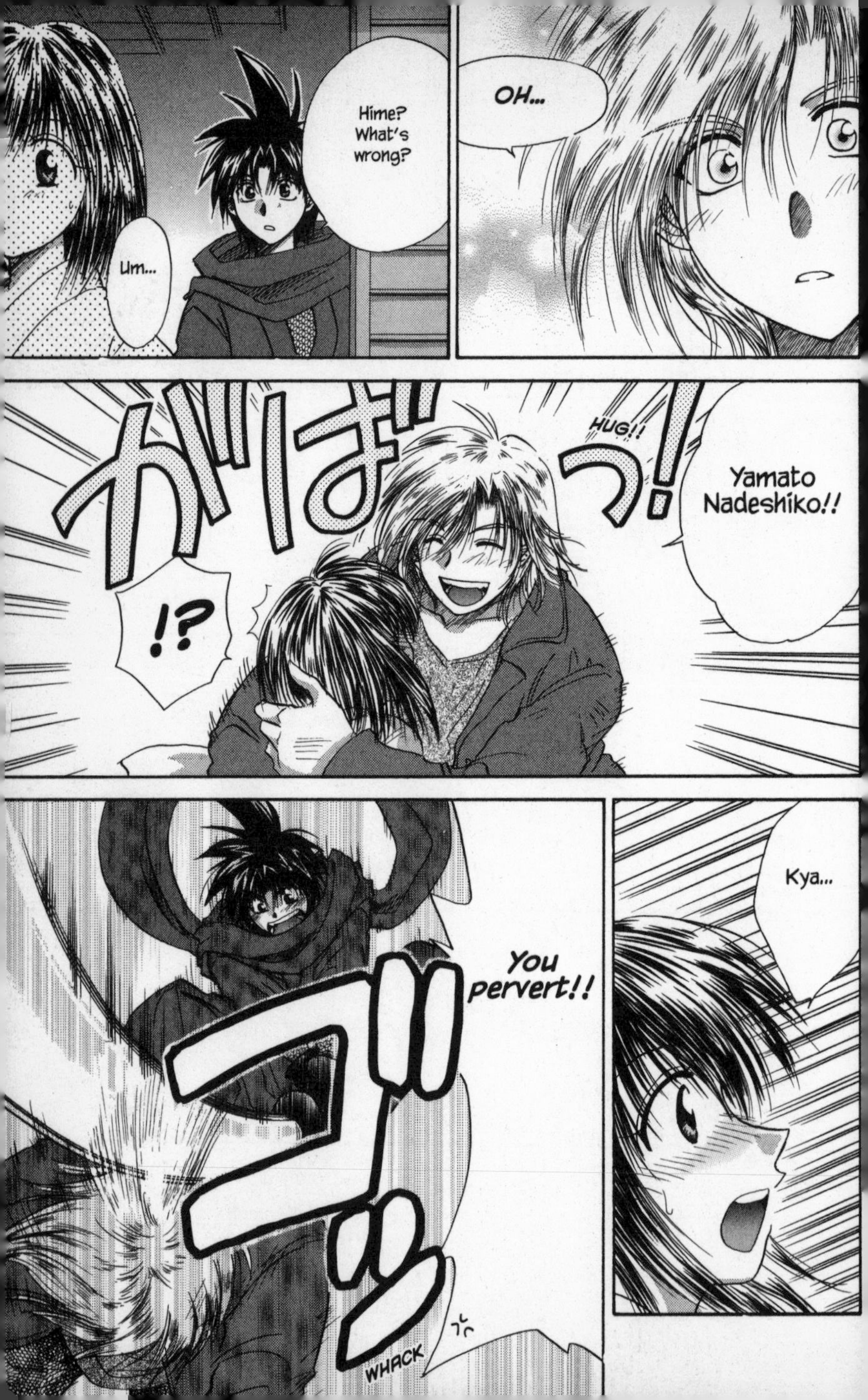
OH...
Hime? What's wrong?
Um...
Yamato Nadeshiko!!
HUG!!
がばっ!
!?
Kya...
You pervert!!
ゴッ
WHACK

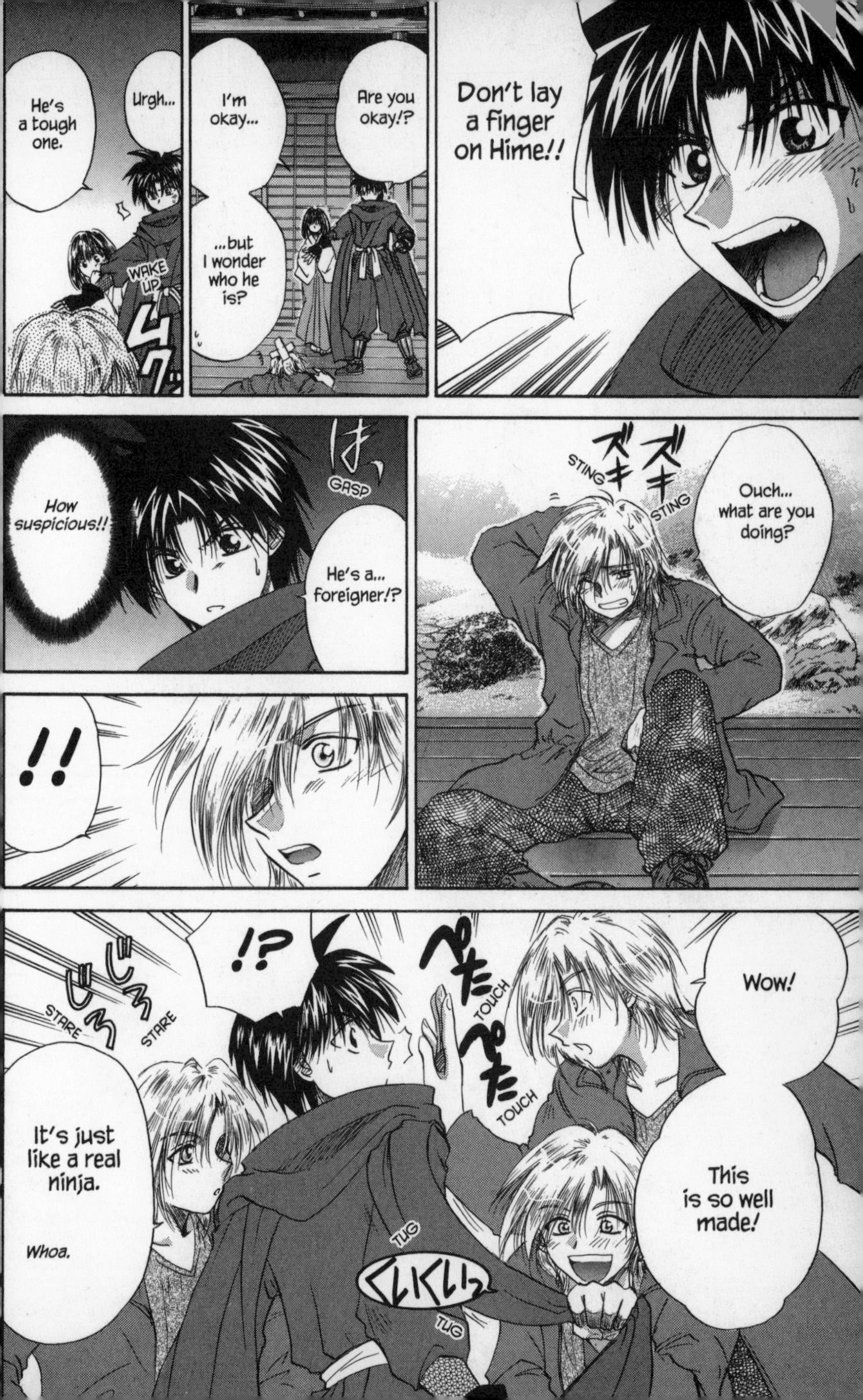
Don't lay a finger on Hime!!
Are you okay!?
I'm okay...
...but I wonder who he is?
Urgh...
He's a tough one.
WAKE UP
ズキ ズキ
STING STING
Ouch... what are you doing?
は
GASP
He's a... foreigner!?
How suspicious!!
!!
Wow!
This is so well made!
ぺた ぺた
TOUCH TOUCH
!?
じろ じろ
STARE STARE
It's just like a real ninja.
Whoa.
くいくいっ
TUG TUG

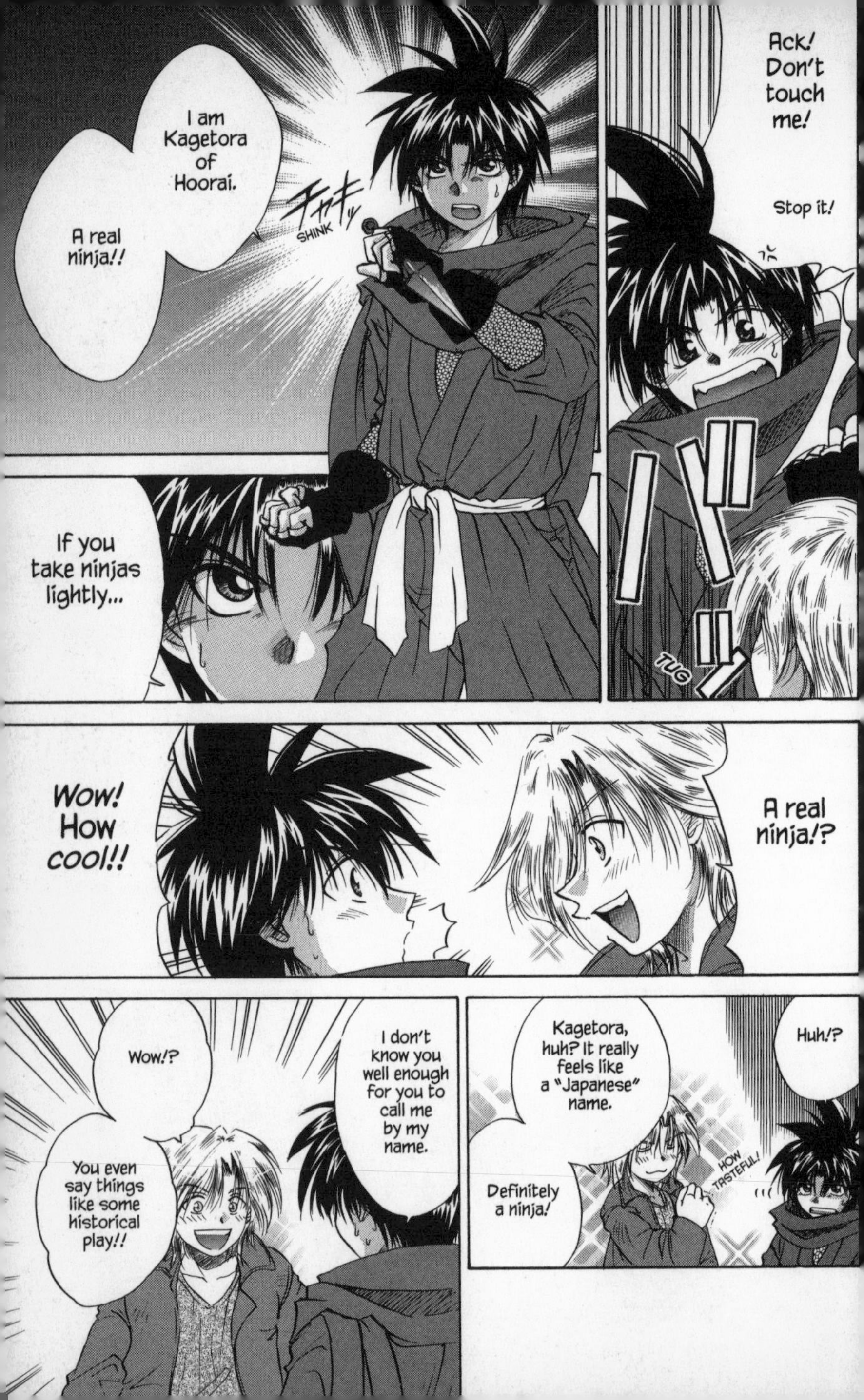
Ack! Don't touch me!
Stop it!
TUG
I am Kagetora of Hoorai.
A real ninja!!
チャキッ
SHINK
If you take ninjas lightly...
A real ninja!?
Wow! How cool!!
Huh!?
Kagetora, huh? It really feels like a "Japanese" name.
HOW TASTEFUL!
Definitely a ninja!
I don't know you well enough for you to call me by my name.
Wow!?
You even say things like some historical play!!

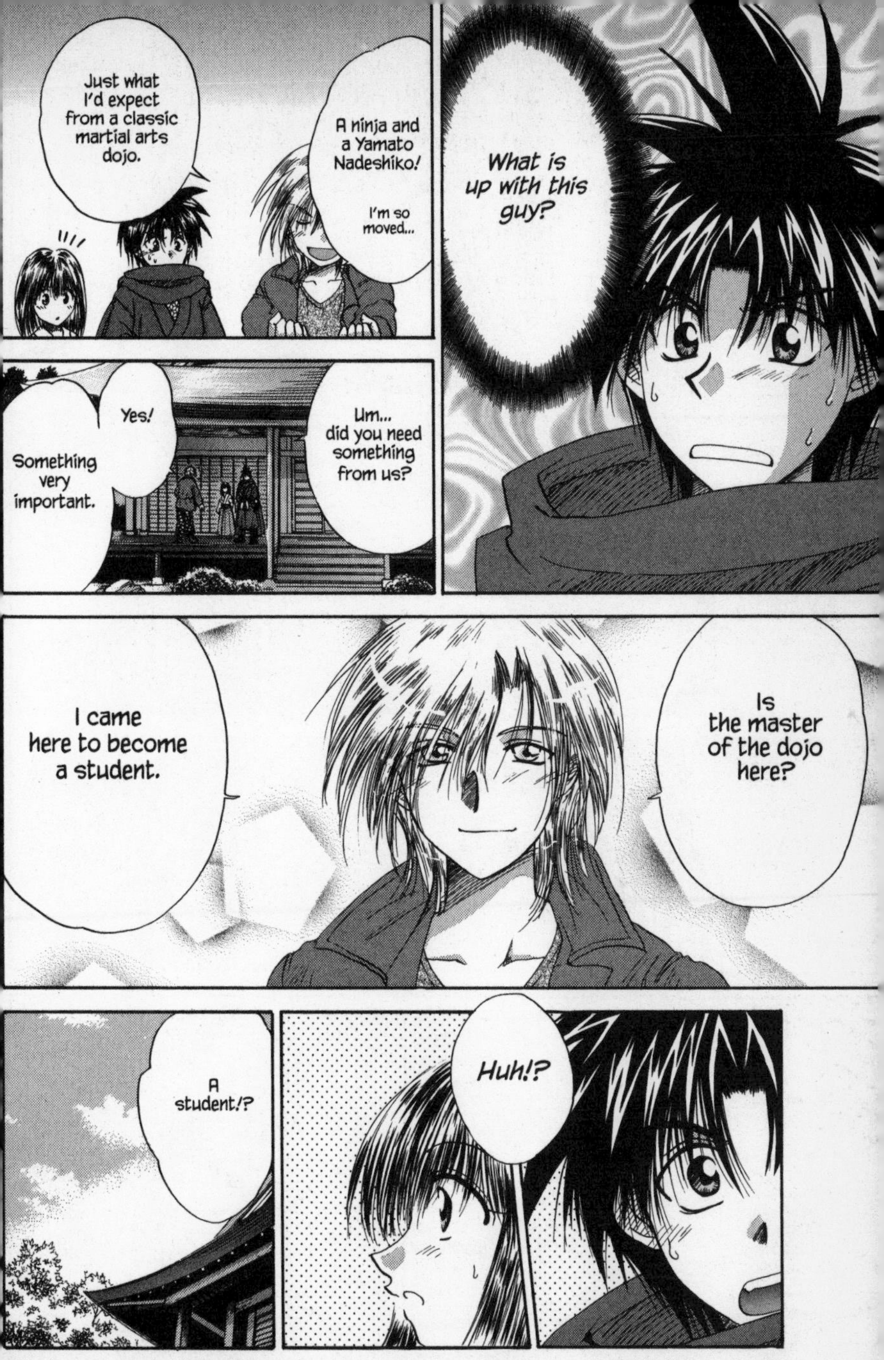
What is up with this guy?
A ninja and a Yamato Nadeshiko!
I'm so moved...
Just what I'd expect from a classic martial arts dojo.
Um... did you need something from us?
Yes!
Something very important.
Is the master of the dojo here?
I came here to become a student.
Huh!?
A student!?

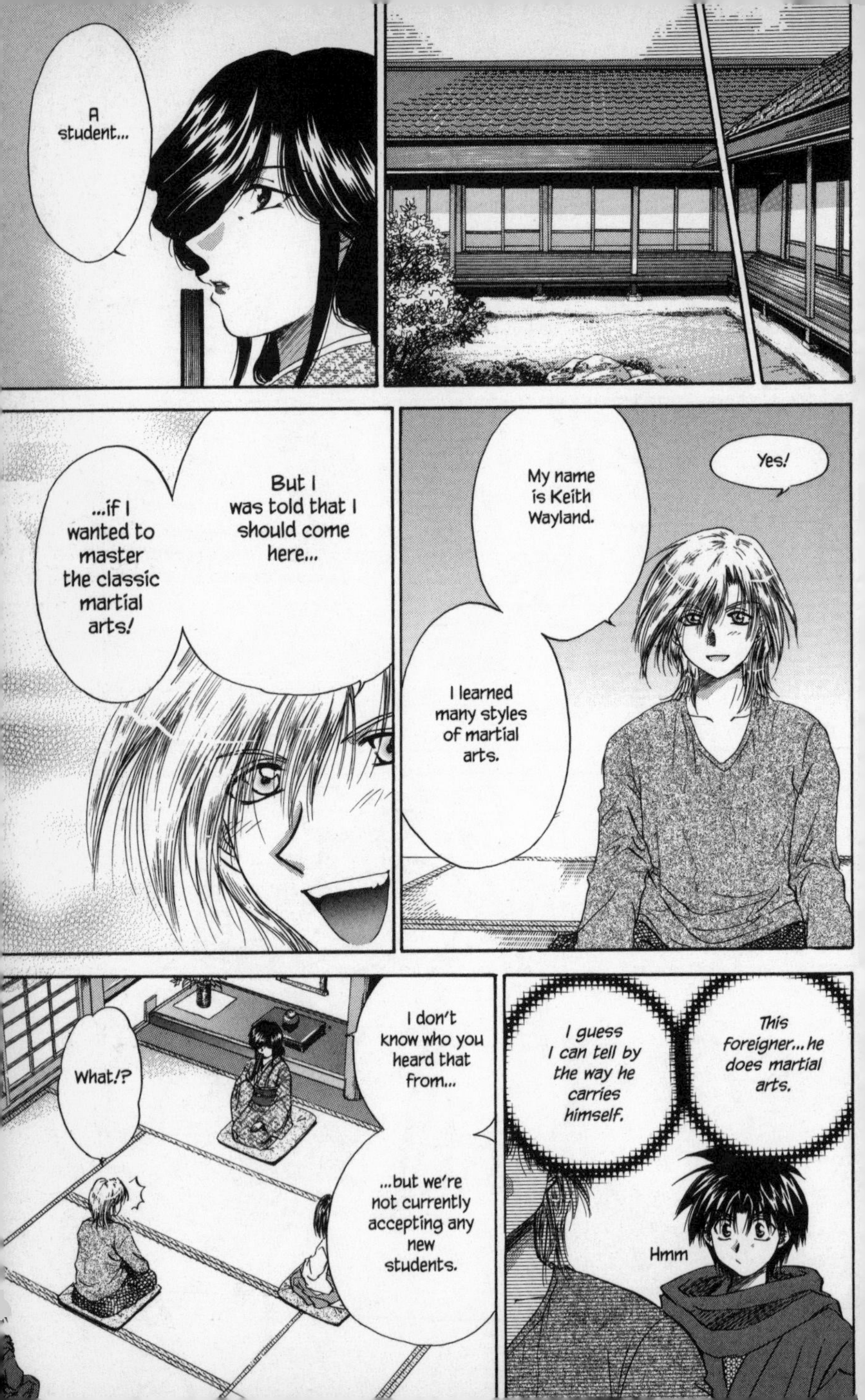
A student...
Yes!
My name is Keith Wayland.
I learned many styles of martial arts.
But I was told that I should come here...
...if I wanted to master the classic martial arts!
This foreigner...he does martial arts.
I guess I can tell by the way he carries himself.
Hmm
I don't know who you heard that from...
...but we're not currently accepting any new students.
What!?

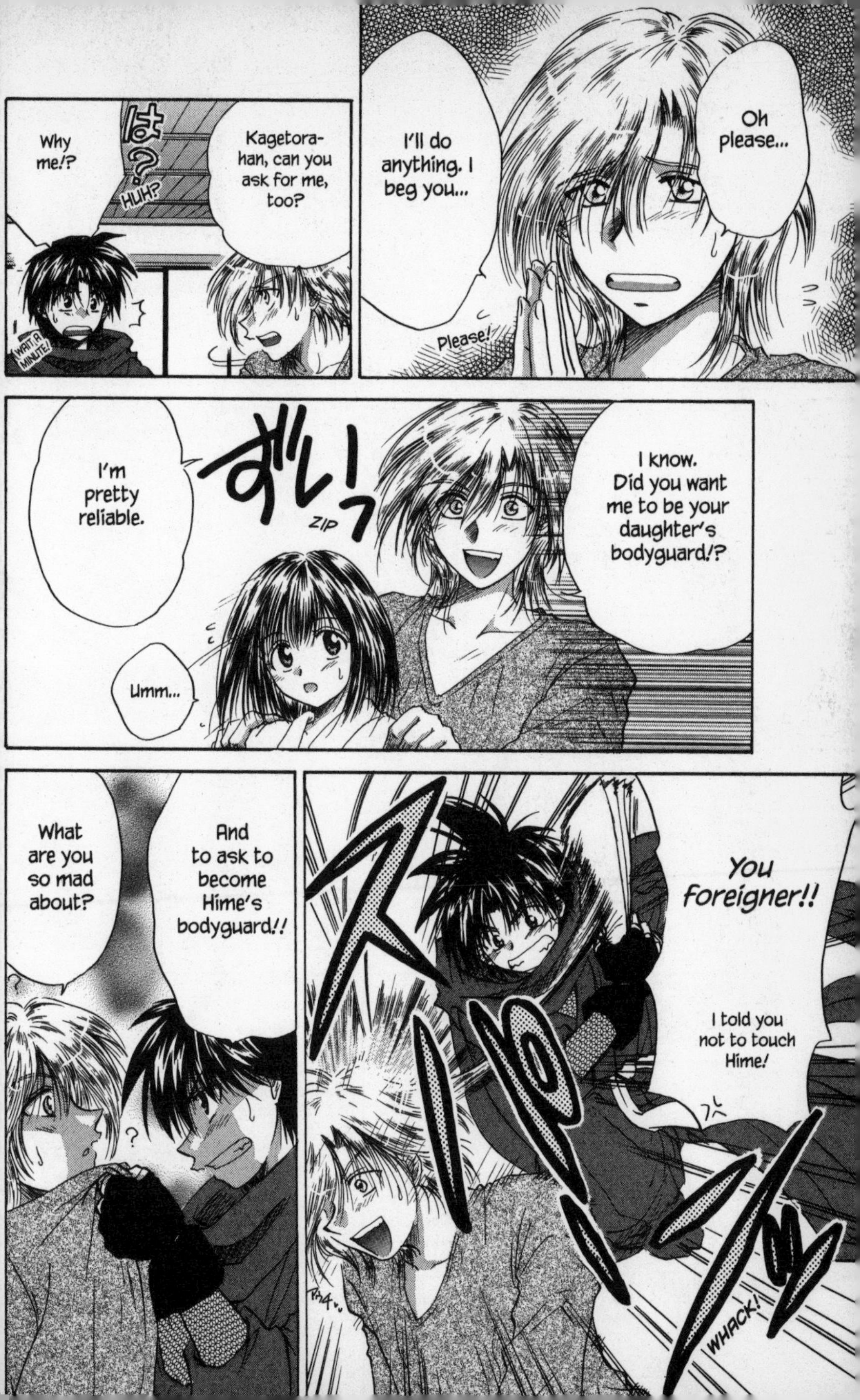
Oh please...
I'll do anything. I beg you...
Please!
Kagetora-han, can you ask for me, too?
は？
HUH?
Why me!?
WAIT A MINUTE!
I know. Did you want me to be your daughter's bodyguard!?
ずいっ
ZIP
I'm pretty reliable.
Umm...
You foreigner!!
I told you not to touch Hime!
WHACK!
And to ask to become Hime's bodyguard!!
What are you so mad about?

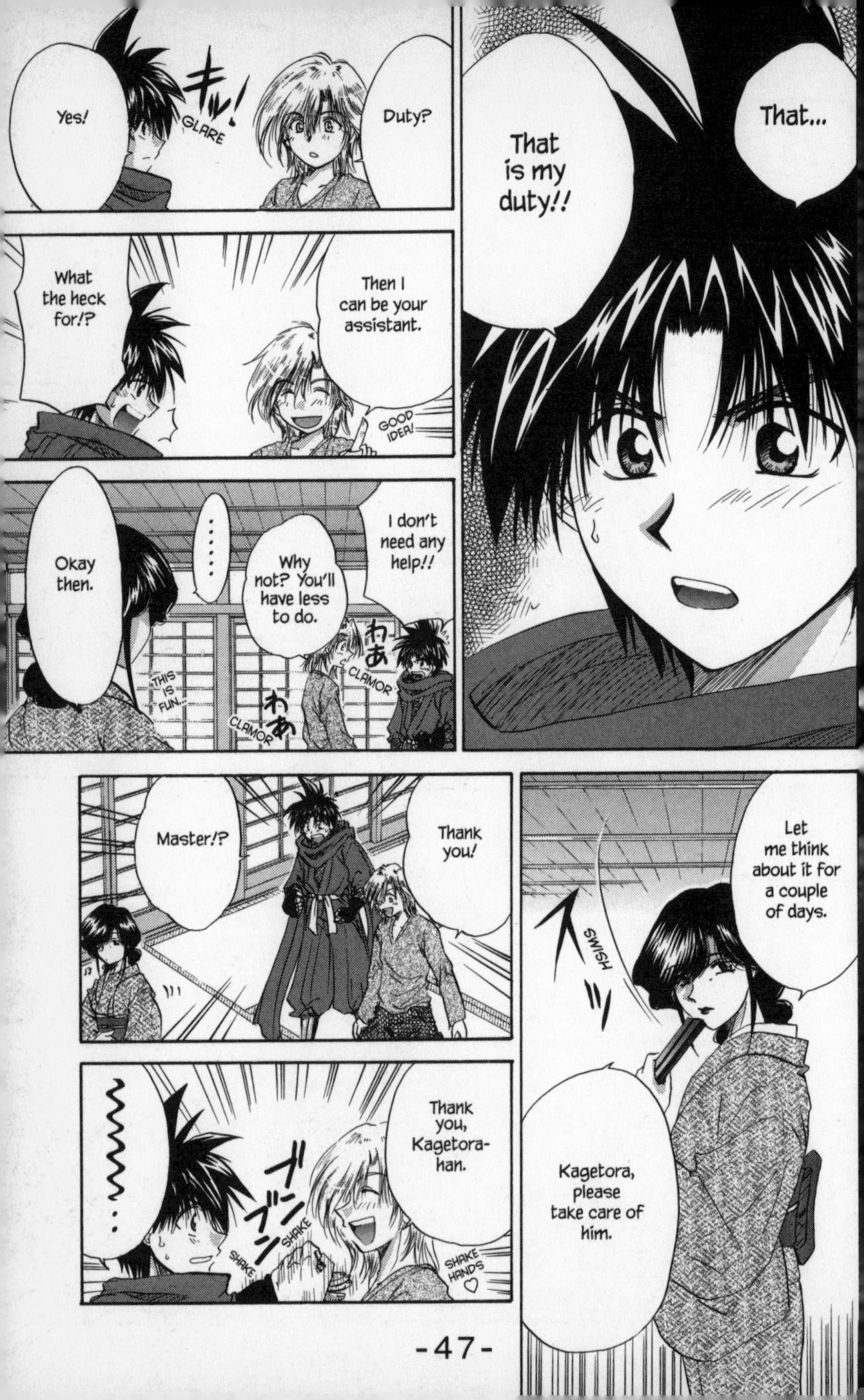
That...
That is my duty!!
Duty?
GLARE
Yes!
Then I can be your assistant.
GOOD IDEA!
What the heck for!?
I don't need any help!!
Why not? You'll have less to do.
CLAMOR
CLAMOR
......
THIS IS FUN...
Okay then.
Let me think about it for a couple of days.
SWISH
Kagetora, please take care of him.
Thank you!
Master!?
Thank you, Kagetora-han.
SHAKE HANDS
SHAKE
SHAKE
......

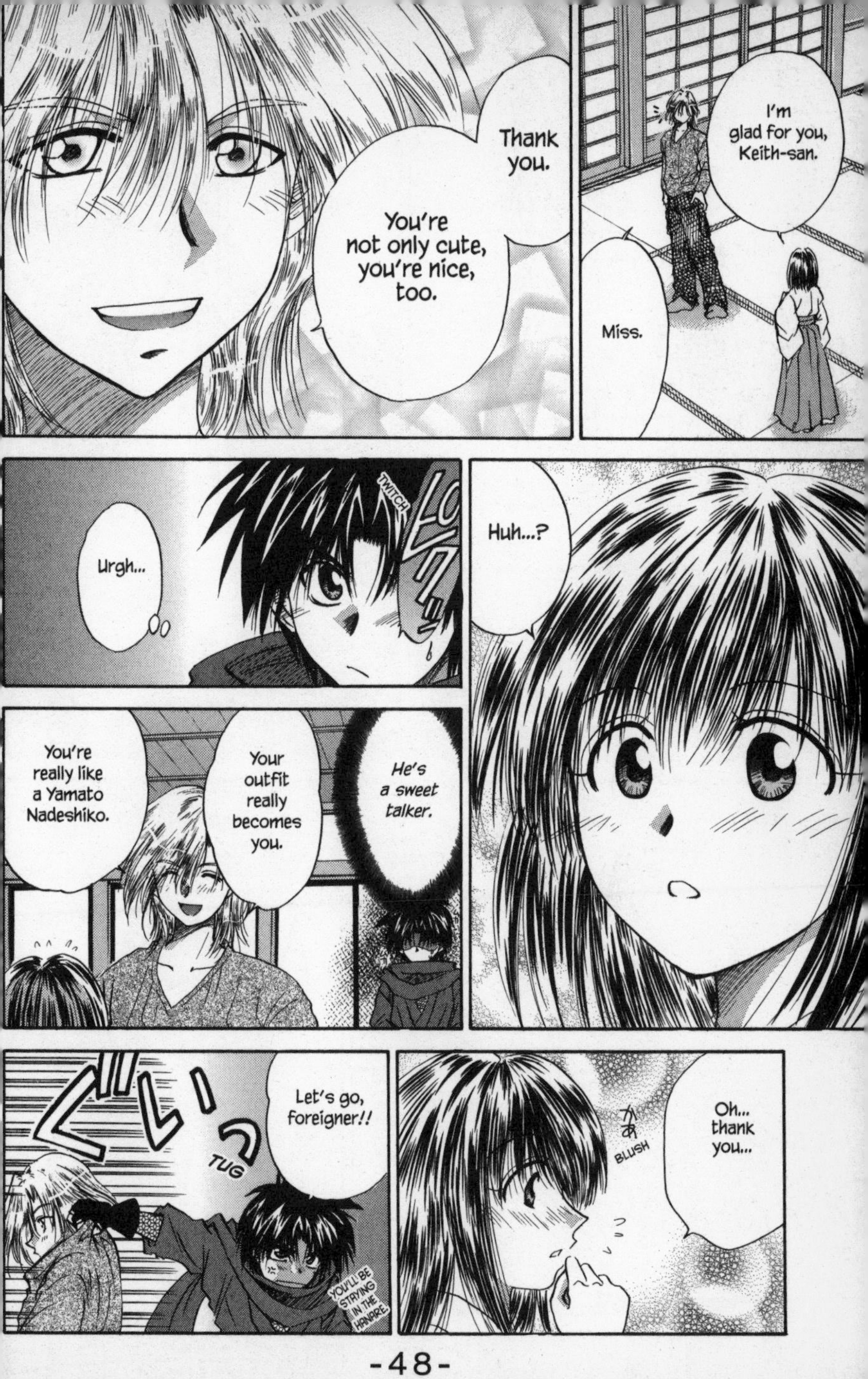
I'm glad for you, Keith-san.
Miss.
Thank you.
You're not only cute, you're nice, too.
Huh...?
TWITCH
Urgh...
He's a sweet talker.
Your outfit really becomes you.
You're really like a Yamato Nadeshiko.
BLUSH
Oh... thank you...
Let's go, foreigner!!
TUG
YOU'LL BE STAYING IN THE HANARE.

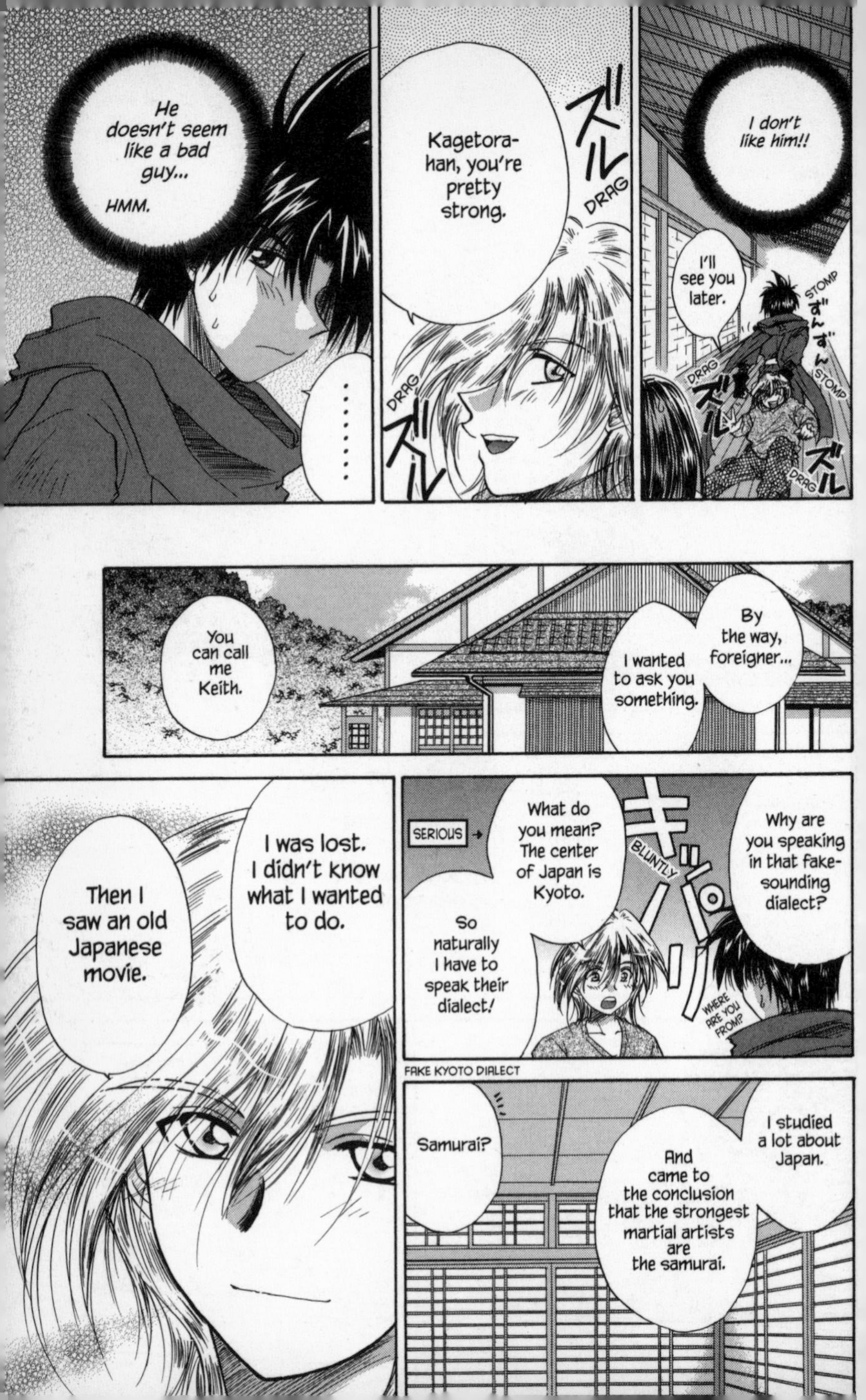

I don't like him!!
I'll see you later.
STOMP
ずんずん
STOMP
DRAG
ズル
DRAG
ズル
Kagetora-han, you're pretty strong.
ズル
DRAG
DRAG
ズル
He doesn't seem like a bad guy...
HMM.
......
By the way, foreigner...
I wanted to ask you something.
You can call me Keith.
Why are you speaking in that fake-sounding dialect?
WHERE ARE YOU FROM?
SERIOUS →
What do you mean? The center of Japan is Kyoto.
キッパリ
BLUNTLY
So naturally I have to speak their dialect!
FAKE KYOTO DIALECT
I studied a lot about Japan.
And came to the conclusion that the strongest martial artists are the samurai.
Samurai?
I was lost. I didn't know what I wanted to do.
Then I saw an old Japanese movie.

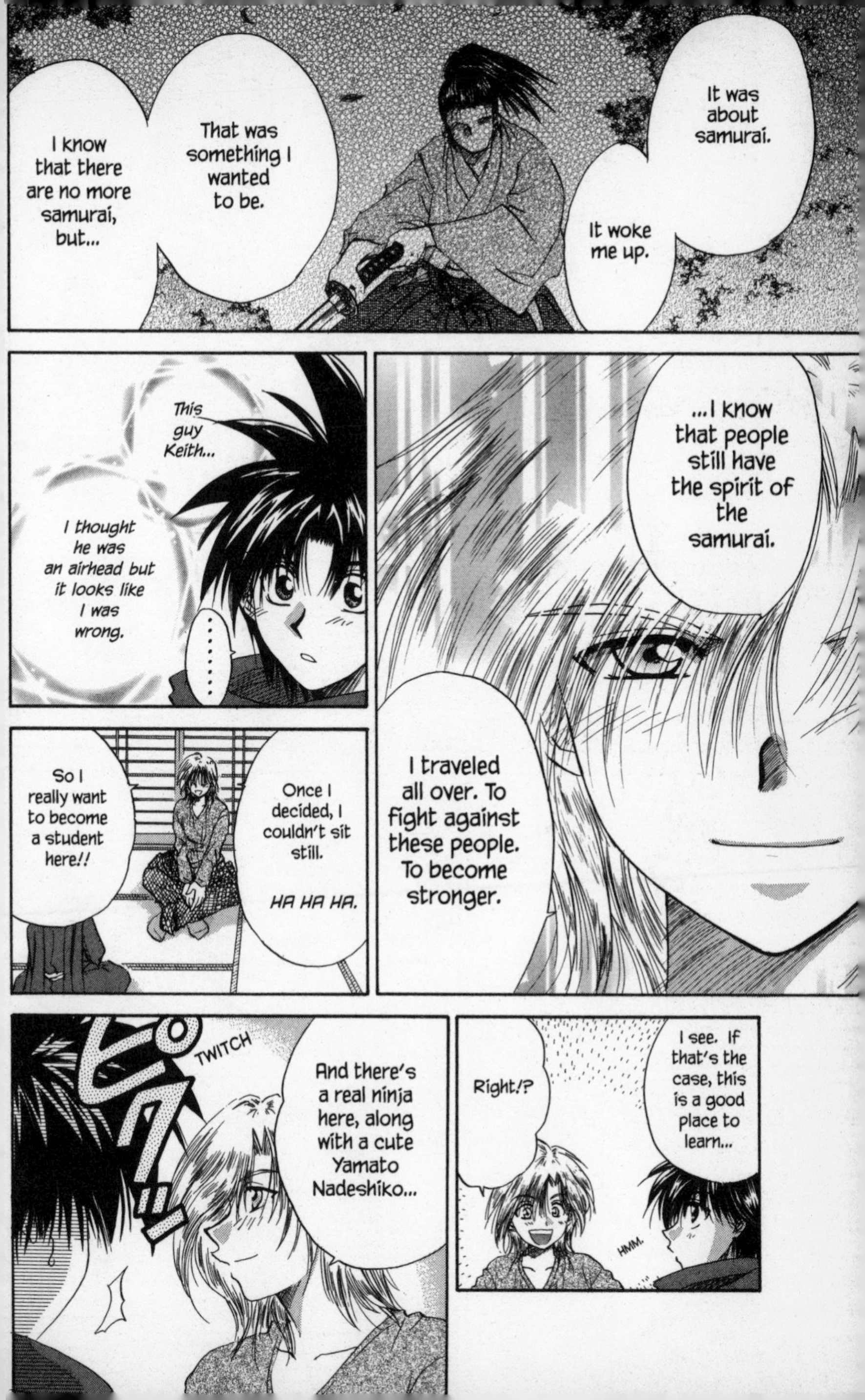

It was about samurai.
It woke me up.
That was something I wanted to be.
I know that there are no more samurai, but...
...I know that people still have the spirit of the samurai.
I traveled all over. To fight against these people. To become stronger.
This guy Keith...
I thought he was an airhead but it looks like I was wrong.
......
Once I decided, I couldn't sit still.
HA HA HA.
So I really want to become a student here!!
I see. If that's the case, this is a good place to learn...
HMM.
Right!?
And there's a real ninja here, along with a cute Yamato Nadeshiko...
TWITCH

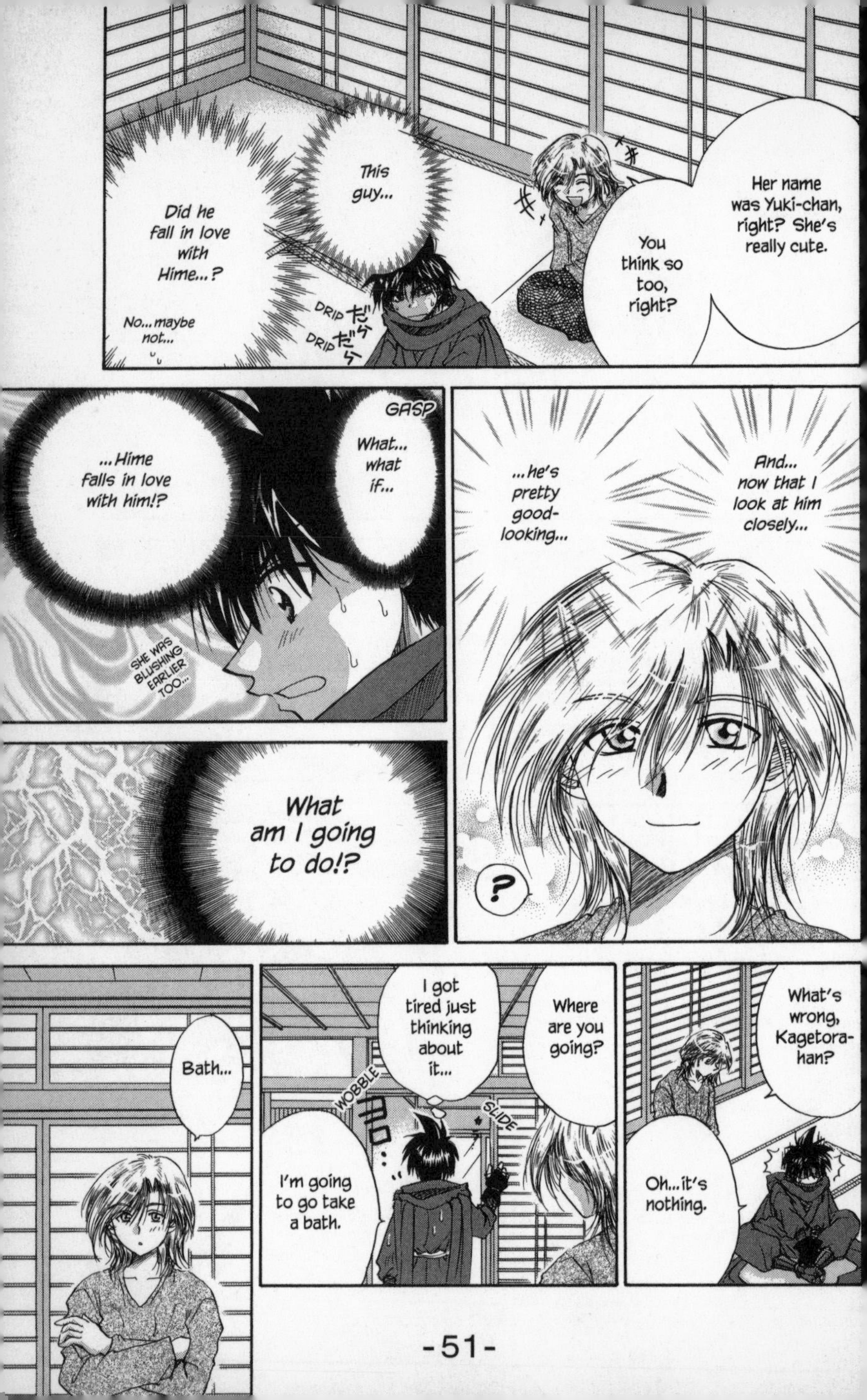

Her name was Yuki-chan, right? She's really cute.
You think so too, right?
This guy...
Did he fall in love with Hime...?
No...maybe not...
DRIP
DRIP
And... now that I look at him closely...
...he's pretty good-looking...
?
GASP
What... what if...
...Hime falls in love with him!?
SHE WAS BLUSHING EARLIER TOO...
What am I going to do!?
What's wrong, Kagetora-han?
Oh...it's nothing.
Where are you going?
I got tired just thinking about it...
SLIDE
WOBBLE
I'm going to go take a bath.
Bath...

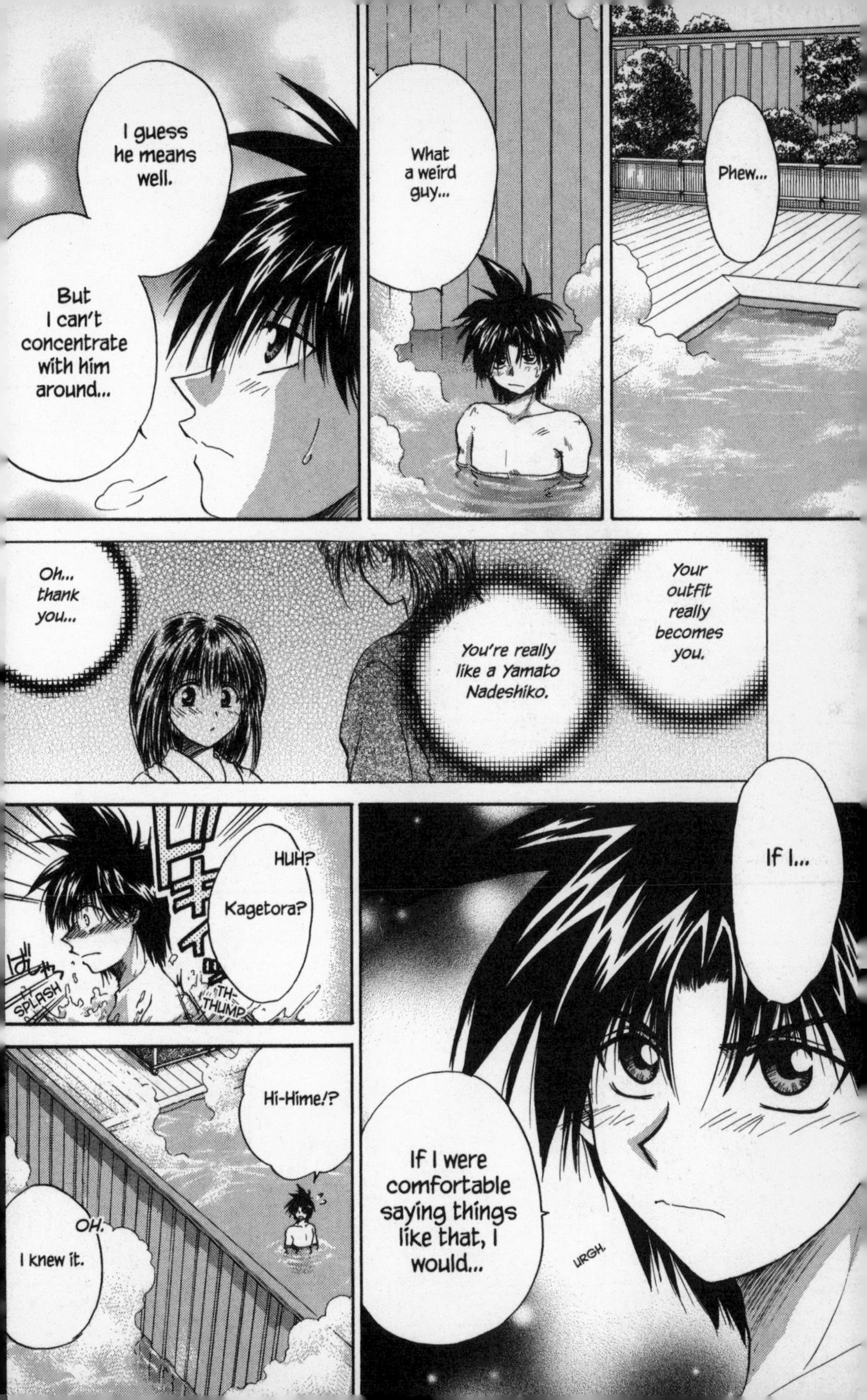
Phew...
What a weird guy...
I guess he means well.
But I can't concentrate with him around...
Your outfit really becomes you.
You're really like a Yamato Nadeshiko.
Oh... thank you...
If I...
If I were comfortable saying things like that, I would...
URGH.
HUH?
Kagetora?
TH-THUMP
SPLASH
Hi-Hime!?
OH.
I knew it.

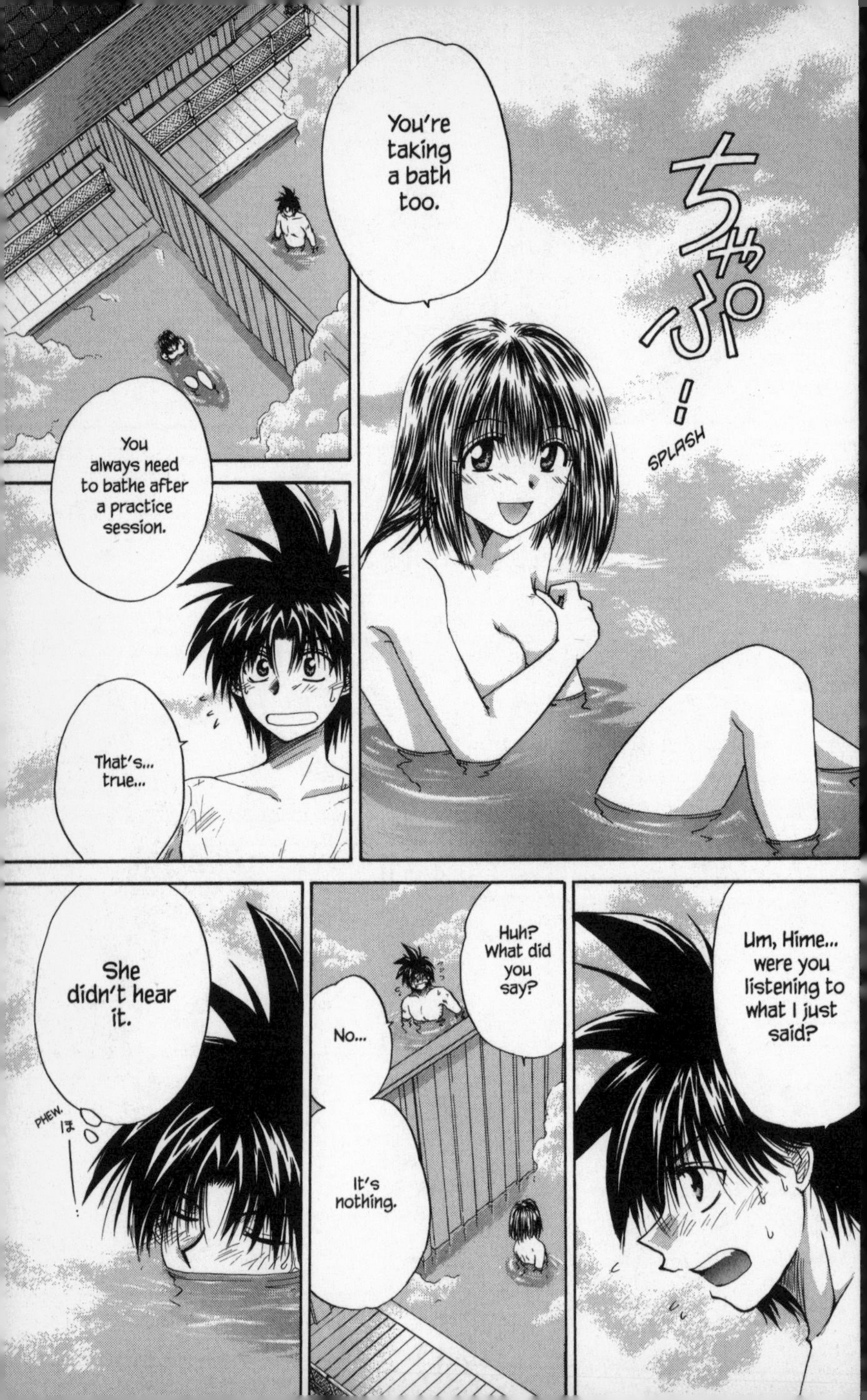
ちゅぷ!!
SPLASH
You're taking a bath too.
You always need to bathe after a practice session.
That's... true...
Um, Hime... were you listening to what I just said?
Huh? What did you say?
No...
It's nothing.
She didn't hear it.
PHEW. ほ

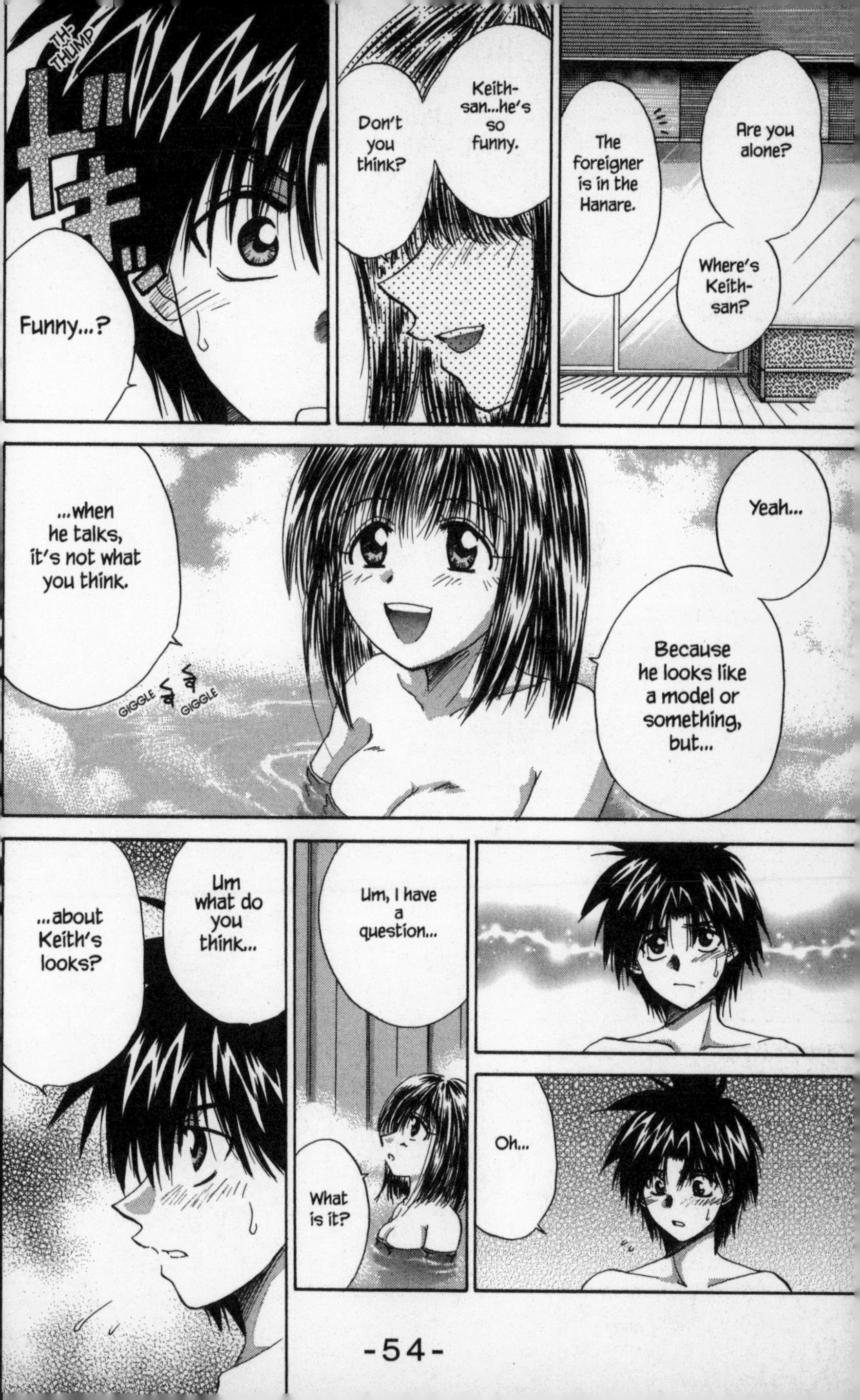
Are you alone?
Where's Keith-san?
The foreigner is in the Hanare.
Keith-san...he's so funny.
Don't you think?
TH-THUMP
Funny...?
Yeah...
Because he looks like a model or something, but...
...when he talks, it's not what you think.
GIGGLE GIGGLE
Oh...
Um, I have a question...
What is it?
Um what do you think...
...about Keith's looks?

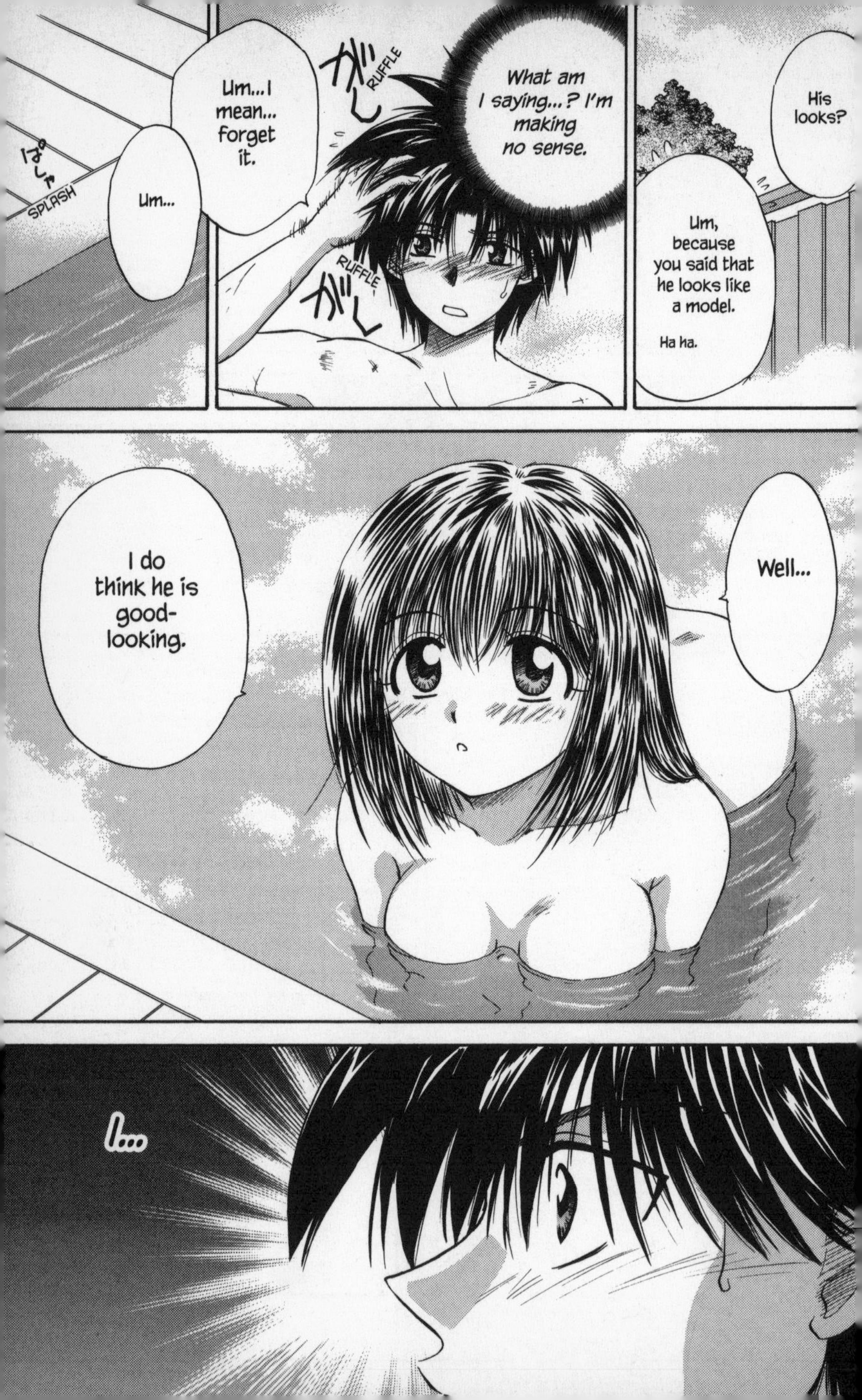
His looks?
Um, because you said that he looks like a model.
Ha ha.
What am I saying...? I'm making no sense.
がし RUFFLE
がし RUFFLE
Um...I mean...forget it.
Um...
ぱしゃ SPLASH
Well...
I do think he is good-looking.
I...

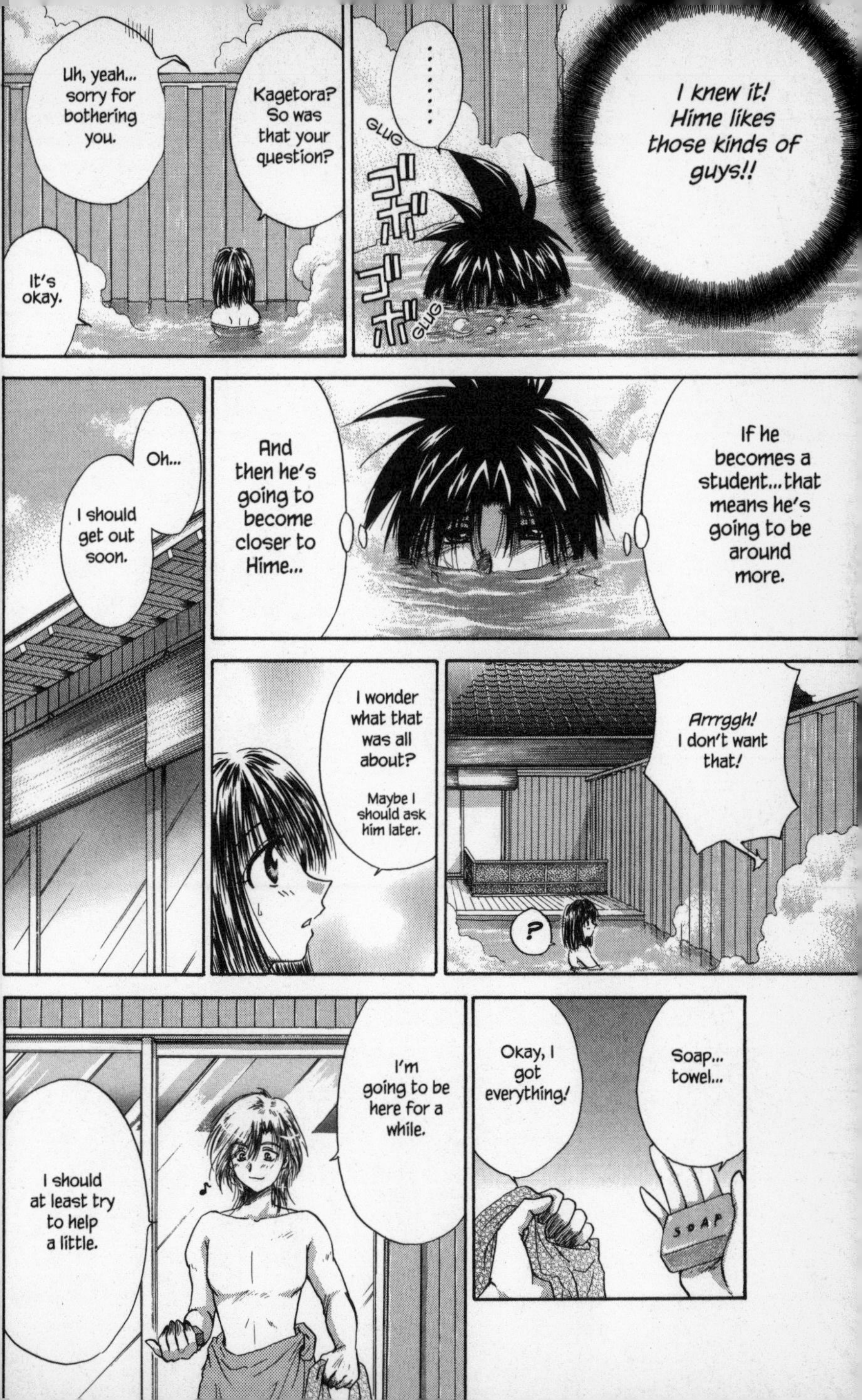
I knew it! Hime likes those kinds of guys!!
......
GLUG
ゴボゴボ
GLUG
Kagetora? So was that your question?
Uh, yeah... sorry for bothering you.
It's okay.
If he becomes a student...that means he's going to be around more.
And then he's going to become closer to Hime...
Arrrggh! I don't want that!
?
I wonder what that was all about?
Maybe I should ask him later.
Oh...
I should get out soon.
Soap... towel...
Okay, I got everything!
SOAP
I'm going to be here for a while.
I should at least try to help a little.

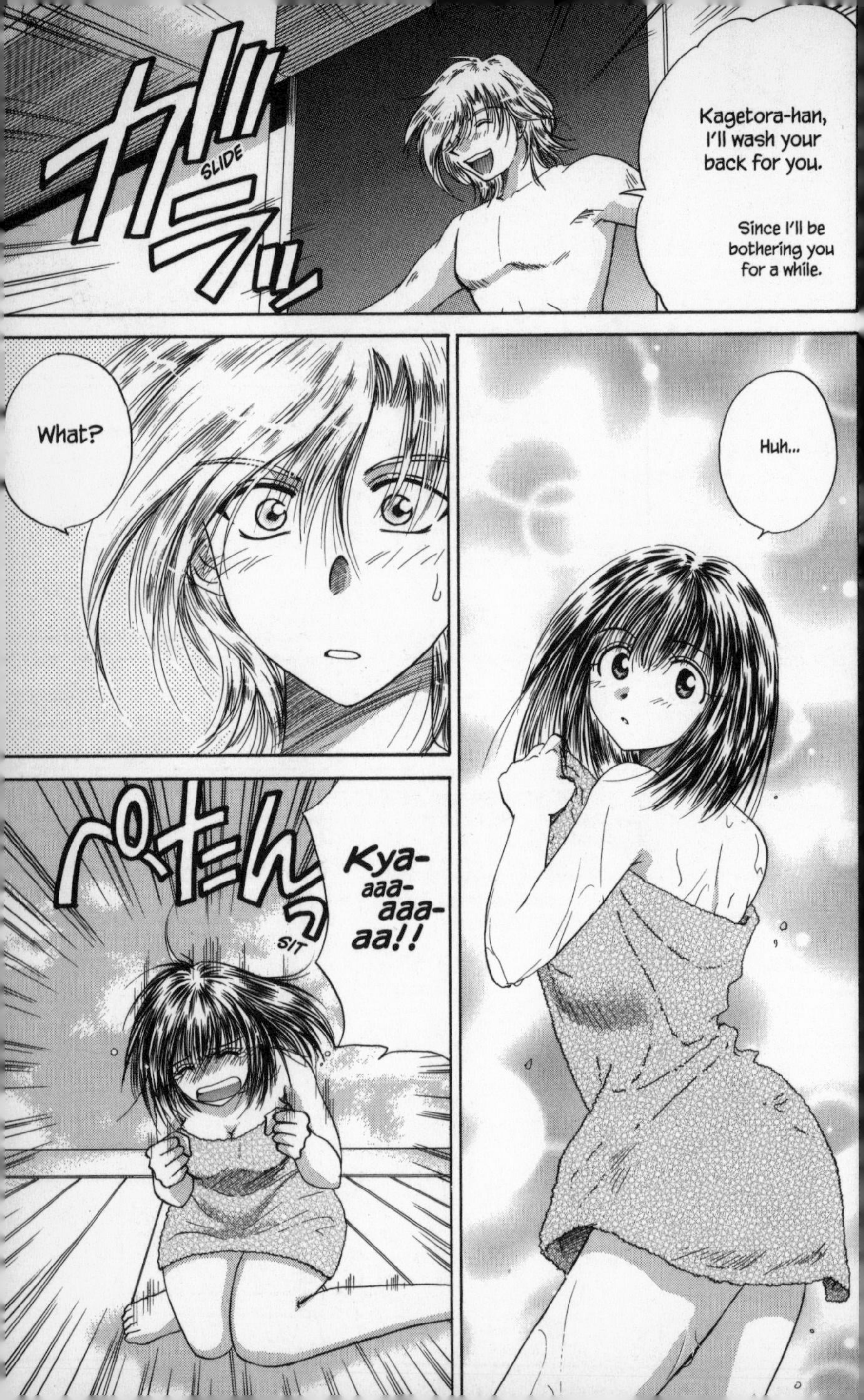
Kagetora-han, I'll wash your back for you.
Since I'll be bothering you for a while.
カラッ
SLIDE
Huh...
What?
Kya-aaa-aaa-aa!!
ぺたんっ
SIT

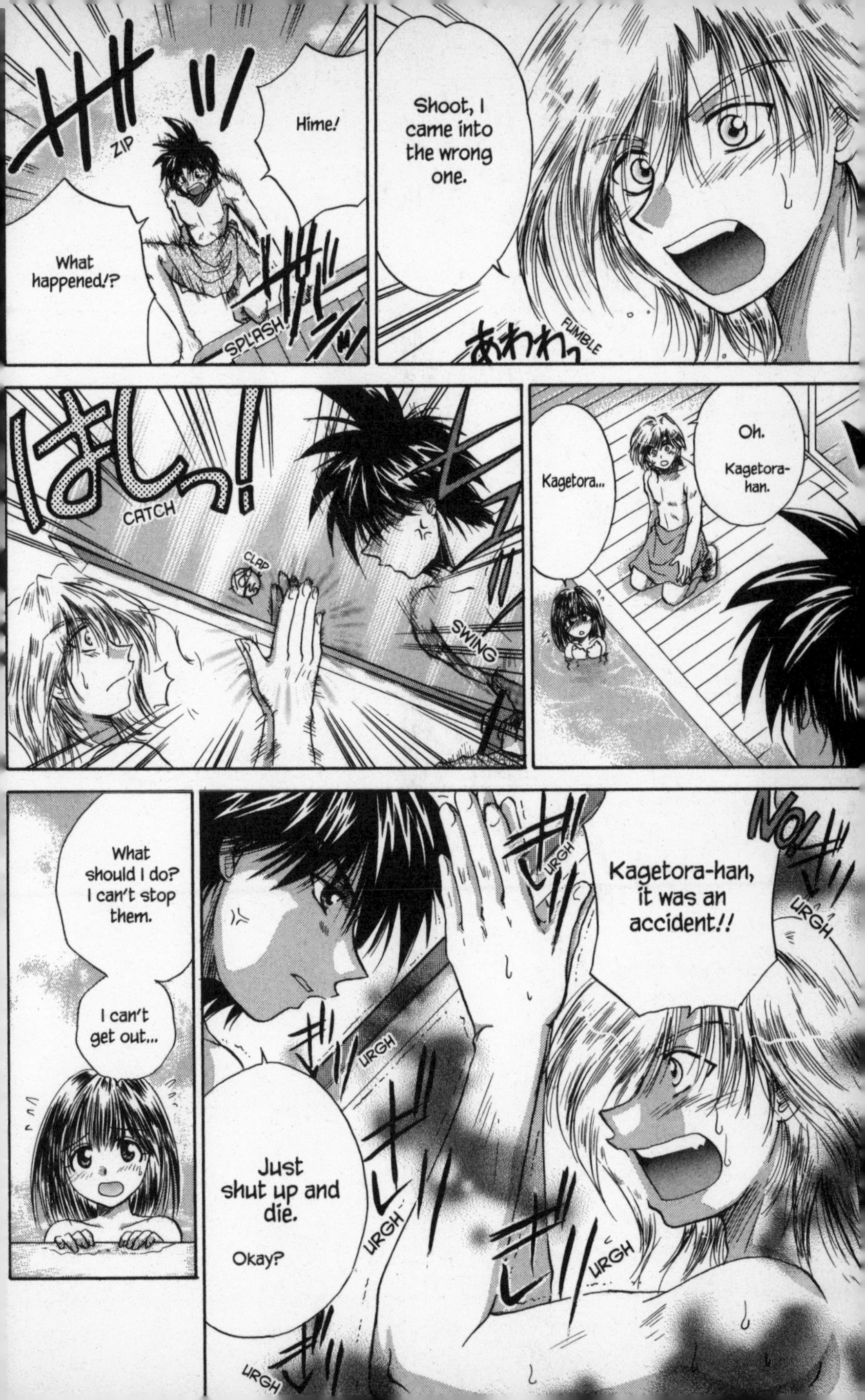

Shoot, I came into the wrong one.
あわわっ
FUMBLE
Hime!
ZIP
What happened!?
SPLASH
Oh.
Kagetora-han.
Kagetora...
はしっ!
CATCH
CLAP
SWING
Kagetora-han, it was an accident!!
NO!
URGH
URGH
Just shut up and die.
Okay?
URGH
URGH
URGH
URGH
What should I do? I can't stop them.
I can't get out...

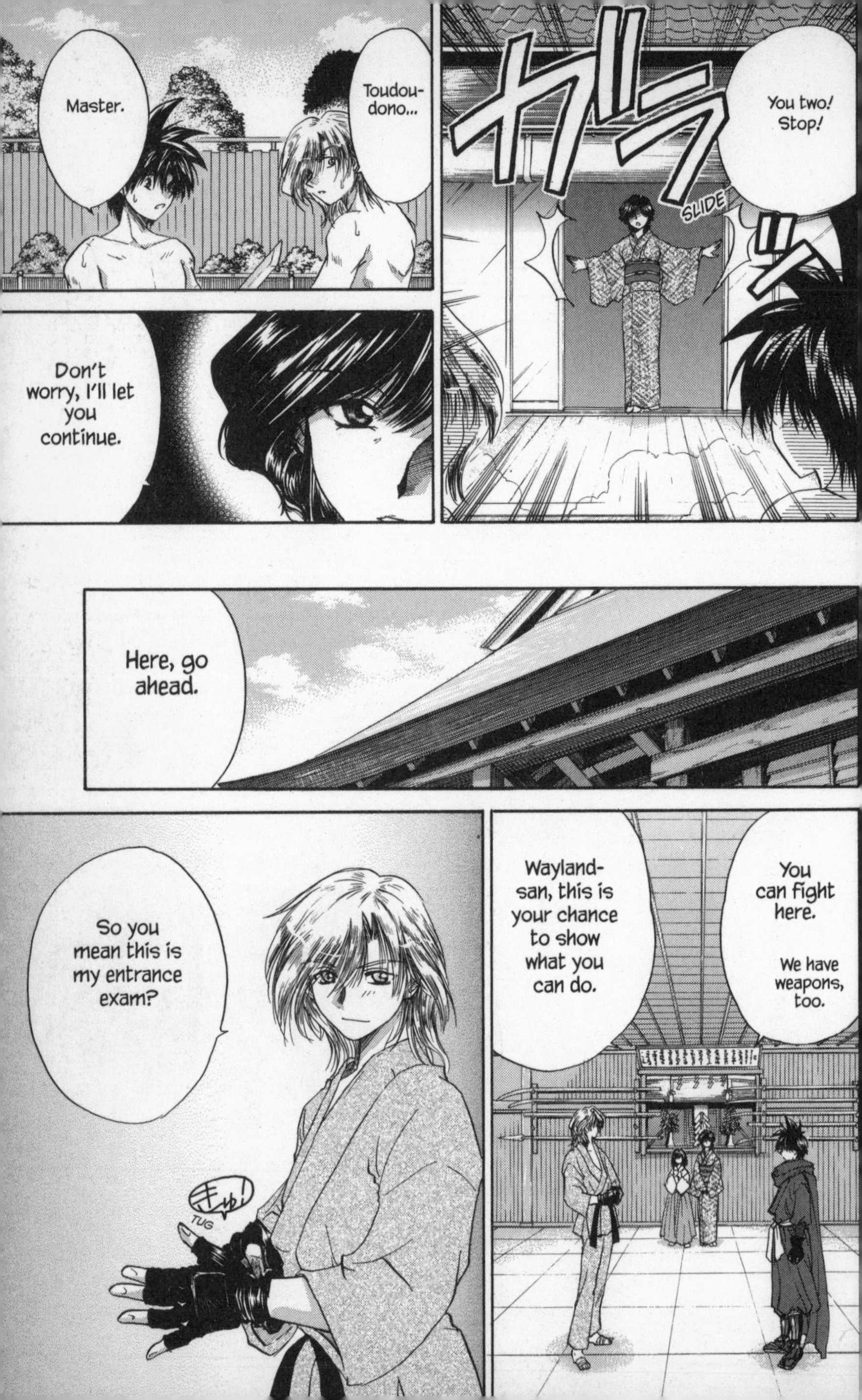
You two! Stop!
SLIDE
Toudou-dono...
Master.
Don't worry, I'll let you continue.
Here, go ahead.
You can fight here.
We have weapons, too.
Wayland-san, this is your chance to show what you can do.
So you mean this is my entrance exam?
TUG

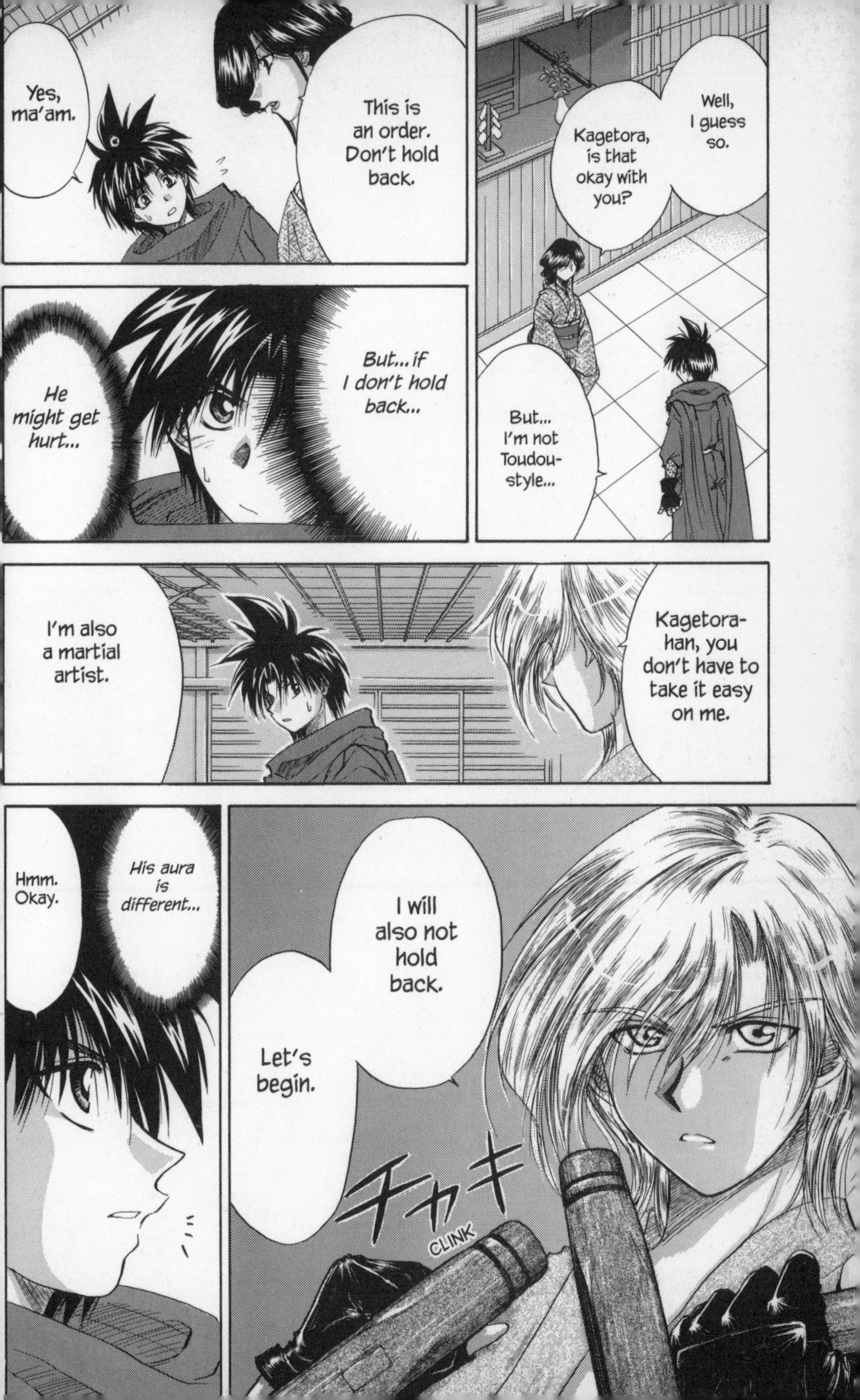
Well, I guess so.
Kagetora, is that okay with you?
But... I'm not Toudou-style...
This is an order. Don't hold back.
Yes, ma'am.
But...if I don't hold back...
He might get hurt...
Kagetora-han, you don't have to take it easy on me.
I'm also a martial artist.
I will also not hold back.
Let's begin.
チャキ
CLINK
His aura is different...
Hmm. Okay.

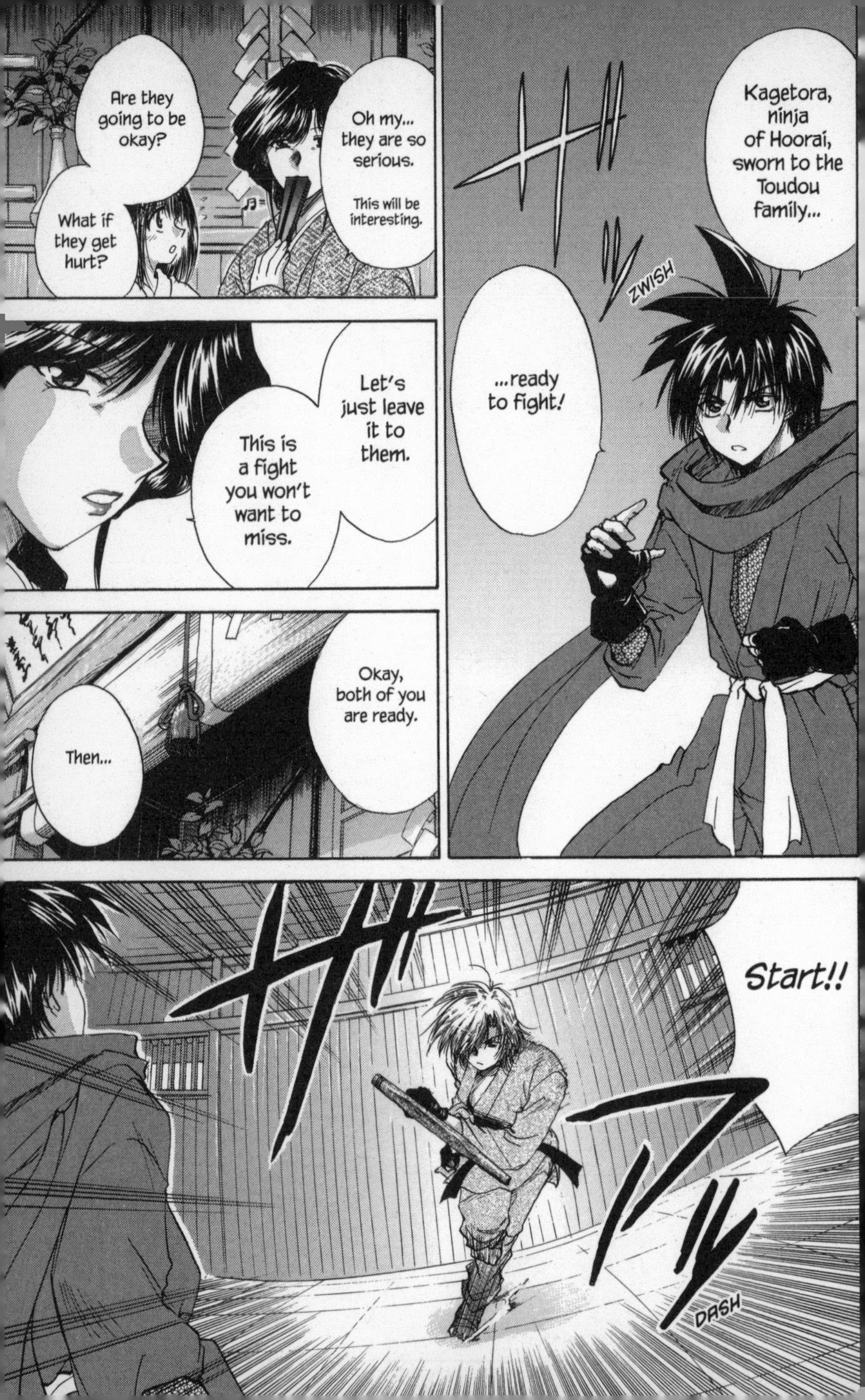
Kagetora, ninja of Hoorai, sworn to the Toudou family...
ZWISH
...ready to fight!
Oh my... they are so serious.
This will be interesting.
Are they going to be okay?
What if they get hurt?
Let's just leave it to them.
This is a fight you won't want to miss.
Okay, both of you are ready.
Then...
Start!!
DASH

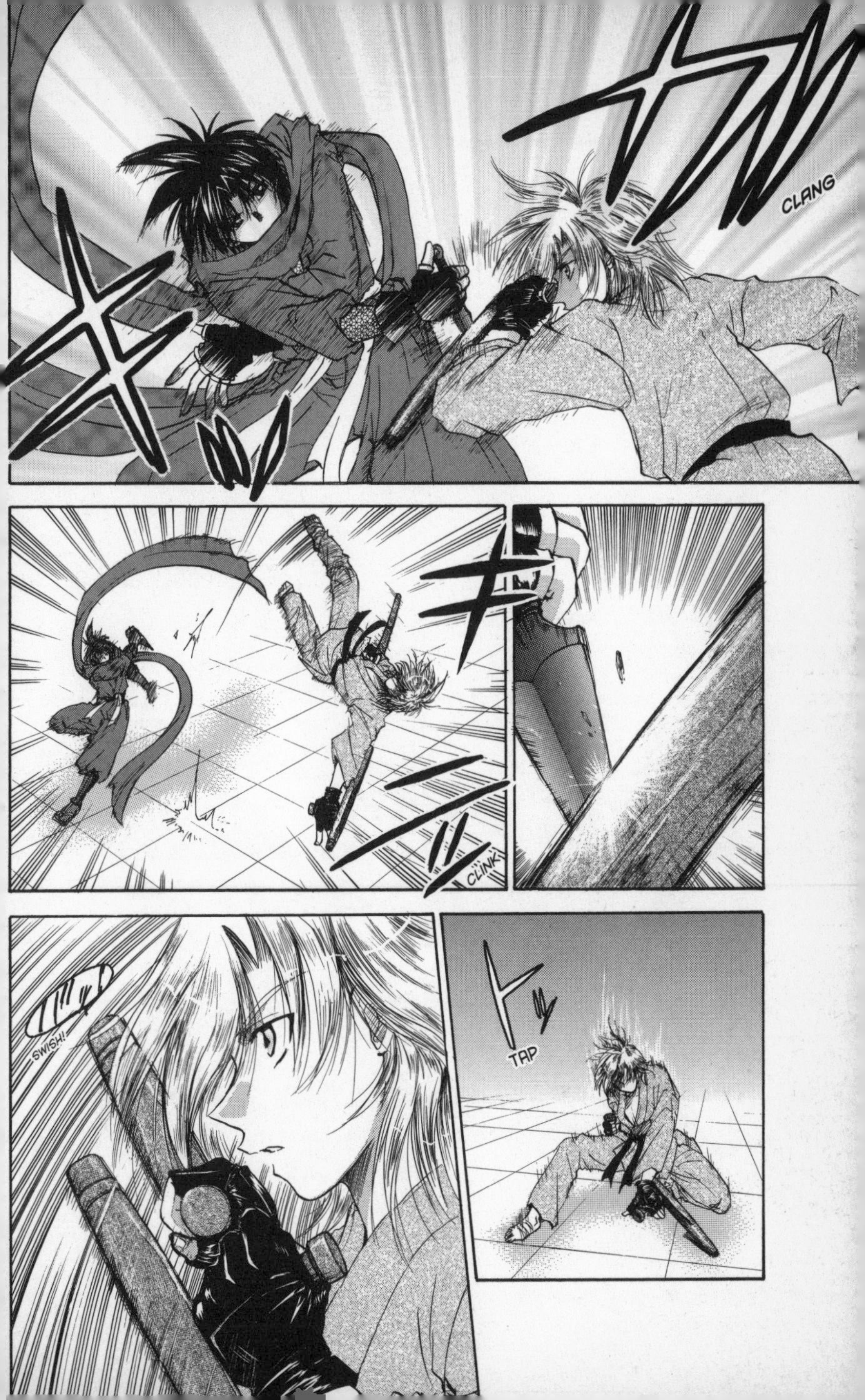
CLANG
CLINK
TAP
SWISH!

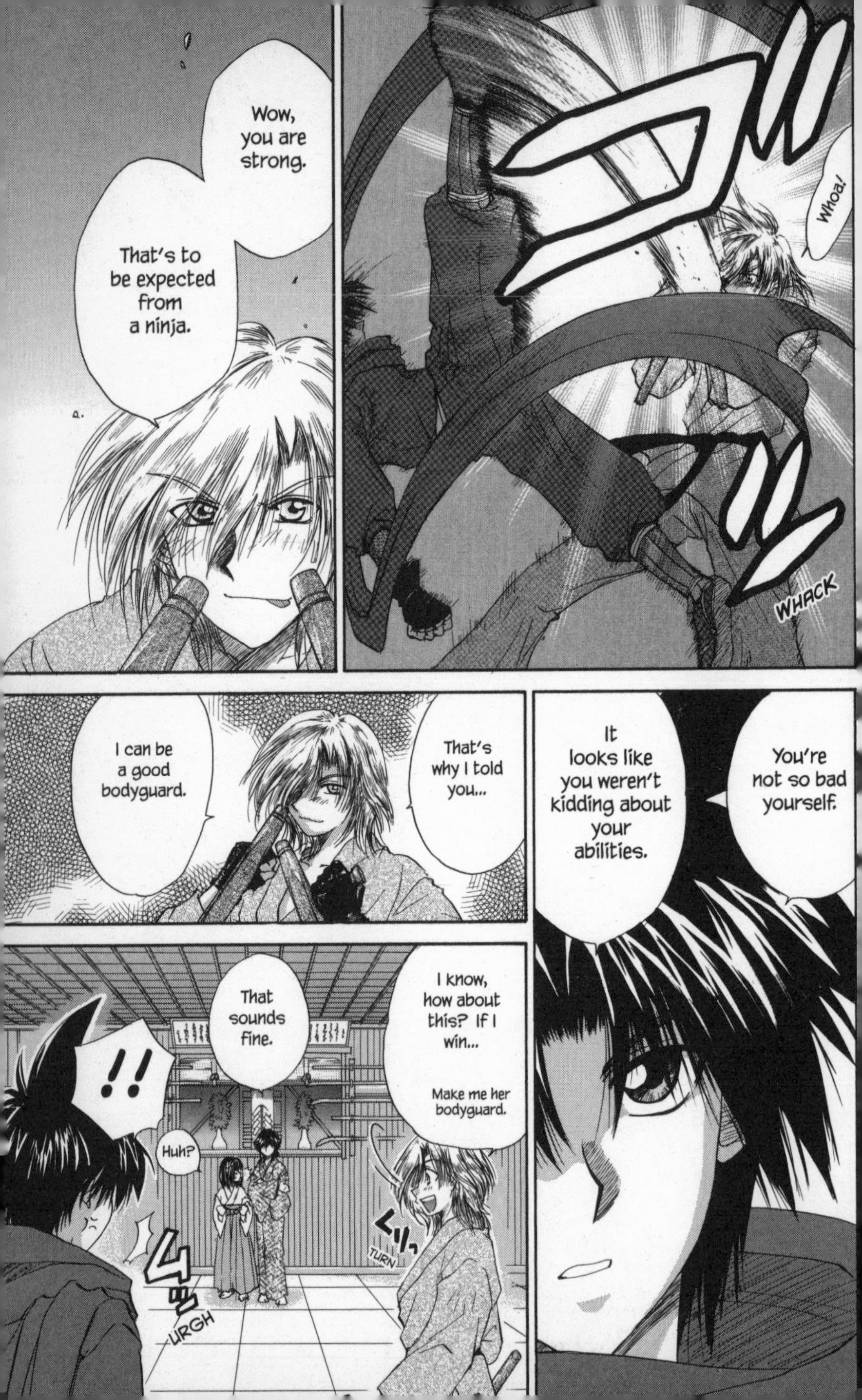
Whoa!
WHACK
Wow, you are strong.
That's to be expected from a ninja.
You're not so bad yourself.
It looks like you weren't kidding about your abilities.
That's why I told you...
I can be a good bodyguard.
I know, how about this? If I win...
Make me her bodyguard.
TURN
That sounds fine.
Huh?
!!
URGH

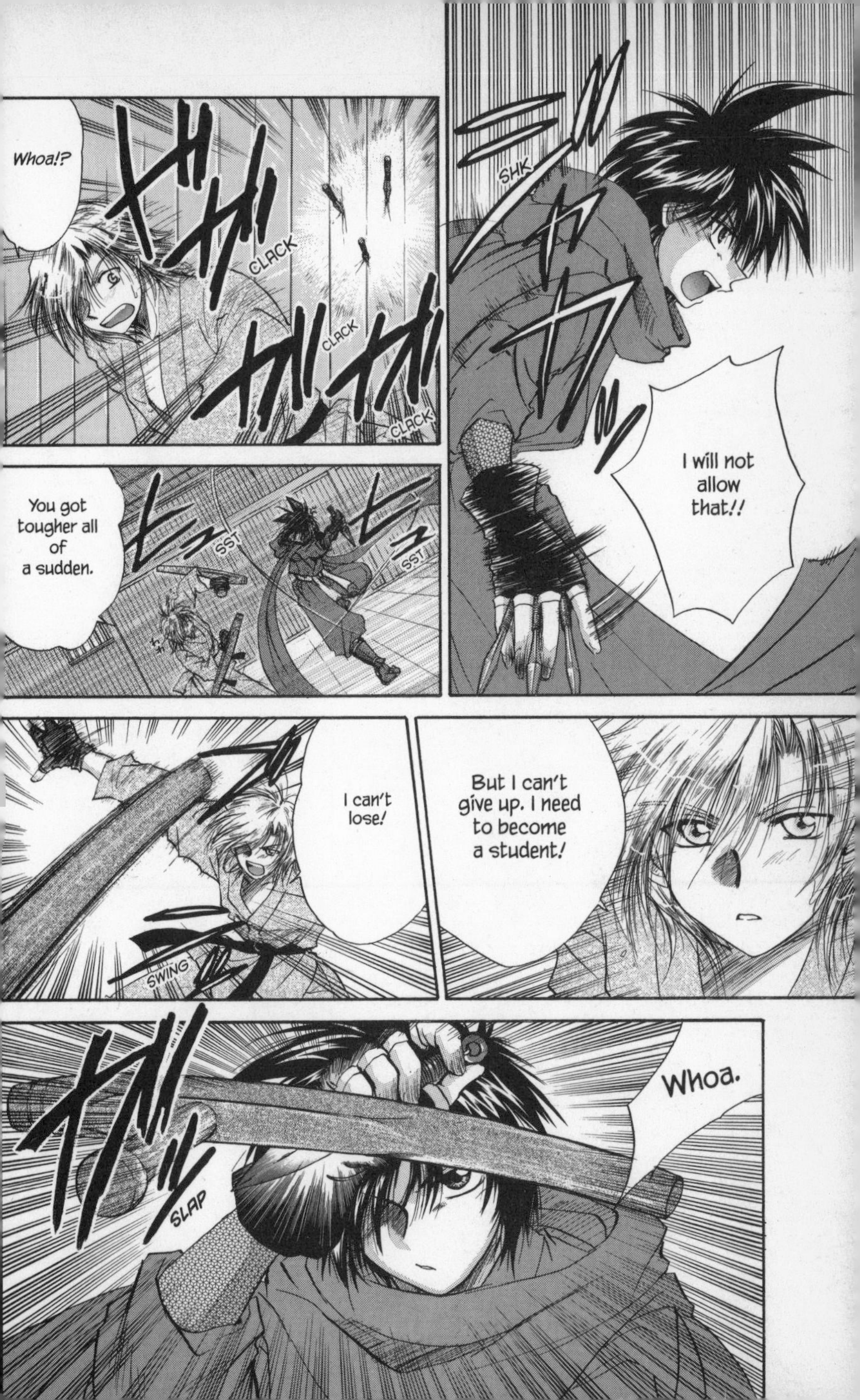
SHK
I will not allow that!!
Whoa!?
CLACK
CLACK
CLACK
You got tougher all of a sudden.
SST
SST
But I can't give up. I need to become a student!
I can't lose!
SWING
Whoa.
SLAP

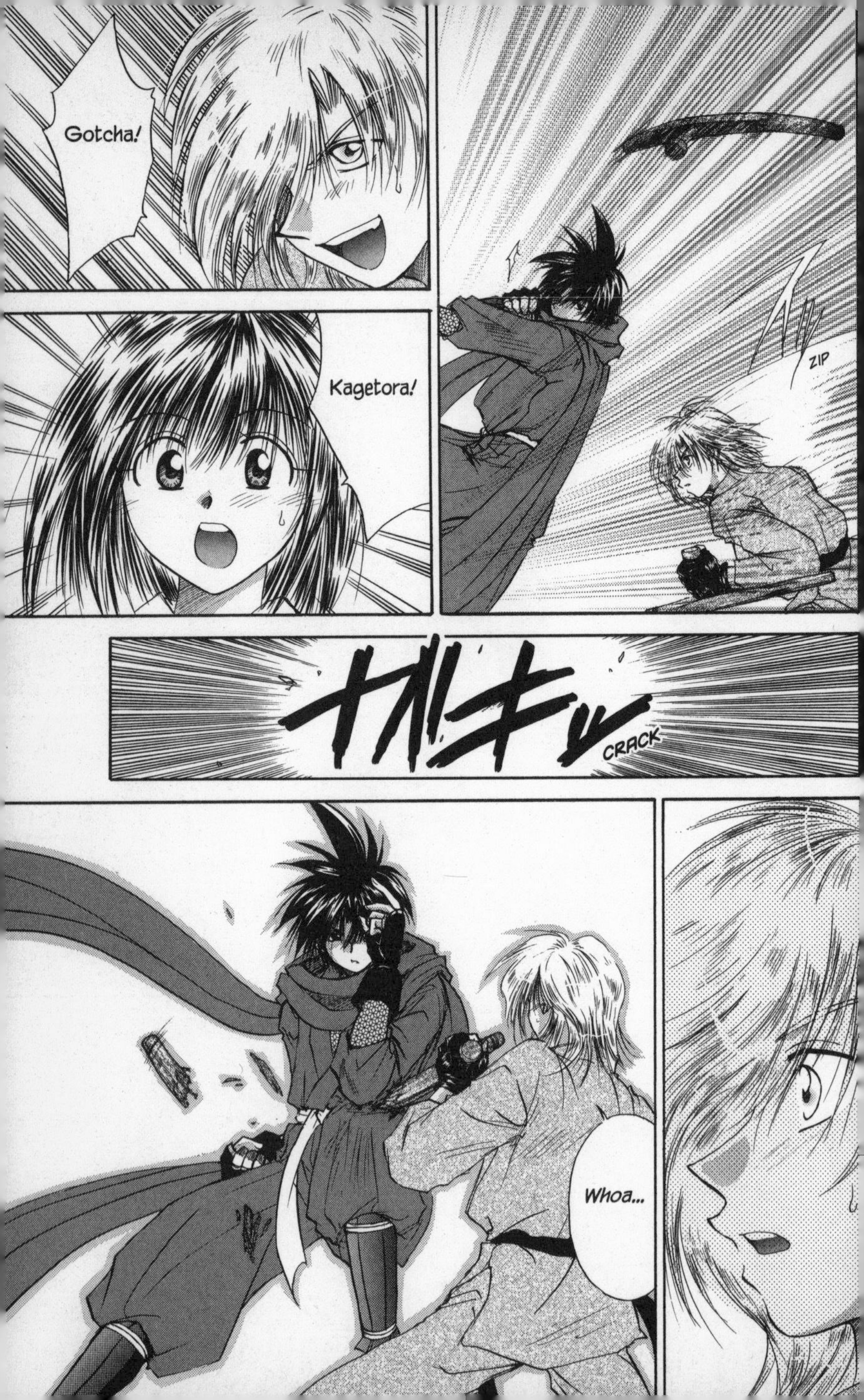
ZIP
Gotcha!
Kagetora!
CRACK
Whoa...

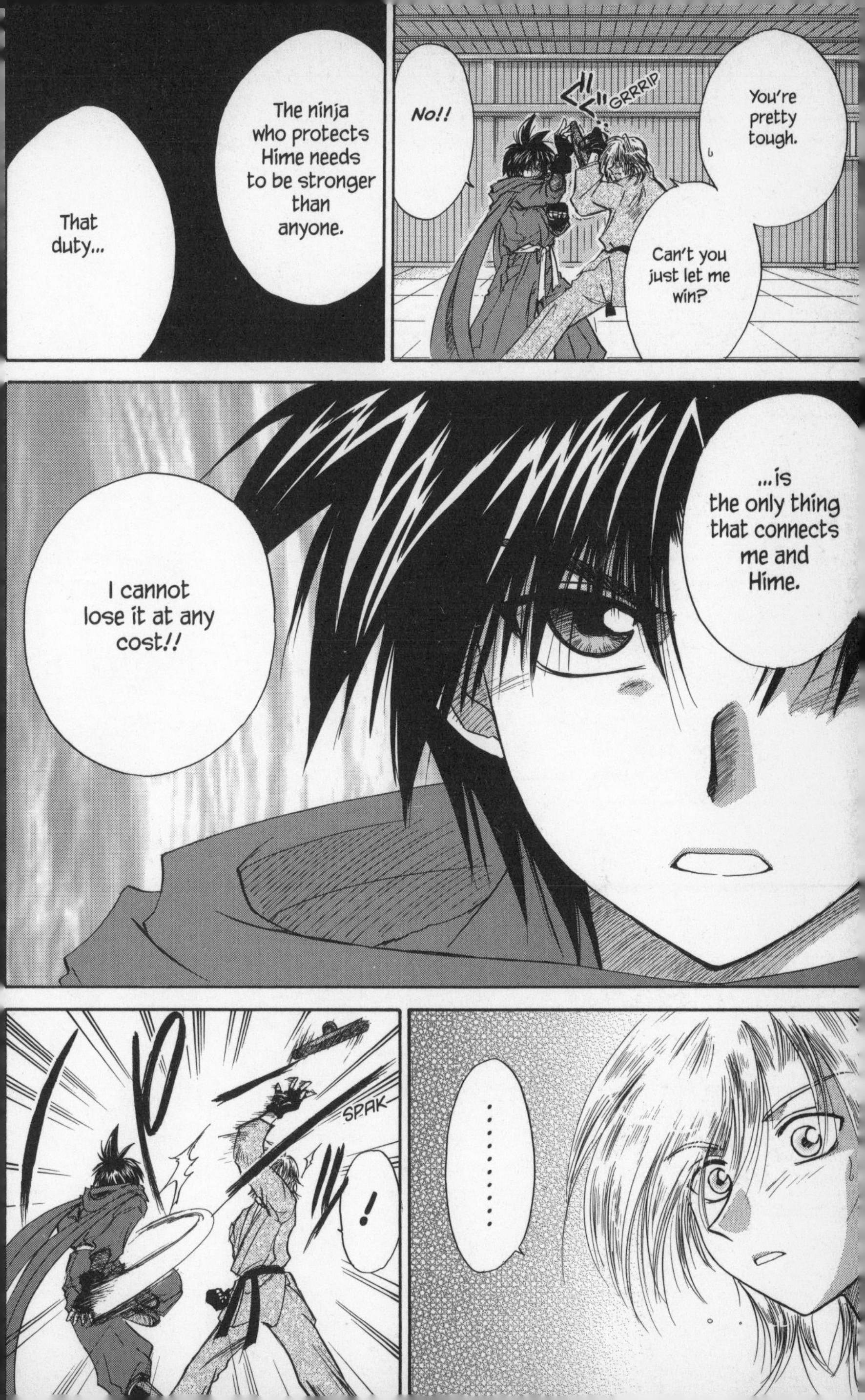
You're pretty tough.
Can't you just let me win?
GRRRIP
No!!
The ninja who protects Hime needs to be stronger than anyone.
That duty...
...is the only thing that connects me and Hime.
I cannot lose it at any cost!!
....
SPAK
!

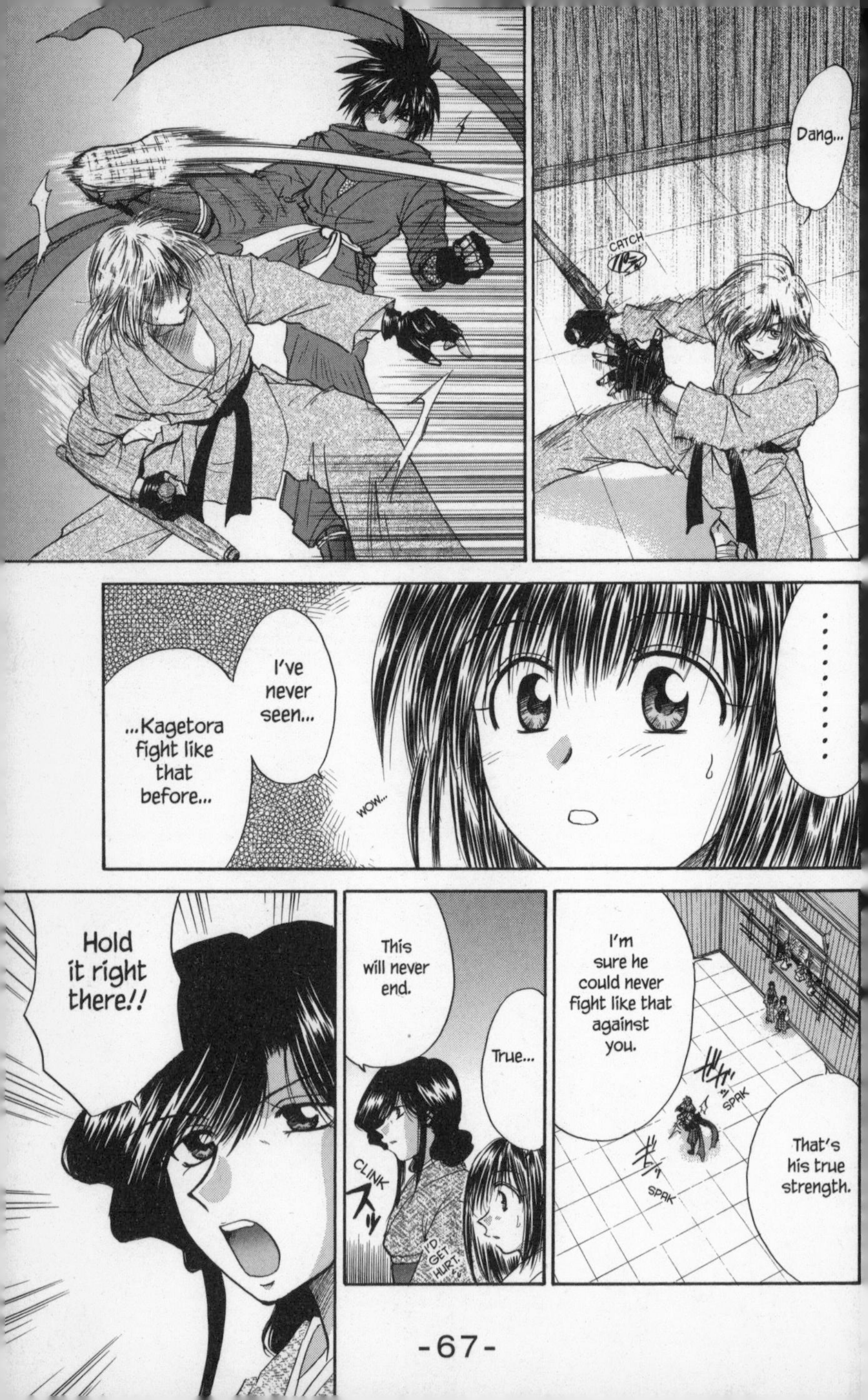

Dang...
CATCH
......
I've never seen...
...Kagetora fight like that before...
WOW...
I'm sure he could never fight like that against you.
SPAK
SPAK
That's his true strength.
This will never end.
True...
CLINK
I'D GET HURT.
Hold it right there!!

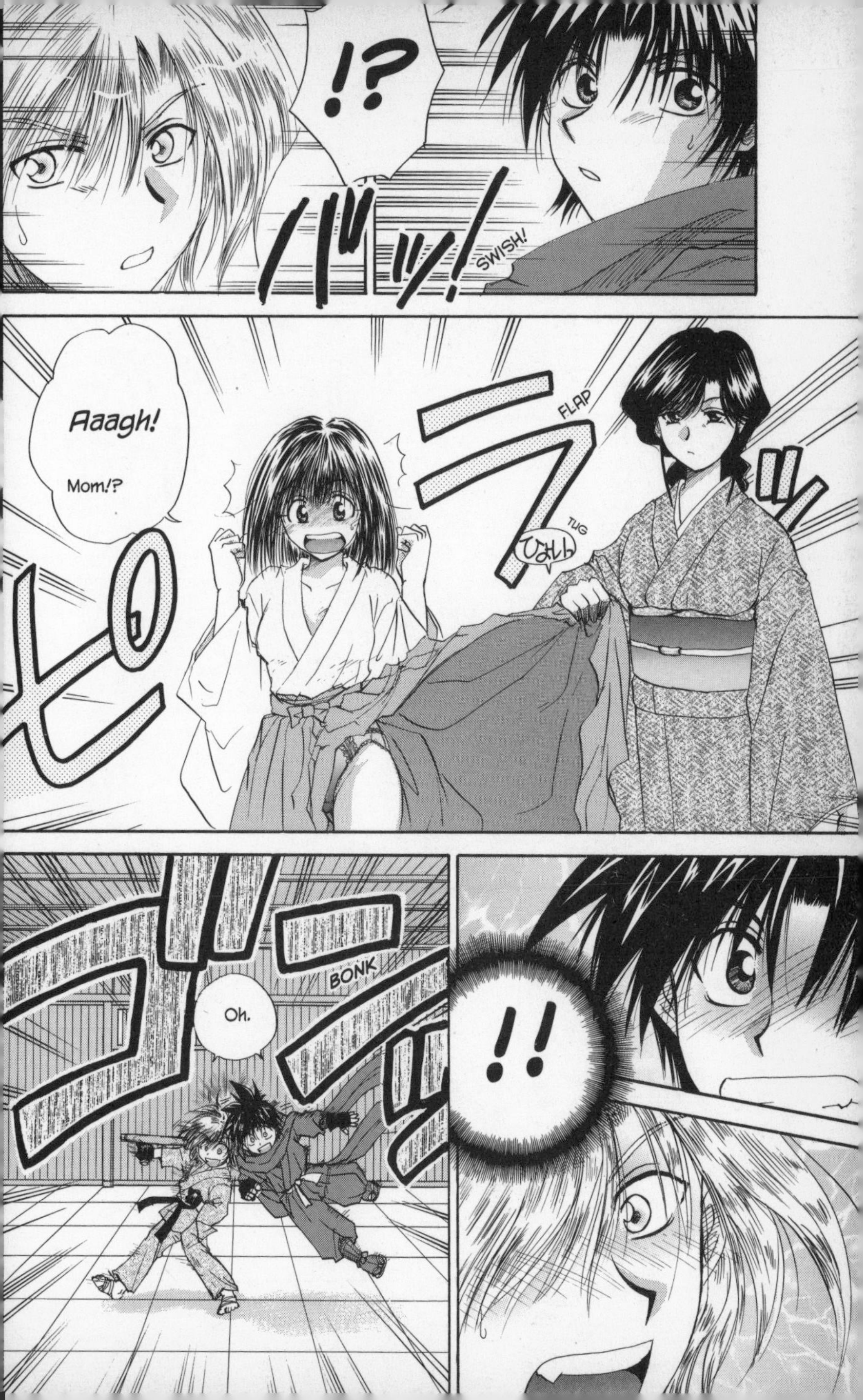

SWISH!
バッ!
!?
FLAP
TUG
Aaagh!
Mom!?
!!
BONK
Oh.

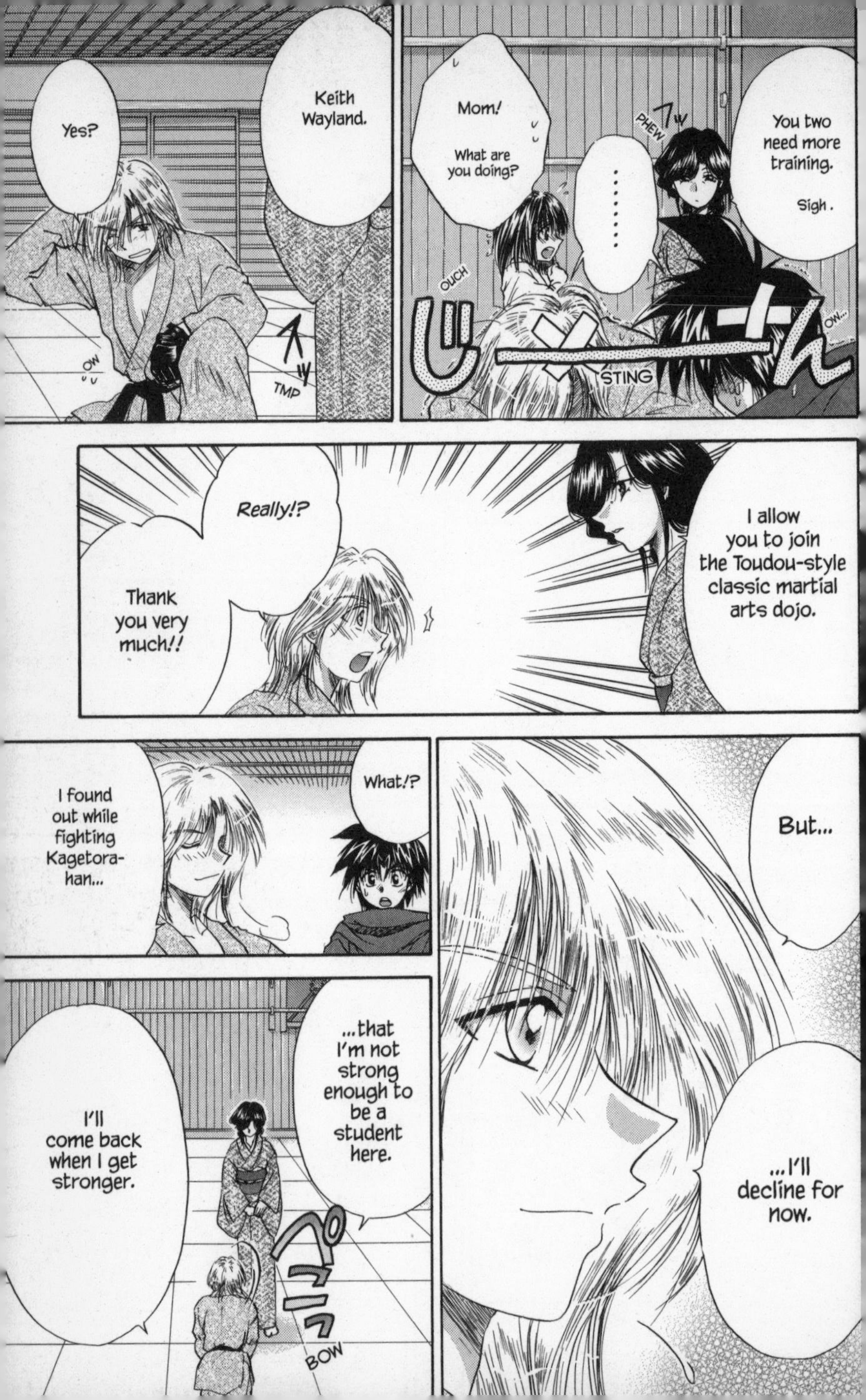
You two need more training.
Sigh.
PHEW
......
Mom!
What are you doing?
OUCH
STING
OW...
Keith Wayland.
Yes?
TMP
OW
I allow you to join the Toudou-style classic martial arts dojo.
Really!?
Thank you very much!!
But...
...I'll decline for now.
What!?
I found out while fighting Kagetora-han...
...that I'm not strong enough to be a student here.
I'll come back when I get stronger.
BOW

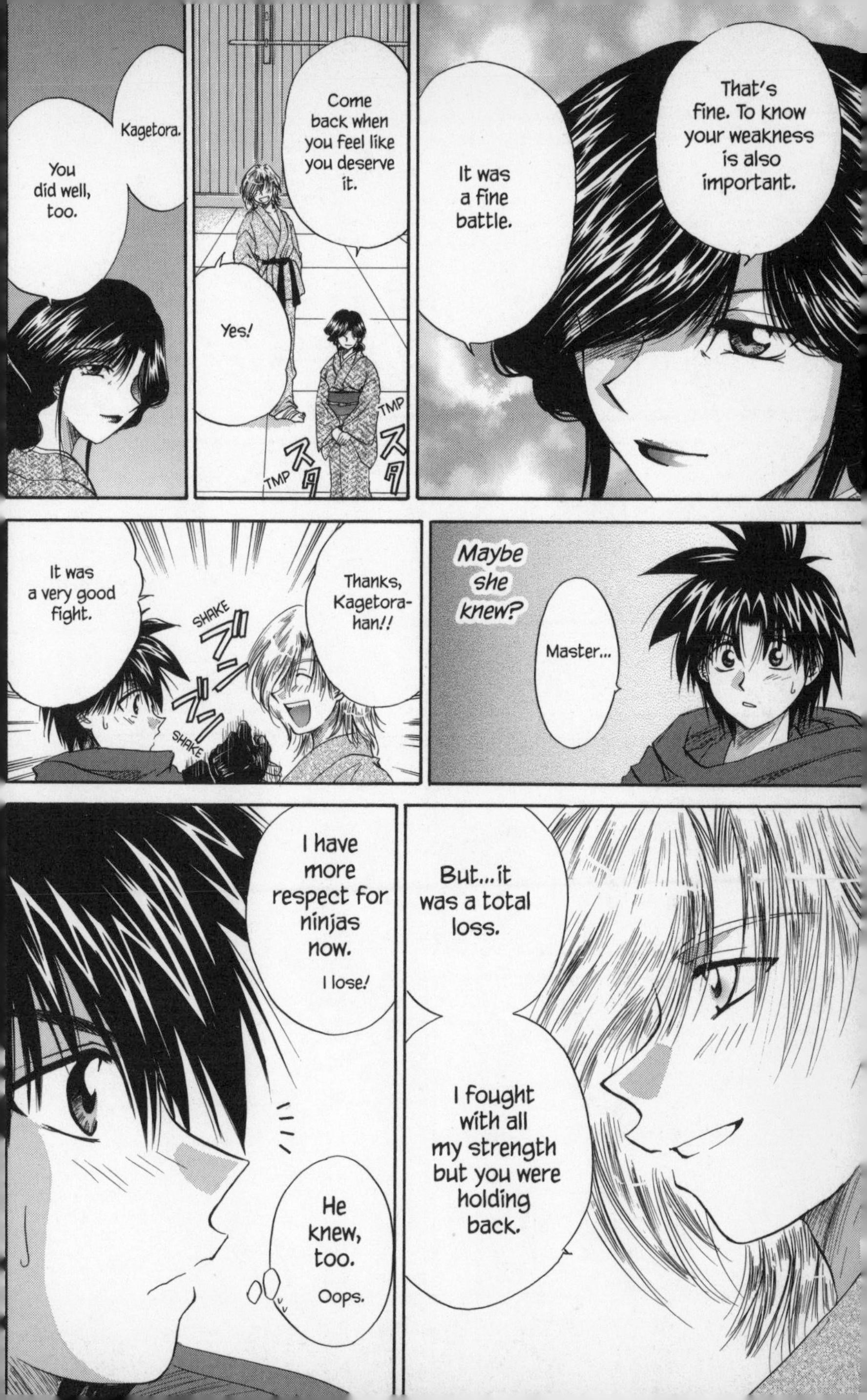
That's fine. To know your weakness is also important.
It was a fine battle.
Come back when you feel like you deserve it.
Yes!
TMP
スタ
TMP
スタ
Kagetora.
You did well, too.
Maybe she knew?
Master...
Thanks, Kagetora-han!!
SHAKE
SHAKE
It was a very good fight.
But...it was a total loss.
I fought with all my strength but you were holding back.
I have more respect for ninjas now.
I lose!
He knew, too.
Oops.

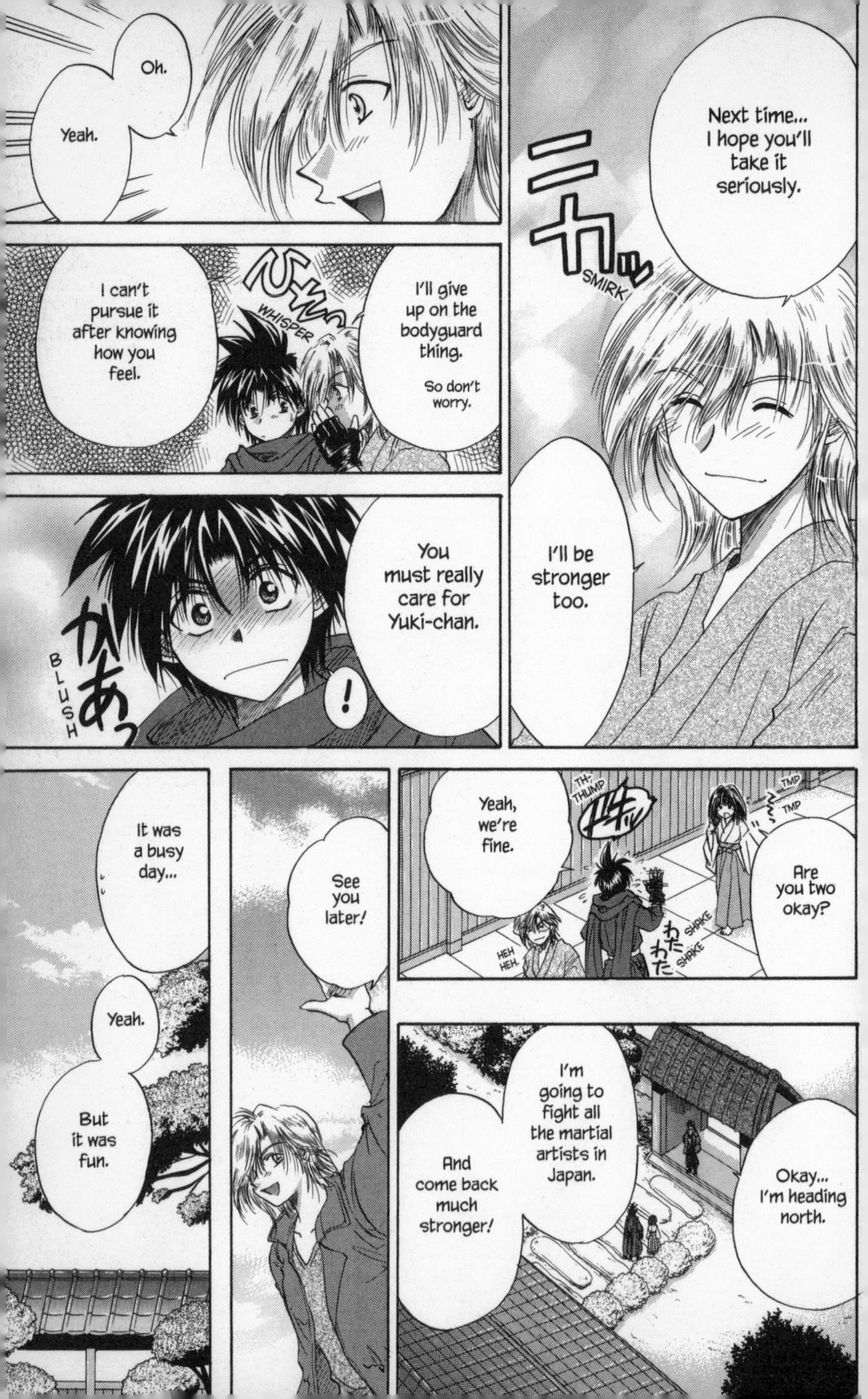
Next time... I hope you'll take it seriously.
ニカッ
SMIRK
I'll be stronger too.
Oh.
Yeah.
WHISPER
I'll give up on the bodyguard thing.
So don't worry.
I can't pursue it after knowing how you feel.
You must really care for Yuki-chan.
!
かあっ
BLUSH
TMP
TMP
Are you two okay?
TH-THUMP
Yeah, we're fine.
わたわた
SHAKE SHAKE
HEH HEH.
Okay... I'm heading north.
I'm going to fight all the martial artists in Japan.
And come back much stronger!
See you later!
It was a busy day...
Yeah.
But it was fun.

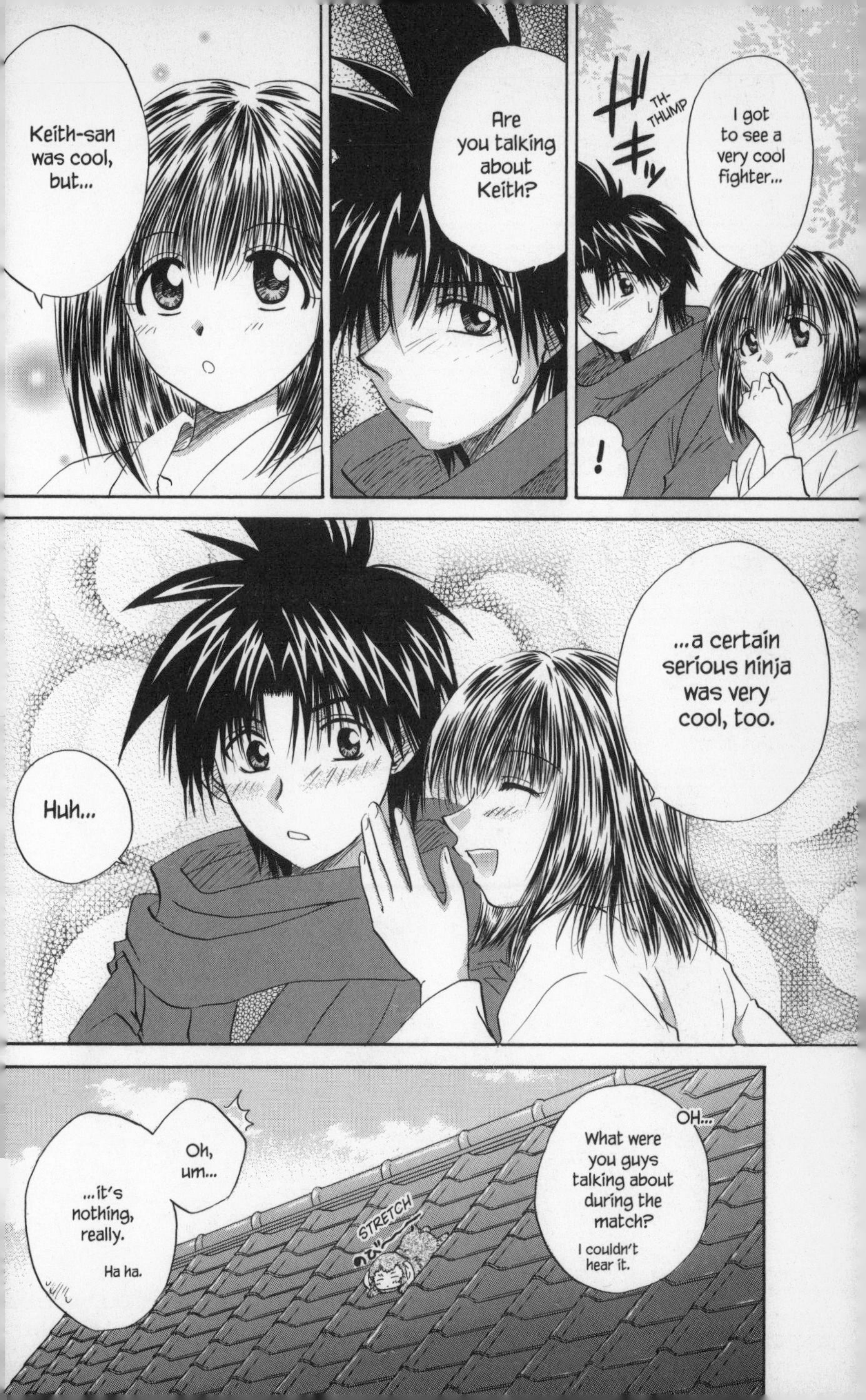

I got to see a very cool fighter...
TH-THUMP
!
Are you talking about Keith?
Keith-san was cool, but...
...a certain serious ninja was very cool, too.
Huh...
OH...
What were you guys talking about during the match?
I couldn't hear it.
STRETCH
Oh, um...
...it's nothing, really.
Ha ha.

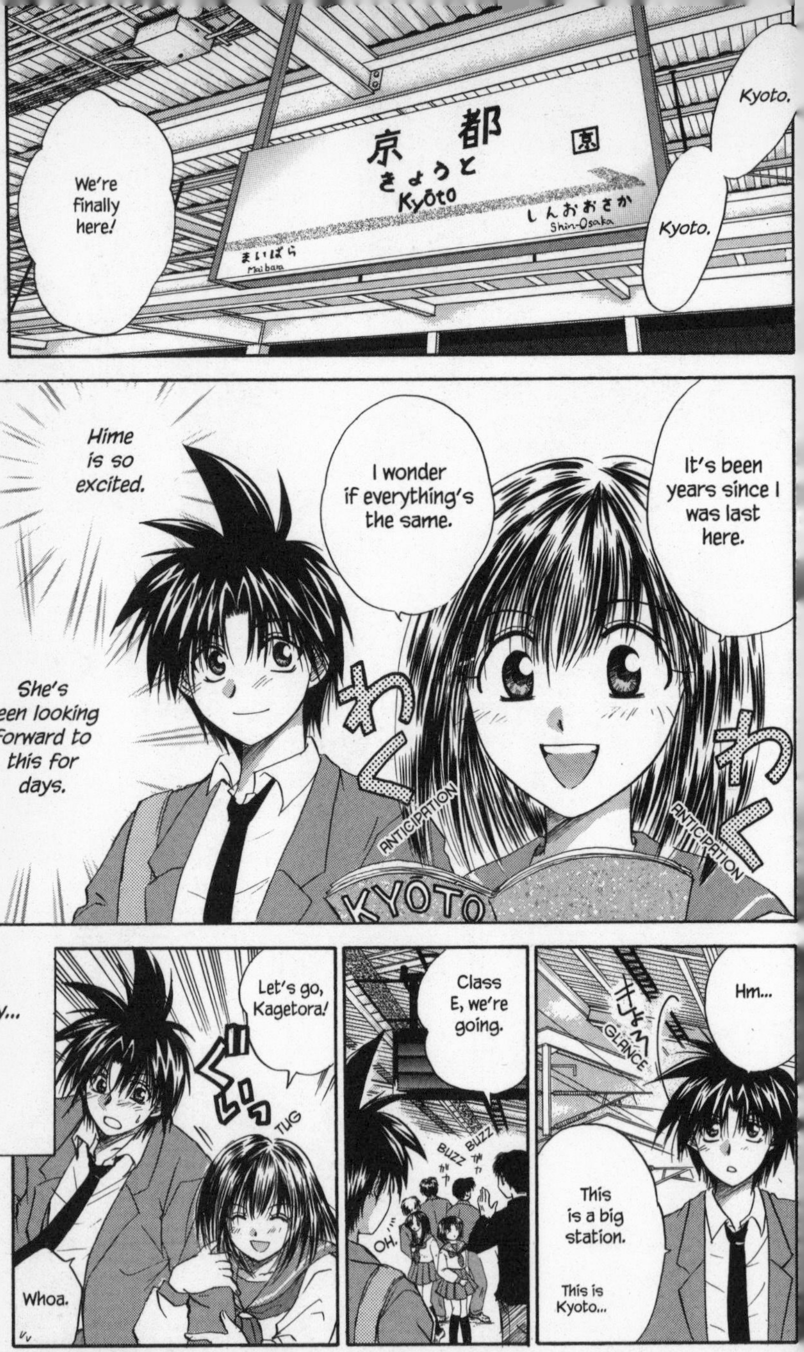
Kyoto.
Kyoto.
京都
きょうと
Kyōto
しんおおさか
Shin-Osaka
まいばら
Maibara
We're finally here!
It's been years since I was last here.
I wonder if everything's the same.
わく
ANTICIPATION
わく
ANTICIPATION
KYOTO
Hime is so excited.
She's been looking forward to this for days.
Hm...
GLANCE
This is a big station.
This is Kyoto...
Class E, we're going.
BUZZ
BUZZ
OH.
Let's go, Kagetora!
TUG
Whoa.
Today...

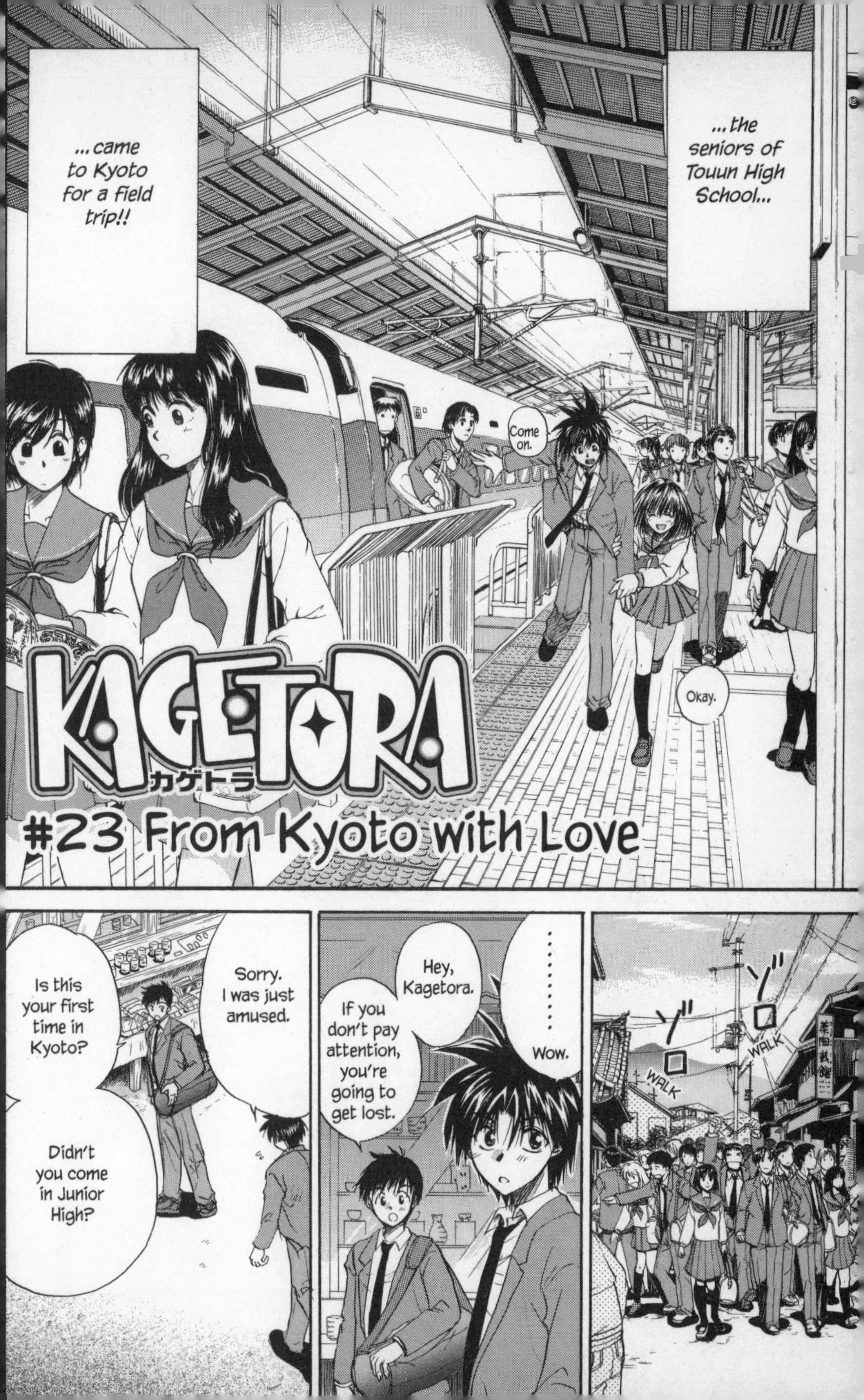
...the seniors of Touun High School...
...came to Kyoto for a field trip!!
Come on.
Okay.
KAGETORA
カゲトラ
#23 From Kyoto with Love
ゾロ
WALK
ゾロ
WALK
......
Wow.
Hey, Kagetora.
If you don't pay attention, you're going to get lost.
Sorry. I was just amused.
Is this your first time in Kyoto?
Didn't you come in Junior High?

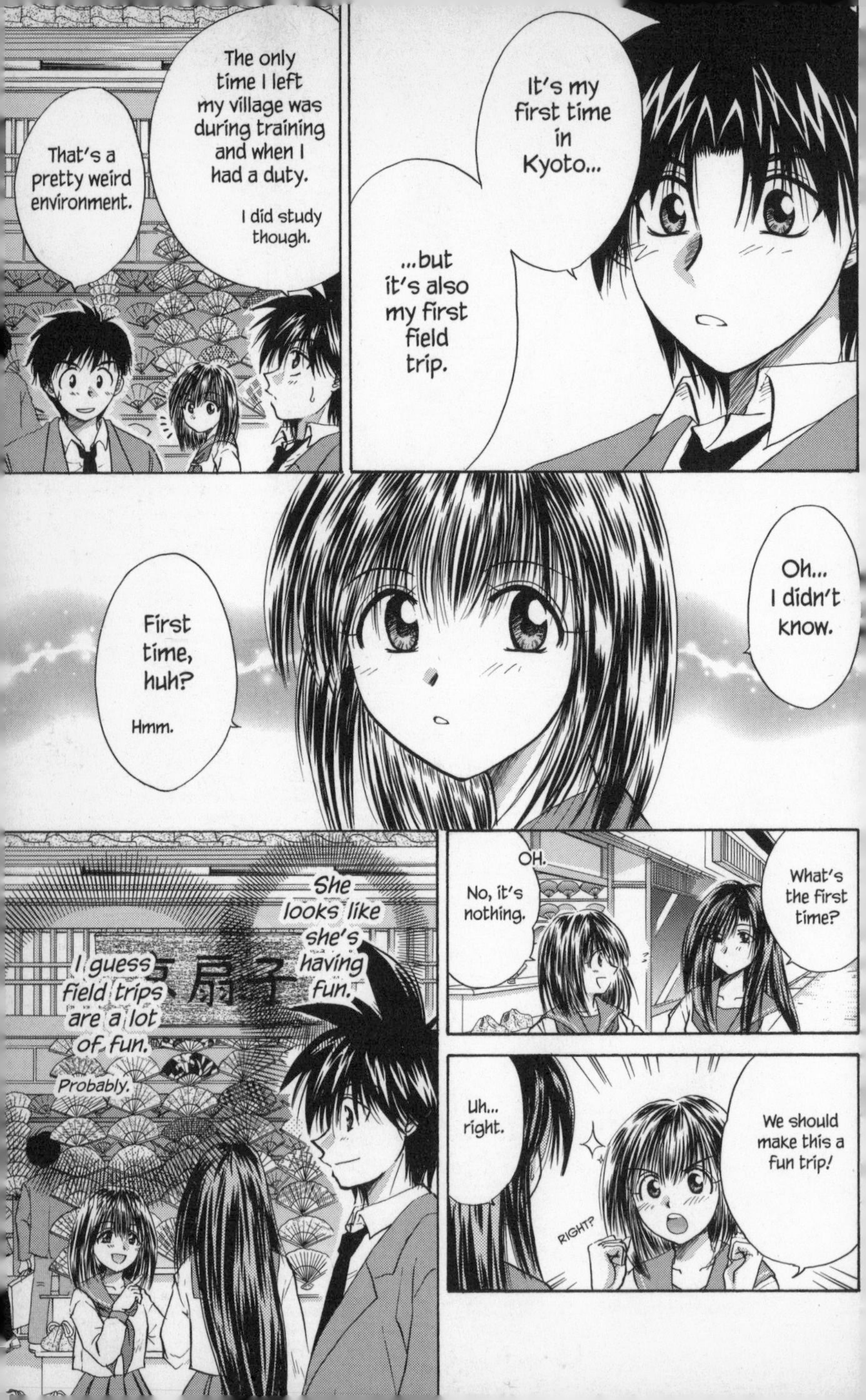

It's my first time in Kyoto...
...but it's also my first field trip.
The only time I left my village was during training and when I had a duty.
I did study though.
That's a pretty weird environment.
Oh... I didn't know.
First time, huh?
Hmm.
What's the first time?
OH.
No, it's nothing.
We should make this a fun trip!
RIGHT?
Uh... right.
She looks like she's having fun.
I guess field trips are a lot of fun.
Probably.

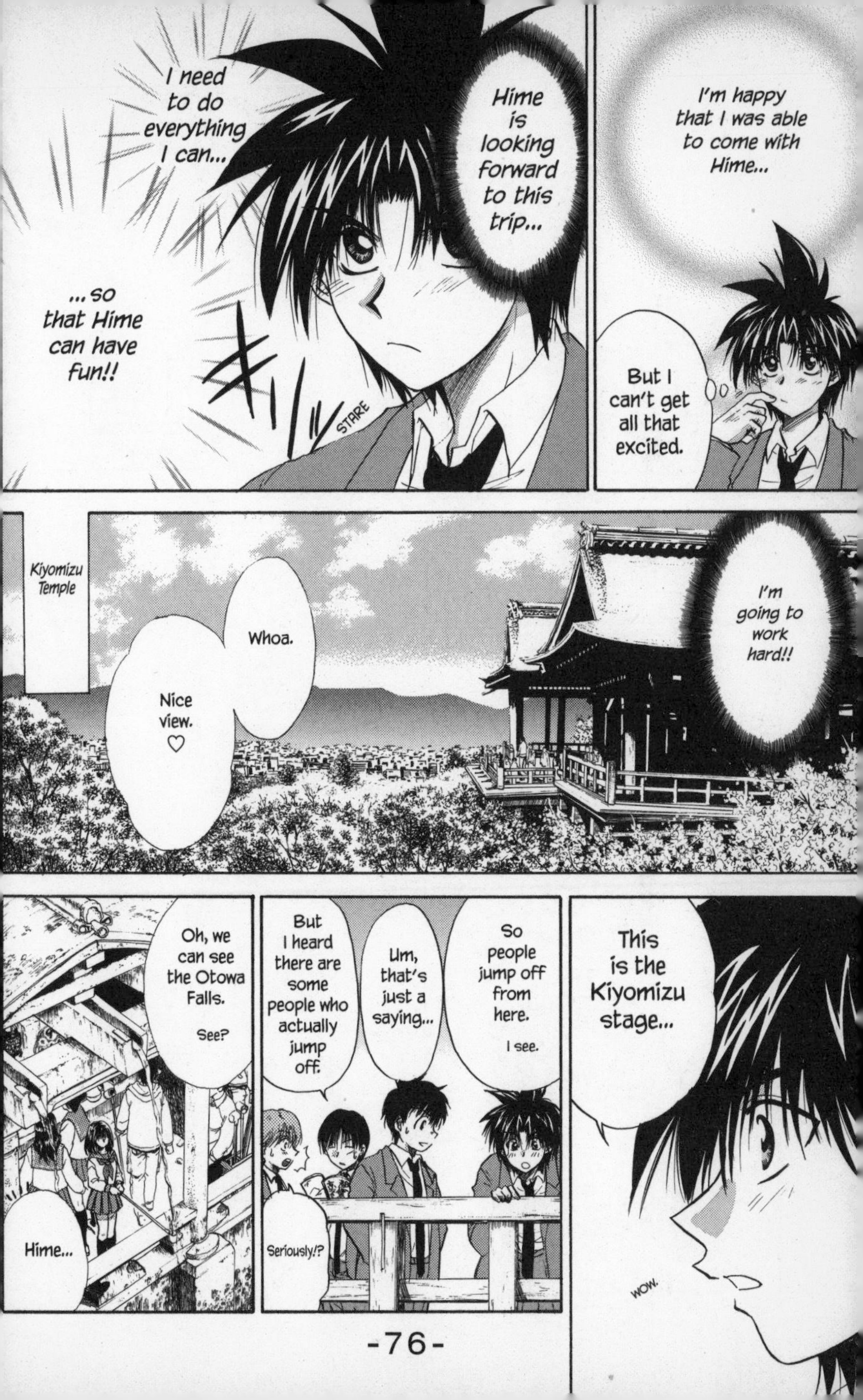
I'm happy that I was able to come with Hime...
But I can't get all that excited.
Hime is looking forward to this trip...
I need to do everything I can...
...so that Hime can have fun!!
STARE
I'm going to work hard!!
Whoa.
Nice view. ♡
Kiyomizu Temple
This is the Kiyomizu stage...
WOW.
So people jump off from here.
I see.
Um, that's just a saying...
But I heard there are some people who actually jump off.
Seriously!?
Oh, we can see the Otowa Falls.
See?
Hime...

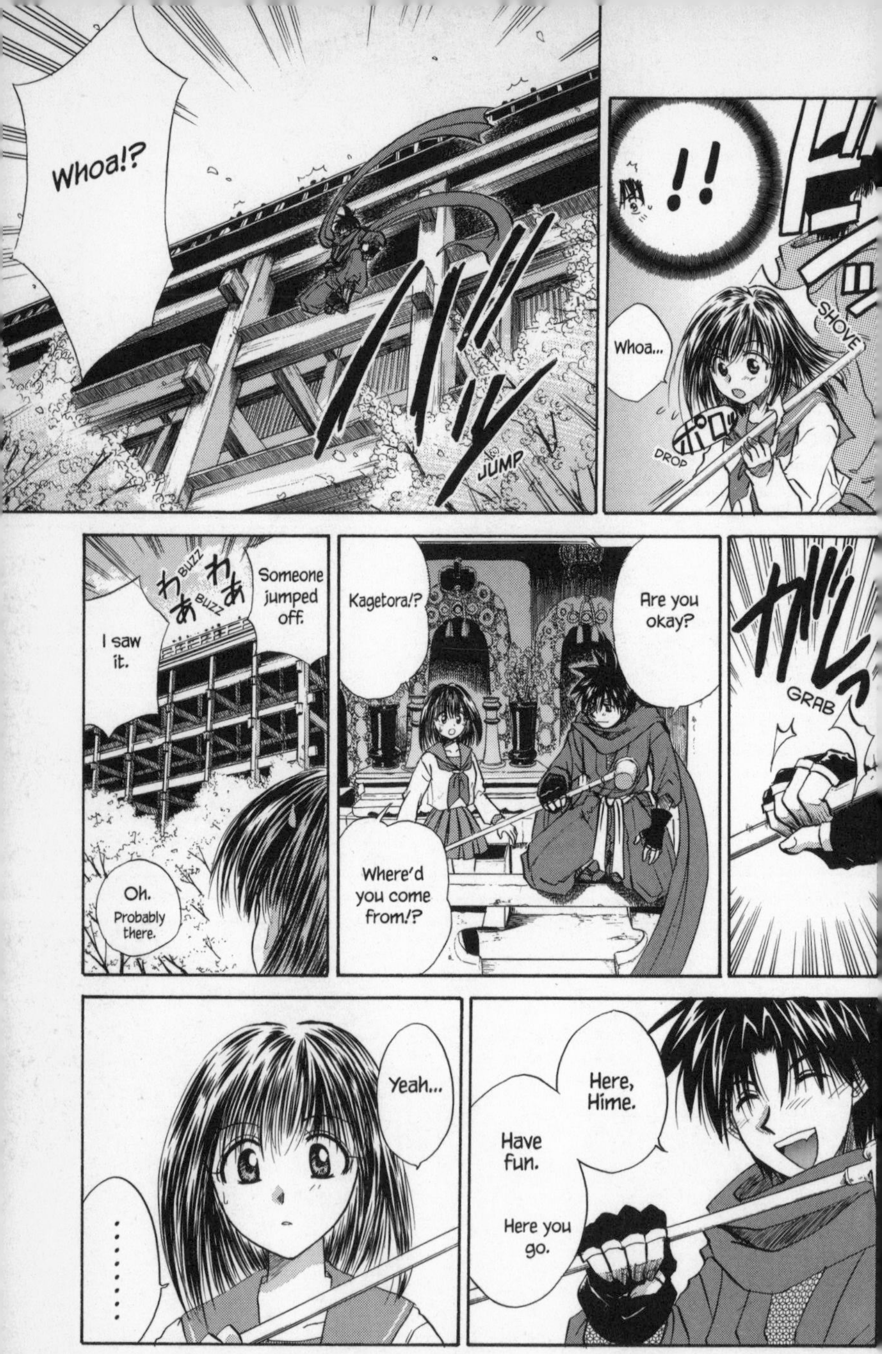
!!
SHOVE
Whoa...
DROP
Whoa!?
JUMP
GRAB
Are you okay?
Kagetora!?
Where'd you come from!?
Someone jumped off.
BUZZ BUZZ
I saw it.
Oh. Probably there.
Here, Hime.
Have fun.
Here you go.
Yeah...
......

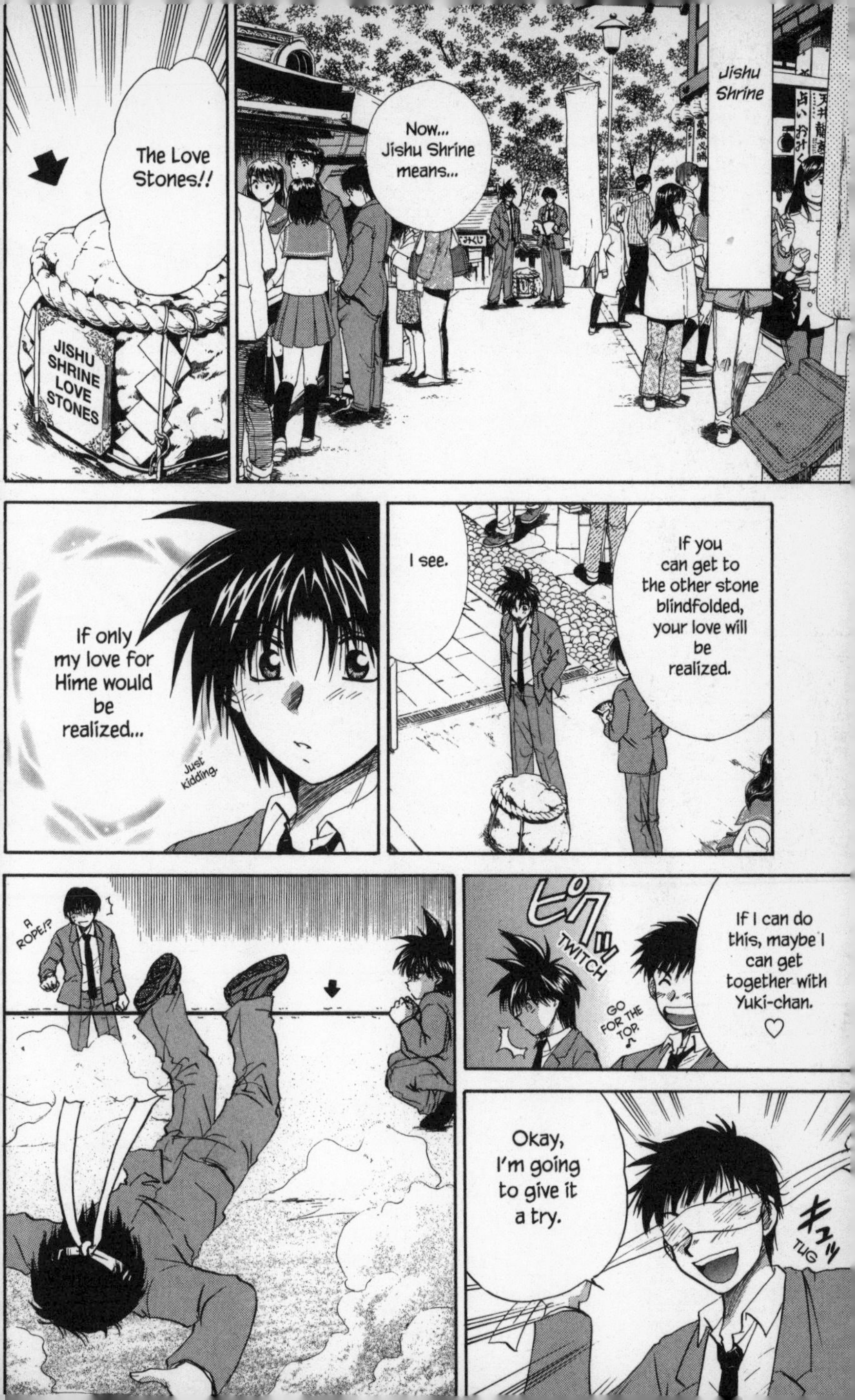

Jishu Shrine
Now... Jishu Shrine means...
The Love Stones!!
JISHU SHRINE LOVE STONES
If you can get to the other stone blindfolded, your love will be realized.
I see.
If only my love for Hime would be realized...
Just kidding.
If I can do this, maybe I can get together with Yuki-chan. ♡
TWITCH
GO FOR THE TOP. ♪
Okay, I'm going to give it a try.
TUG
A ROPE!?

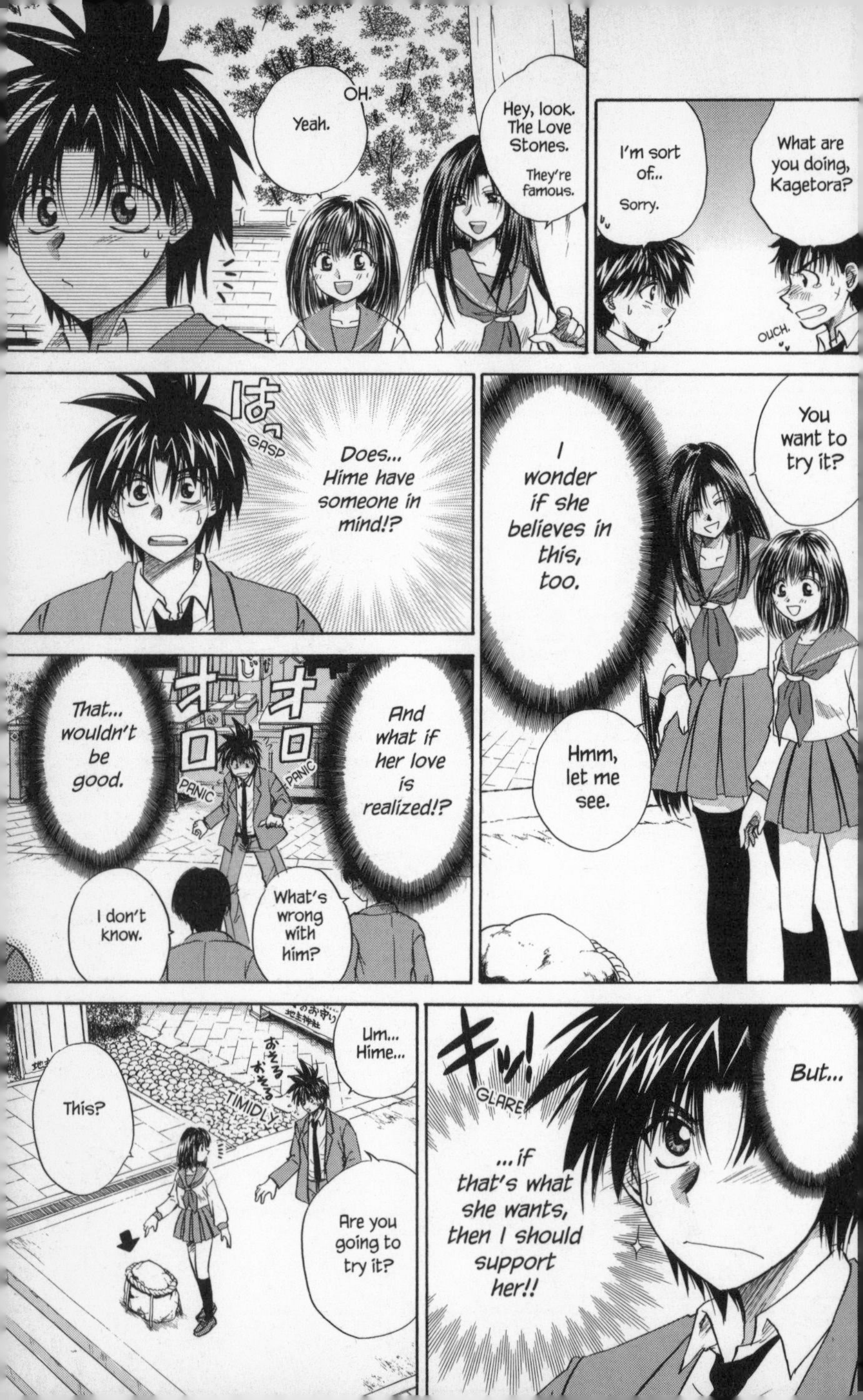

What are you doing, Kagetora?
I'm sort of...
Sorry.
OUCH.
Hey, look. The Love Stones.
They're famous.
OH.
Yeah.
You want to try it?
I wonder if she believes in this, too.
Hmm, let me see.
はっ
GASP
Does... Hime have someone in mind!?
And what if her love is realized!?
オロ
PANIC
オロ
PANIC
That... wouldn't be good.
What's wrong with him?
I don't know.
But...
キッ!
GLARE
...if that's what she wants, then I should support her!!
Um... Hime...
おそるおそる
TIMIDLY
This?
Are you going to try it?

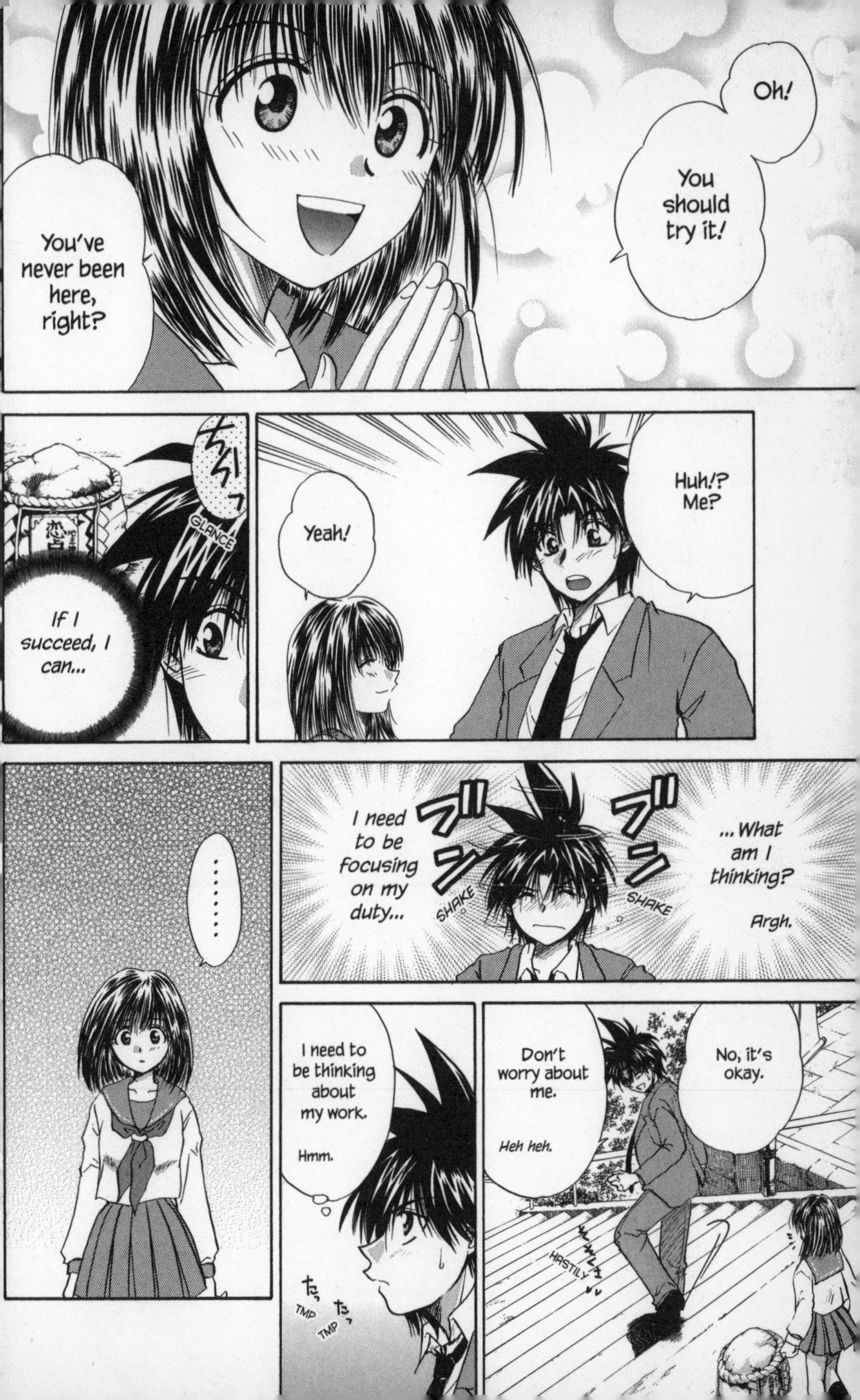
Oh!
You should try it!
You've never been here, right?
Huh!? Me?
Yeah!
GLANCE
If I succeed, I can...
...What am I thinking?
Argh.
SHAKE
SHAKE
I need to be focusing on my duty...
No, it's okay.
Don't worry about me.
Heh heh.
HASTILY
I need to be thinking about my work.
Hmm.
TMP
TMP
......

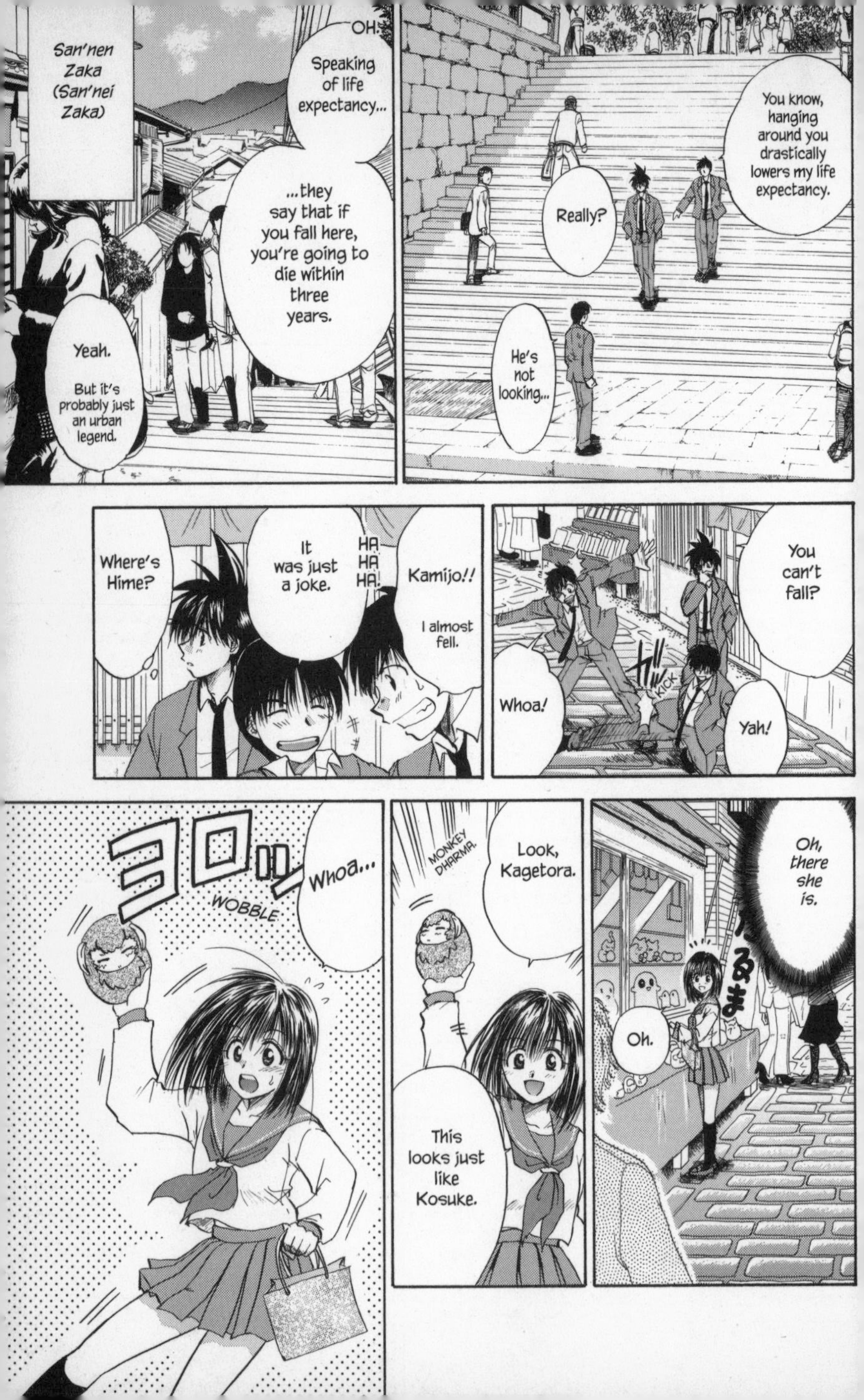
You know, hanging around you drastically lowers my life expectancy.
Really?
He's not looking...
OH! Speaking of life expectancy...
San'nen Zaka (San'nei Zaka)
...they say that if you fall here, you're going to die within three years.
Yeah. But it's probably just an urban legend.
You can't fall?
Whoa!
KICK
Yah!
Kamijo!!
I almost fell.
HA HA HA!
It was just a joke.
Where's Hime?
Oh, there she is.
Oh.
Look, Kagetora.
MONKEY D'HARMA.
This looks just like Kosuke.
Whoa...
WOBBLE

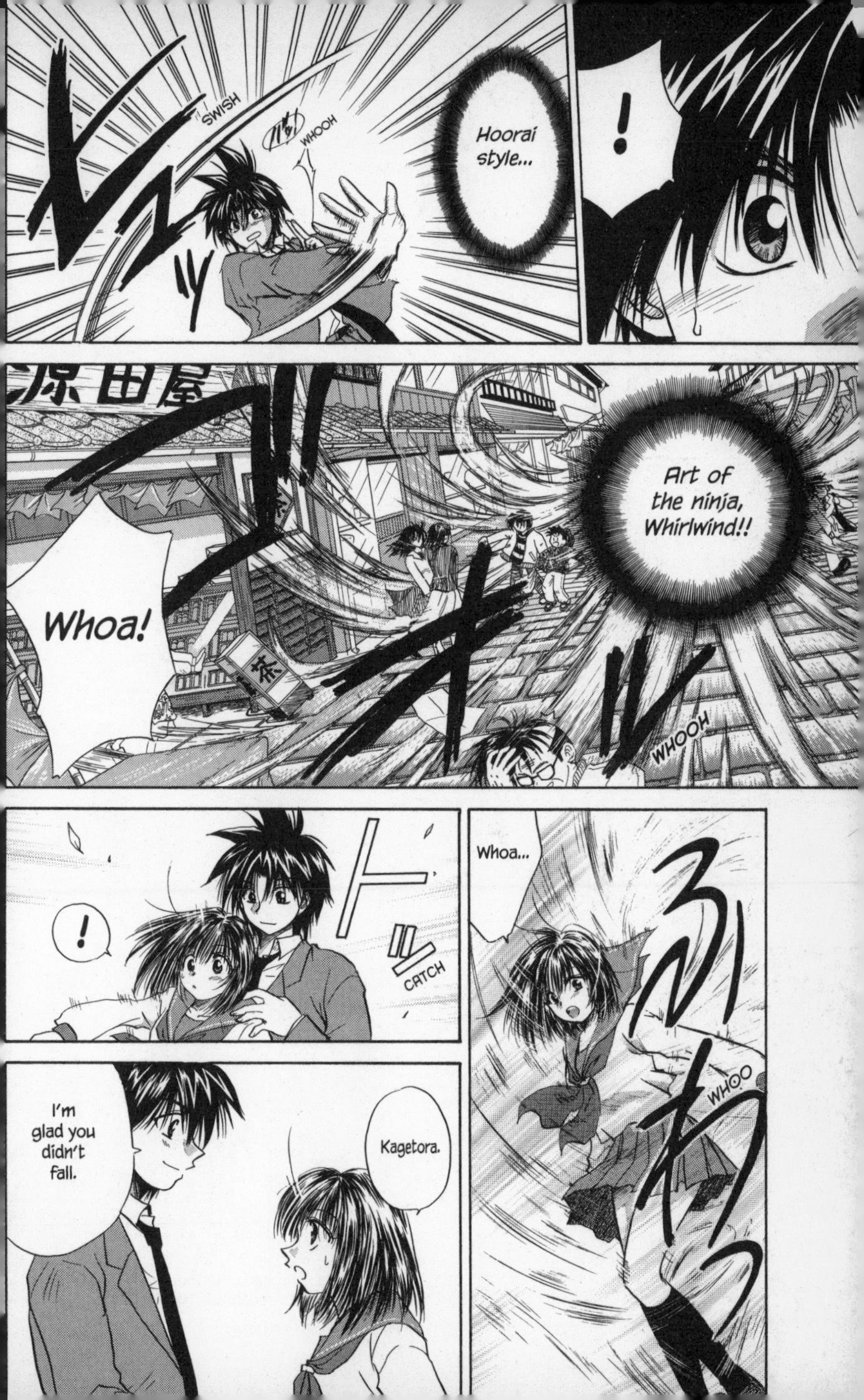
!
Hoorai style...
WHOOH
SWISH
Art of the ninja, Whirlwind!!
Whoa!
WHOOH
Whoa...
WHOO
!
CATCH
Kagetora.
I'm glad you didn't fall.

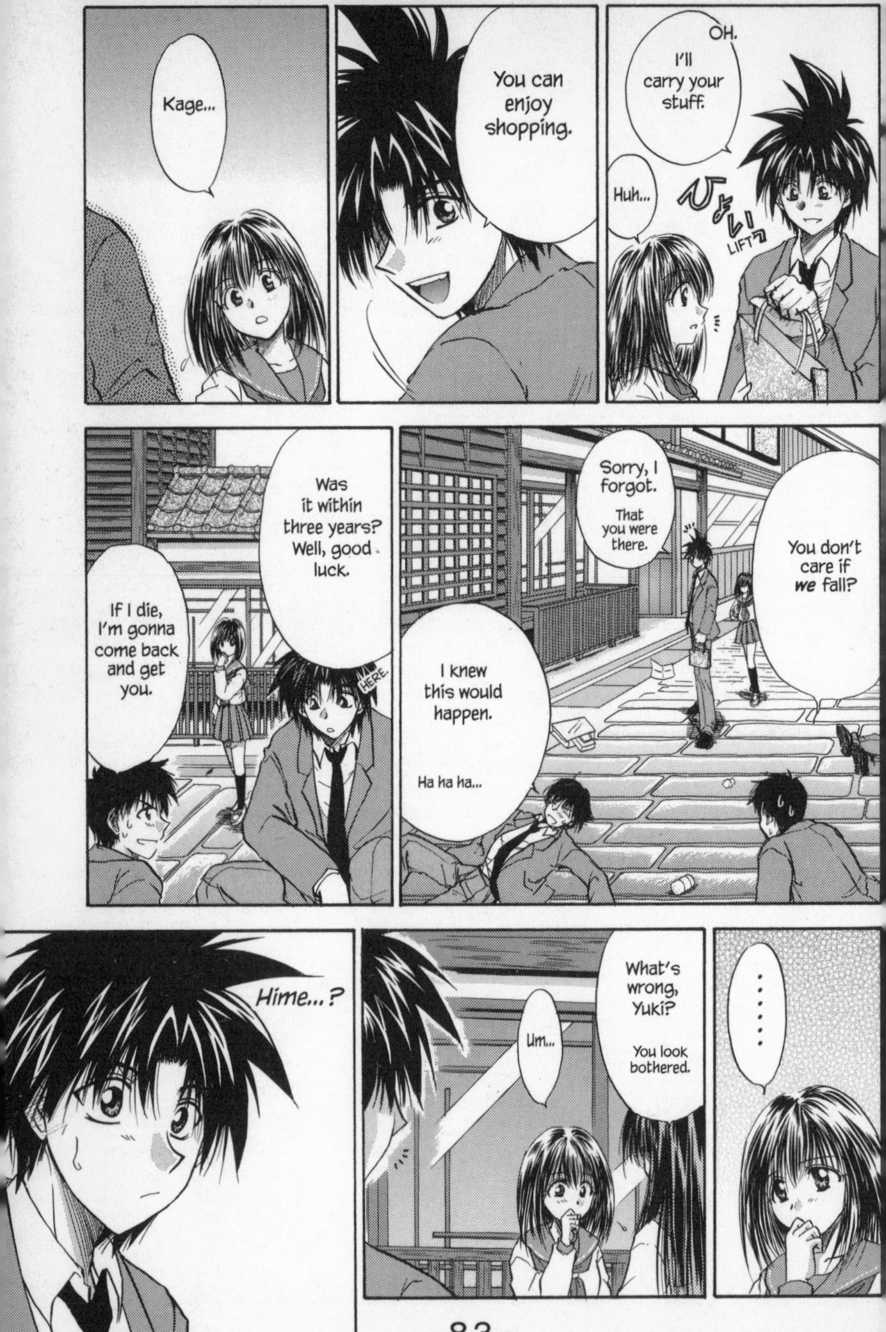
OH.
I'll carry your stuff.
Huh...
ひょい
LIFT
You can enjoy shopping.
Kage...
You don't care if *we* fall?
Sorry, I forgot.
That you were there.
I knew this would happen.
Ha ha ha...
Was it within three years? Well, good luck.
HERE.
If I die, I'm gonna come back and get you.
......
What's wrong, Yuki?
You look bothered.
Um...
Hime...?

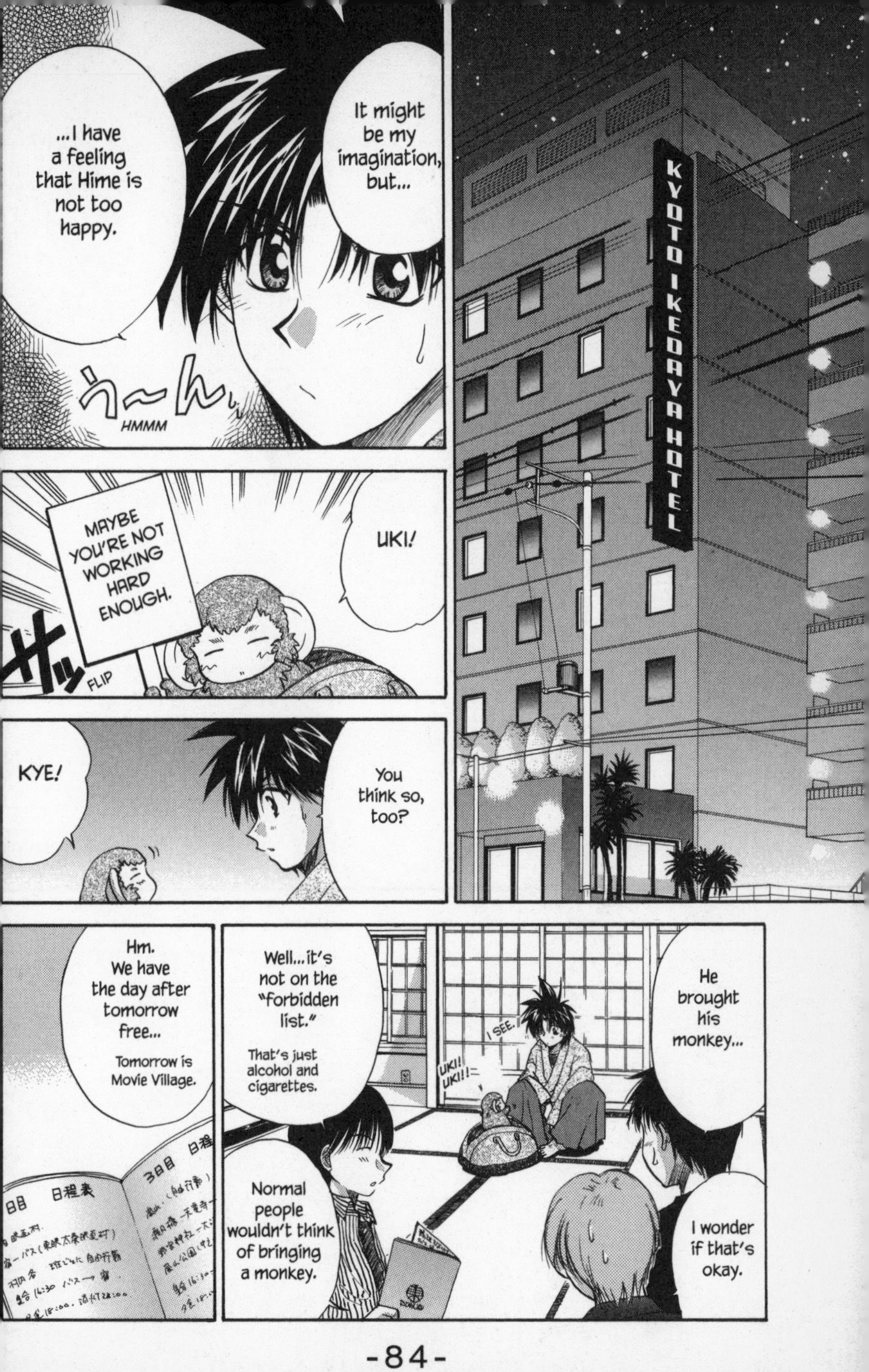
KYOTO IKEDAYA HOTEL
It might be my imagination, but...
...I have a feeling that Hime is not too happy.
うーん
HMMM
UKI!
MAYBE YOU'RE NOT WORKING HARD ENOUGH.
ザッ
FLIP
You think so, too?
KYE!
He brought his monkey...
Well...it's not on the "forbidden list."
That's just alcohol and cigarettes.
I SEE.
UKI! UKI!!
I wonder if that's okay.
Normal people wouldn't think of bringing a monkey.
Hm. We have the day after tomorrow free...
Tomorrow is Movie Village.
日程表
日程

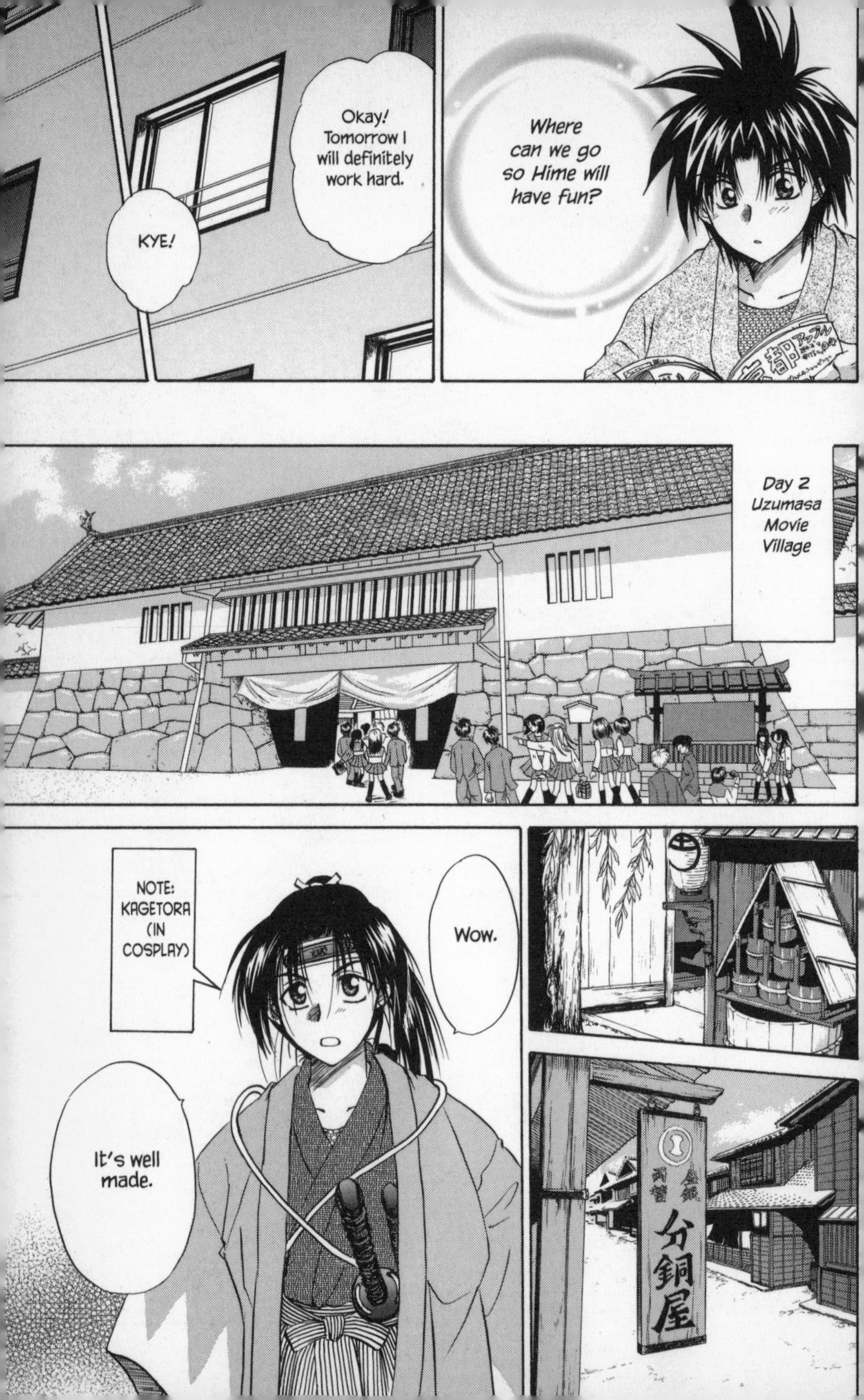
Where can we go so Hime will have fun?
Okay! Tomorrow I will definitely work hard.
KYE!
Day 2 Uzumasa Movie Village
両替 金銀
分銅屋
Wow.
NOTE: KAGETORA (IN COSPLAY)
It's well made.

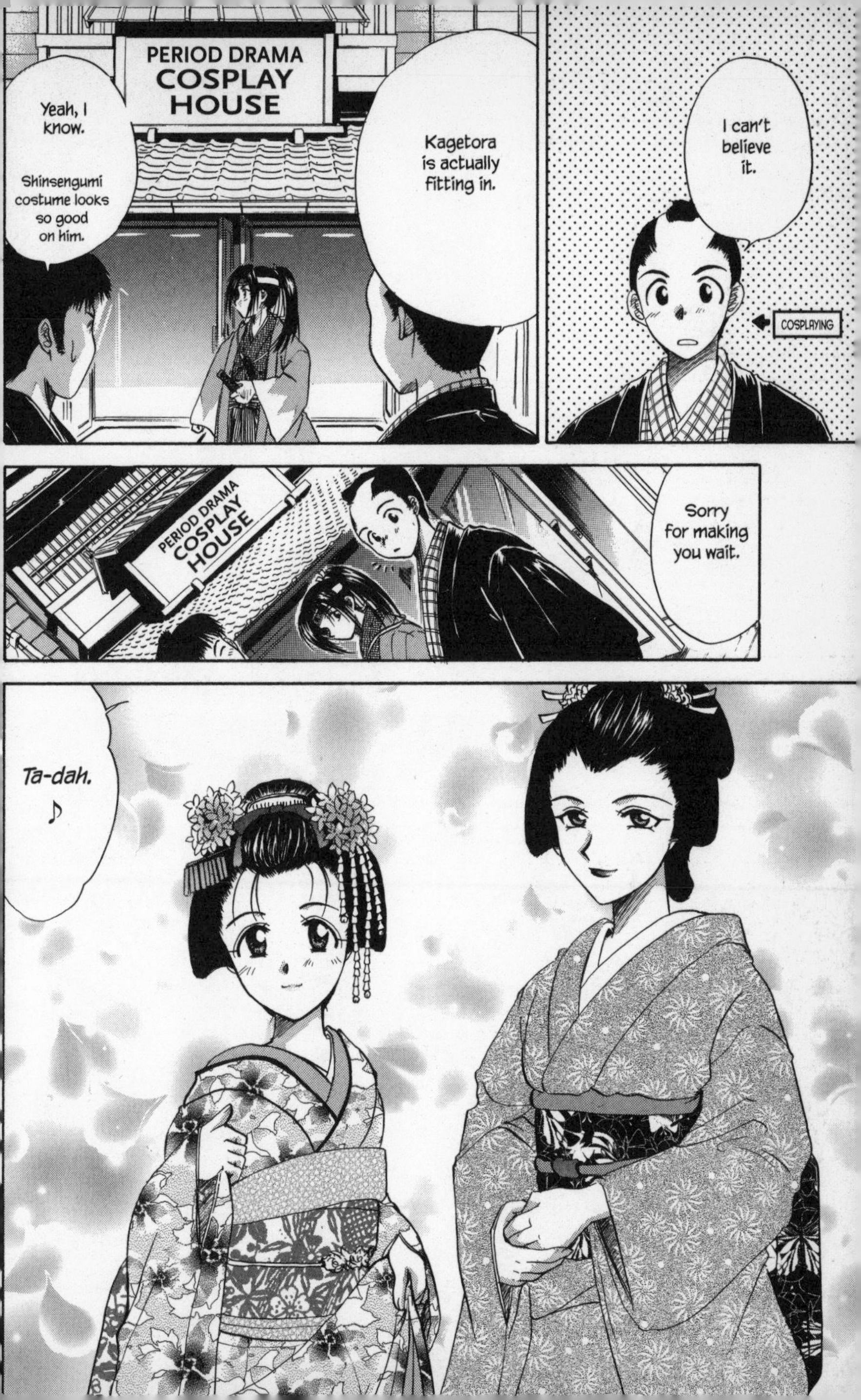
I can't believe it.
COSPLAYING
PERIOD DRAMA COSPLAY HOUSE
Kagetora is actually fitting in.
Yeah, I know.
Shinsengumi costume looks so good on him.
Sorry for making you wait.
PERIOD DRAMA COSPLAY HOUSE
Ta-dah. ♪

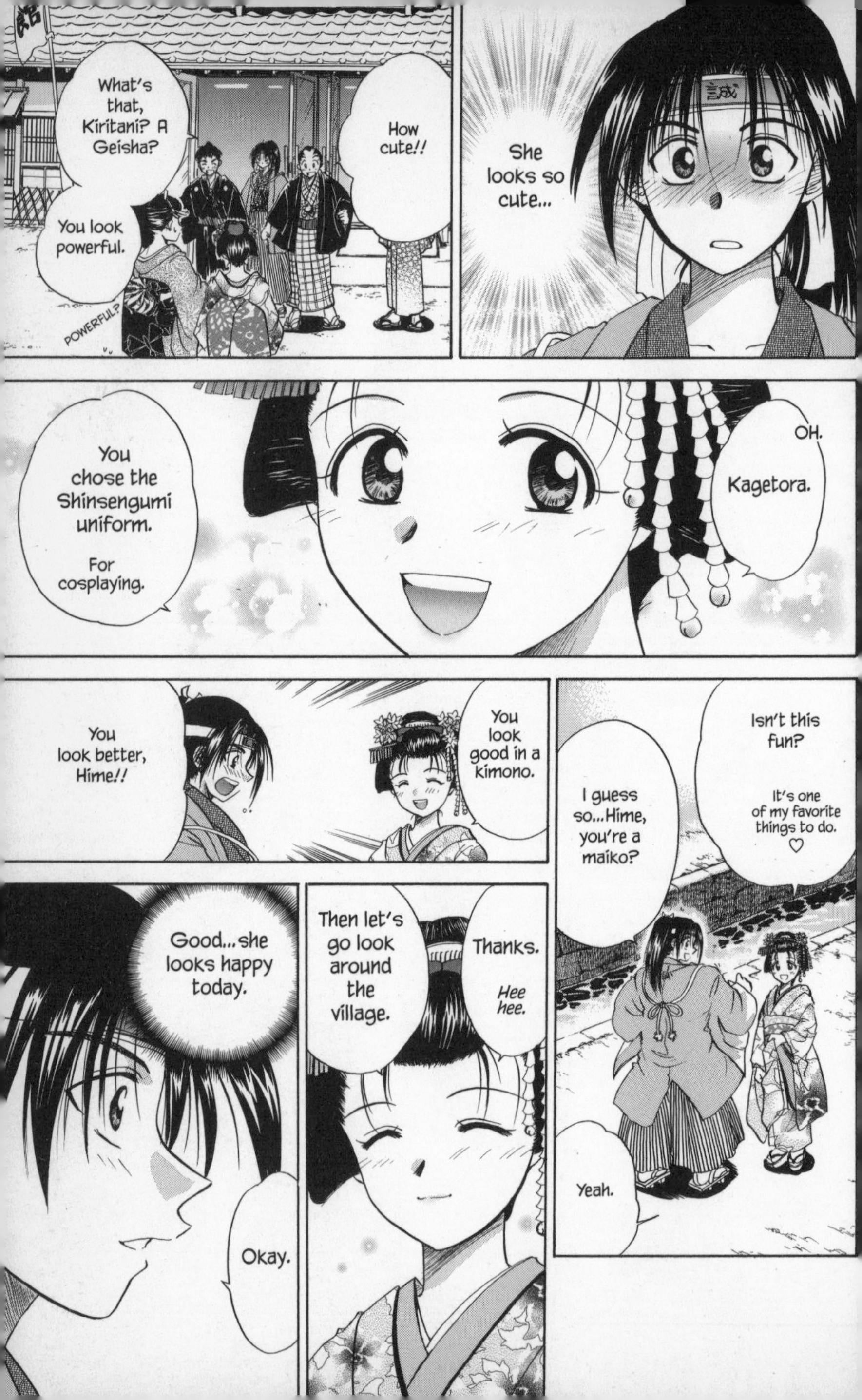
She looks so cute...
How cute!!
What's that, Kiritani? A Geisha?
You look powerful.
POWERFUL?
OH.
Kagetora.
You chose the Shinsengumi uniform.
For cosplaying.
Isn't this fun?
It's one of my favorite things to do. ♡
I guess so...Hime, you're a maiko?
Yeah.
You look good in a kimono.
You look better, Hime!!
Thanks.
Hee hee.
Then let's go look around the village.
Good...she looks happy today.
Okay.

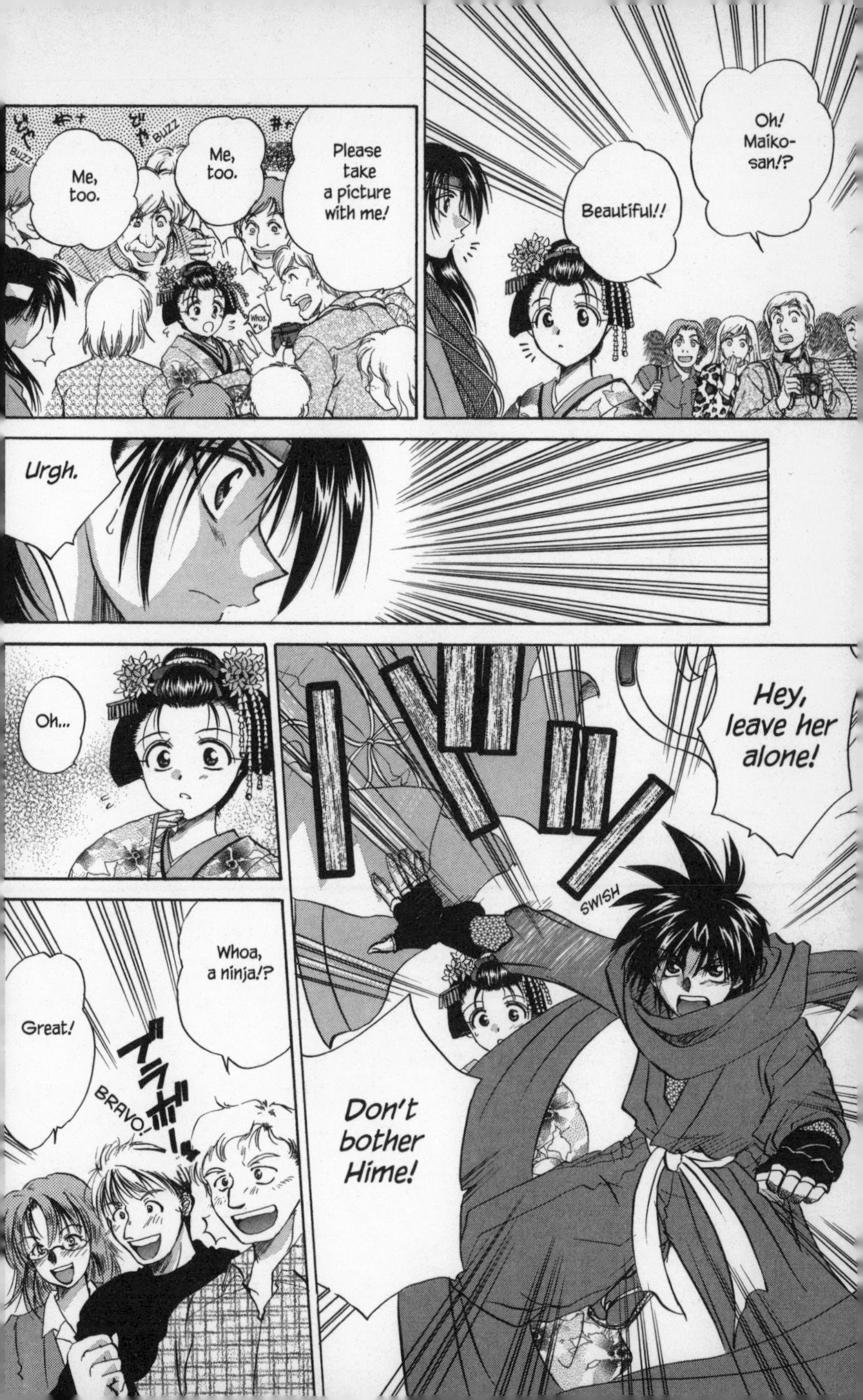
Oh! Maiko-san!?
Beautiful!!
Please take a picture with me!
Me, too.
BUZZ
Me, too.
BUZZ
Urgh.
Hey, leave her alone!
SWISH
Don't bother Hime!
Oh...
Whoa, a ninja!?
Great!
BRAVO!

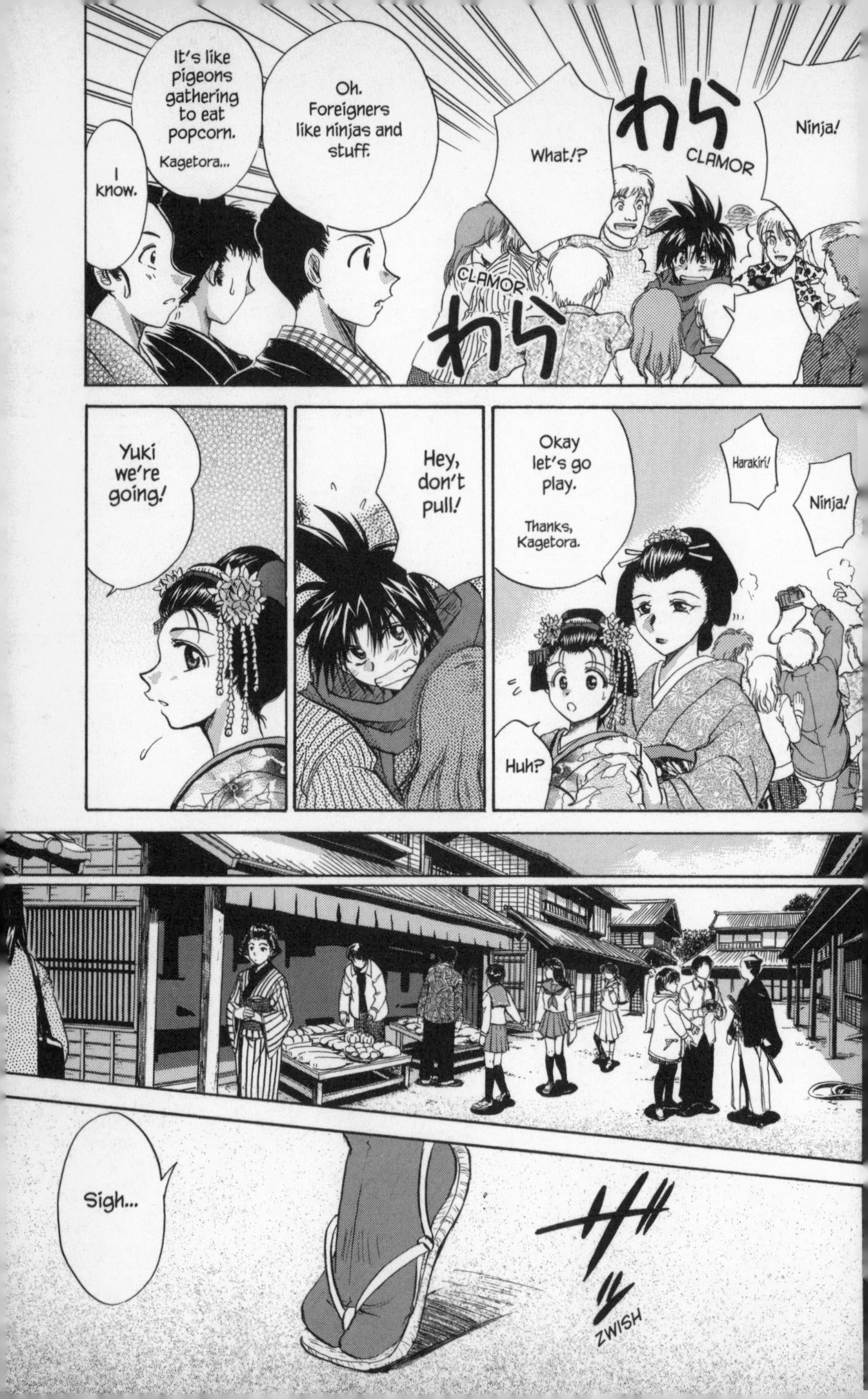
Ninja!
わら
CLAMOR
What!?
Oh. Foreigners like ninjas and stuff.
It's like pigeons gathering to eat popcorn.
Kagetora...
I know.
CLAMOR
わら
Ninja!
Harakiri!
Okay let's go play.
Thanks, Kagetora.
Huh?
Hey, don't pull!
Yuki we're going!
ZWISH
Sigh...

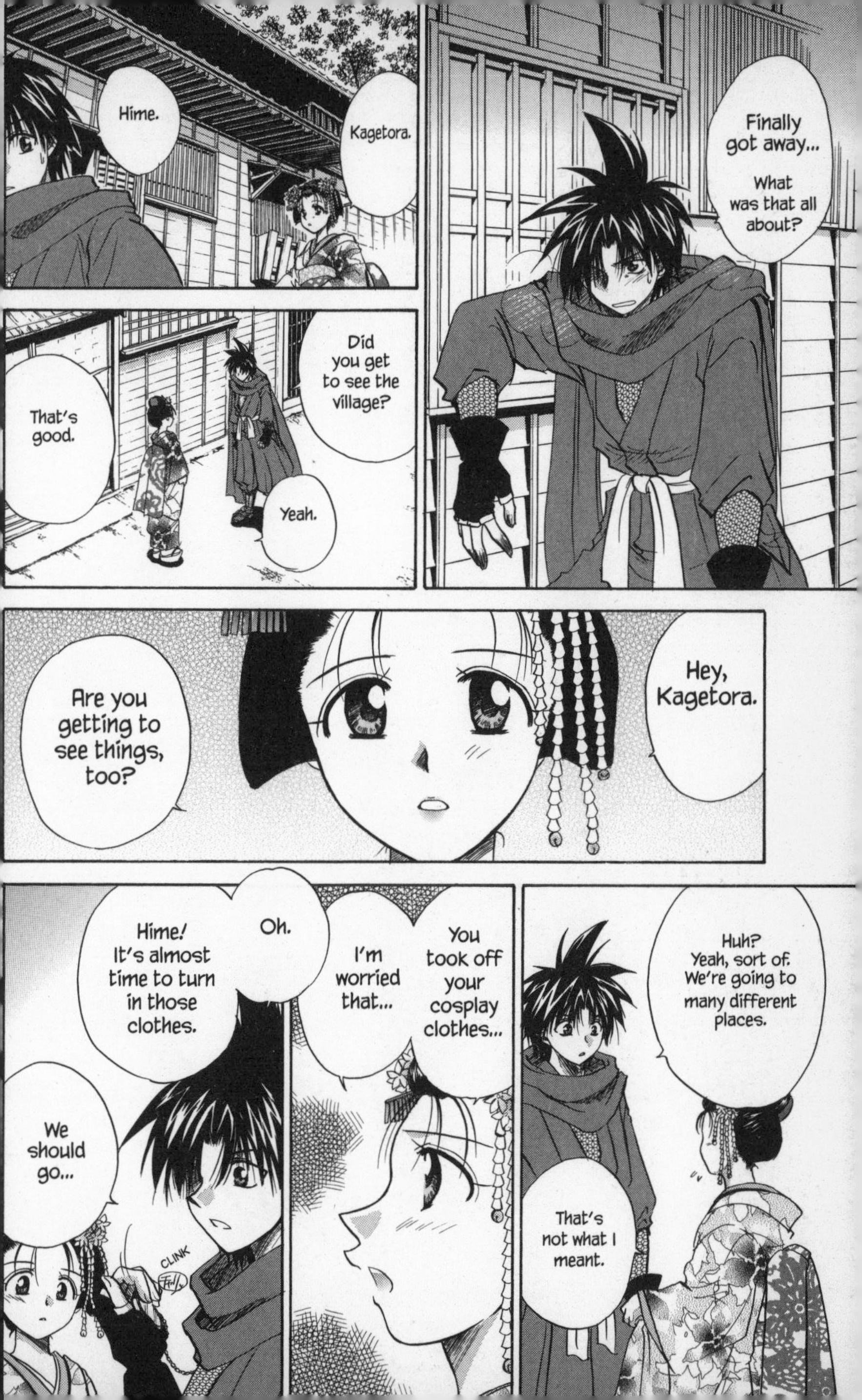
Finally got away...
What was that all about?
Kagetora.
Hime.
Did you get to see the village?
Yeah.
That's good.
Hey, Kagetora.
Are you getting to see things, too?
Huh? Yeah, sort of. We're going to many different places.
That's not what I meant.
You took off your cosplay clothes...
I'm worried that...
Oh.
Hime! It's almost time to turn in those clothes.
We should go...
CLINK

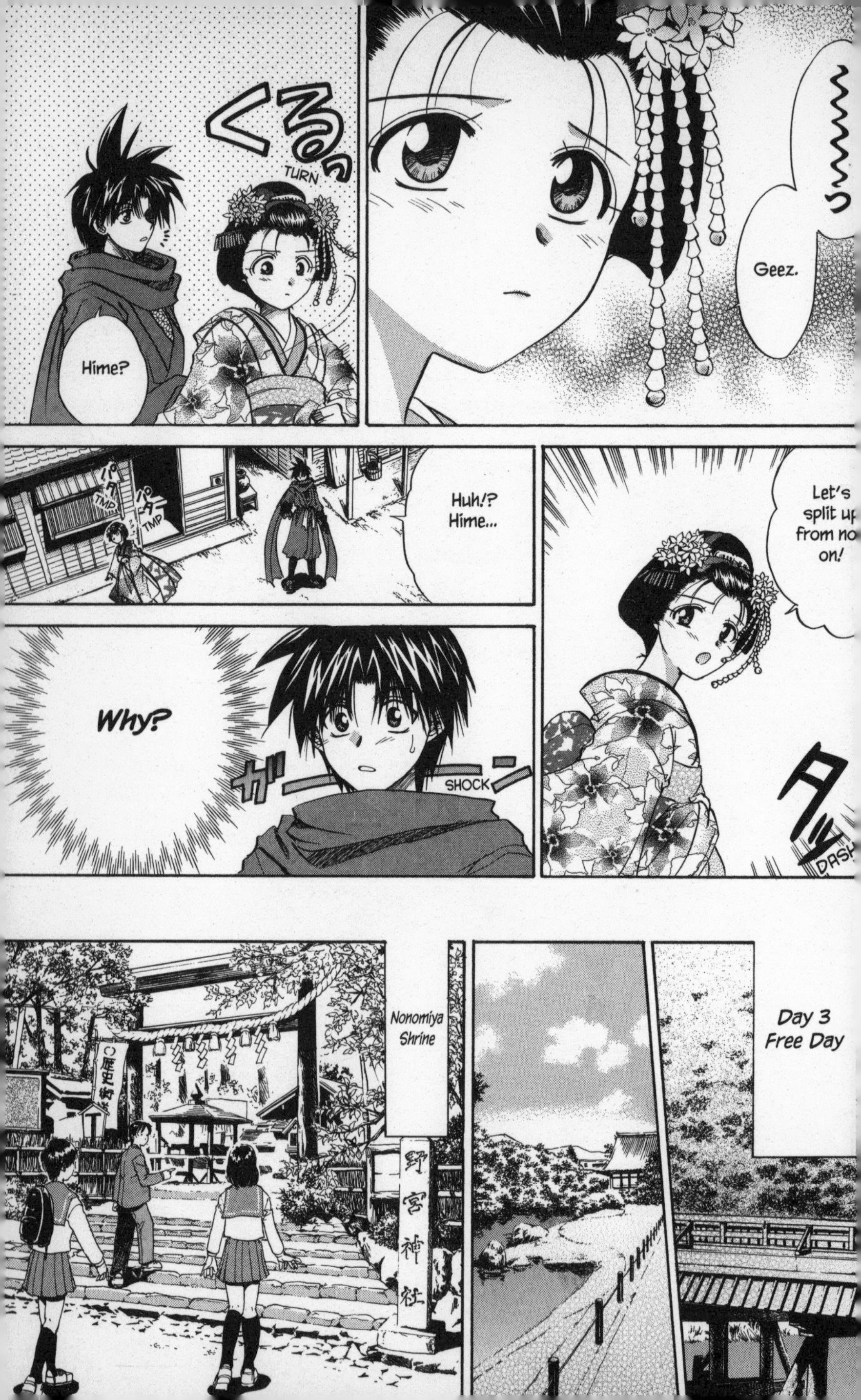
ううう
Geez.
くるっ
TURN
Hime?
Let's split u from no on!
タッ
DAS
Huh!? Hime...
パタ
TMP
パタ
TMP
Why?
ガーン
SHOCK
Day 3 Free Day
Nonomiya Shrine
野宮神社

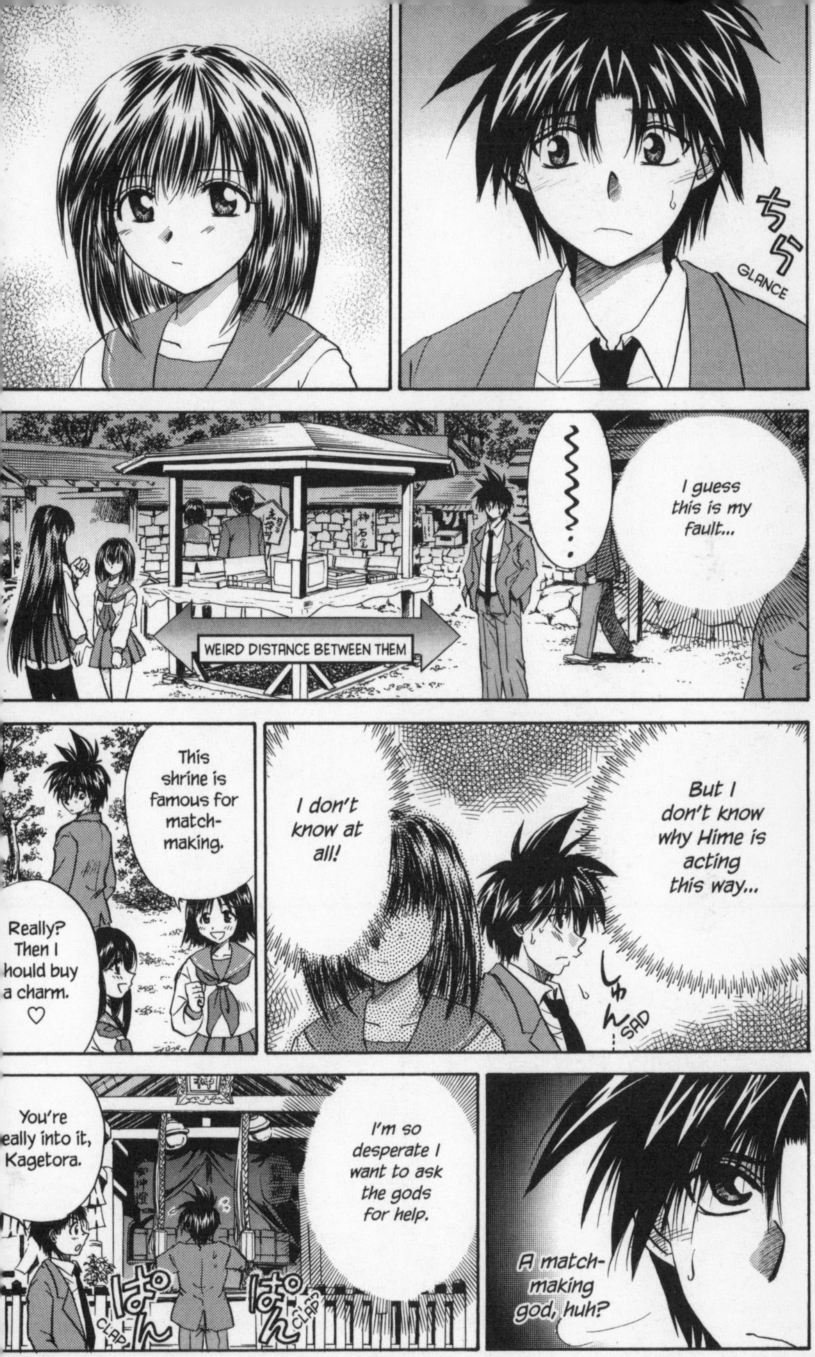
ちら
GLANCE
I guess this is my fault...
WEIRD DISTANCE BETWEEN THEM
But I don't know why Hime is acting this way...
I don't know at all!
しゅん
SAD
This shrine is famous for match-making.
Really? Then I hould buy a charm. ♡
A match-making god, huh?
I'm so desperate I want to ask the gods for help.
You're eally into it, Kagetora.
ぱん
CLAP
ぱん
CLAP

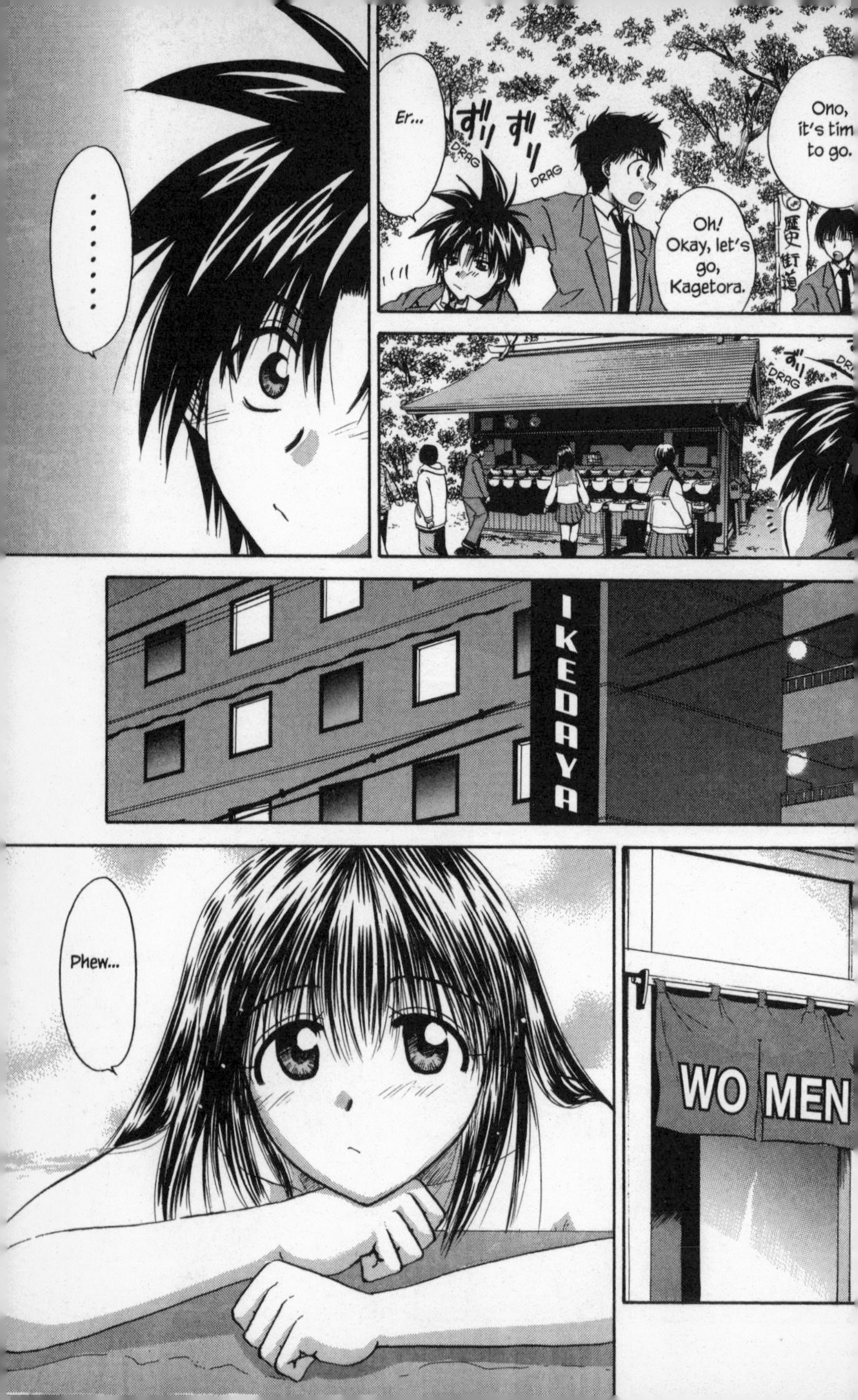
Ono, it's tim to go.
Oh! Okay, let's go, Kagetora.
DRAG
DRAG
Er...
DRAG
DRAG
....
IKEDAYA
WO MEN
Phew...

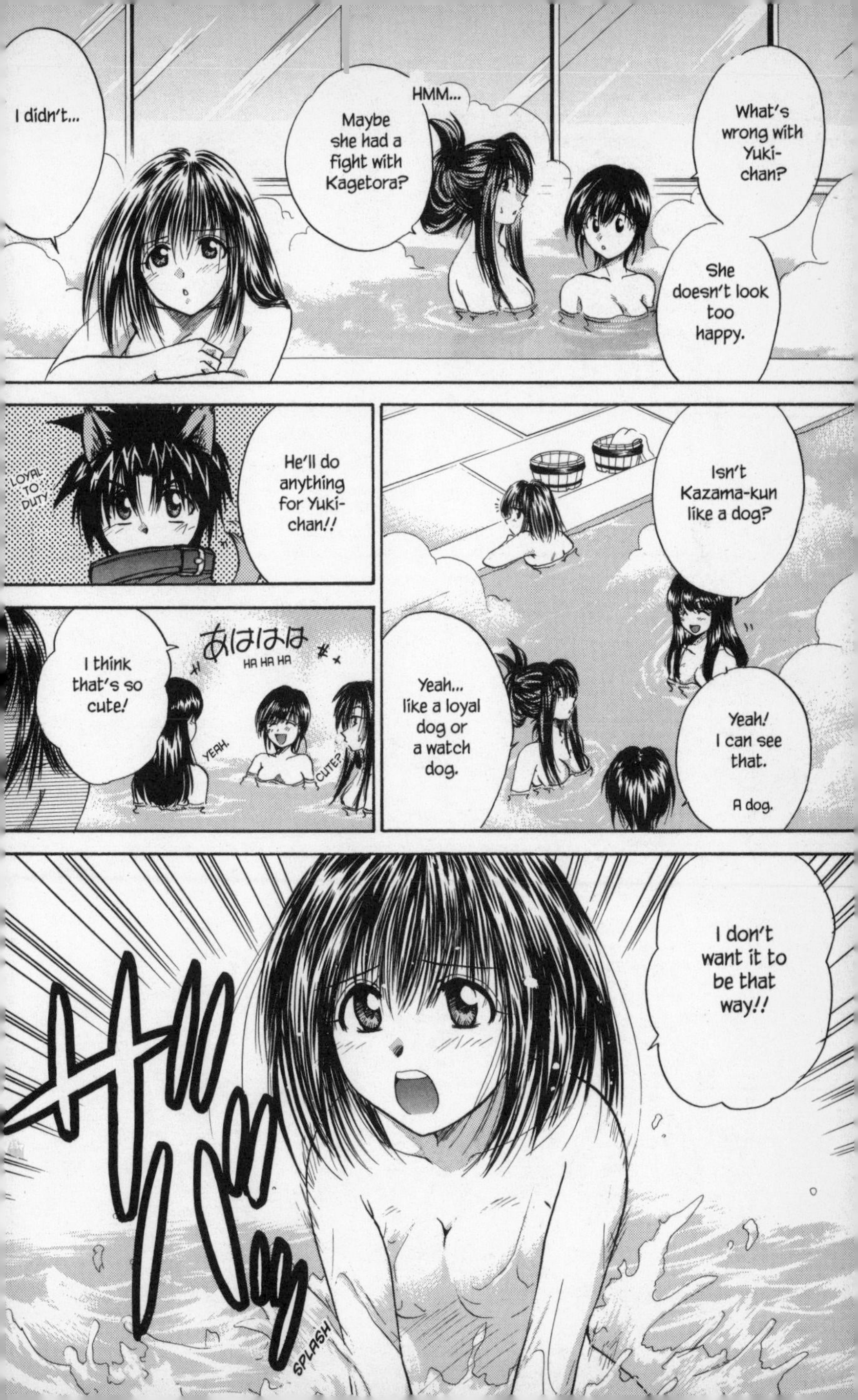
What's wrong with Yuki-chan?
She doesn't look too happy.
HMM...
Maybe she had a fight with Kagetora?
I didn't...
Isn't Kazama-kun like a dog?
Yeah! I can see that.
A dog.
Yeah... like a loyal dog or a watch dog.
He'll do anything for Yuki-chan!!
LOYAL TO DUTY
あははは
HA HA HA
CUTE?
YEAH.
I think that's so cute!
I don't want it to be that way!!
SPLASH

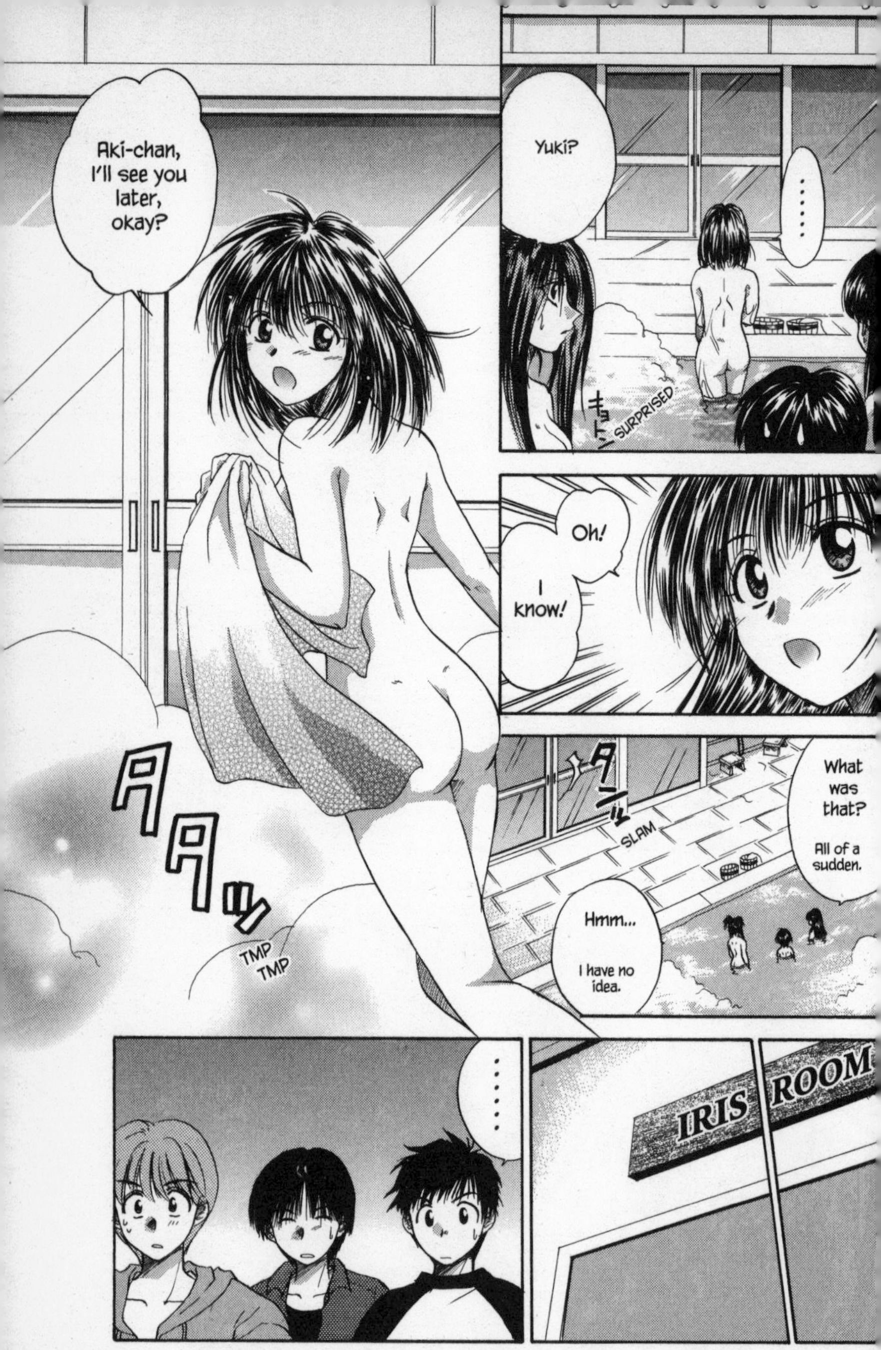
Yuki?
......
SURPRISED
Oh!
I know!
What was that?
All of a sudden.
SLAM
Hmm...
I have no idea.
Aki-chan, I'll see you later, okay?
TMP TMP
IRIS ROOM
......

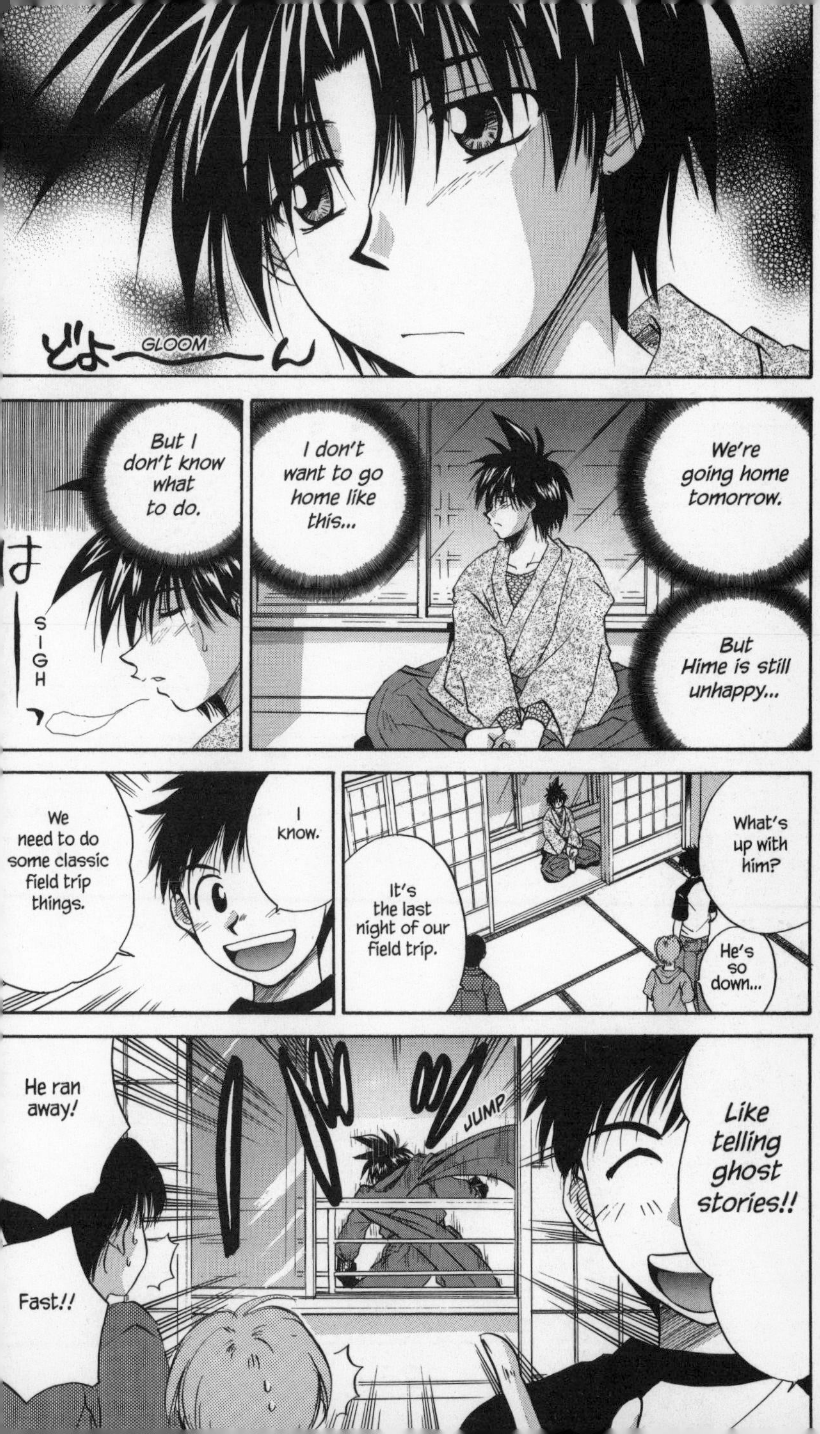

どよ〜〜ん GLOOM
We're going home tomorrow.
But Hime is still unhappy...
I don't want to go home like this...
But I don't know what to do.
はー SIGH
What's up with him?
He's so down...
It's the last night of our field trip.
I know.
We need to do some classic field trip things.
Like telling ghost stories!!
JUMP
He ran away!
Fast!!

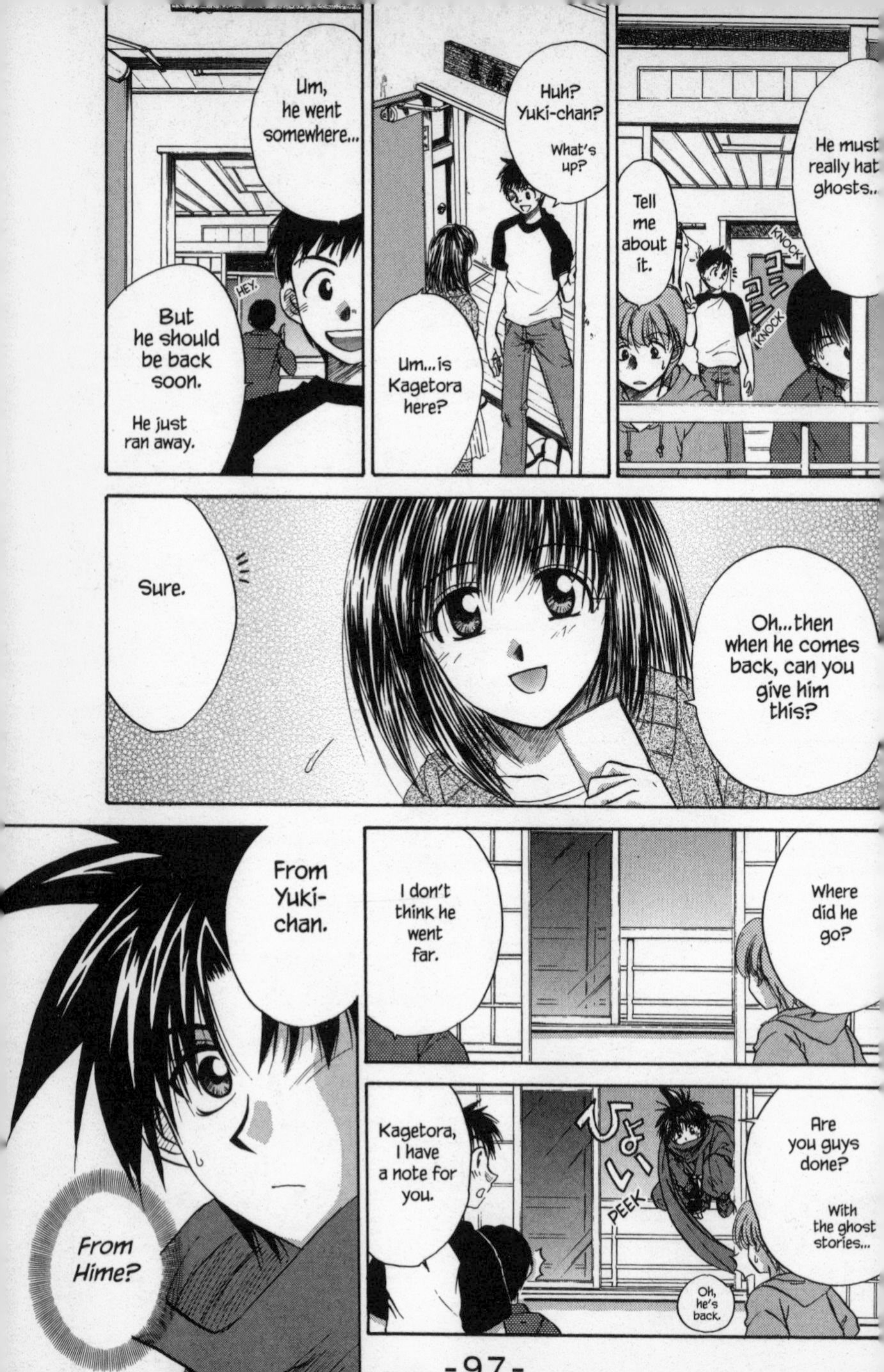
He must really hat ghosts..
KNOCK
KNOCK
Tell me about it.
Huh? Yuki-chan?
What's up?
Um...is Kagetora here?
Um, he went somewhere...
HEY.
But he should be back soon.
He just ran away.
Oh...then when he comes back, can you give him this?
Sure.
Where did he go?
I don't think he went far.
Are you guys done?
With the ghost stories...
Oh, he's back.
PEEK
Kagetora, I have a note for you.
From Yuki-chan.
From Hime?

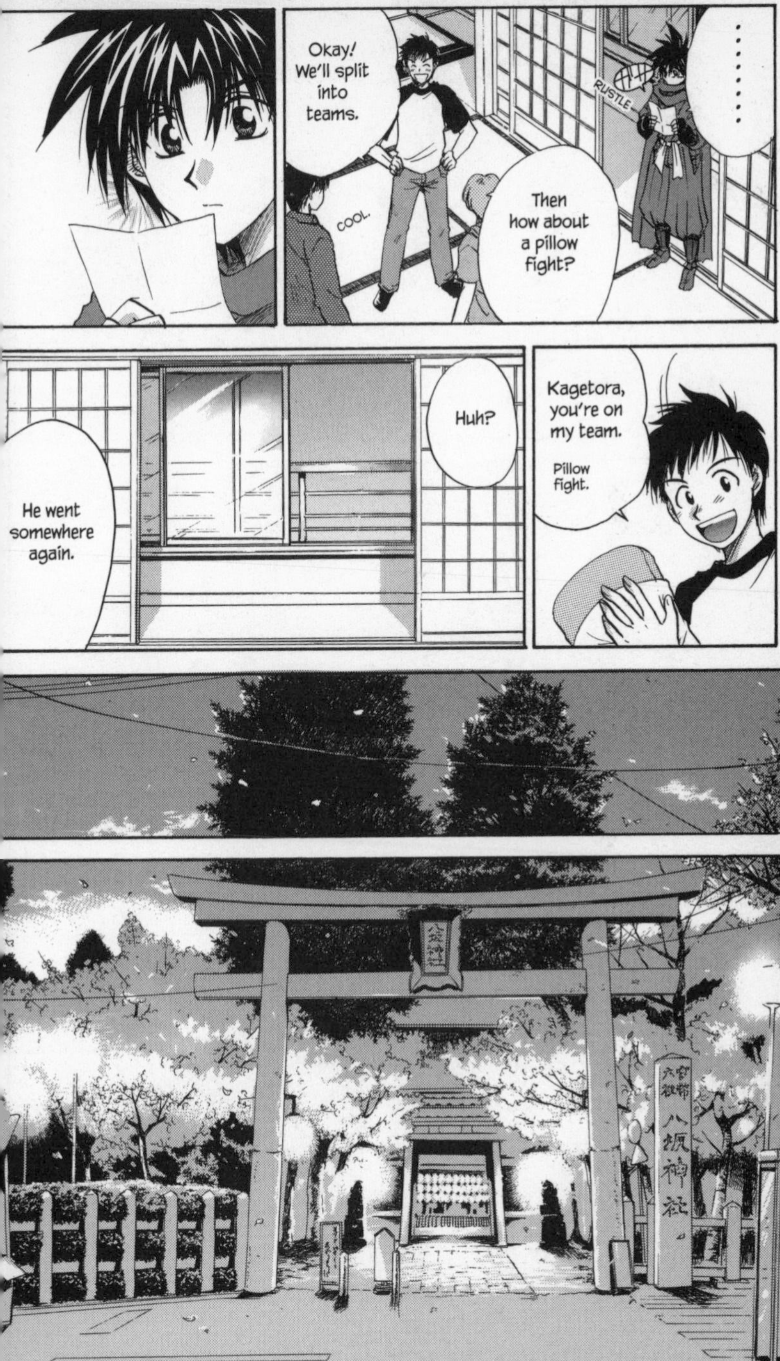

......
RUSTLE
Okay! We'll split into teams.
Then how about a pillow fight?
COOL.
Kagetora, you're on my team.
Pillow fight.
Huh?
He went somewhere again.

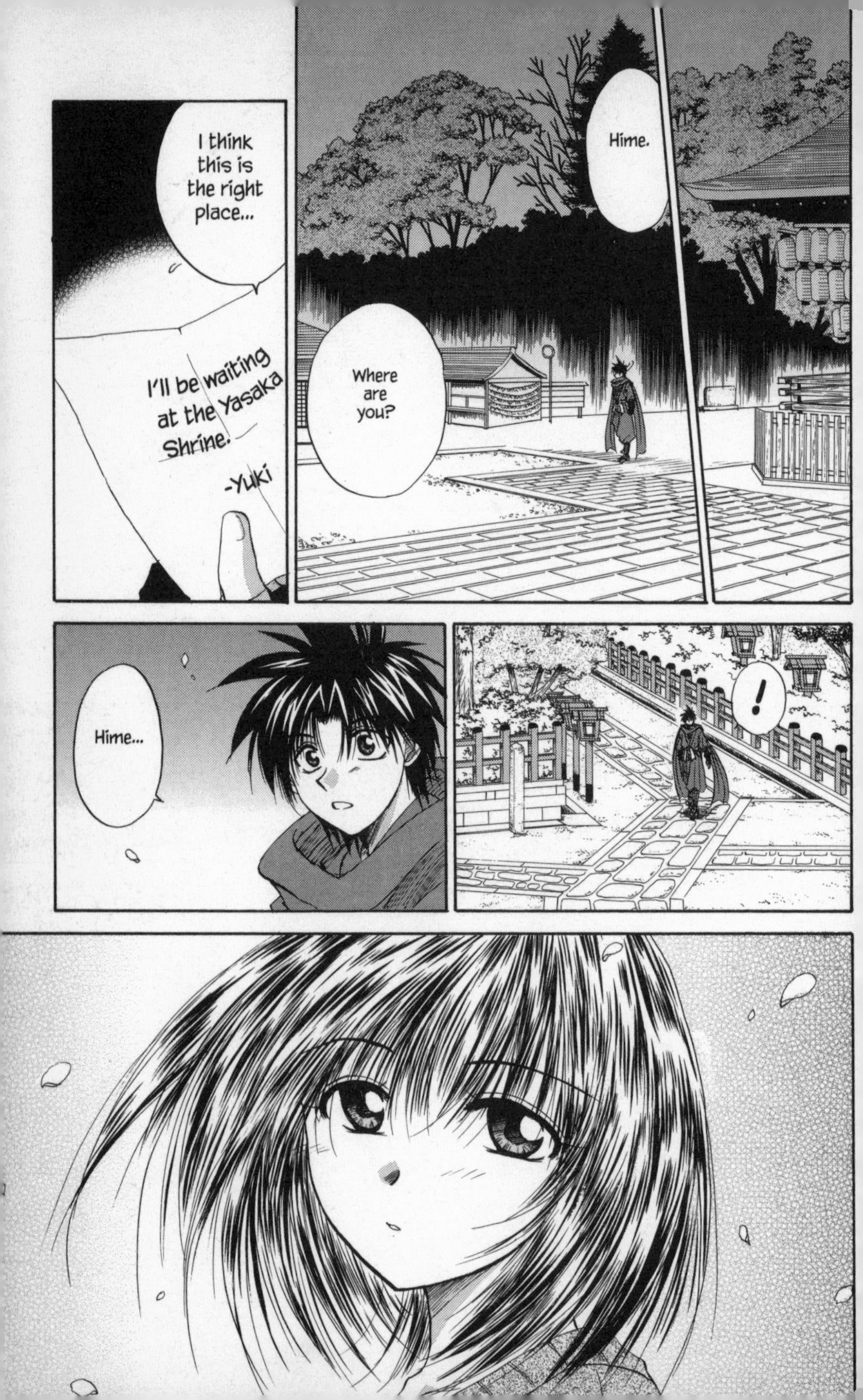
Hime.
Where are you?
I think this is the right place...
I'll be waiting at the Yasaka Shrine.
-Yuki
!
Hime...

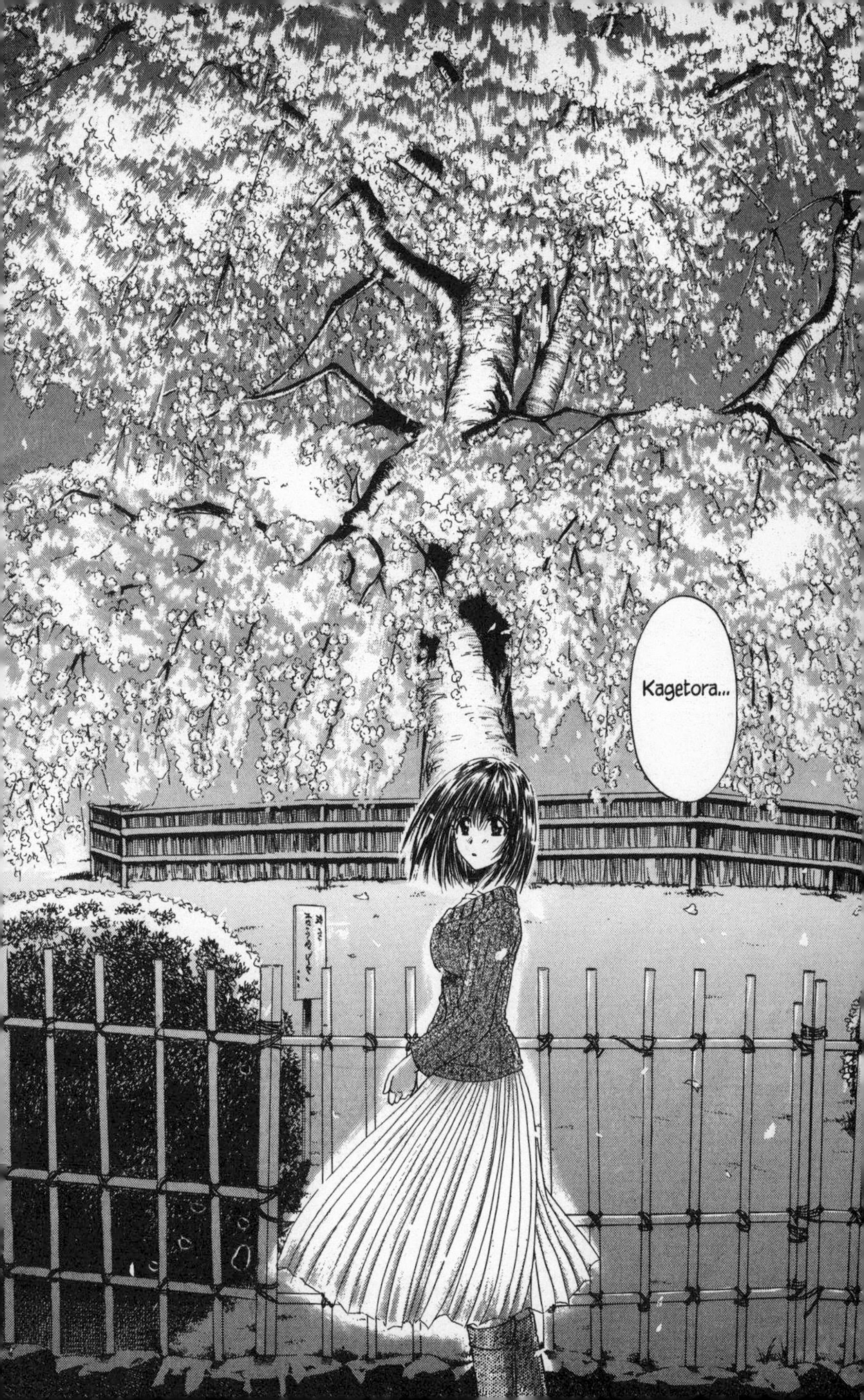
Kagetora...

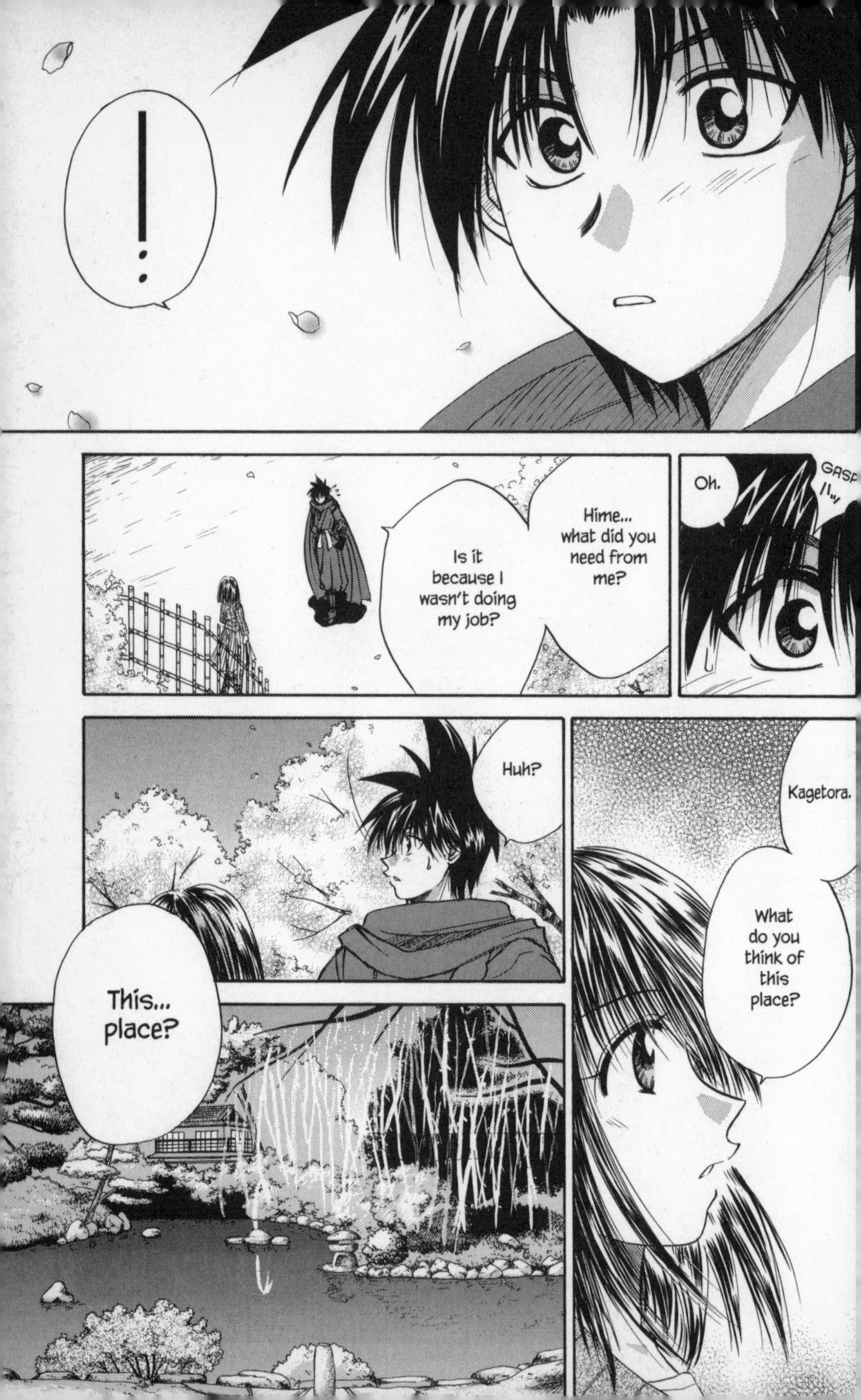
!
Oh.
GASP
Hime... what did you need from me?
Is it because I wasn't doing my job?
Kagetora.
What do you think of this place?
Huh?
This... place?

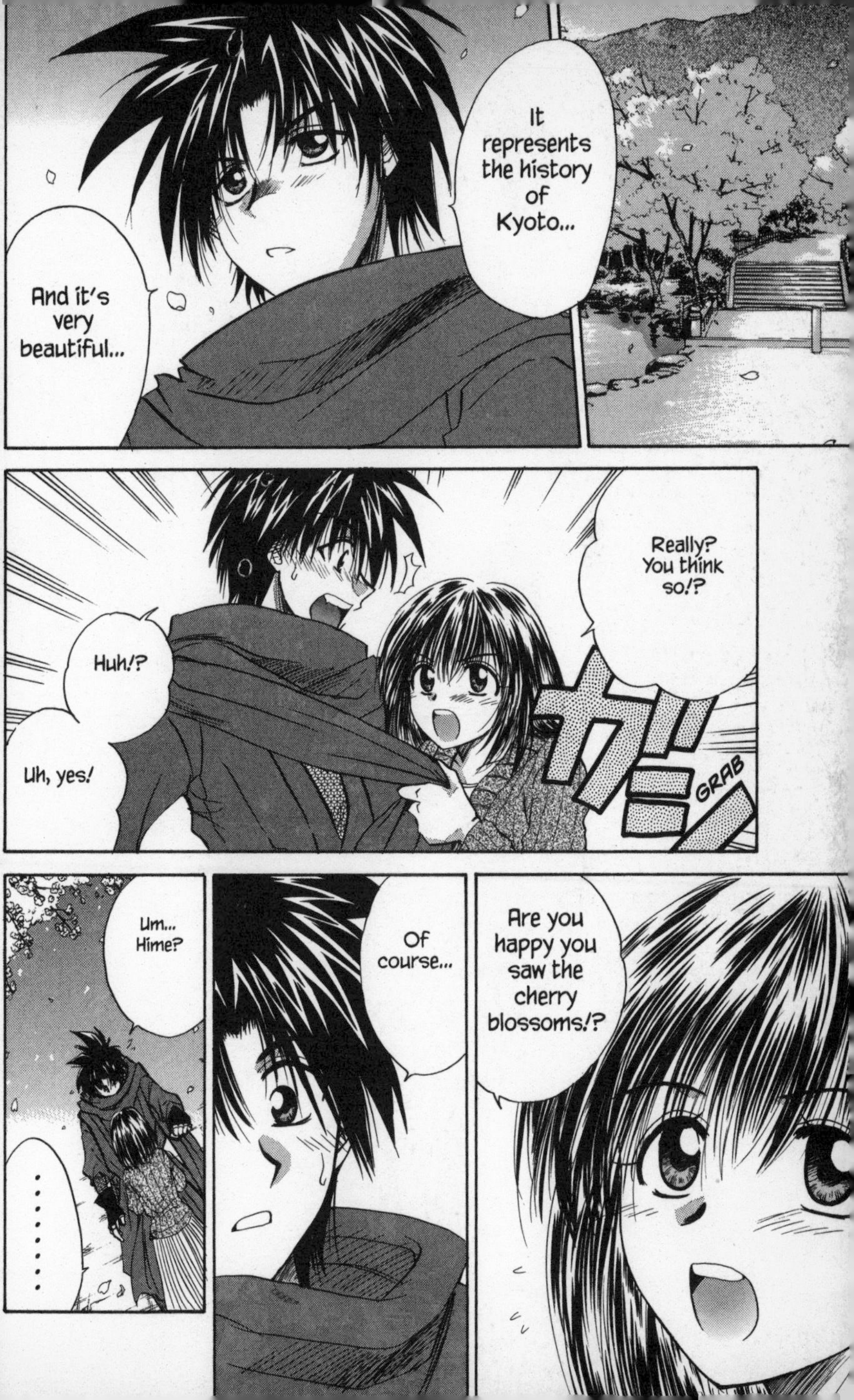

It represents the history of Kyoto...
And it's very beautiful...
Really? You think so!?
GRAB
Huh!?
Uh, yes!
Are you happy you saw the cherry blossoms!?
Of course...
Um... Hime?
....

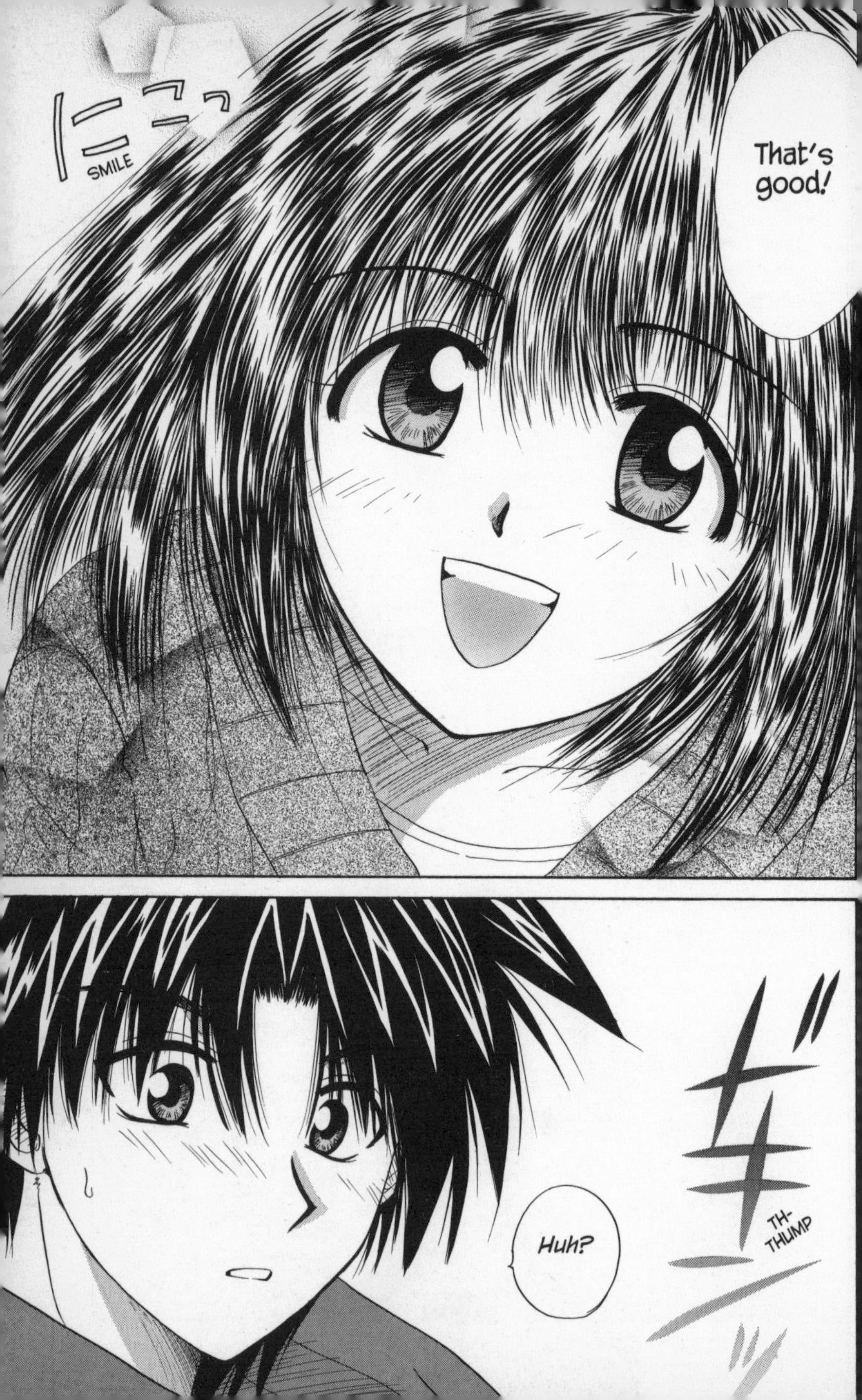
That's good!
にこっ
SMILE
TH-THUMP
Huh?

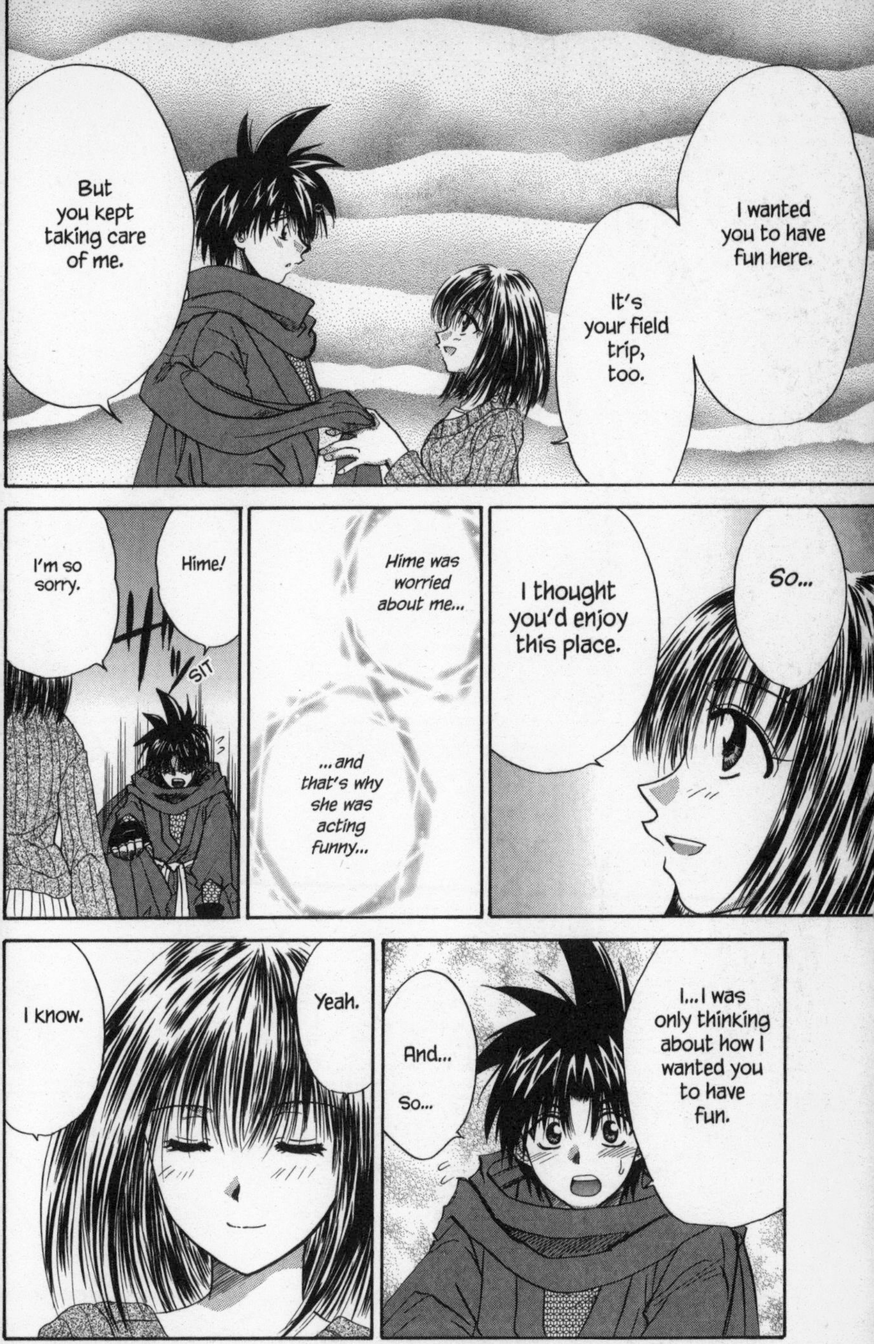
I wanted you to have fun here.
It's your field trip, too.
But you kept taking care of me.
So...
I thought you'd enjoy this place.
Hime was worried about me...
...and that's why she was acting funny...
Hime!
I'm so sorry.
SIT
I...I was only thinking about how I wanted you to have fun.
And...
So...
Yeah.
I know.

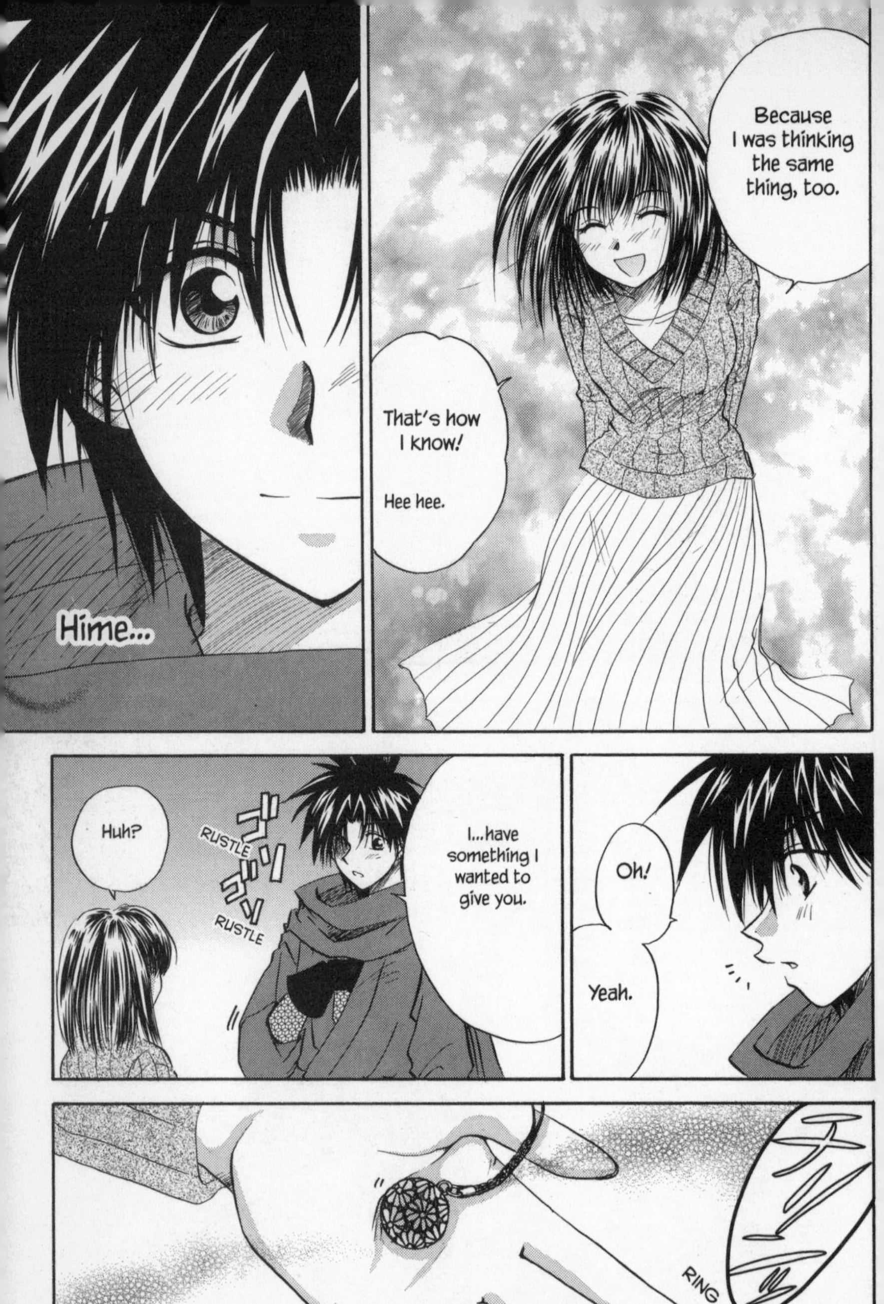
Because I was thinking the same thing, too.
That's how I know!
Hee hee.
Hime...
Oh!
Yeah.
I...have something I wanted to give you.
RUSTLE
RUSTLE
Huh?
RING

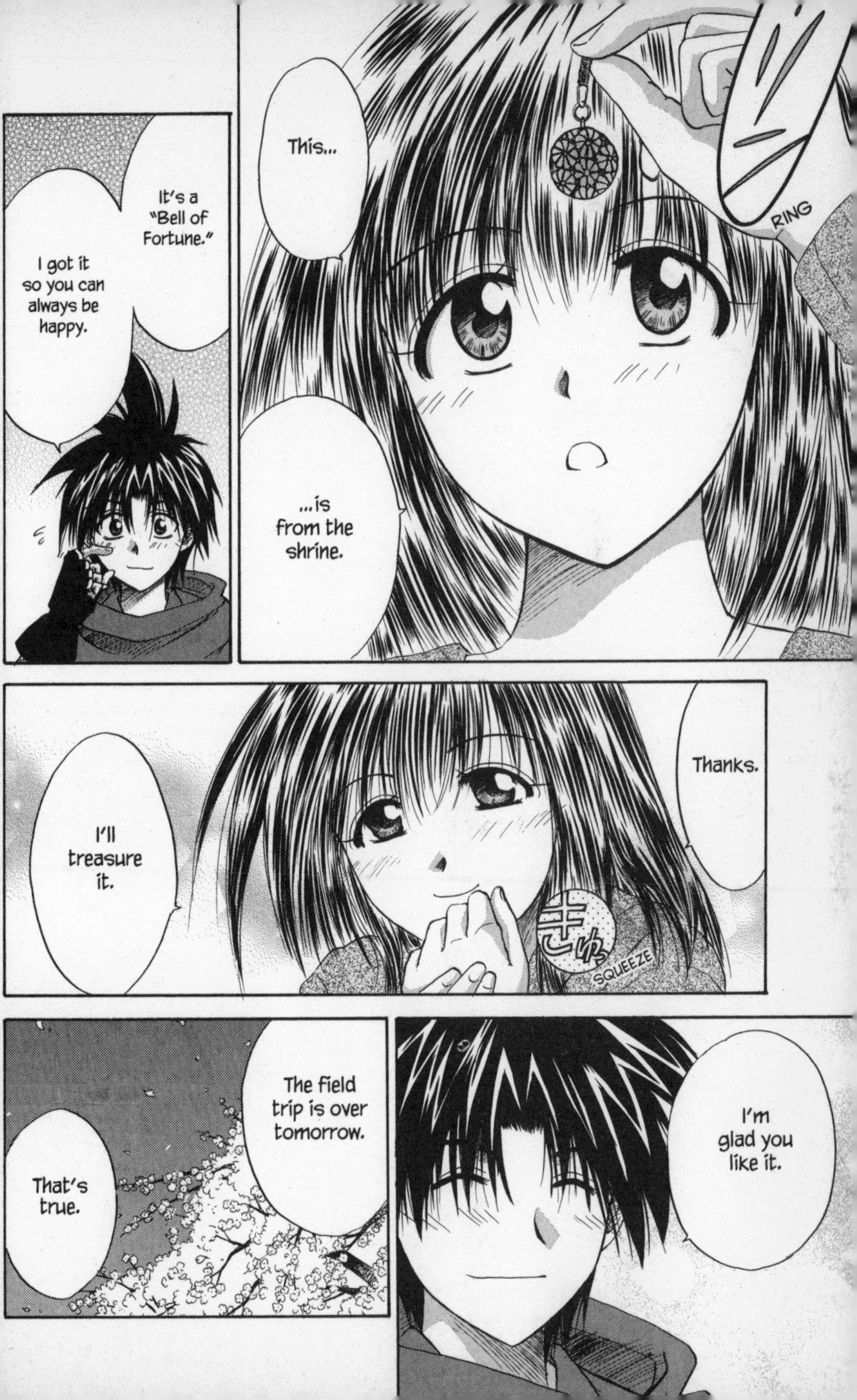
RING
This...
...is from the shrine.
It's a "Bell of Fortune."
I got it so you can always be happy.
Thanks.
きゅ
SQUEEZE
I'll treasure it.
I'm glad you like it.
The field trip is over tomorrow.
That's true.

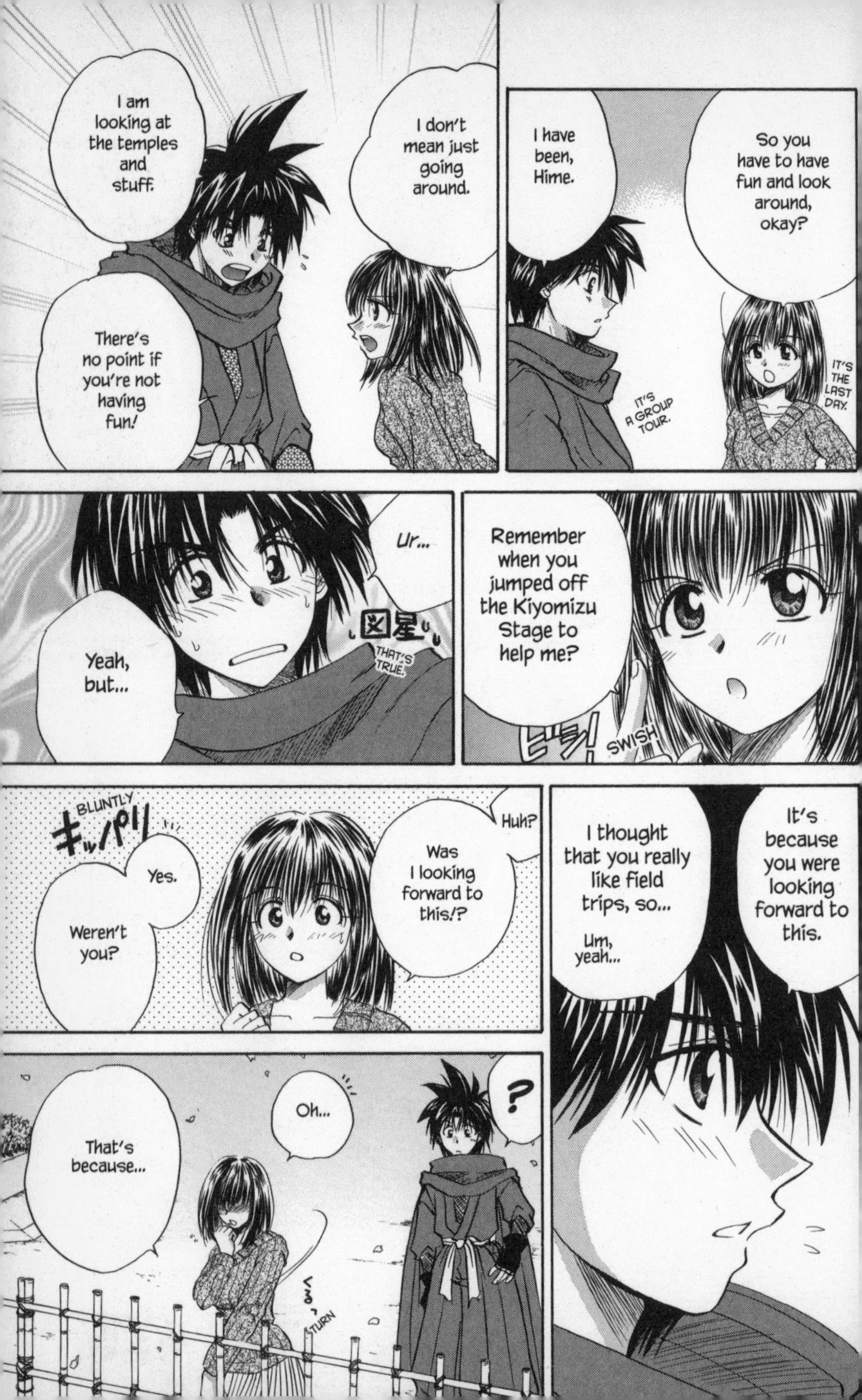
So you have to have fun and look around, okay?
I have been, Hime.
IT'S THE LAST DAY.
IT'S A GROUP TOUR.
I don't mean just going around.
I am looking at the temples and stuff.
There's no point if you're not having fun!
Remember when you jumped off the Kiyomizu Stage to help me?
SWISH
Ur...
THAT'S TRUE.
Yeah, but...
It's because you were looking forward to this.
I thought that you really like field trips, so...
Um, yeah...
Huh?
Was I looking forward to this!?
BLUNTLY
Yes.
Weren't you?
?
Oh...
That's because...
TURN

I was looking forward to it...

...because it was with you...

Hime... what did you say?

It's nothing.

Huh!?

TMP TMP TMP

TH-THUMP

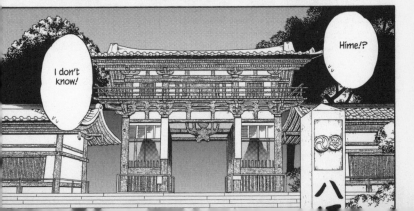

I don't know!

Hime!?

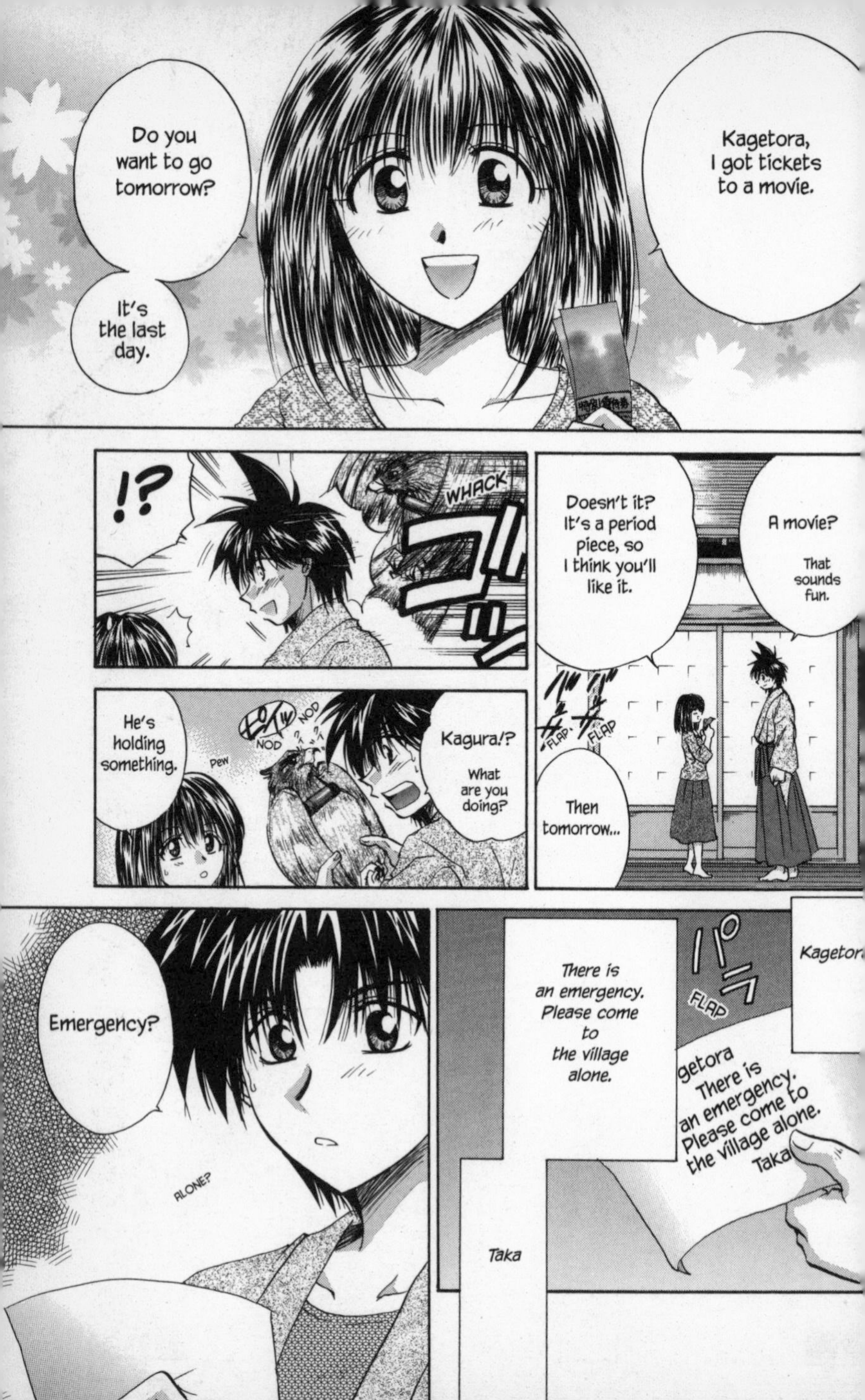
Kagetora, I got tickets to a movie.
Do you want to go tomorrow?
It's the last day.
A movie?
That sounds fun.
Doesn't it? It's a period piece, so I think you'll like it.
FLAP FLAP
Then tomorrow...
!?
WHACK
Kagura!?
What are you doing?
NOD NOD
He's holding something.
Pew
Kagetor
FLAP
getora
There is an emergency. Please come to the village alone.
Taka
There is an emergency. Please come to the village alone.
Taka
Emergency?
ALONE?

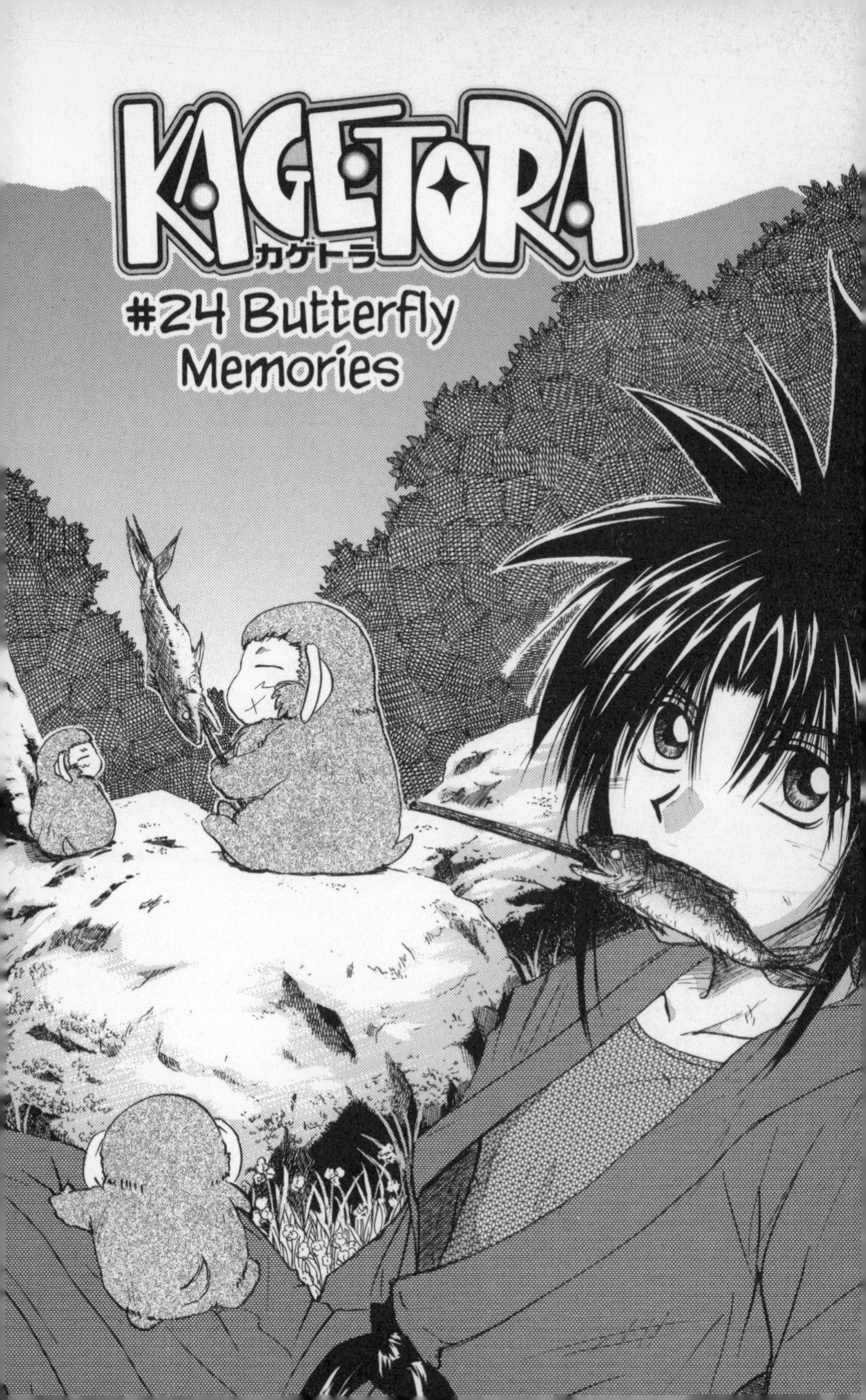
KAGETORA
カゲトラ
#24 Butterfly Memories

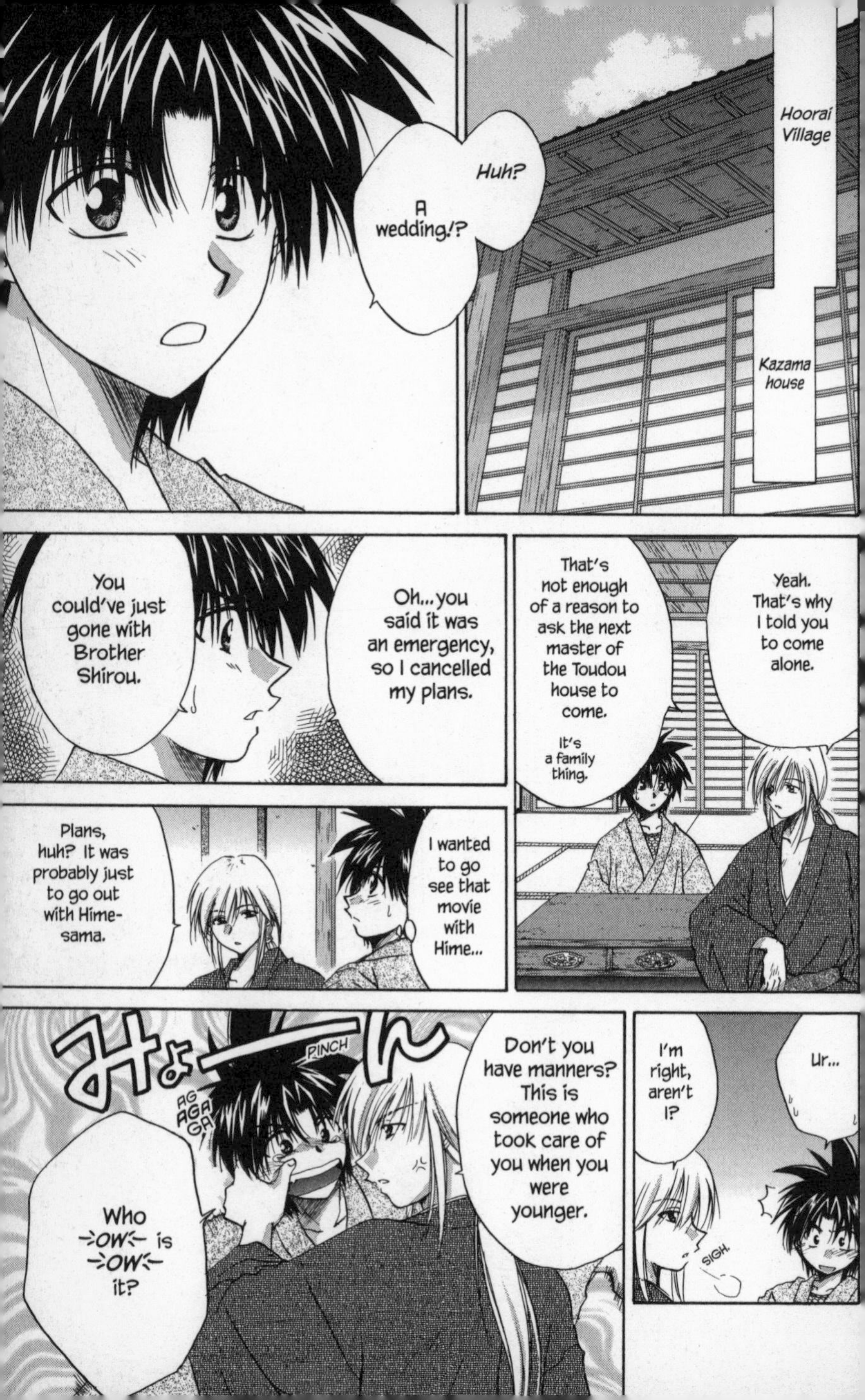
Hoorai Village
Kazama house
Huh?
A wedding!?
Yeah. That's why I told you to come alone.
That's not enough of a reason to ask the next master of the Toudou house to come.
It's a family thing.
Oh...you said it was an emergency, so I cancelled my plans.
You could've just gone with Brother Shirou.
I wanted to go see that movie with Hime...
Plans, huh? It was probably just to go out with Hime-sama.
Ur...
I'm right, aren't I?
SIGH.
Don't you have manners? This is someone who took care of you when you were younger.
PINCH
みょーん
AG AGA GA
Who -OW- is -OW- it?

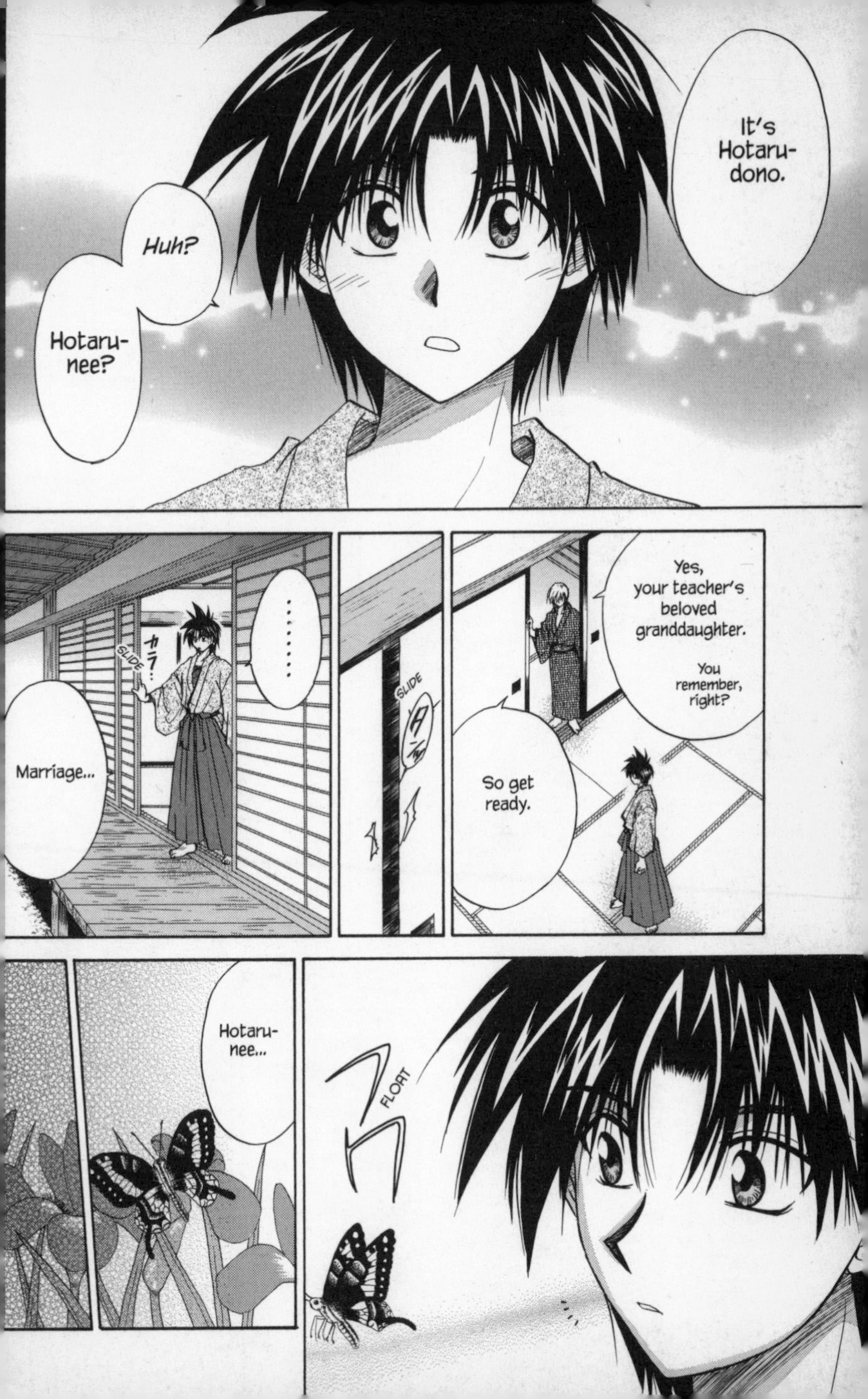
It's Hotaru-dono.
Huh?
Hotaru-nee?
Yes, your teacher's beloved granddaughter.
You remember, right?
So get ready.
SLIDE
......
SLIDE
Marriage...
FLOAT
Hotaru-nee...

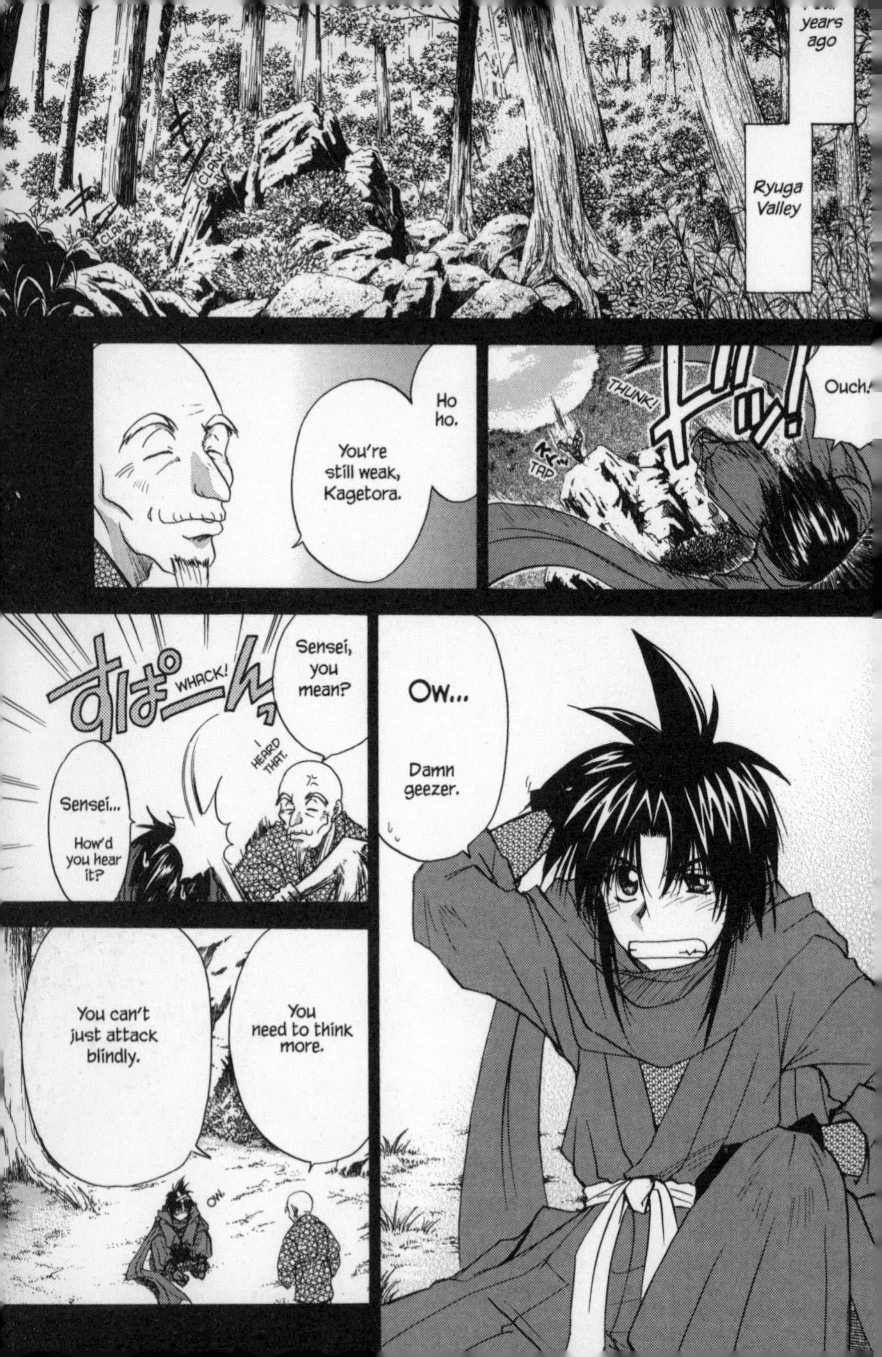

years ago
Ryuga Valley
CLANK
CLANK
Ouch!
THUNK!
TAP
Ho ho.
You're still weak, Kagetora.
Ow...
Damn geezer.
Sensei, you mean?
WHACK!
I HEARD THAT.
Sensei...
How'd you hear it?
You need to think more.
You can't just attack blindly.
OW.

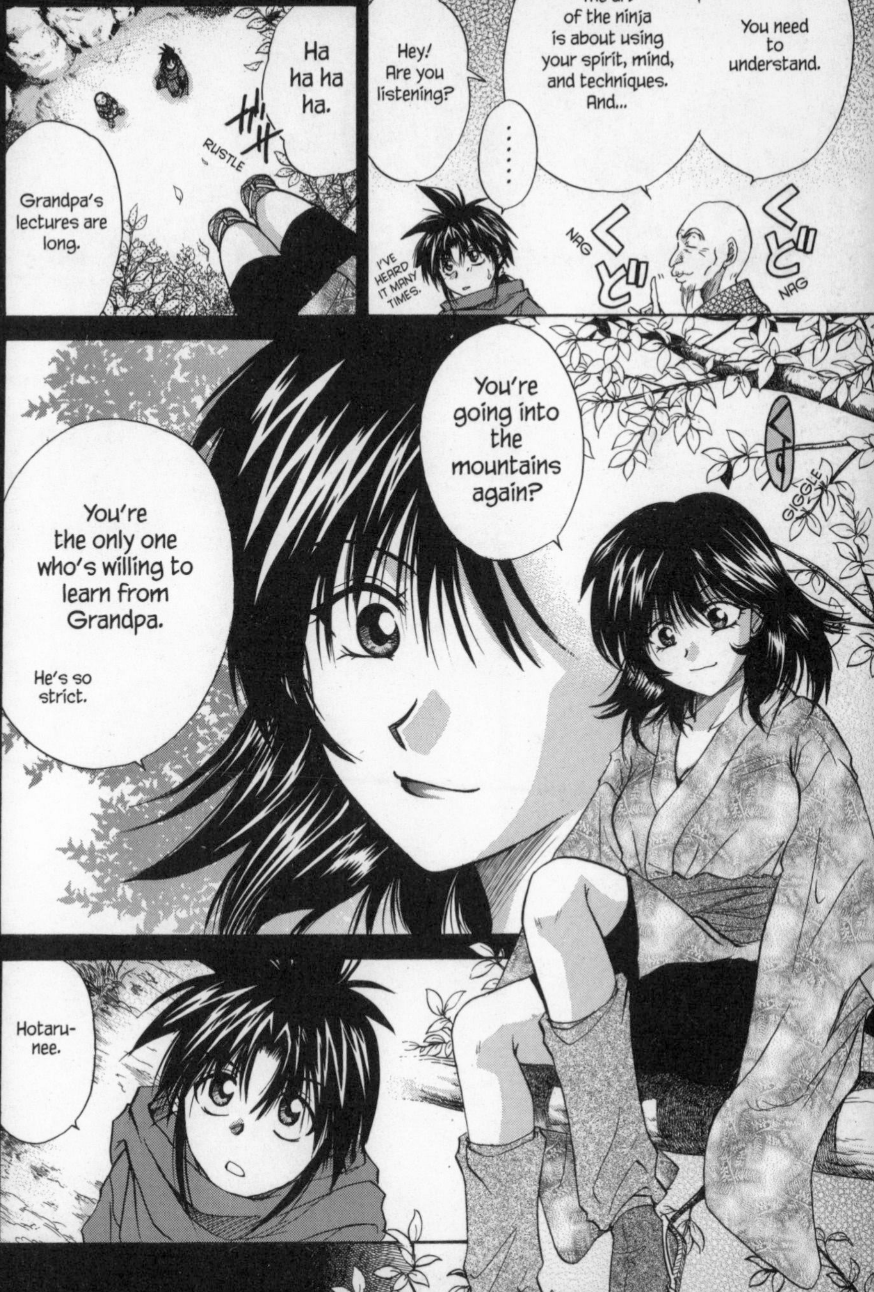
You need to understand.
The art of the ninja is about using your spirit, mind, and techniques. And...
Hey! Are you listening?
......
NAG
NAG
I'VE HEARD IT MANY TIMES.
Ha ha ha ha.
RUSTLE
Grandpa's lectures are long.
You're going into the mountains again?
GIGGLE
You're the only one who's willing to learn from Grandpa.
He's so strict.
Hotaru-nee.

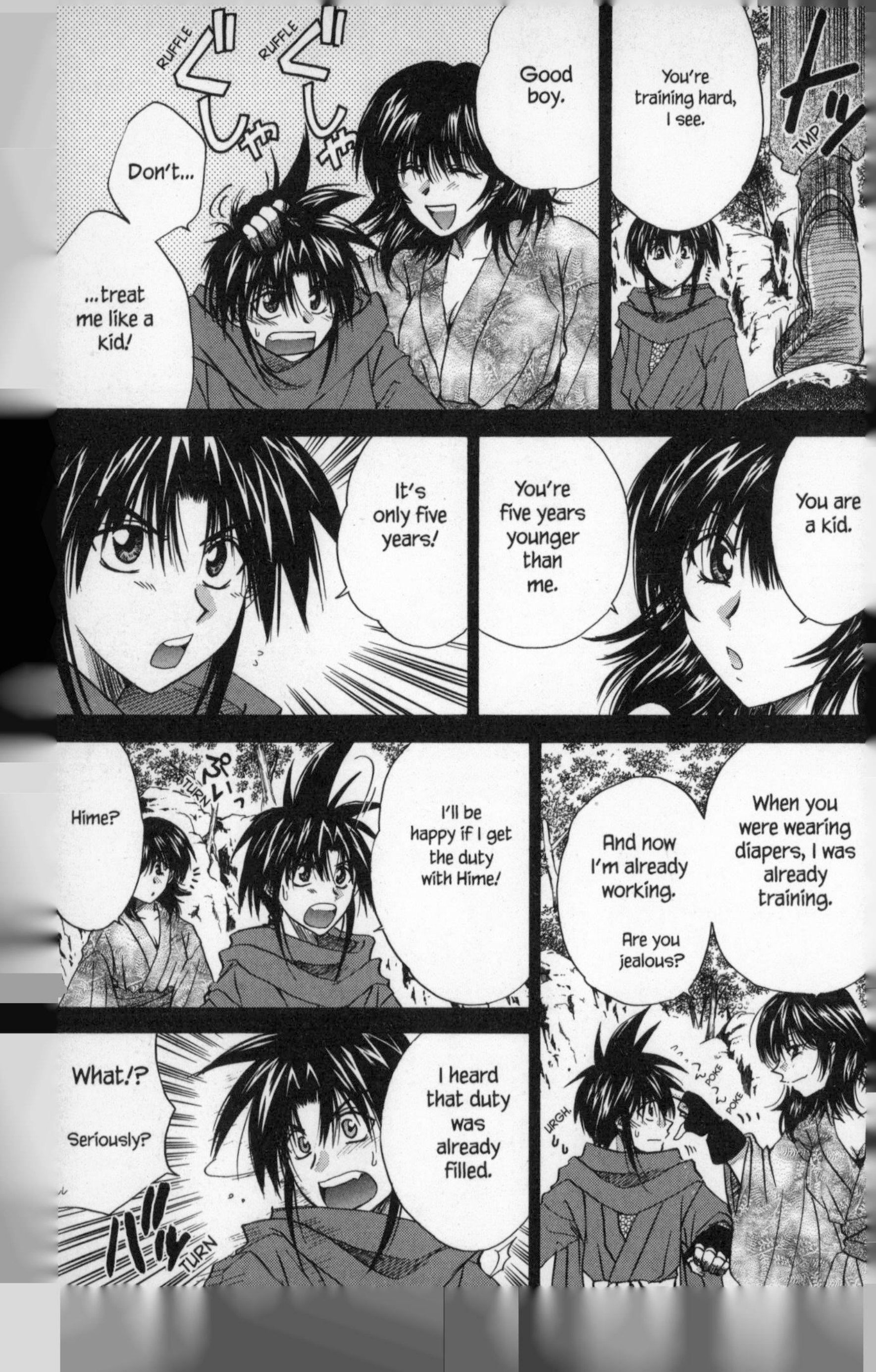
TMP
You're training hard, I see.
Good boy.
RUFFLE
RUFFLE
Don't...
...treat me like a kid!
You are a kid.
You're five years younger than me.
It's only five years!
When you were wearing diapers, I was already training.
And now I'm already working.
Are you jealous?
POKE
POKE
URGH.
I'll be happy if I get the duty with Hime!
TURN
Hime?
I heard that duty was already filled.
What!?
Seriously?
TURN

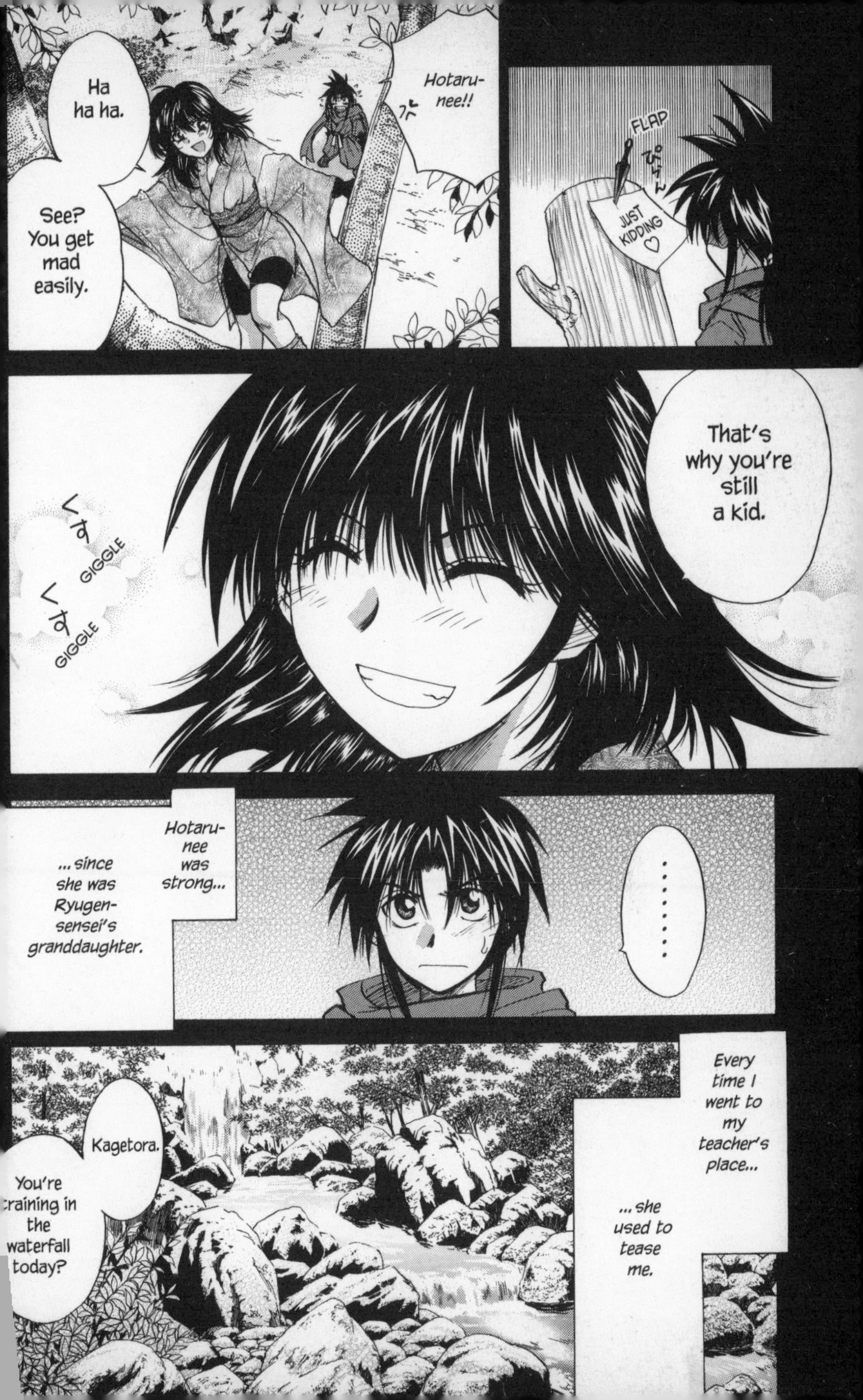
FLAP
JUST KIDDING ♡
Hotaru-nee!!
Ha ha ha.
See? You get mad easily.
That's why you're still a kid.
くす GIGGLE
くす GIGGLE
......
Hotaru-nee was strong...
...since she was Ryugen-sensei's granddaughter.
Every time I went to my teacher's place...
...she used to tease me.
Kagetora.
You're training in the waterfall today?

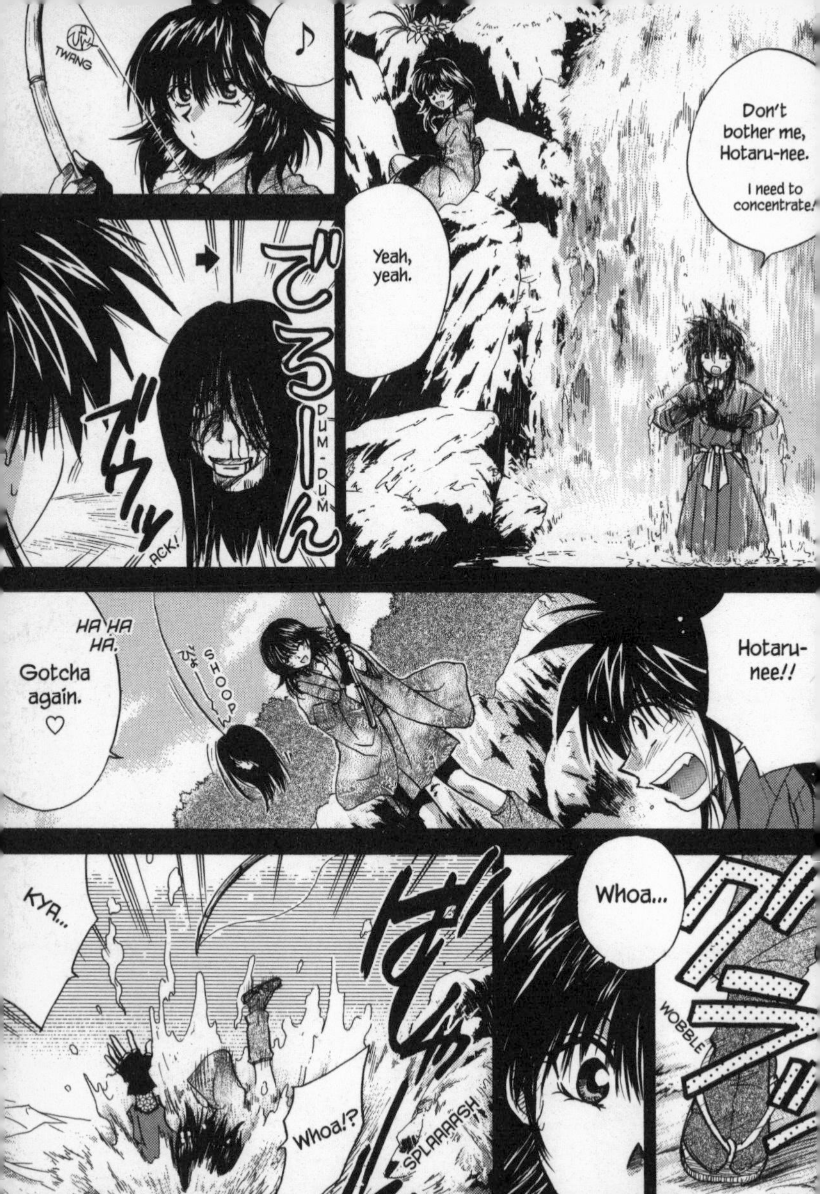

Don't bother me, Hotaru-nee.
I need to concentrate!
Yeah, yeah.
♪
TWANG
でろーん
DUM-DUM
ACK!
Hotaru-nee!!
HA HA HA.
Gotcha again. ♡
SHOOP
Whoa...
WOBBLE
KYA...
SPLAAASH
Whoa!?

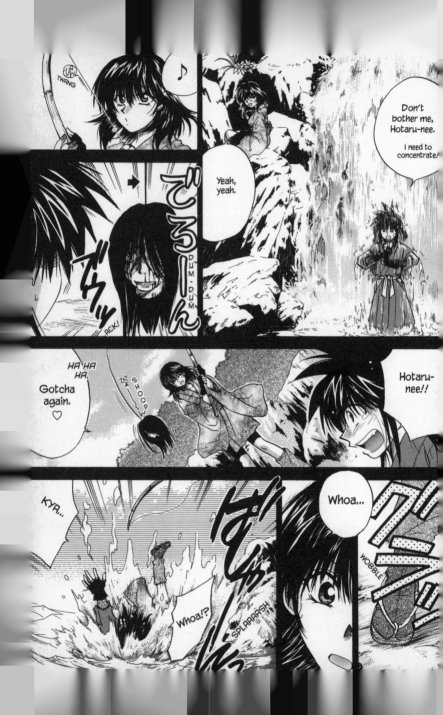

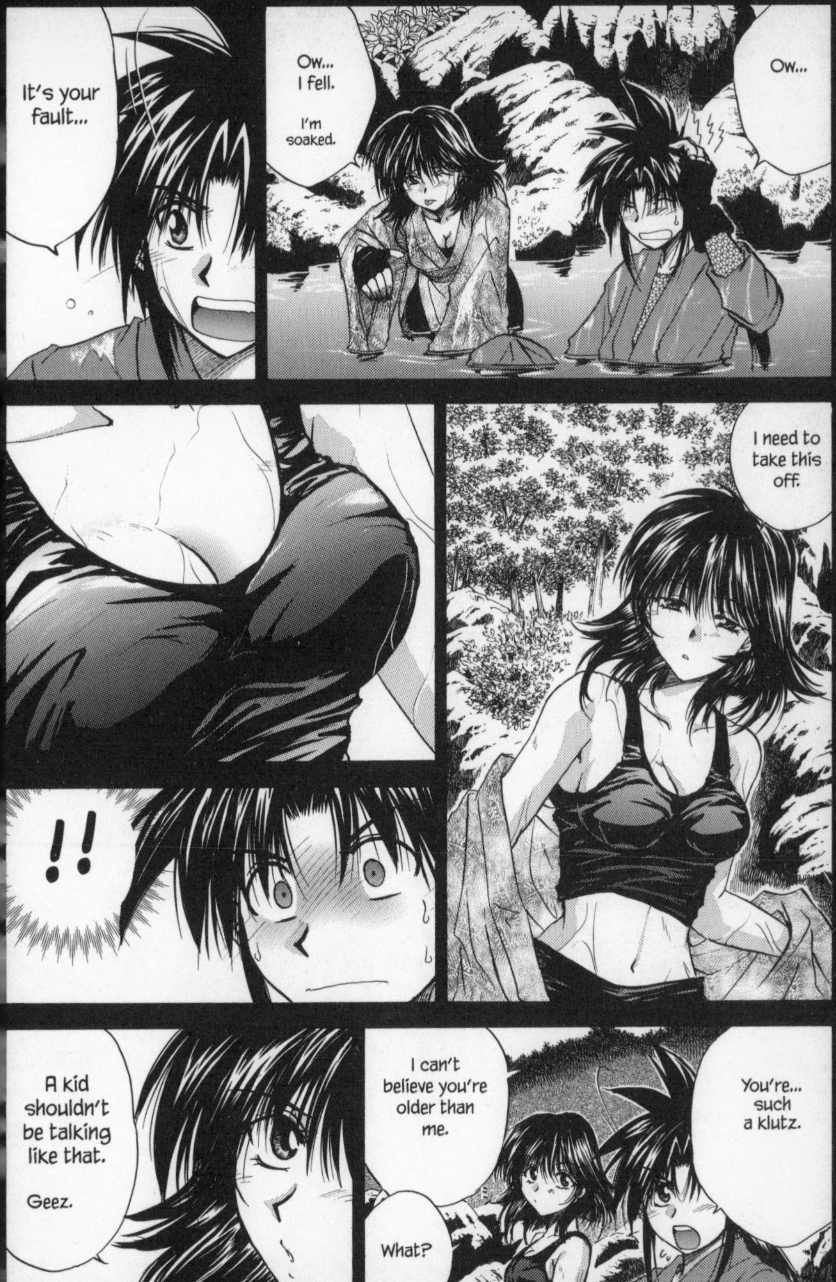
Ow...
Ow... I fell.
I'm soaked.
It's your fault...
I need to take this off.
!!
You're... such a klutz.
I can't believe you're older than me.
What?
A kid shouldn't be talking like that.
Geez.

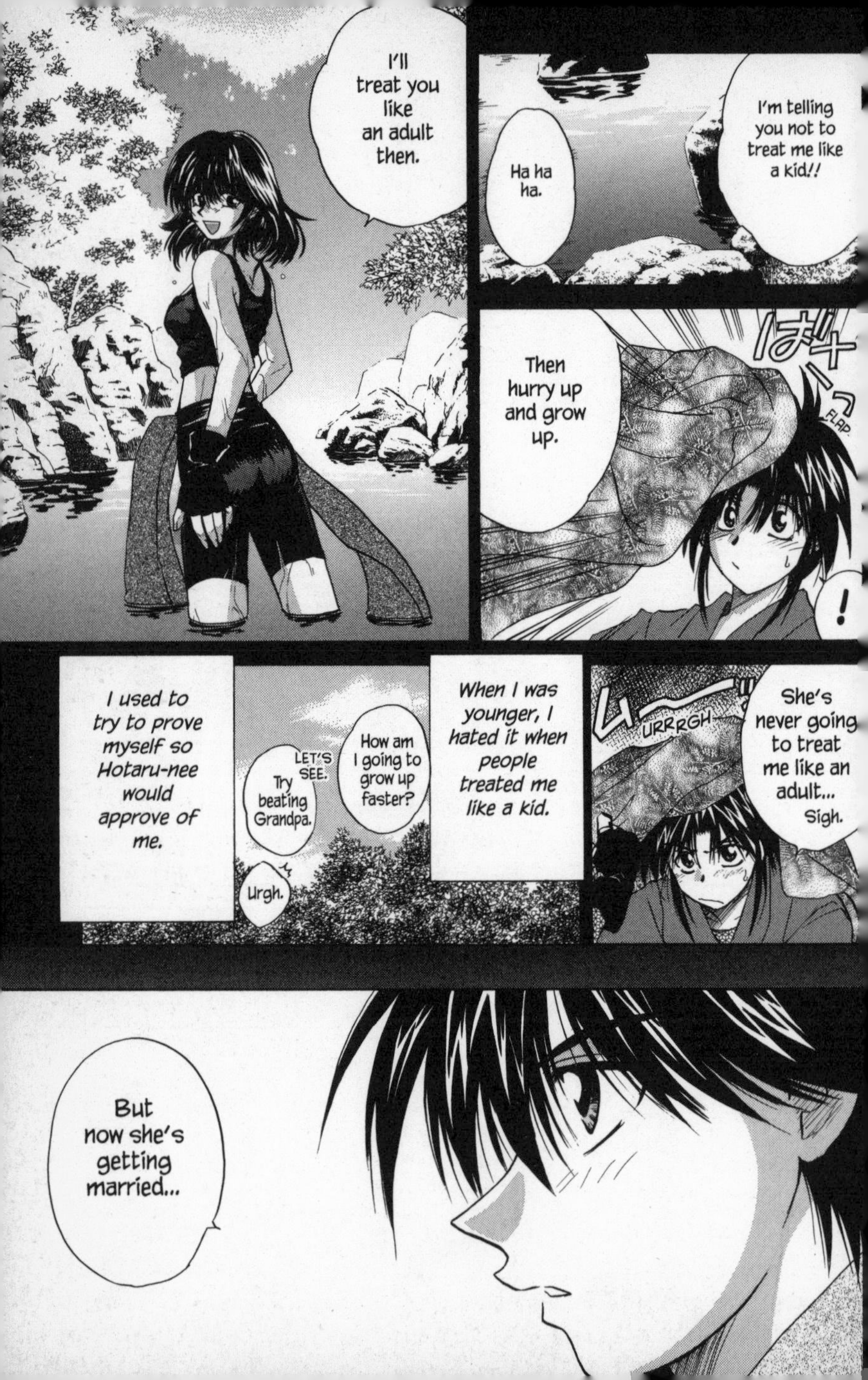
I'm telling you not to treat me like a kid!!
Ha ha ha.
FLAP
Then hurry up and grow up.
!
I'll treat you like an adult then.
URRRGH
She's never going to treat me like an adult... Sigh.
When I was younger, I hated it when people treated me like a kid.
How am I going to grow up faster?
LET'S SEE.
Try beating Grandpa.
Urgh.
I used to try to prove myself so Hotaru-nee would approve of me.
But now she's getting married...

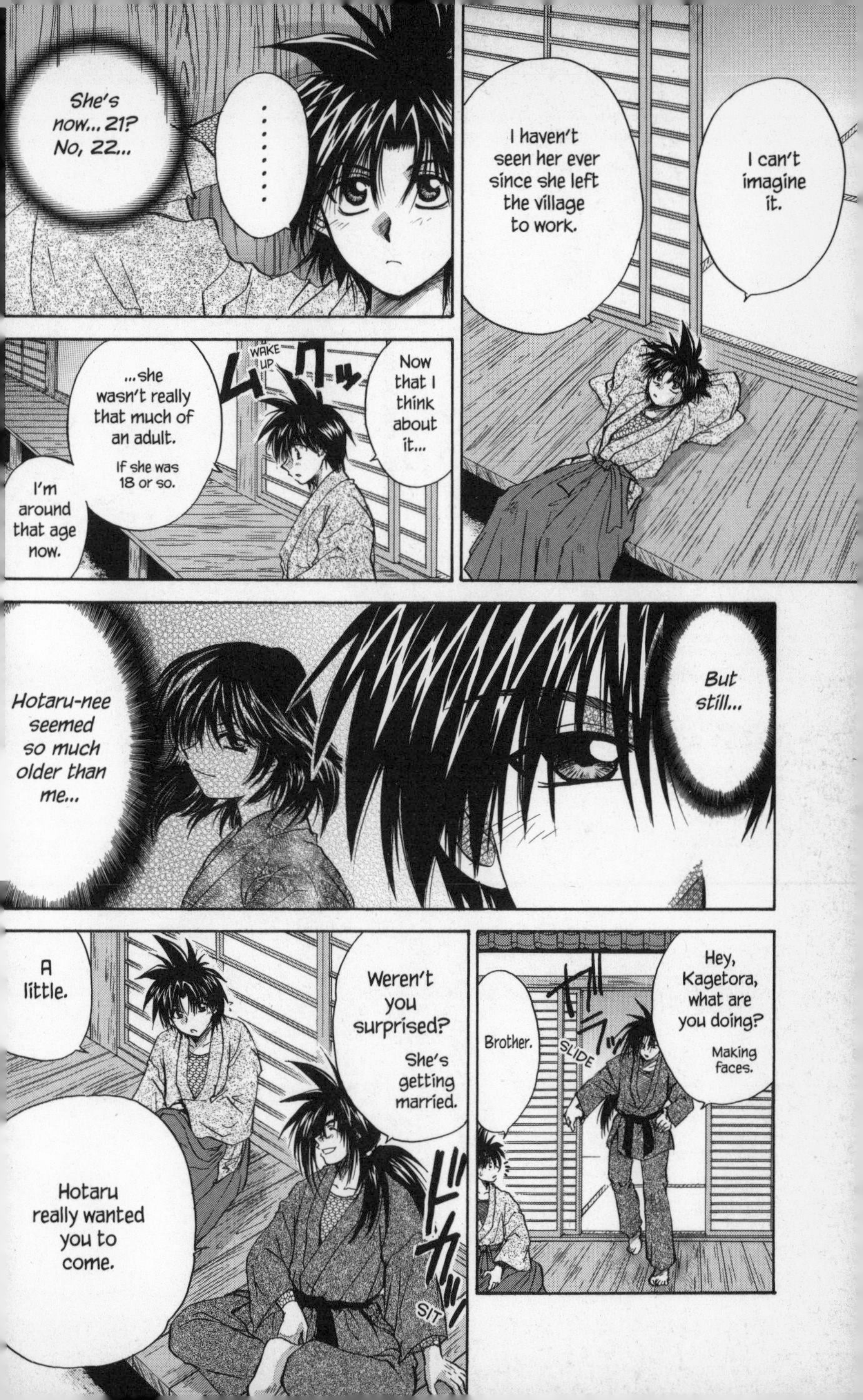
I can't imagine it.
I haven't seen her ever since she left the village to work.
......
She's now... 21? No, 22...
Now that I think about it...
WAKE UP
...she wasn't really that much of an adult.
If she was 18 or so.
I'm around that age now.
But still...
Hotaru-nee seemed so much older than me...
Hey, Kagetora, what are you doing?
Making faces.
SLIDE
Brother.
Weren't you surprised?
She's getting married.
A little.
SIT
Hotaru really wanted you to come.

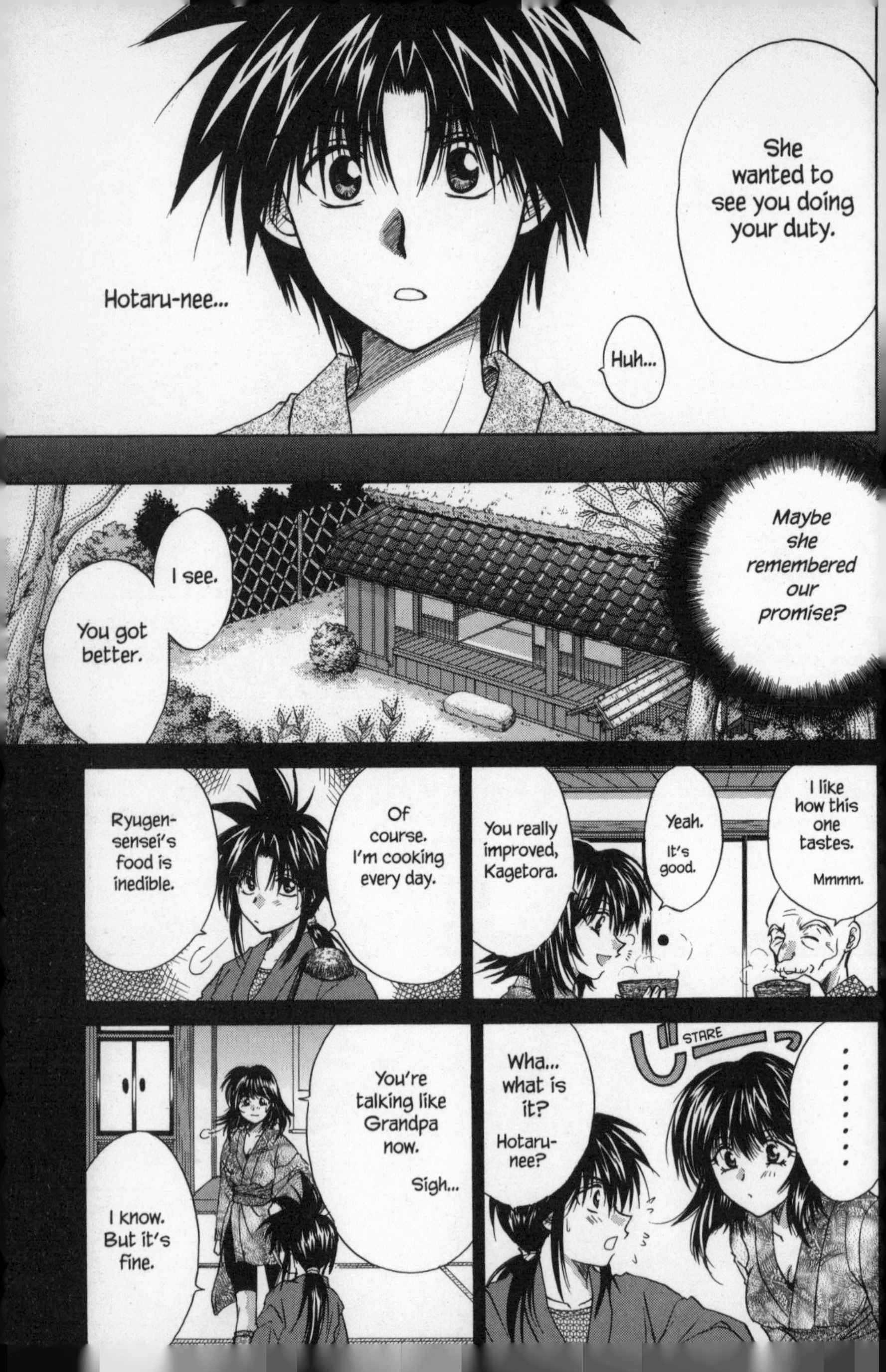
She wanted to see you doing your duty.
Huh...
Hotaru-nee...
Maybe she remembered our promise?
I see.
You got better.
I like how this one tastes.
Mmmm.
Yeah.
It's good.
You really improved, Kagetora.
Of course. I'm cooking every day.
Ryugen-sensei's food is inedible.
....
STARE
Wha... what is it?
Hotaru-nee?
You're talking like Grandpa now.
Sigh...
I know. But it's fine.

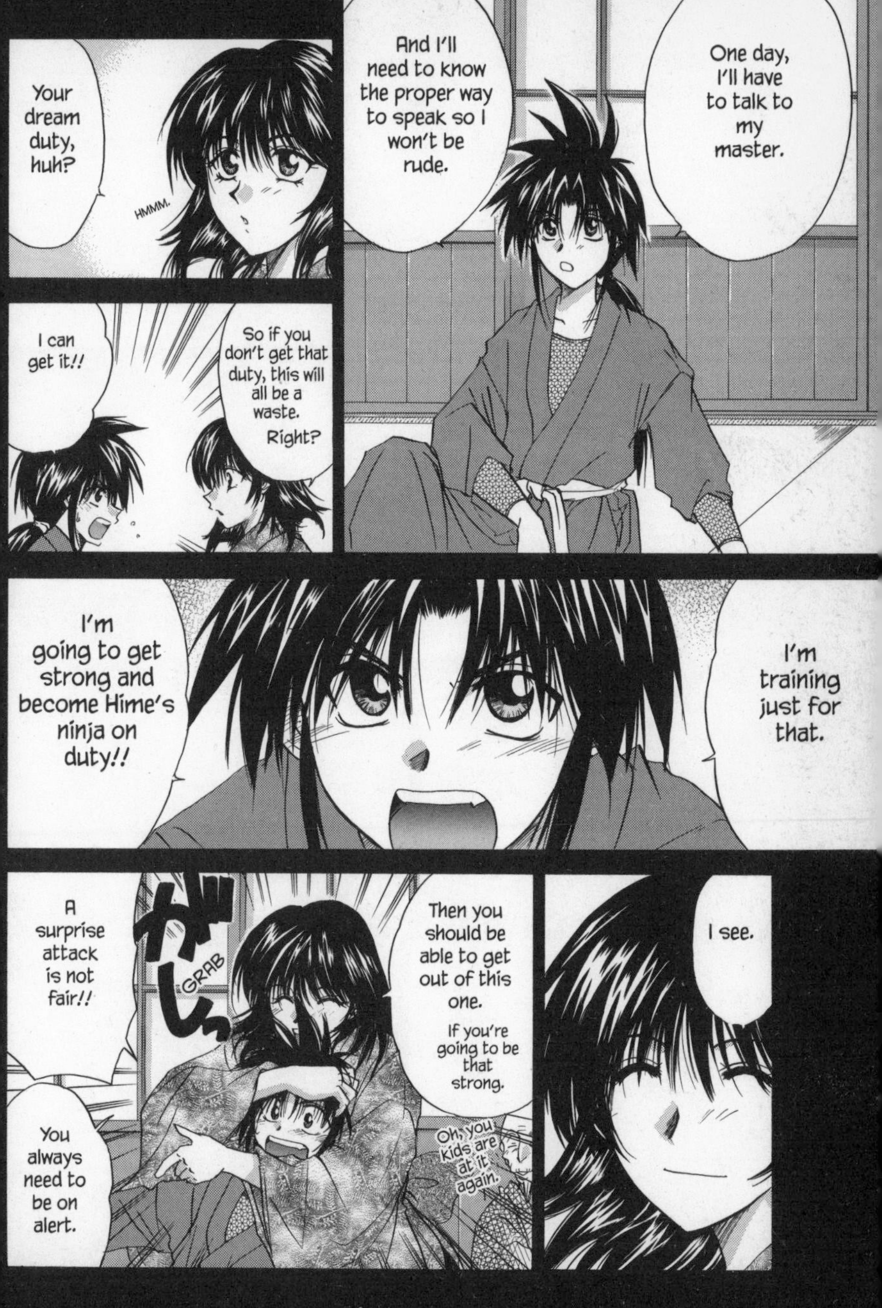
One day, I'll have to talk to my master.
And I'll need to know the proper way to speak so I won't be rude.
Your dream duty, huh?
HMMM.
So if you don't get that duty, this will all be a waste.
Right?
I can get it!!
I'm training just for that.
I'm going to get strong and become Hime's ninja on duty!!
I see.
Then you should be able to get out of this one.
If you're going to be that strong.
GRAB
A surprise attack is not fair!!
Oh, you kids are at it again.
You always need to be on alert.

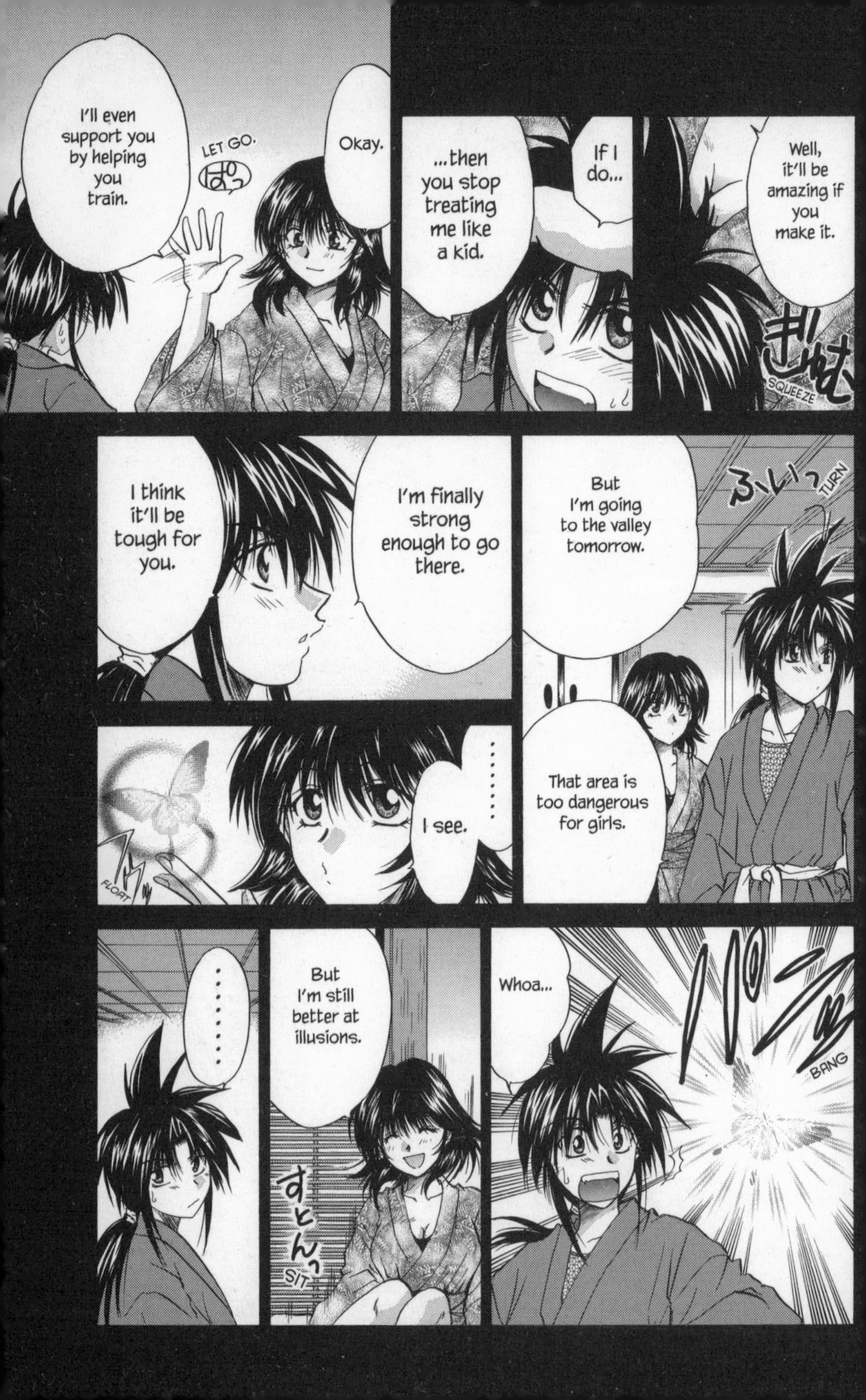
Well, it'll be amazing if you make it.
SQUEEZE
If I do...
...then you stop treating me like a kid.
Okay.
ぱっ
LET GO.
I'll even support you by helping you train.
ふいっ
TURN
But I'm going to the valley tomorrow.
That area is too dangerous for girls.
I'm finally strong enough to go there.
I think it'll be tough for you.
......
I see.
FLOAT
BANG
Whoa...
But I'm still better at illusions.
すとんっ
SIT
......

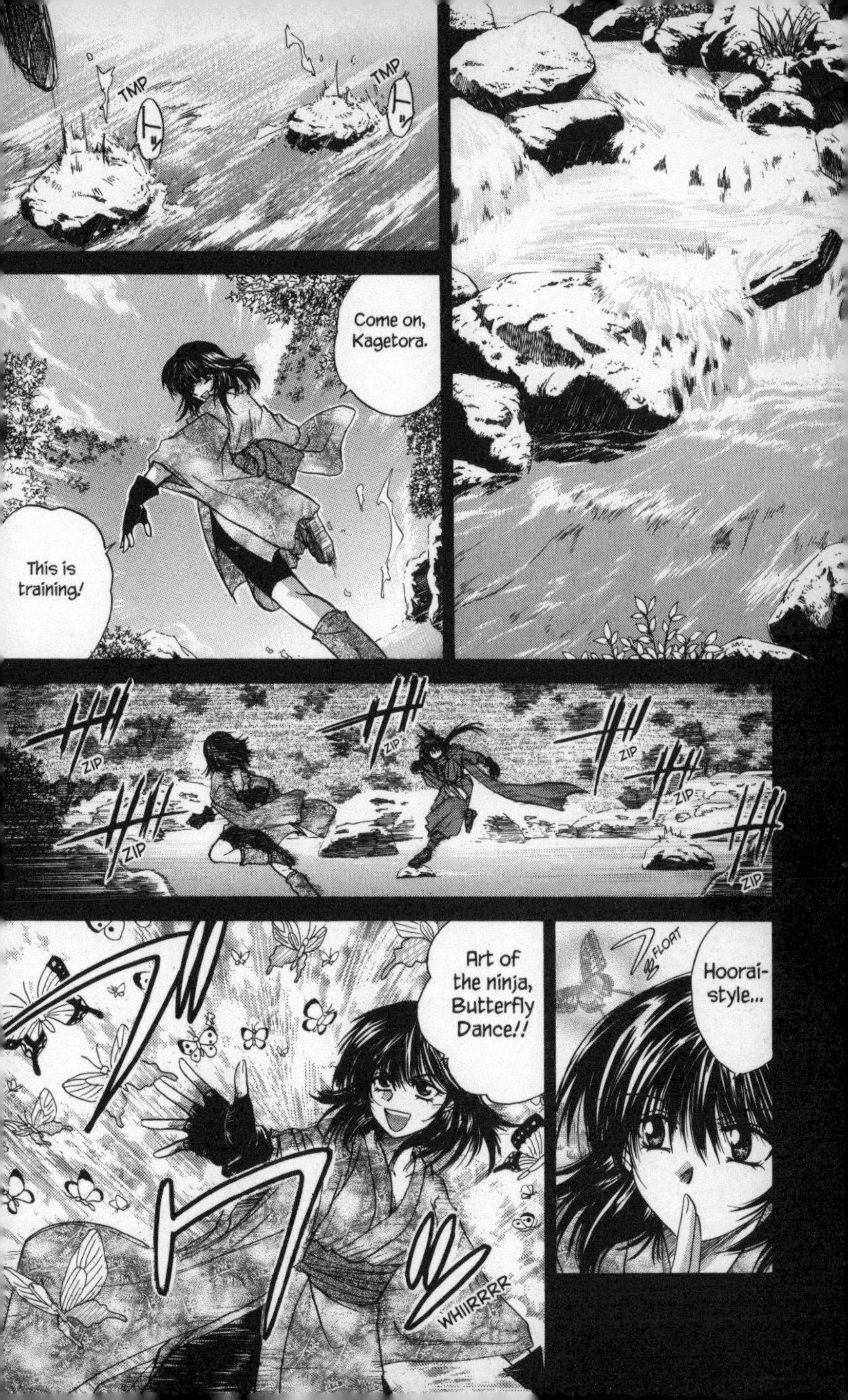
TMP
TMP
Come on, Kagetora.
This is training!
ZIP
ZIP
ZIP
ZIP
ZIP
ZIP
FLOAT
Hoorai-style...
Art of the ninja, Butterfly Dance!!
WHIIRRRR

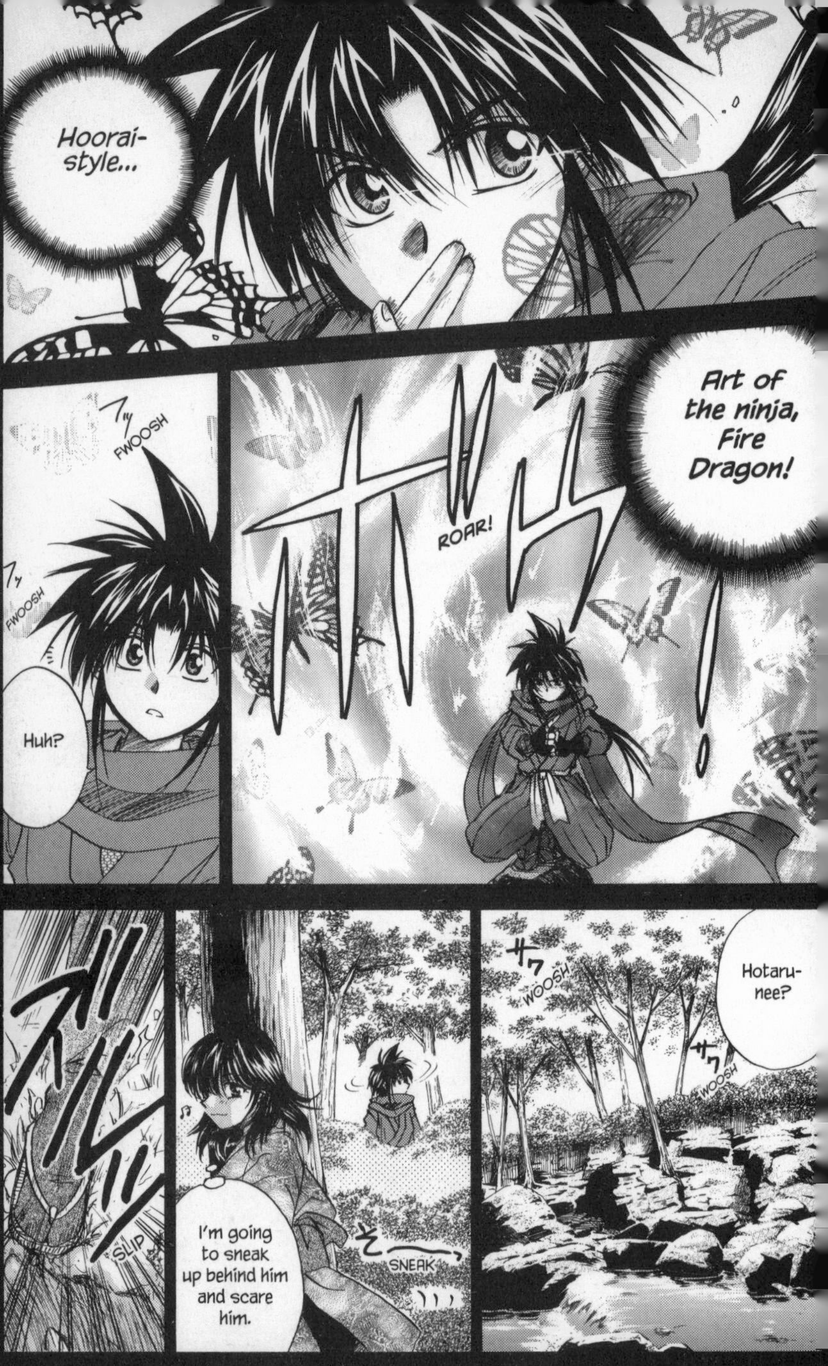
Hoorai-style...
Art of the ninja, Fire Dragon!
ROAR!
FWOOSH
FWOOSH
Huh?
WOOSH
Hotaru-nee?
WOOSH
I'm going to sneak up behind him and scare him.
SNEAK
SLIP

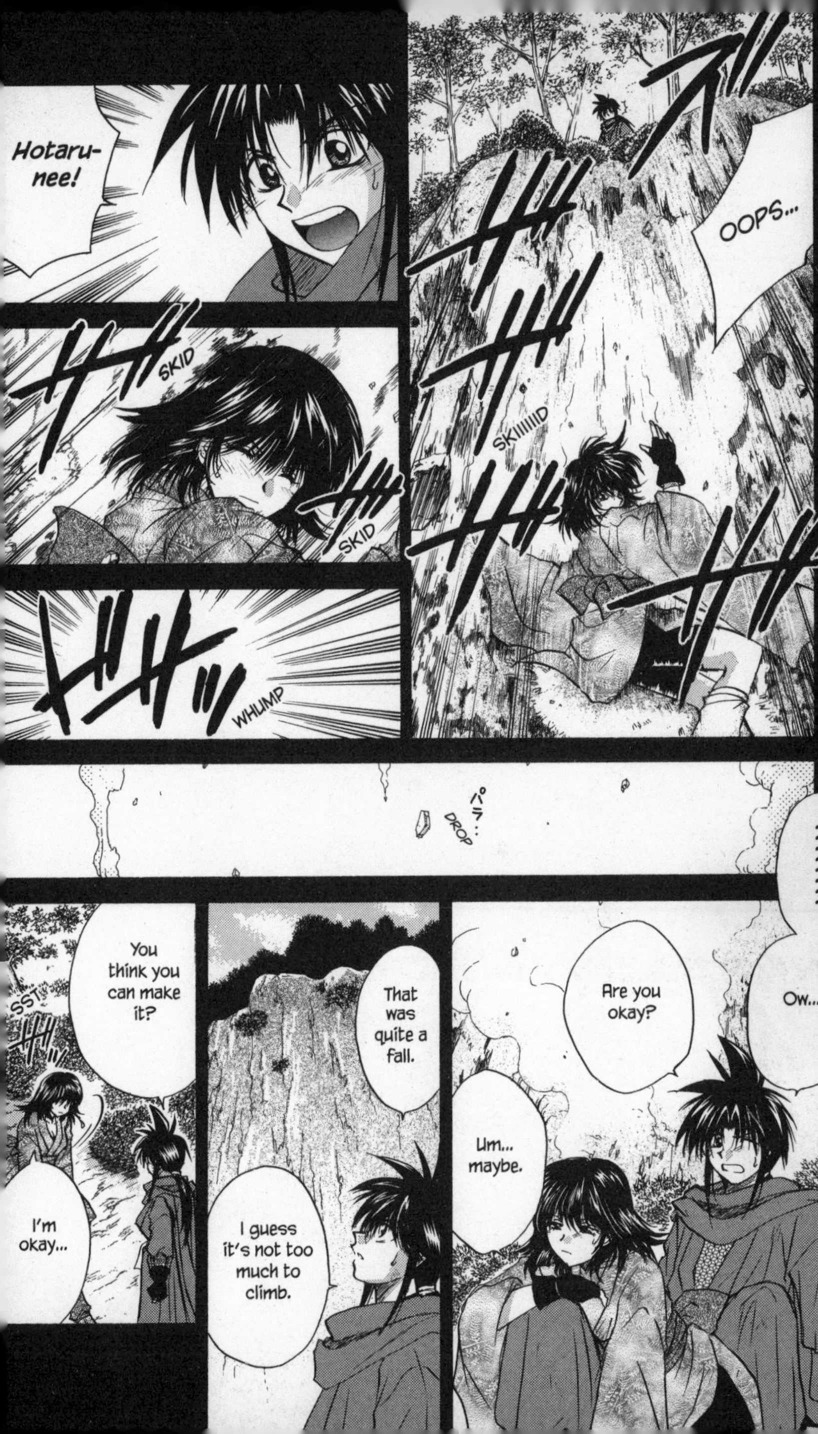
OOPS...
SKIIIIIID
Hotaru-nee!
SKID
SKID
WHUMP
DROP
......
Ow...
Are you okay?
Um... maybe.
That was quite a fall.
I guess it's not too much to climb.
You think you can make it?
SST
I'm okay...

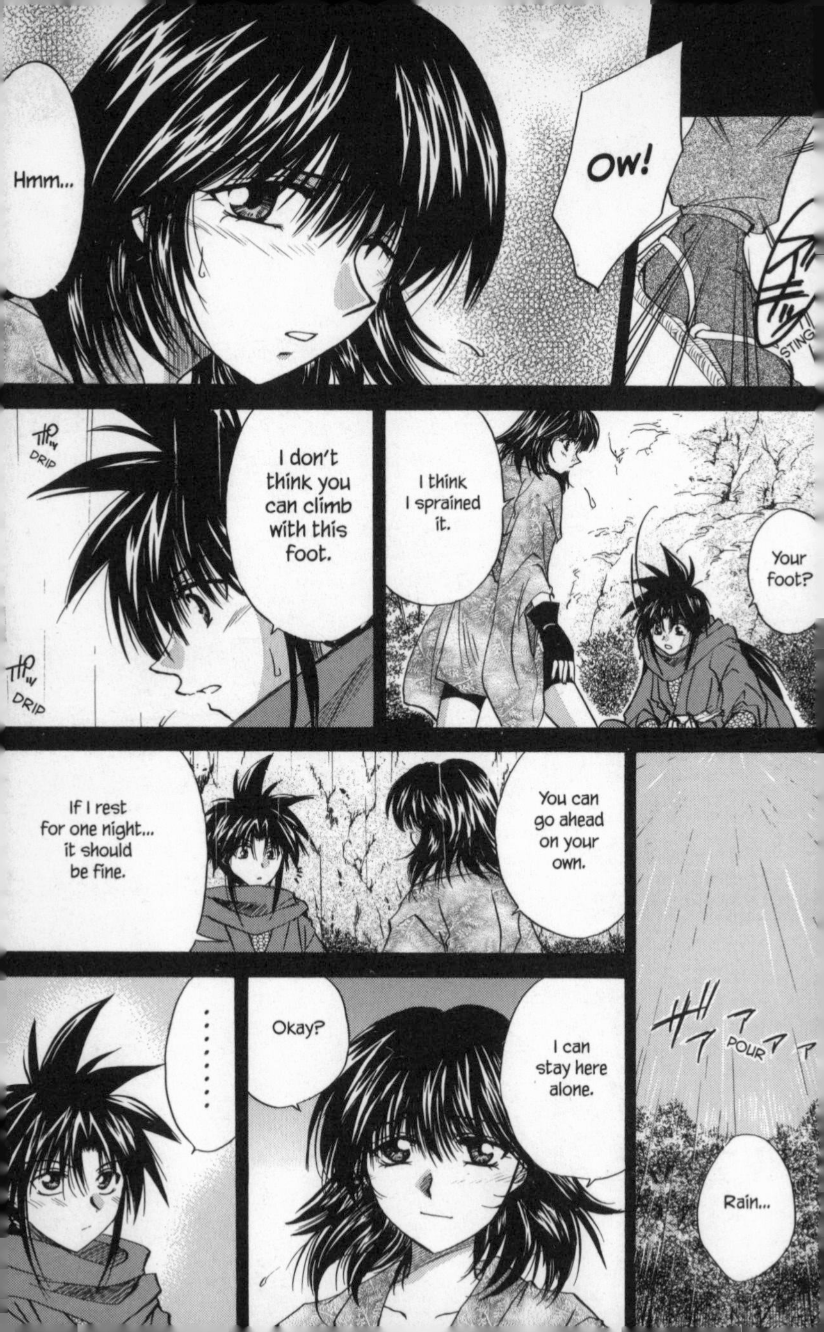
Ow!
STING
Hmm...
Your foot?
I think I sprained it.
I don't think you can climb with this foot.
DRIP
DRIP
POUR
Rain...
You can go ahead on your own.
If I rest for one night... it should be fine.
I can stay here alone.
Okay?
....

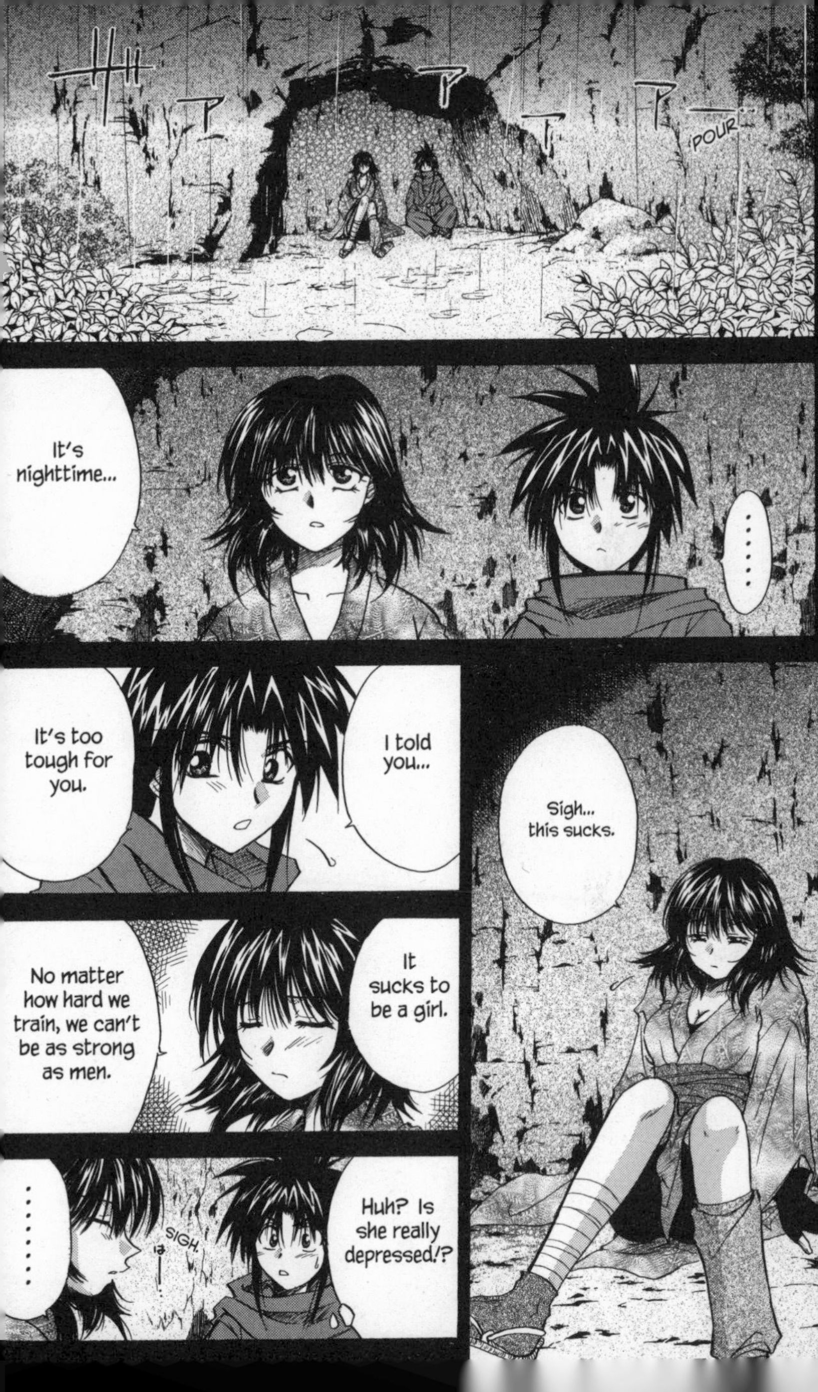
POUR
......
It's nighttime...
Sigh... this sucks.
I told you...
It's too tough for you.
It sucks to be a girl.
No matter how hard we train, we can't be as strong as men.
Huh? Is she really depressed!?
SIGH.
......

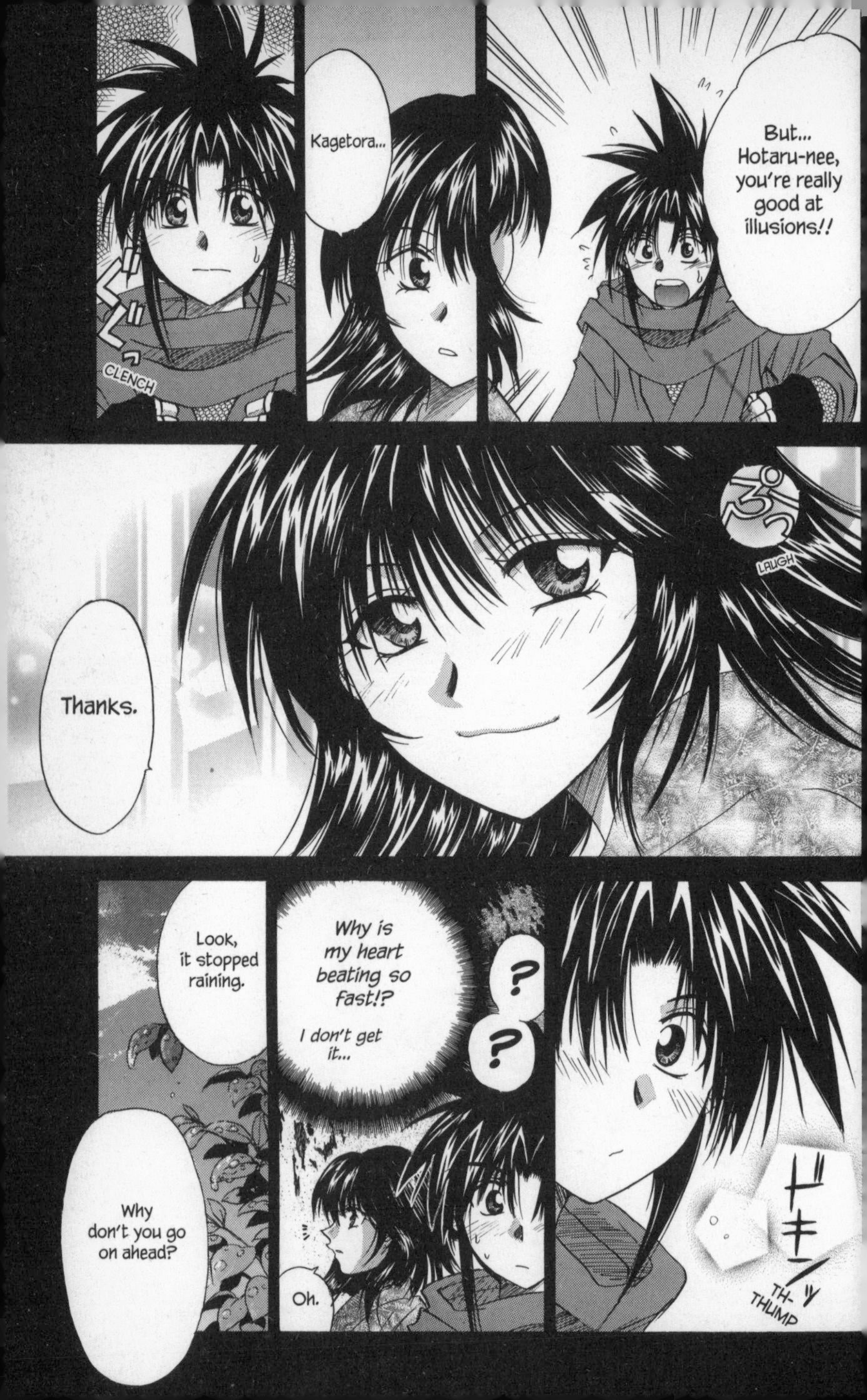
But... Hotaru-nee, you're really good at illusions!!
Kagetora...
CLENCH
LAUGH
Thanks.
TH-THUMP
?
?
Why is my heart beating so fast!?
I don't get it...
Oh.
Look, it stopped raining.
Why don't you go on ahead?

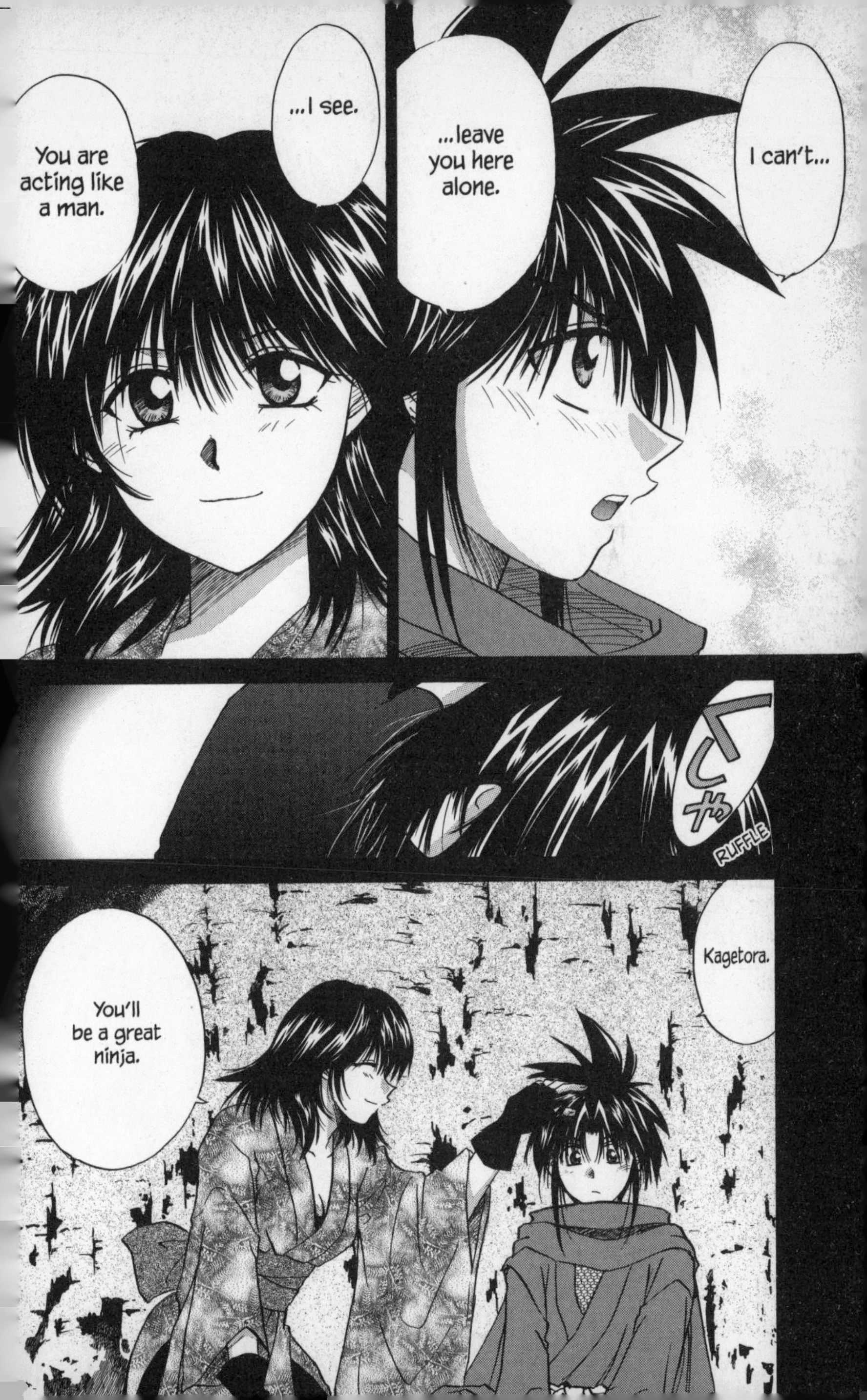
I can't...
...leave you here alone.
...I see.
You are acting like a man.
RUFFLE
Kagetora.
You'll be a great ninja.

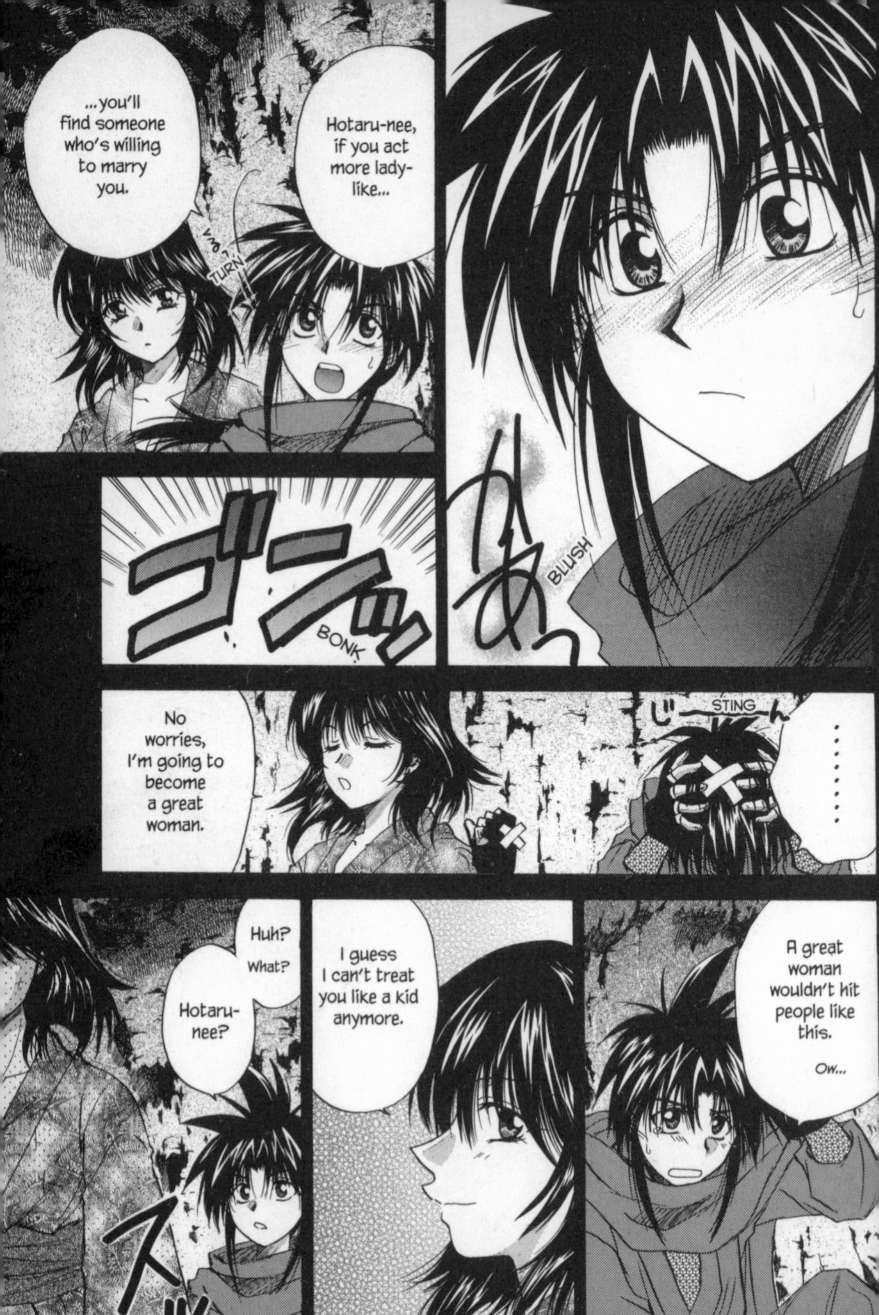
BLUSH
Hotaru-nee, if you act more lady-like...
...you'll find someone who's willing to marry you.
TURN
BONK
STING
......
No worries, I'm going to become a great woman.
A great woman wouldn't hit people like this.
Ow...
I guess I can't treat you like a kid anymore.
Huh? What?
Hotaru-nee?

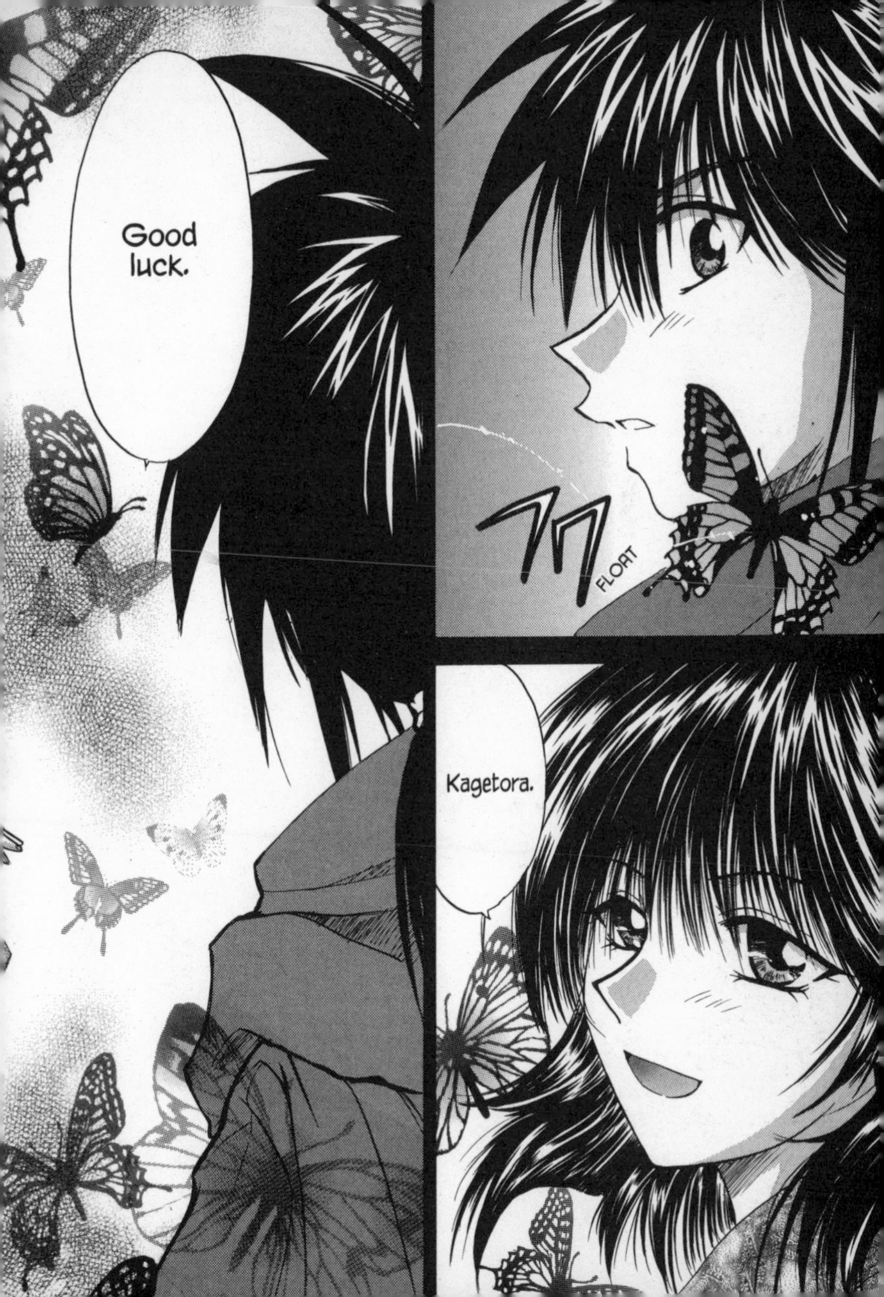
FLOAT
Kagetora.
Good luck.

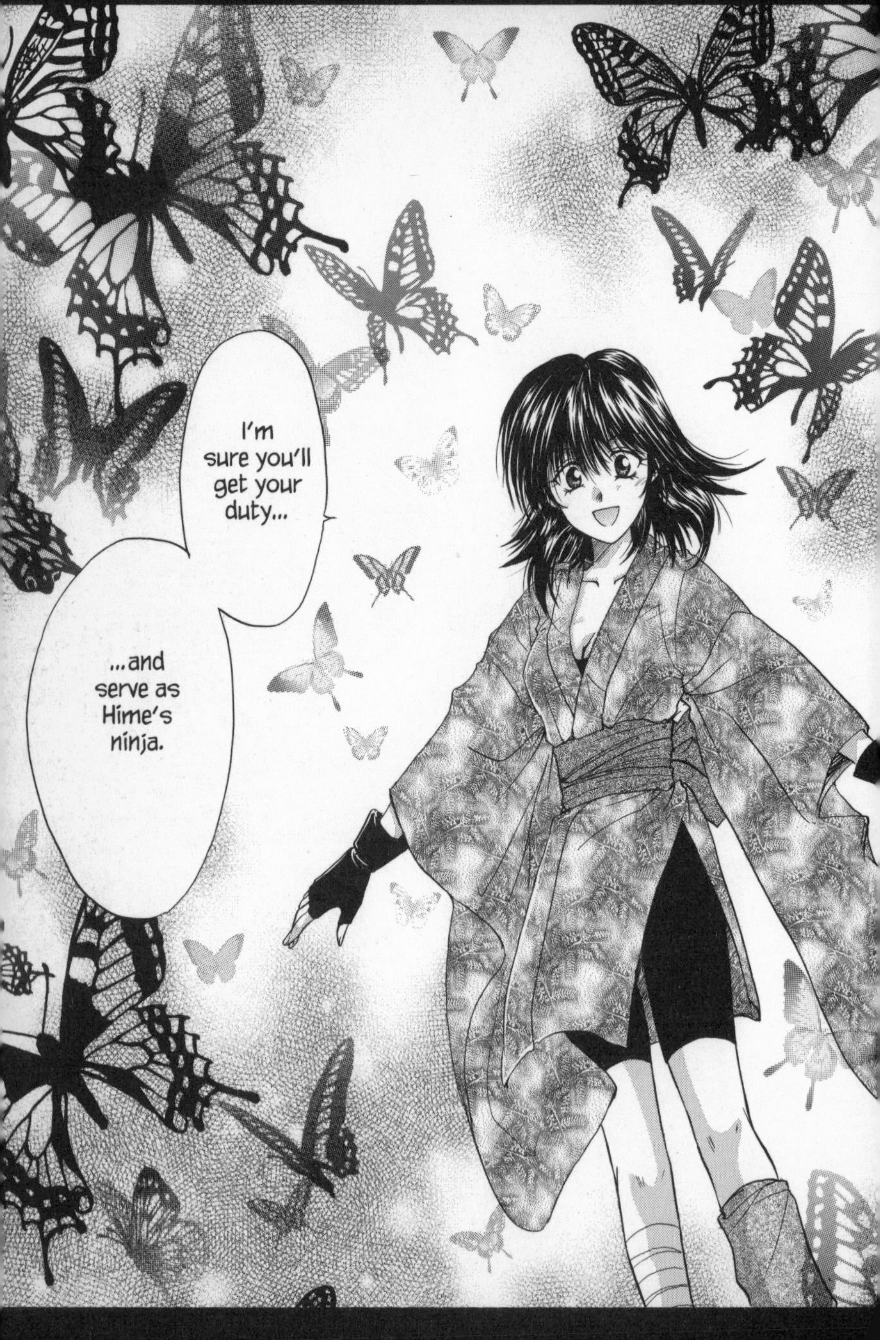
I'm sure you'll get your duty...
...and serve as Hime's ninja.

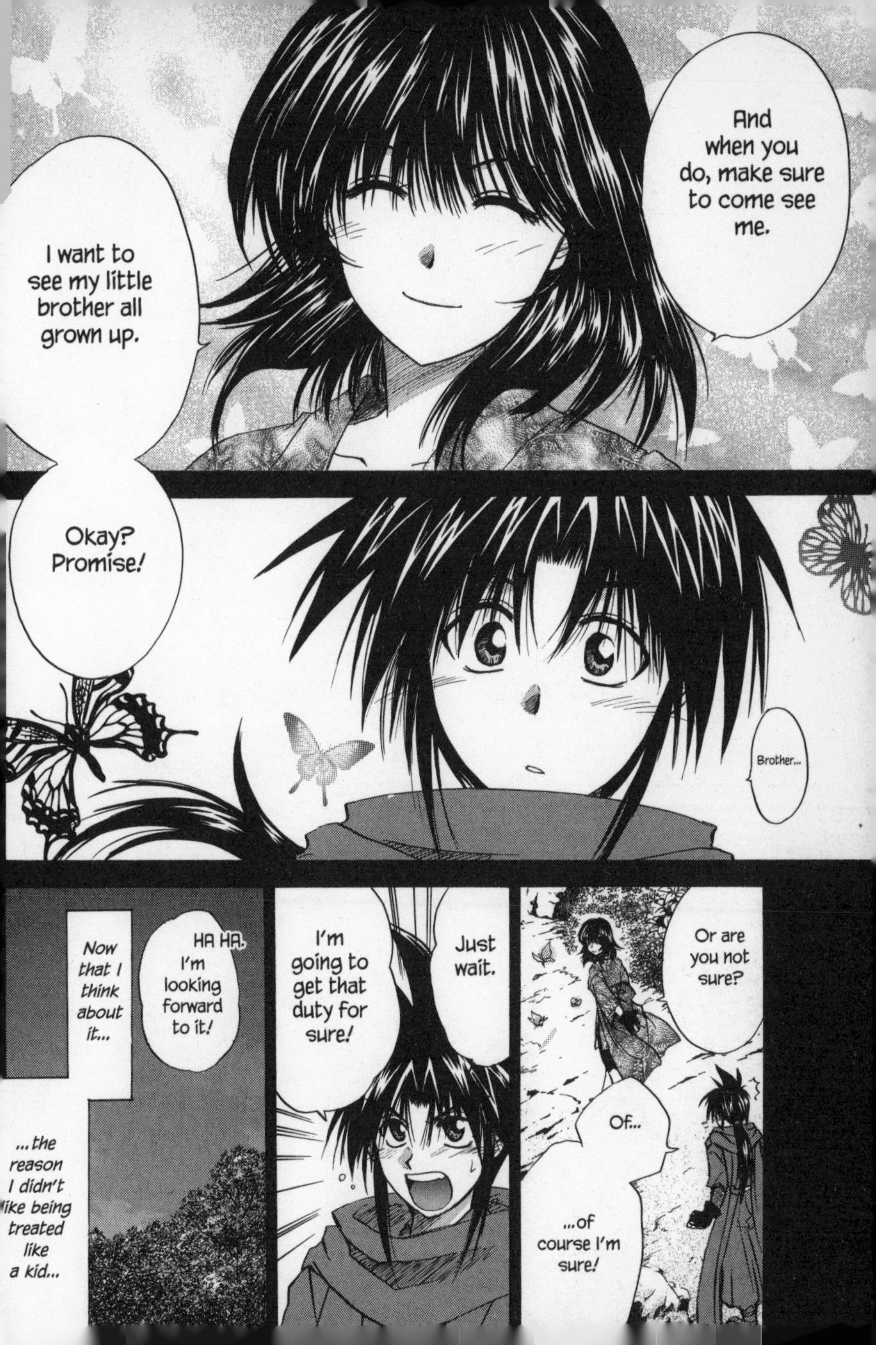
And when you do, make sure to come see me.
I want to see my little brother all grown up.
Okay? Promise!
Brother...
Or are you not sure?
Of...
...of course I'm sure!
Just wait.
I'm going to get that duty for sure!
HA HA. I'm looking forward to it!
Now that I think about it...
...the reason I didn't ike being treated like a kid...

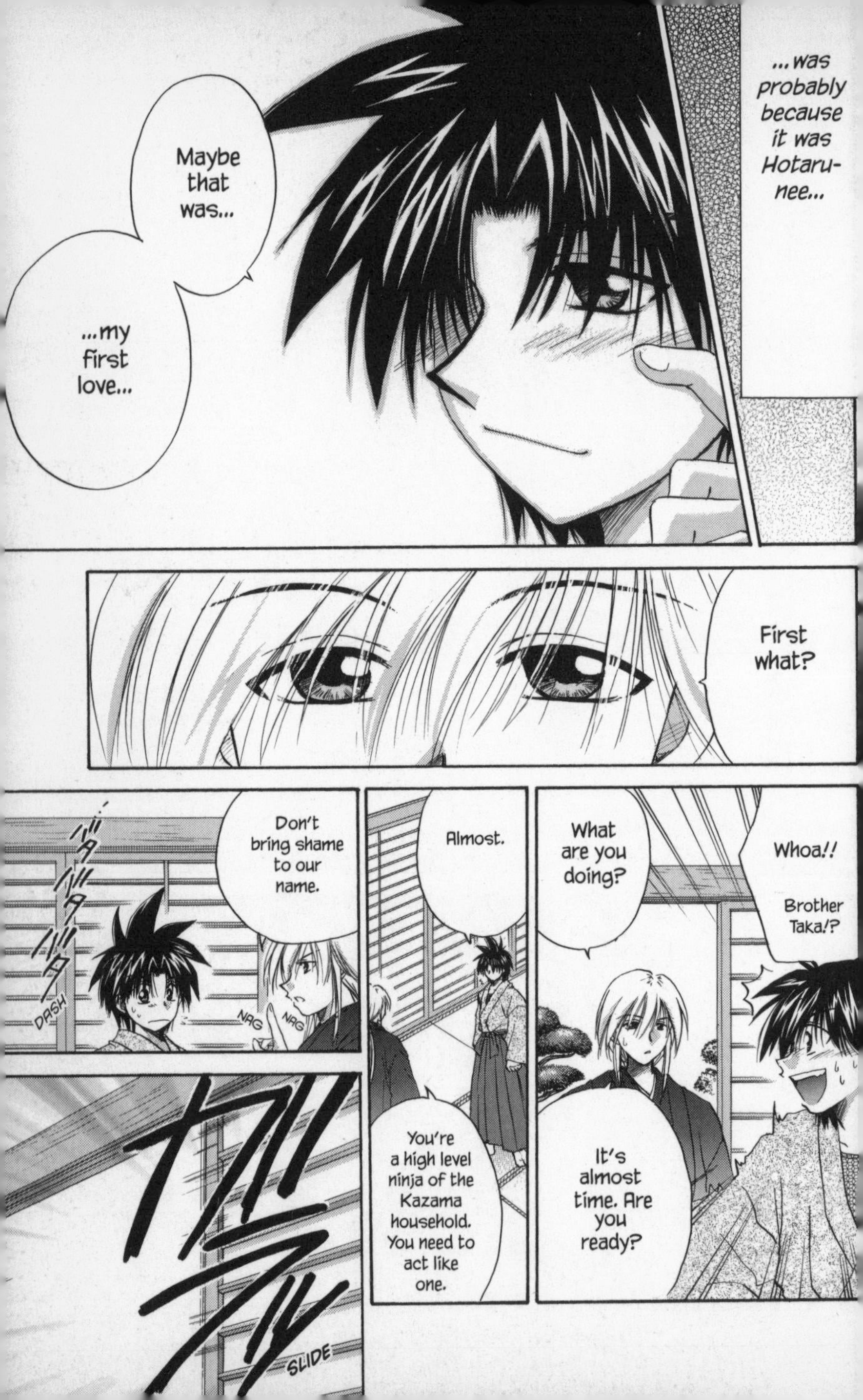
...was probably because it was Hotaru-nee...
Maybe that was...
...my first love...
First what?
Whoa!!
Brother Taka!?
What are you doing?
It's almost time. Are you ready?
Almost.
You're a high level ninja of the Kazama household. You need to act like one.
Don't bring shame to our name.
NAG
NAG
DASH
SLIDE

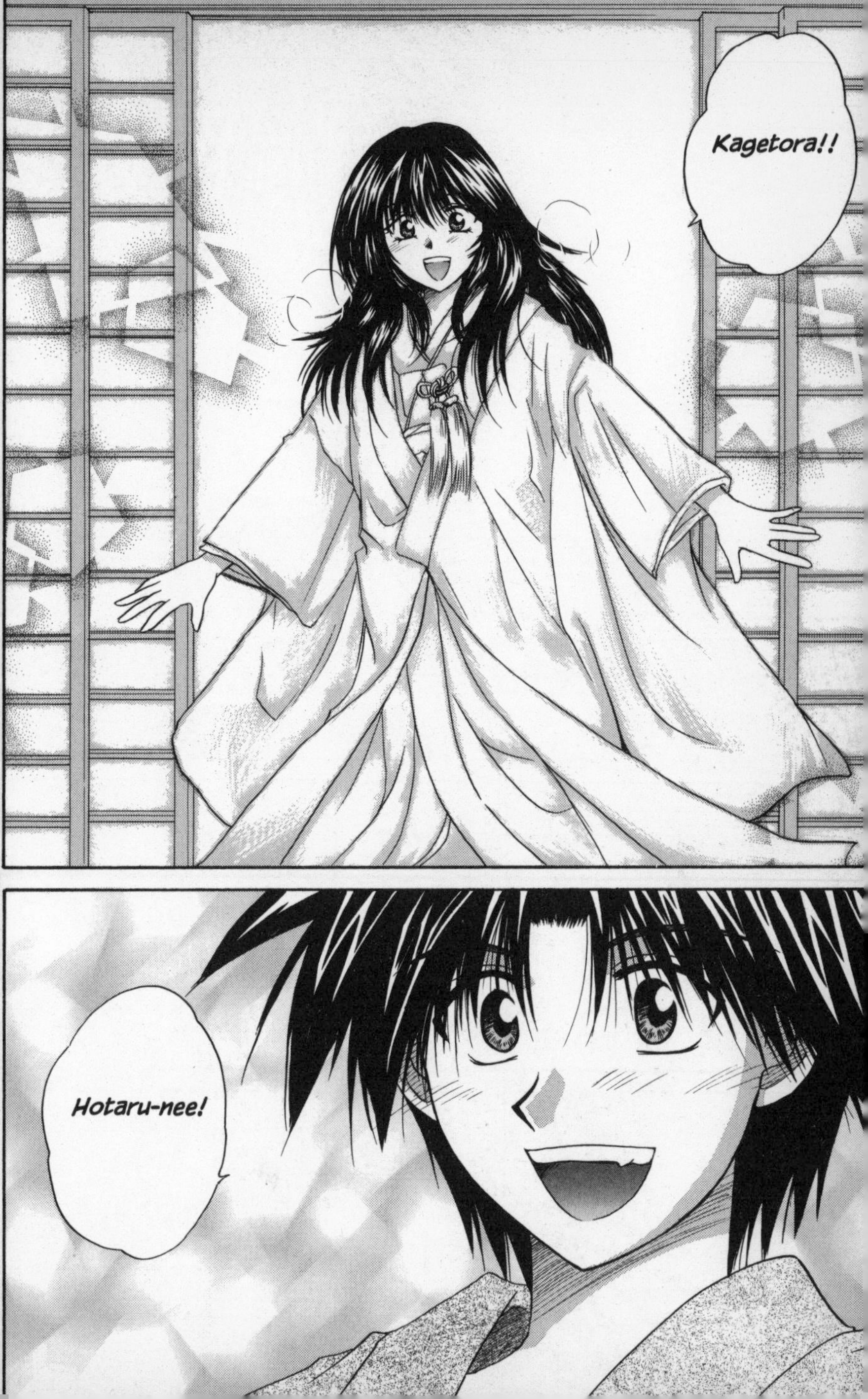
Kagetora!!
Hotaru-nee!

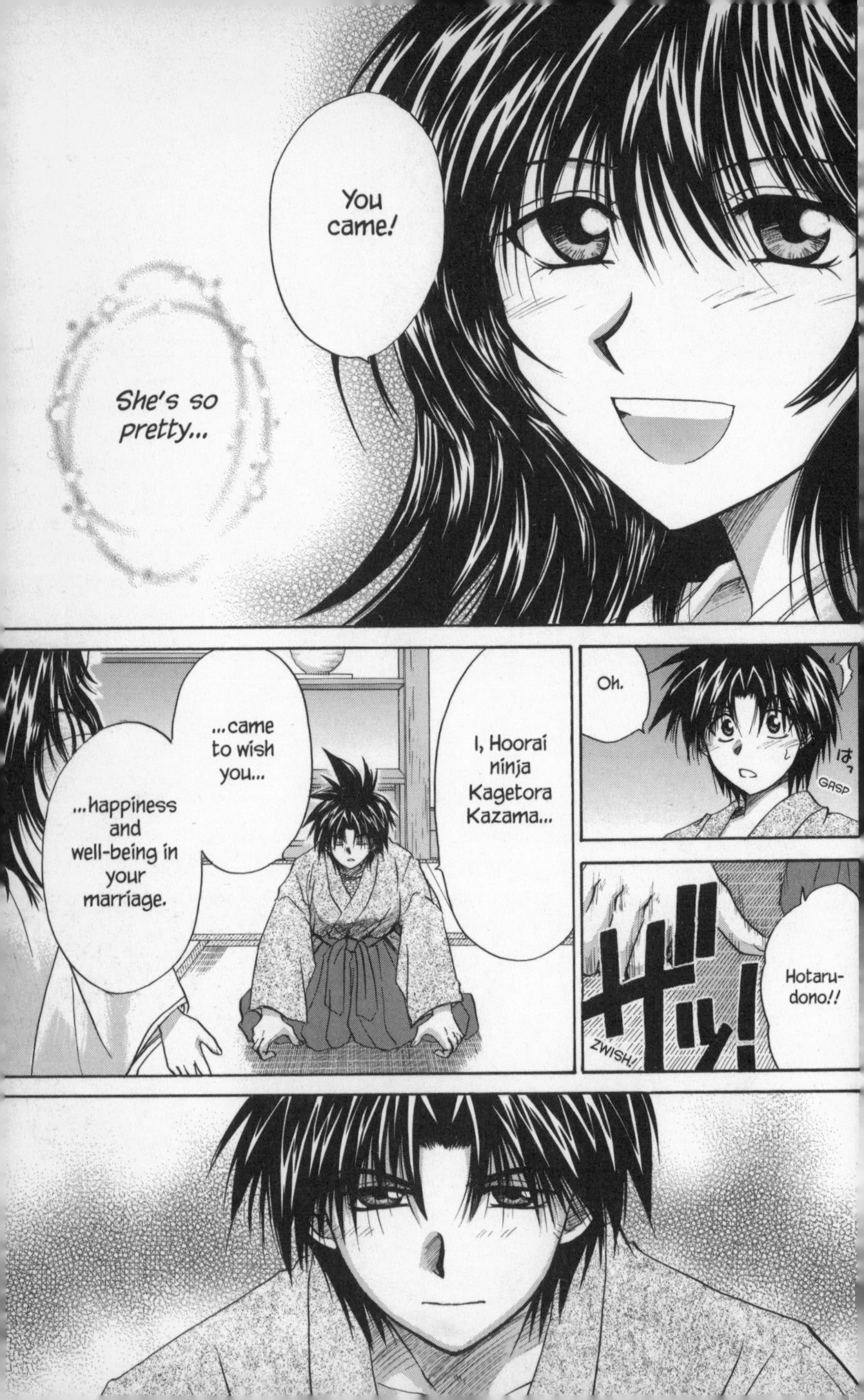
You came!
She's so pretty...
Oh.
はっ
GASP
Hotaru-dono!!
ザッ!
ZWISH!
I, Hoorai ninja Kagetora Kazama...
...came to wish you...
...happiness and well-being in your marriage.

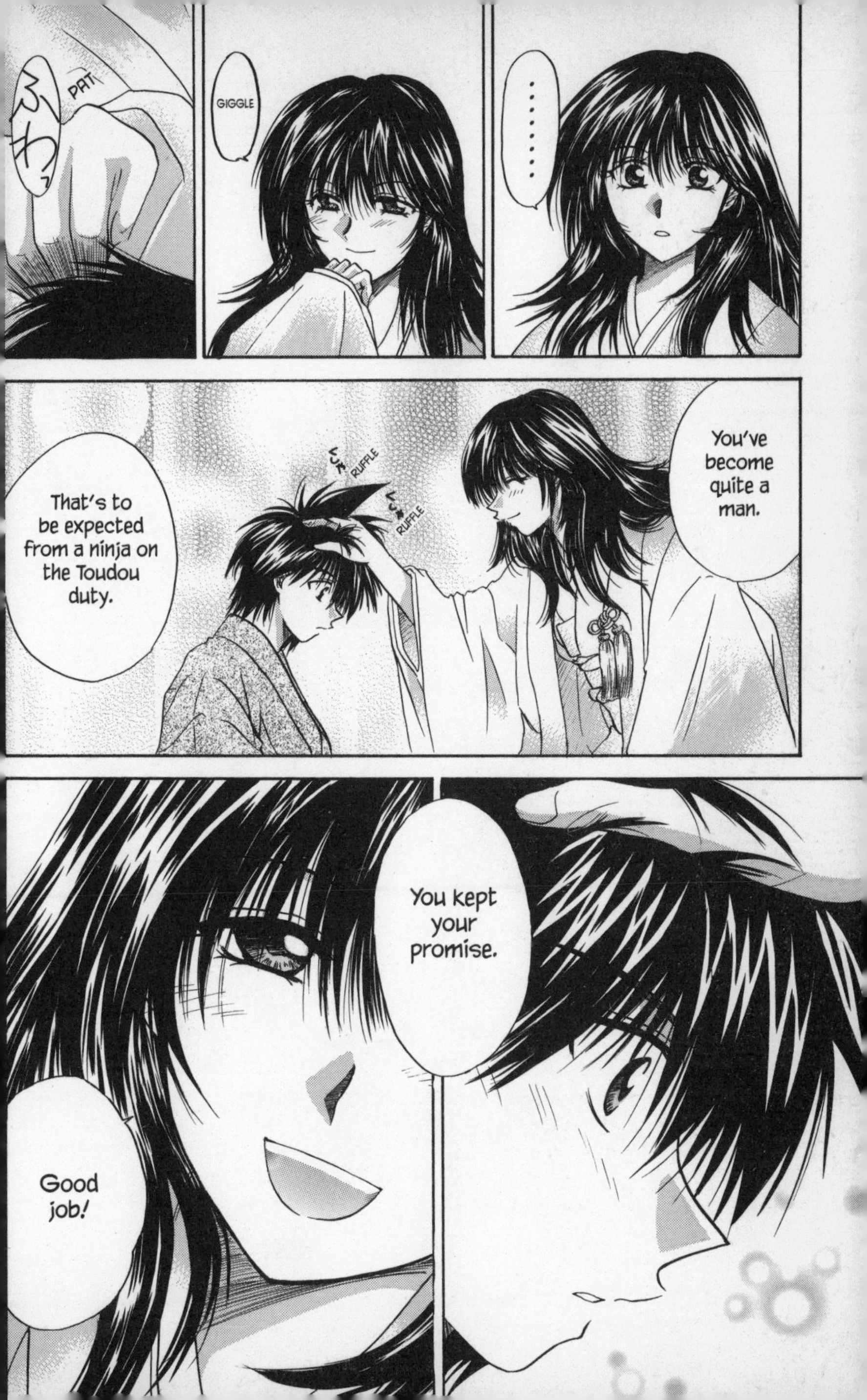
......
GIGGLE
ふわっ
PAT
You've become quite a man.
RUFFLE
RUFFLE
That's to be expected from a ninja on the Toudou duty.
You kept your promise.
Good job!

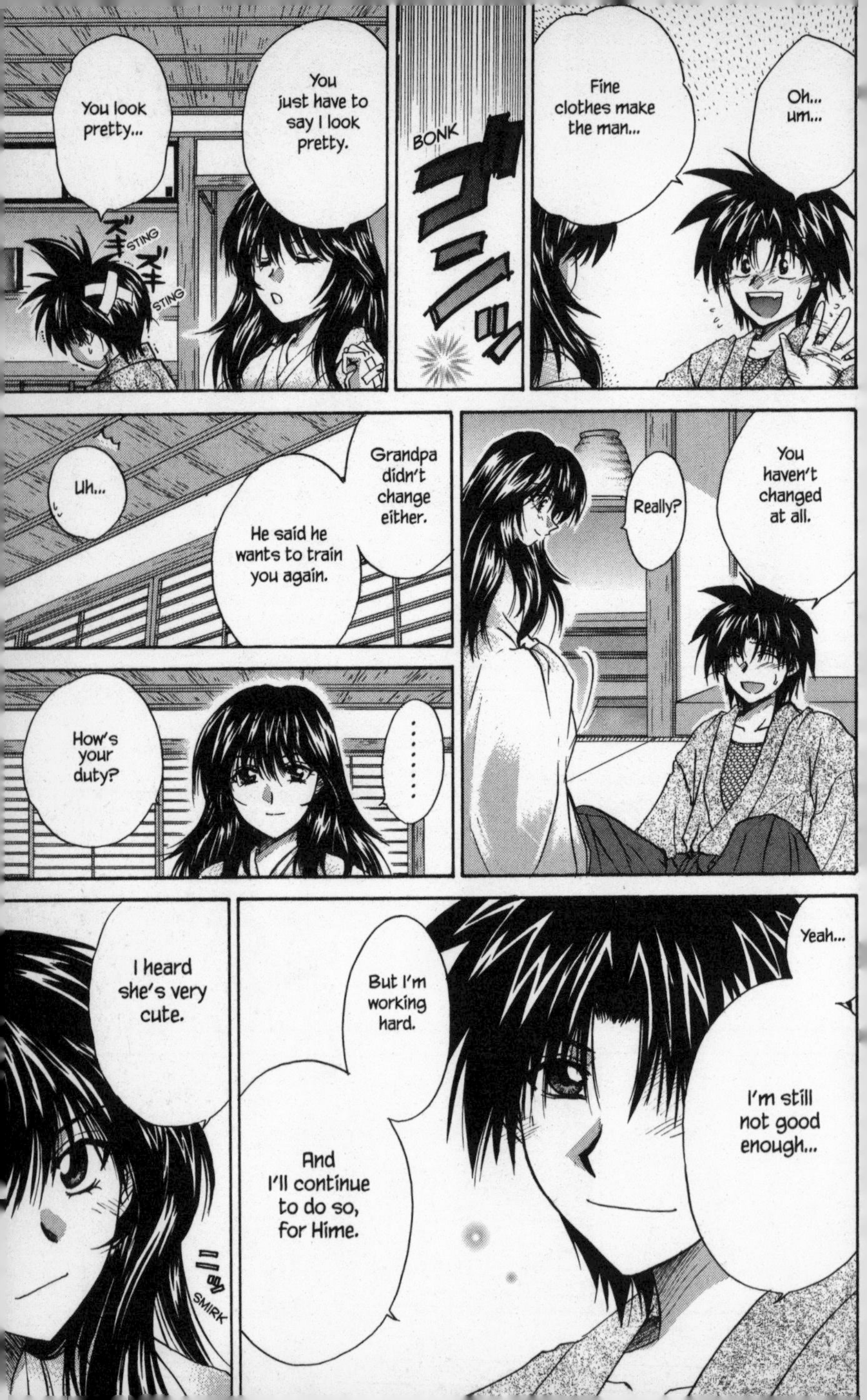
Oh... um...
Fine clothes make the man...
BONK
You just have to say I look pretty.
You look pretty...
STING
STING
You haven't changed at all.
Really?
Grandpa didn't change either.
He said he wants to train you again.
Uh...
......
How's your duty?
Yeah...
I'm still not good enough...
But I'm working hard.
And I'll continue to do so, for Hime.
I heard she's very cute.
SMIRK

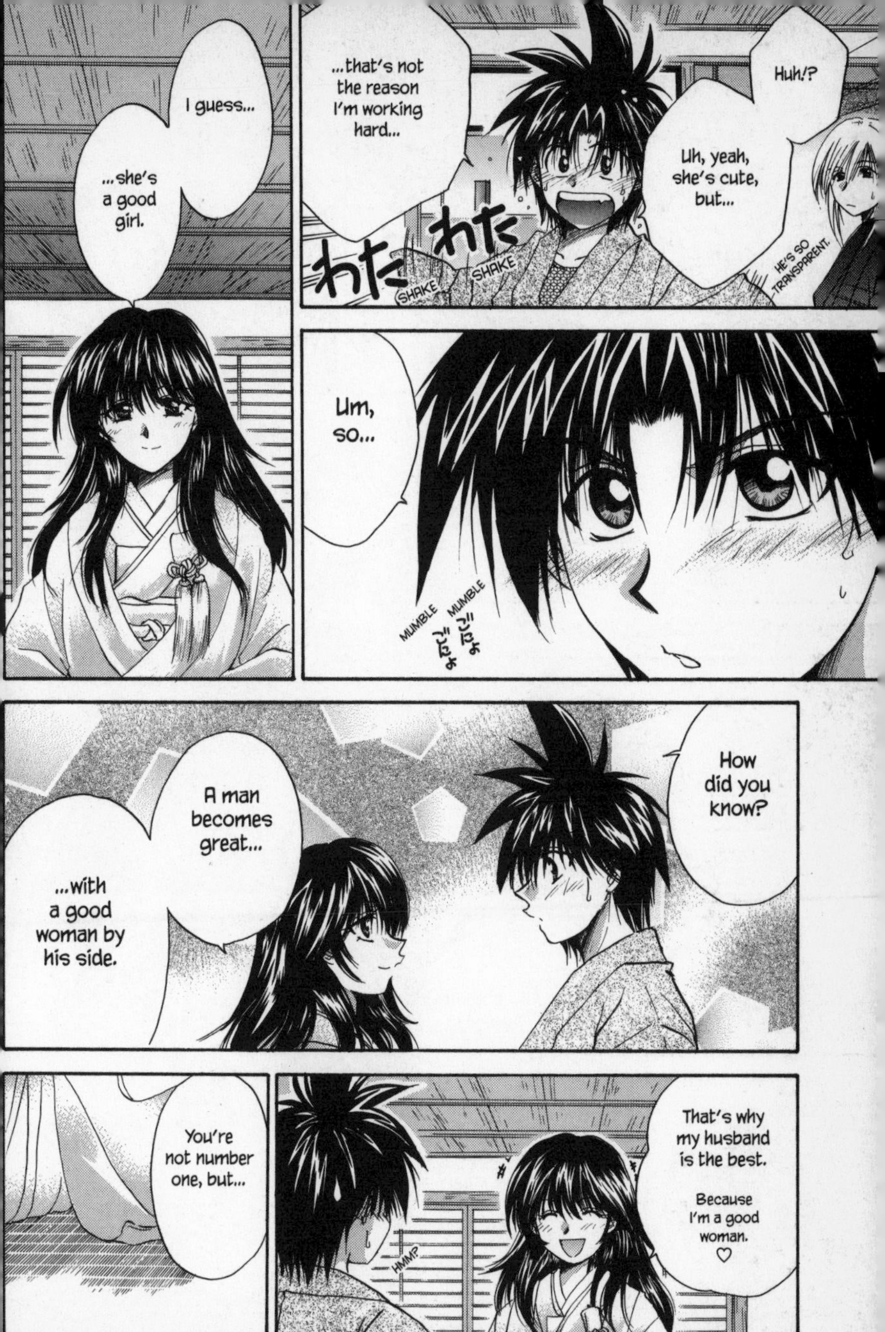
Huh!?
Uh, yeah, she's cute, but...
...that's not the reason I'm working hard...
わた わた
SHAKE SHAKE
HE'S SO TRANSPARENT.
I guess...
...she's a good girl.
Um, so...
ごにょ ごにょ
MUMBLE MUMBLE
How did you know?
A man becomes great...
...with a good woman by his side.
That's why my husband is the best.
Because I'm a good woman. ♡
HMMP?
You're not number one, but...

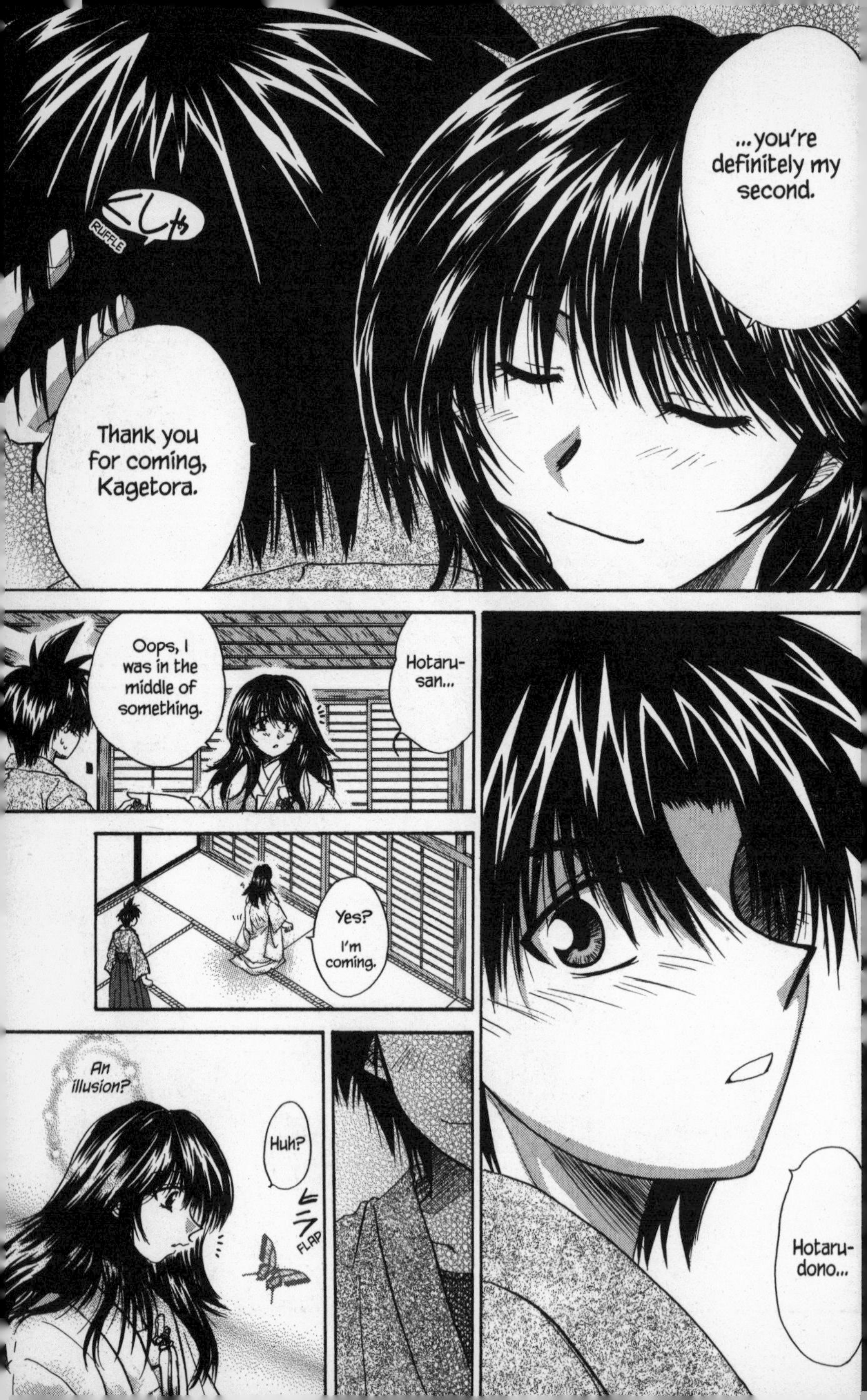

...you're definitely my second.
RUFFLE
Thank you for coming, Kagetora.
Hotaru-dono...
Hotaru-san...
Oops, I was in the middle of something.
Yes? I'm coming.
Huh?
An illusion?
FLAP

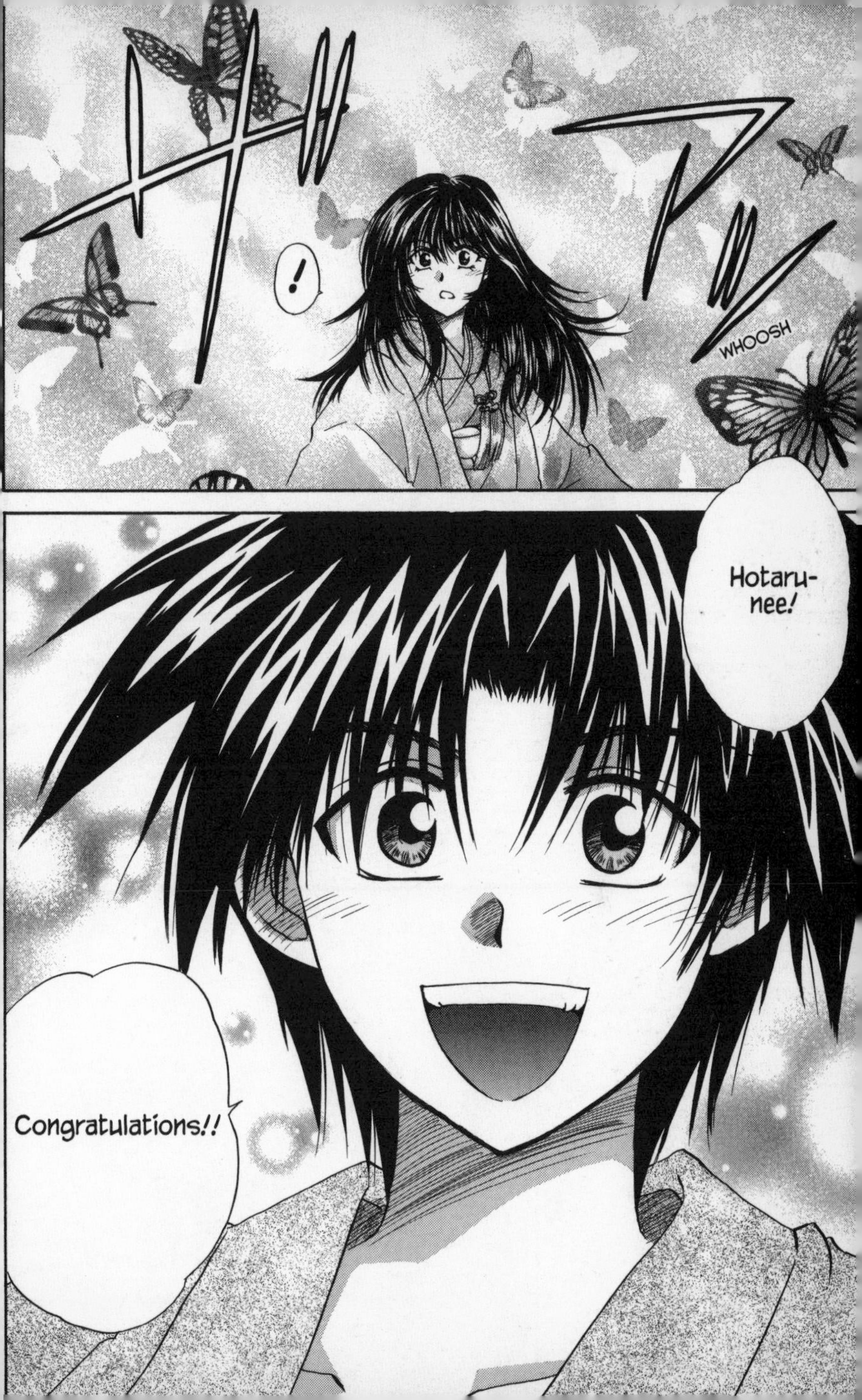
!
WHOOSH
Hotaru-nee!
Congratulations!!

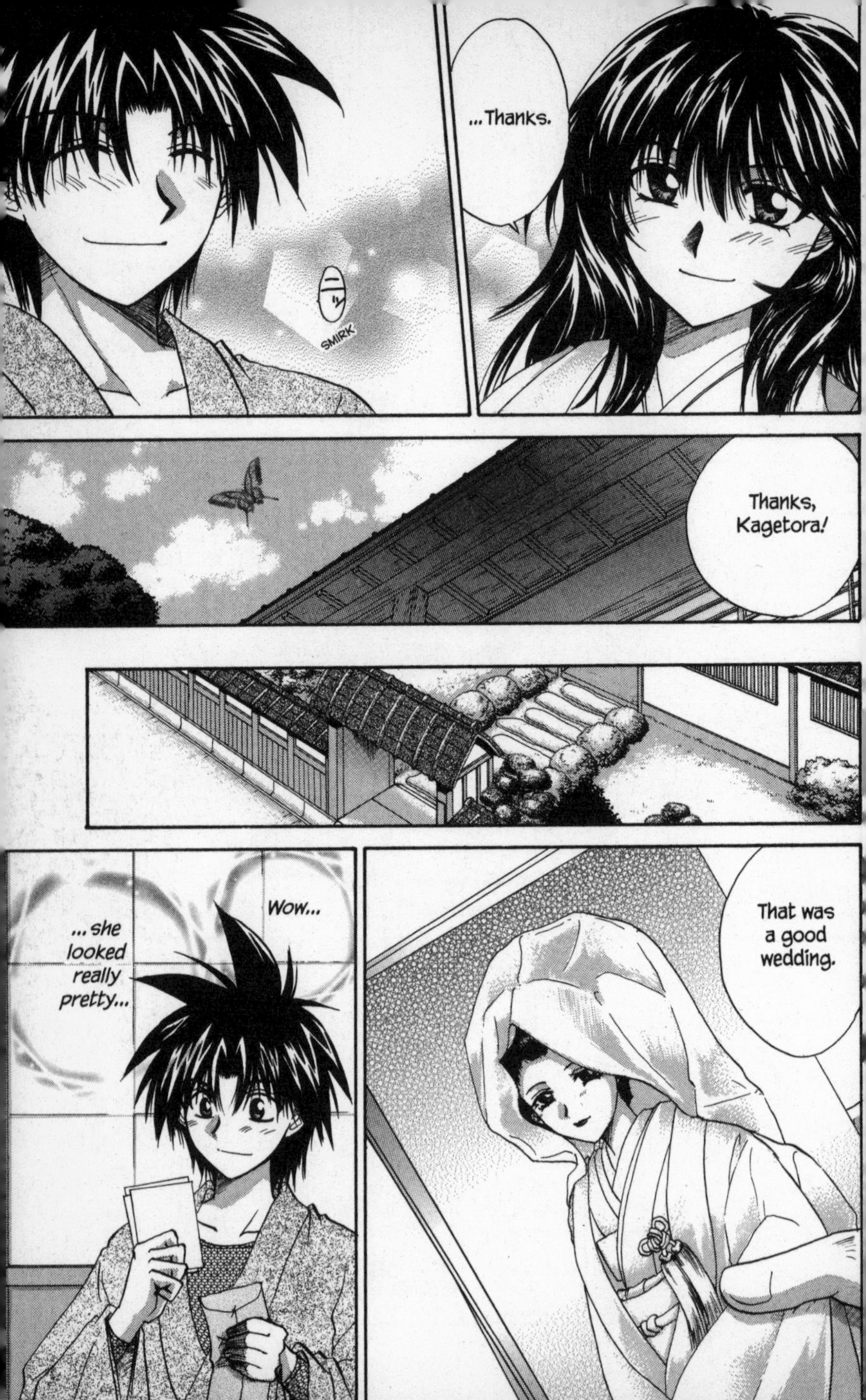
...Thanks.
SMIRK
Thanks, Kagetora!
That was a good wedding.
Wow...
...she looked really pretty...

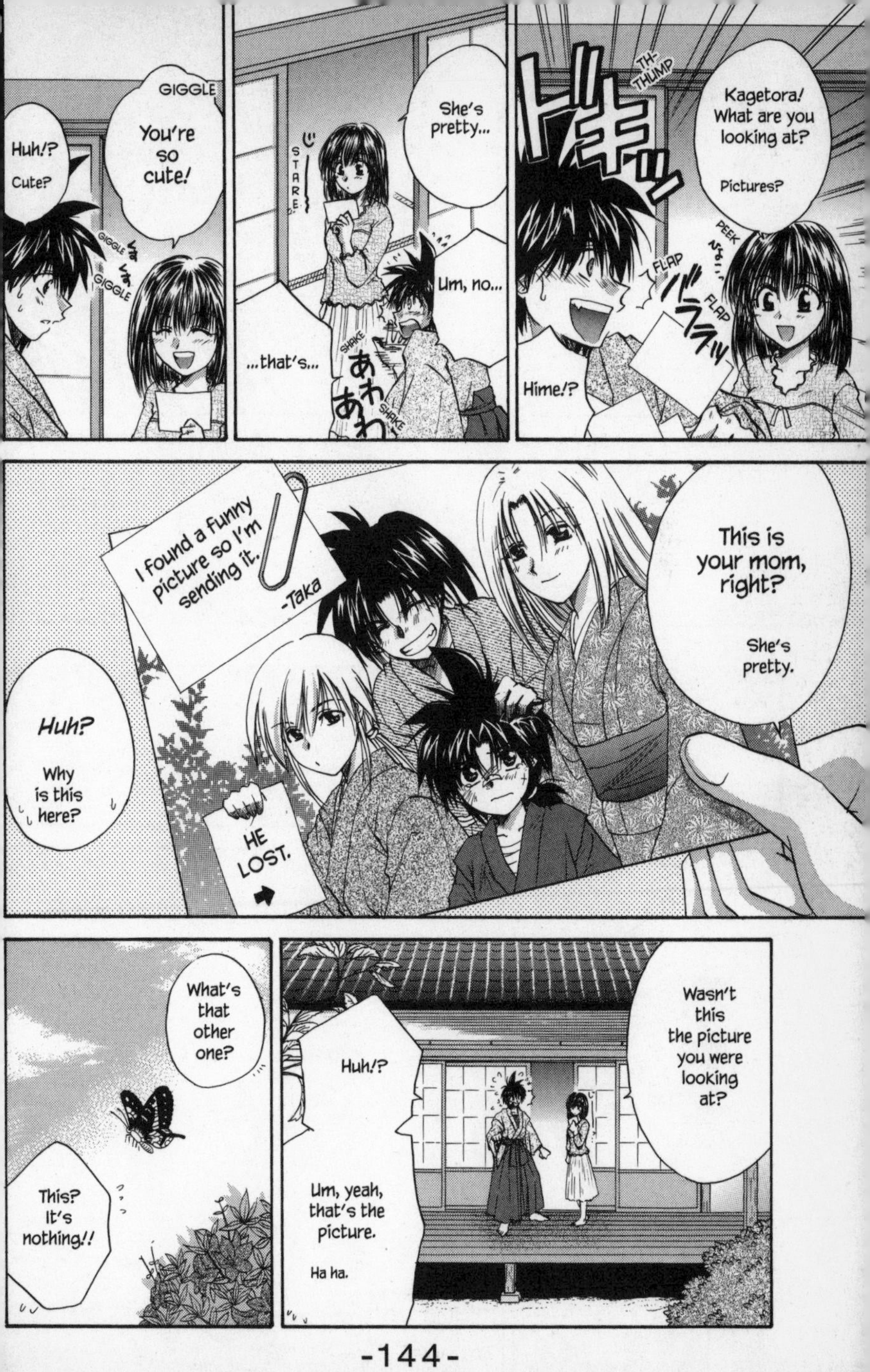
Kagetora! What are you looking at?
Pictures?
PEEK
FLAP
バララッ
FLAP
TH-THUMP
ドキッ
Hime!?
She's pretty...
じ
STARE
Um, no...
...that's...
SHAKE
あわあわ
SHAKE
GIGGLE
You're so cute!
GIGGLE
くすくす
GIGGLE
Huh!? Cute?
This is your mom, right?
She's pretty.
I found a funny picture so I'm sending it. -Taka
HE LOST.
Huh?
Why is this here?
Wasn't this the picture you were looking at?
Huh!?
Um, yeah, that's the picture.
Ha ha.
What's that other one?
This? It's nothing!!

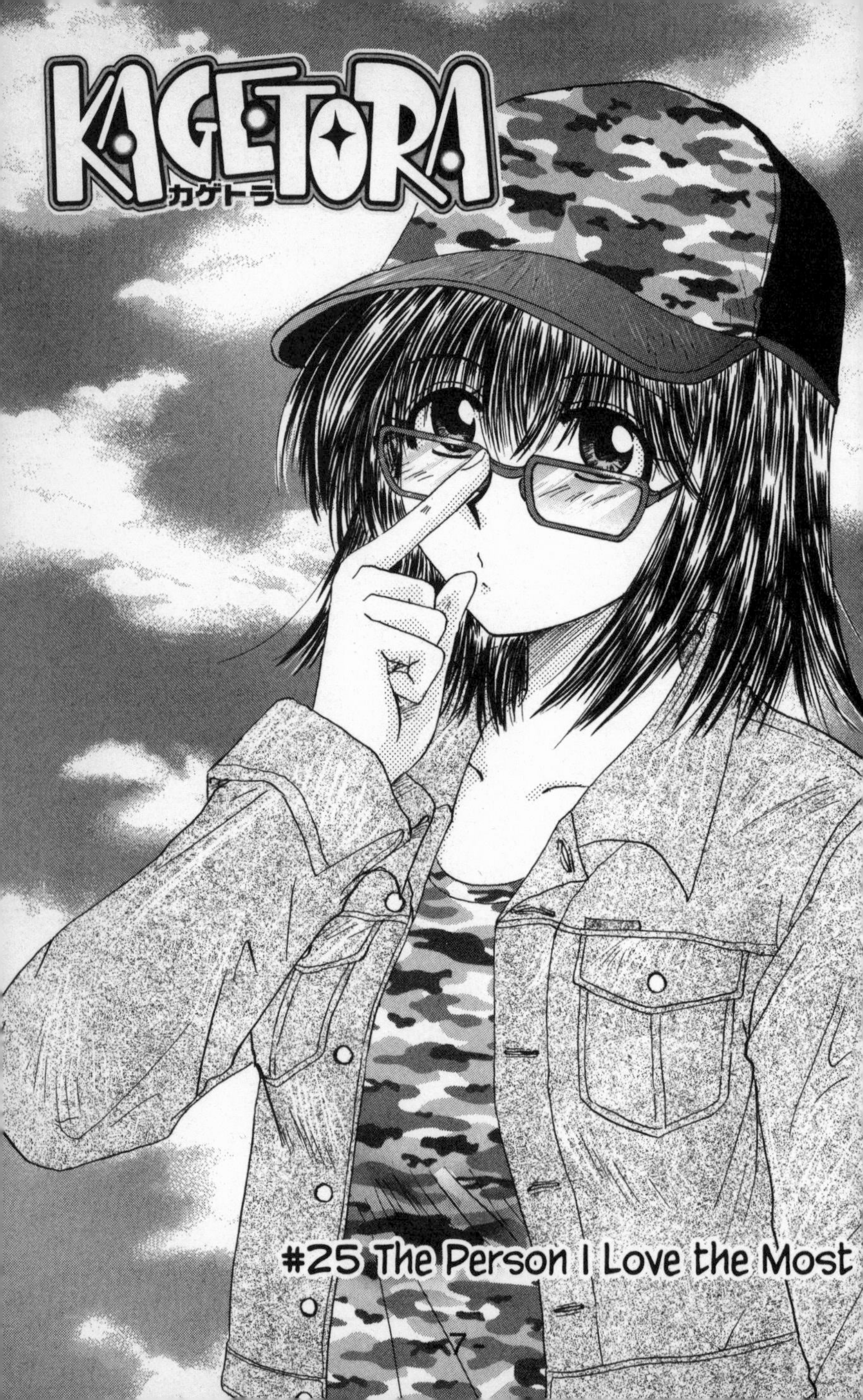
KAGETORA
カゲトラ
#25 The Person I Love the Most

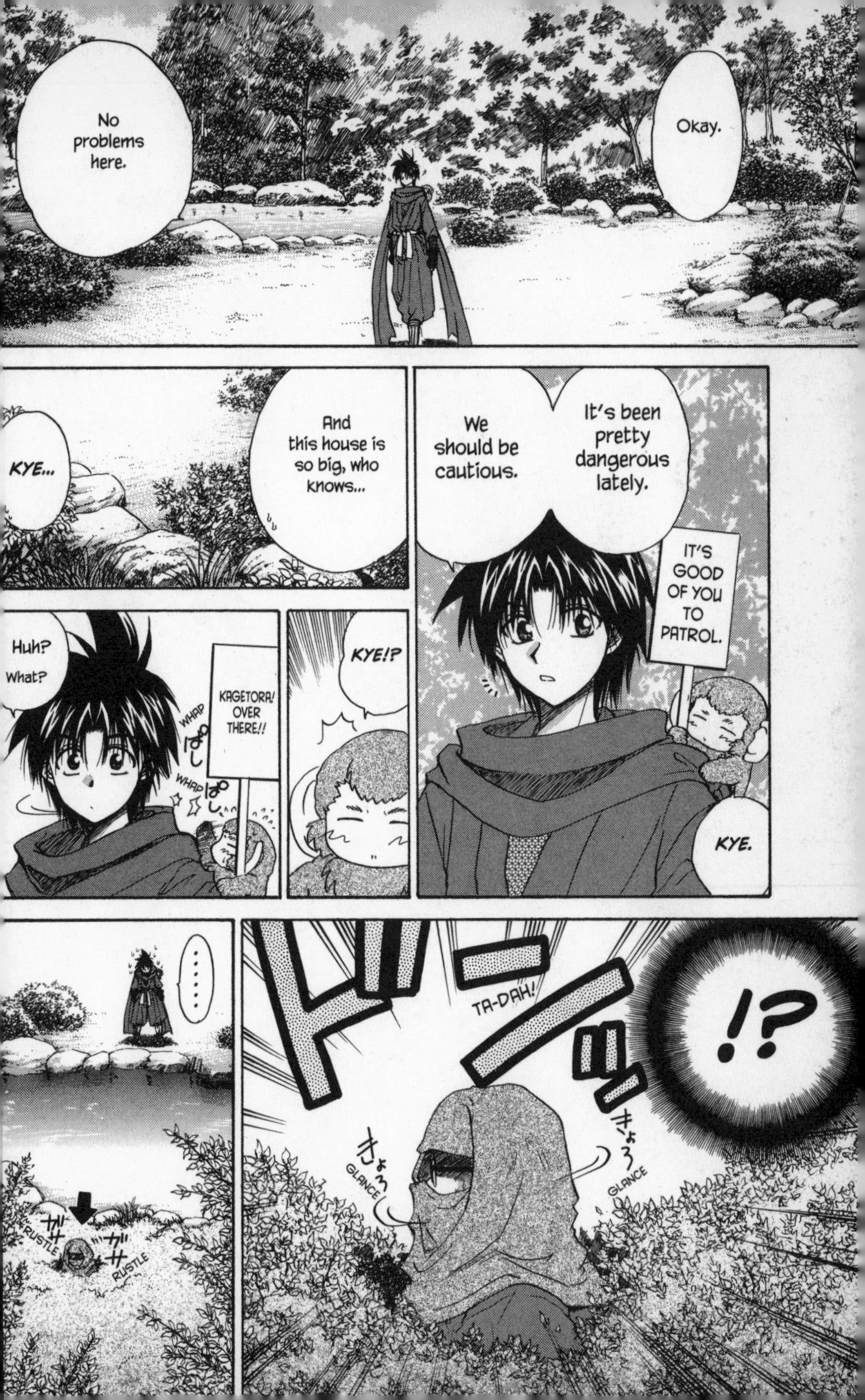
Okay.
No problems here.
It's been pretty dangerous lately.
We should be cautious.
IT'S GOOD OF YOU TO PATROL.
KYE.
And this house is so big, who knows...
KYE...
KYE!?
Huh? What?
KAGETORA! OVER THERE!!
WHAP ぱし
WHAP ぱし
!?
TA-DAH!
きょろ GLANCE
きょろ GLANCE
......
ガサ RUSTLE
ガサ RUSTLE

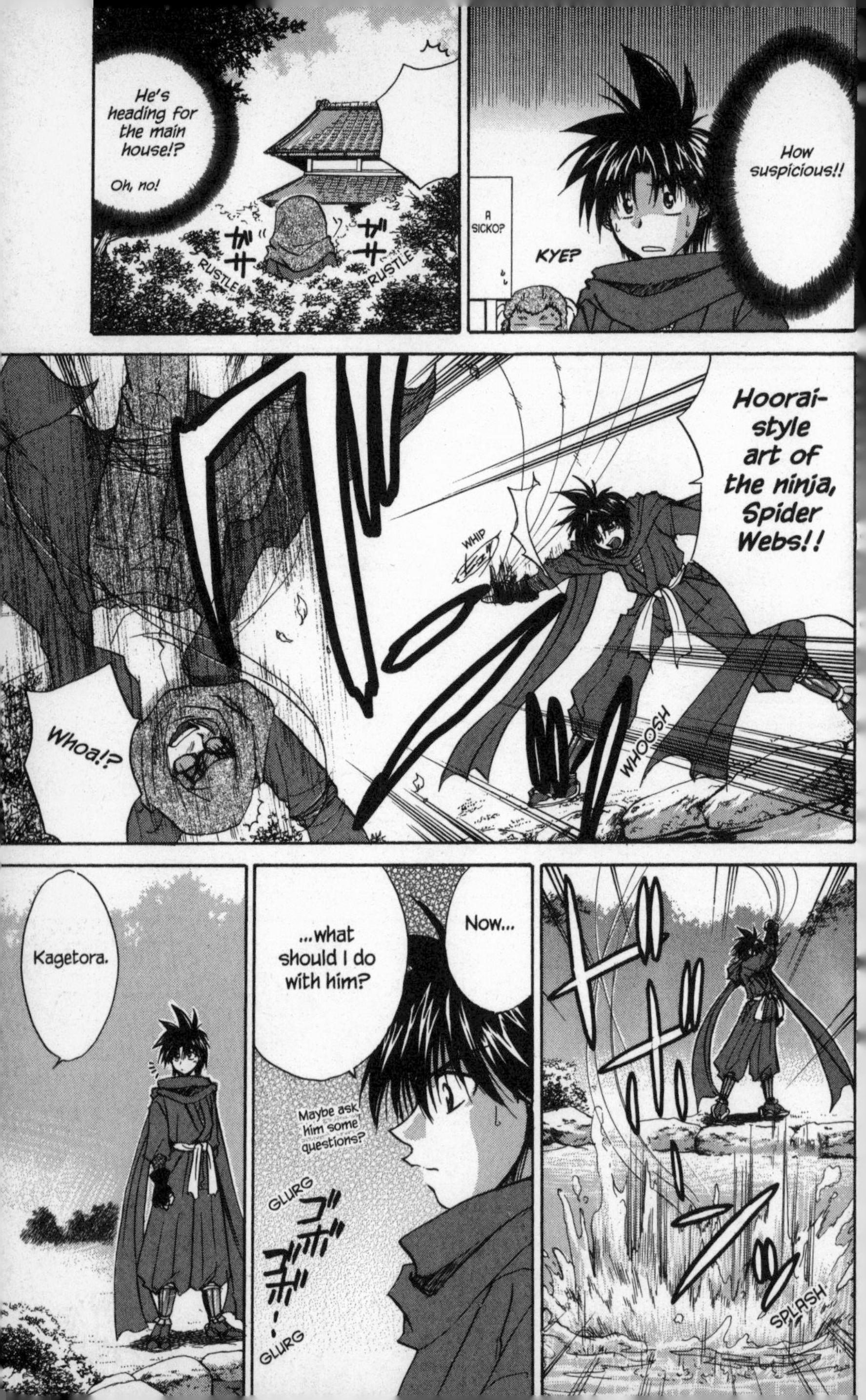
How suspicious!!
KYE?
A SICKO?
He's heading for the main house!?
Oh, no!
RUSTLE
RUSTLE
Hoorai-style art of the ninja, Spider Webs!!
WHIP
WHOOSH
Whoa!?
SPLASH
Now...
...what should I do with him?
Maybe ask him some questions?
GLURG
GLURG
Kagetora.

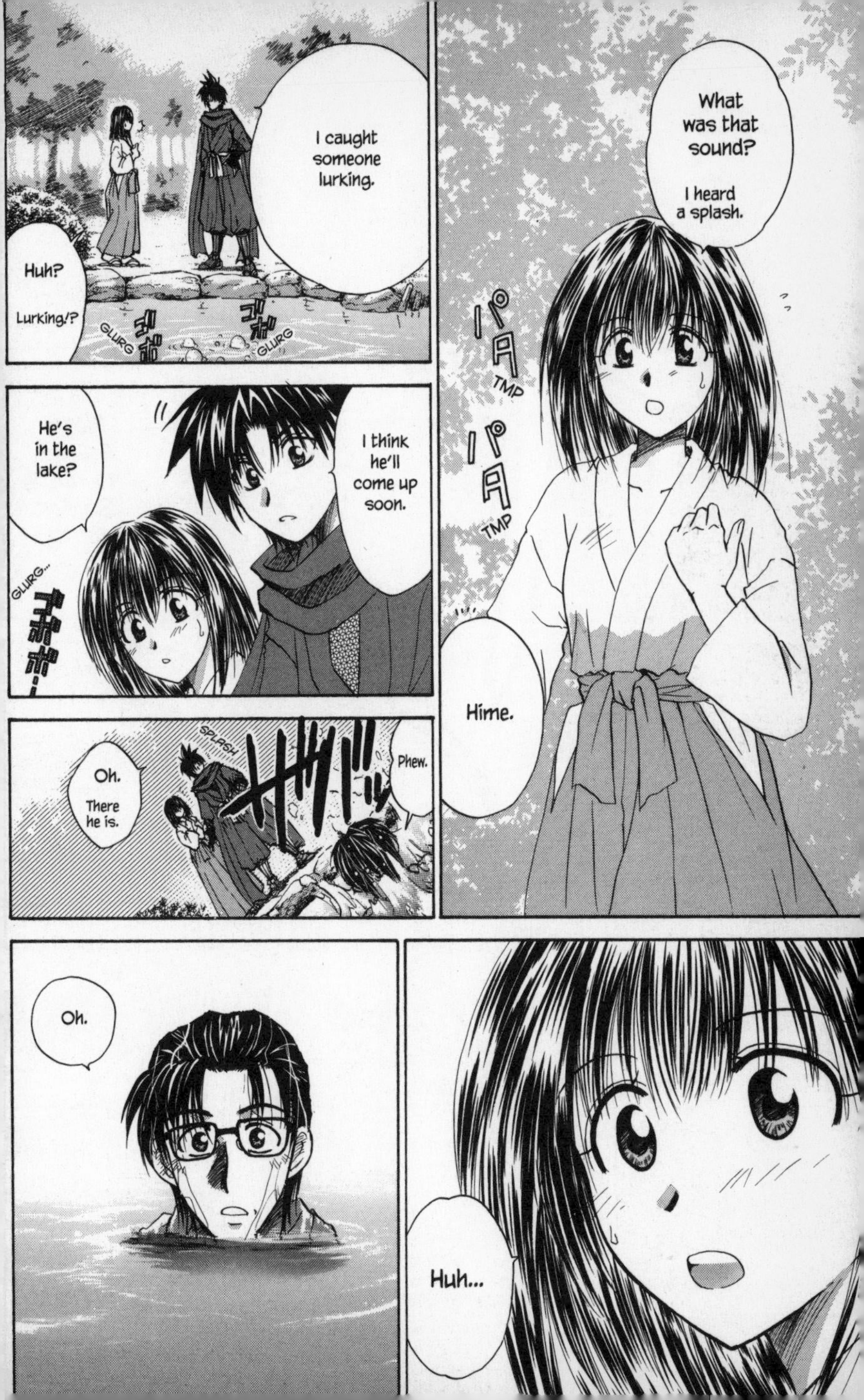
What was that sound?
I heard a splash.
TMP
TMP
Hime.
I caught someone lurking.
Huh?
Lurking!?
GLURG
GLURG
I think he'll come up soon.
He's in the lake?
GLURG...
SPLASH
Phew.
Oh.
There he is.
Huh...
Oh.

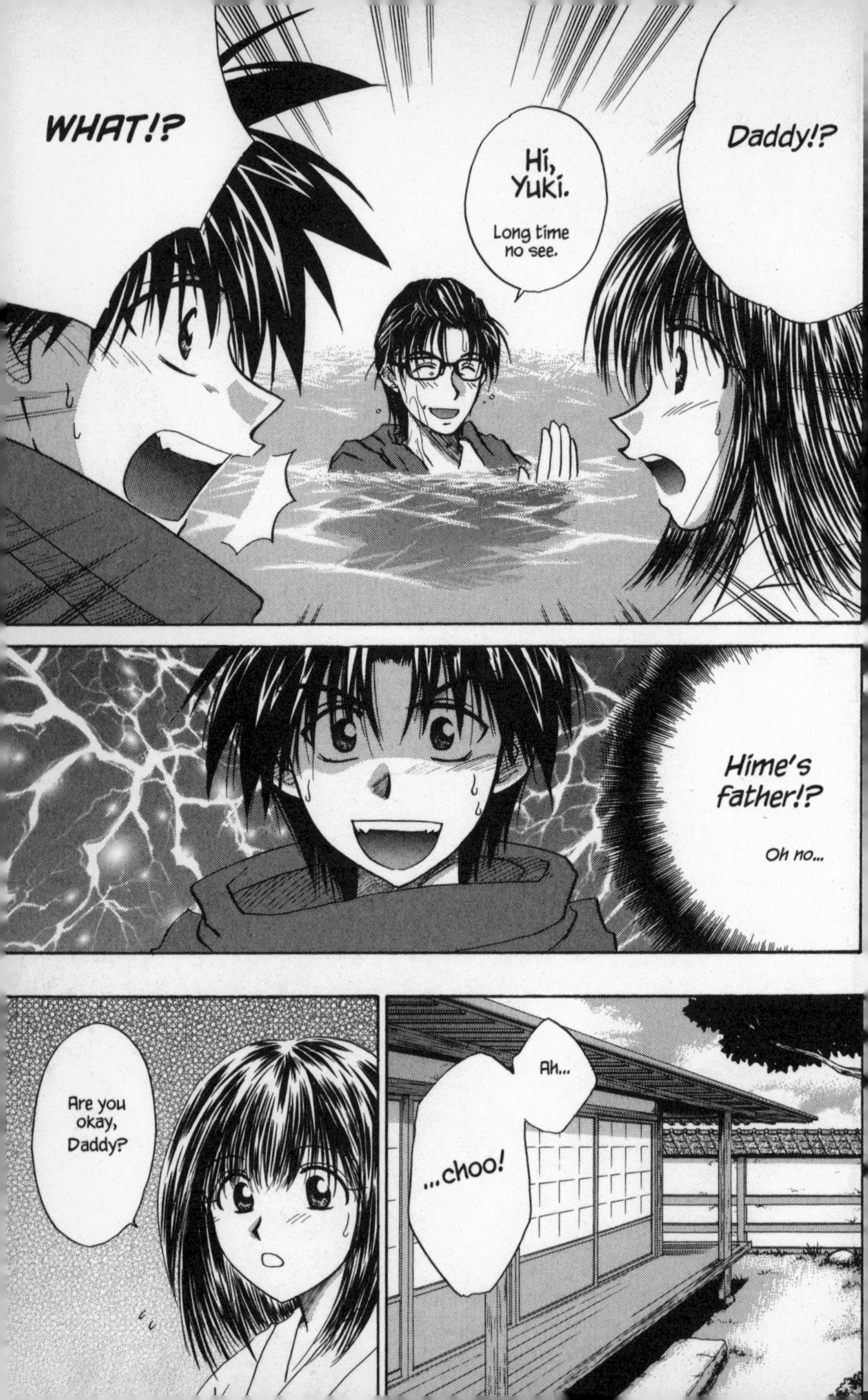
Daddy!?
Hi, Yuki.
Long time no see.
WHAT!?
Hime's father!?
Oh no...
Ah...
...choo!
Are you okay, Daddy?

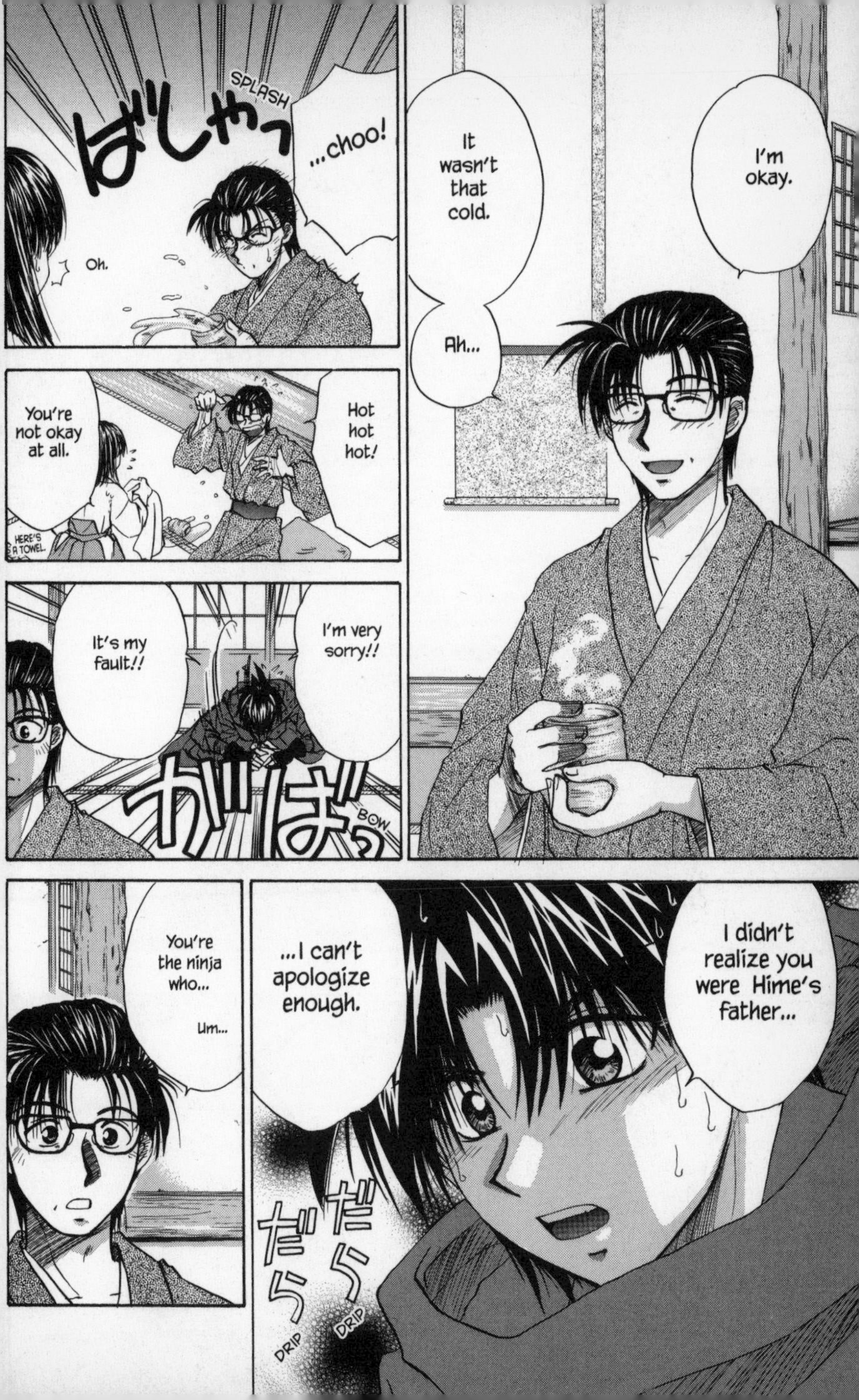
I'm okay.
It wasn't that cold.
Ah...
SPLASH
ばしゃっ
...choo!
Oh.
Hot hot hot!
You're not okay at all.
HERE'S A TOWEL.
I'm very sorry!!
It's my fault!!
がばっ
BOW
I didn't realize you were Hime's father...
...I can't apologize enough.
だらだら
DRIP DRIP
You're the ninja who...
Um...

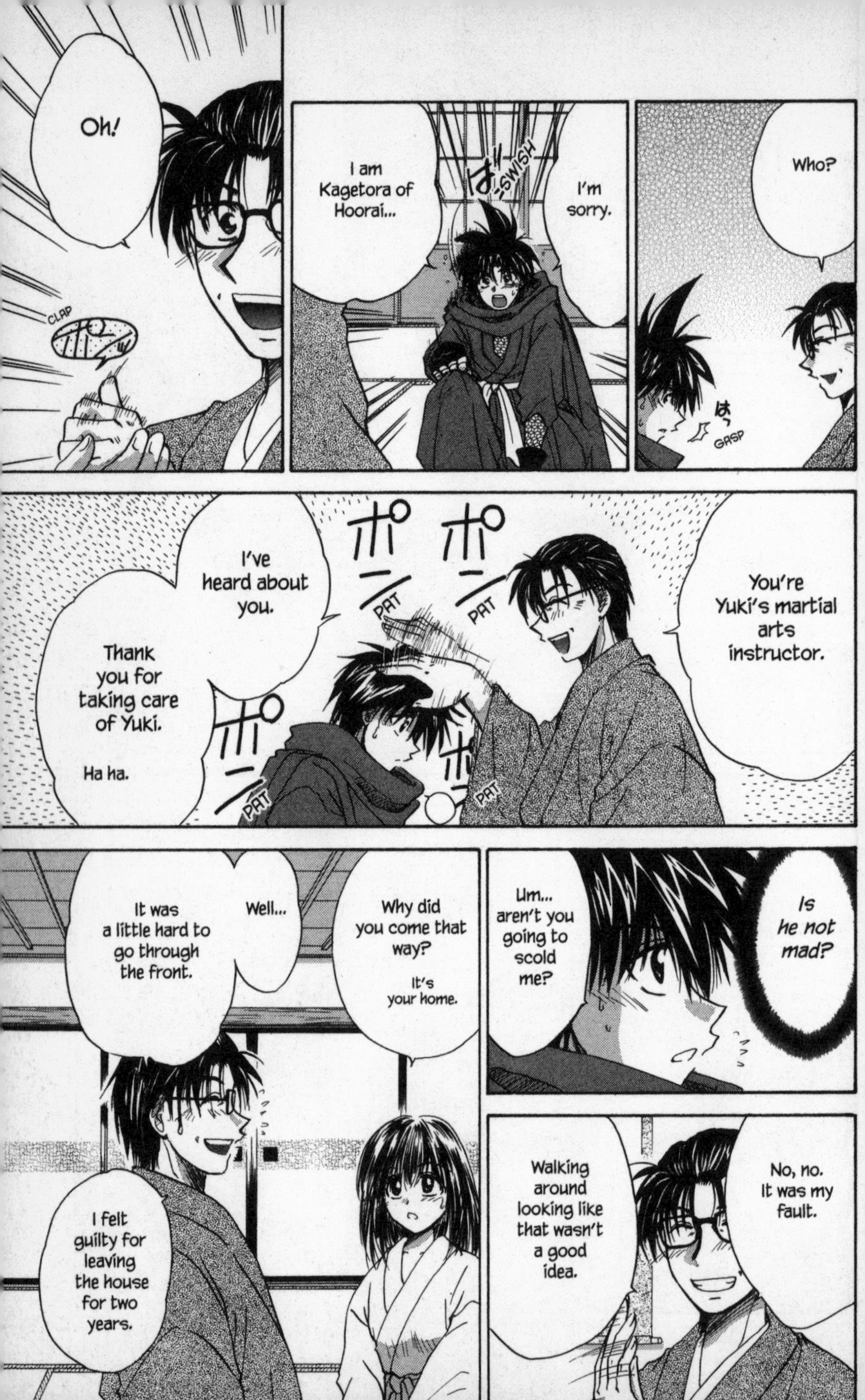
Who?
GASP
I'm sorry.
SWISH
I am Kagetora of Hoorai...
Oh!
CLAP
You're Yuki's martial arts instructor.
PAT
PAT
I've heard about you.
Thank you for taking care of Yuki.
Ha ha.
PAT
PAT
Is he not mad?
Um... aren't you going to scold me?
No, no. It was my fault.
Walking around looking like that wasn't a good idea.
Why did you come that way?
It's your home.
Well...
It was a little hard to go through the front.
I felt guilty for leaving the house for two years.

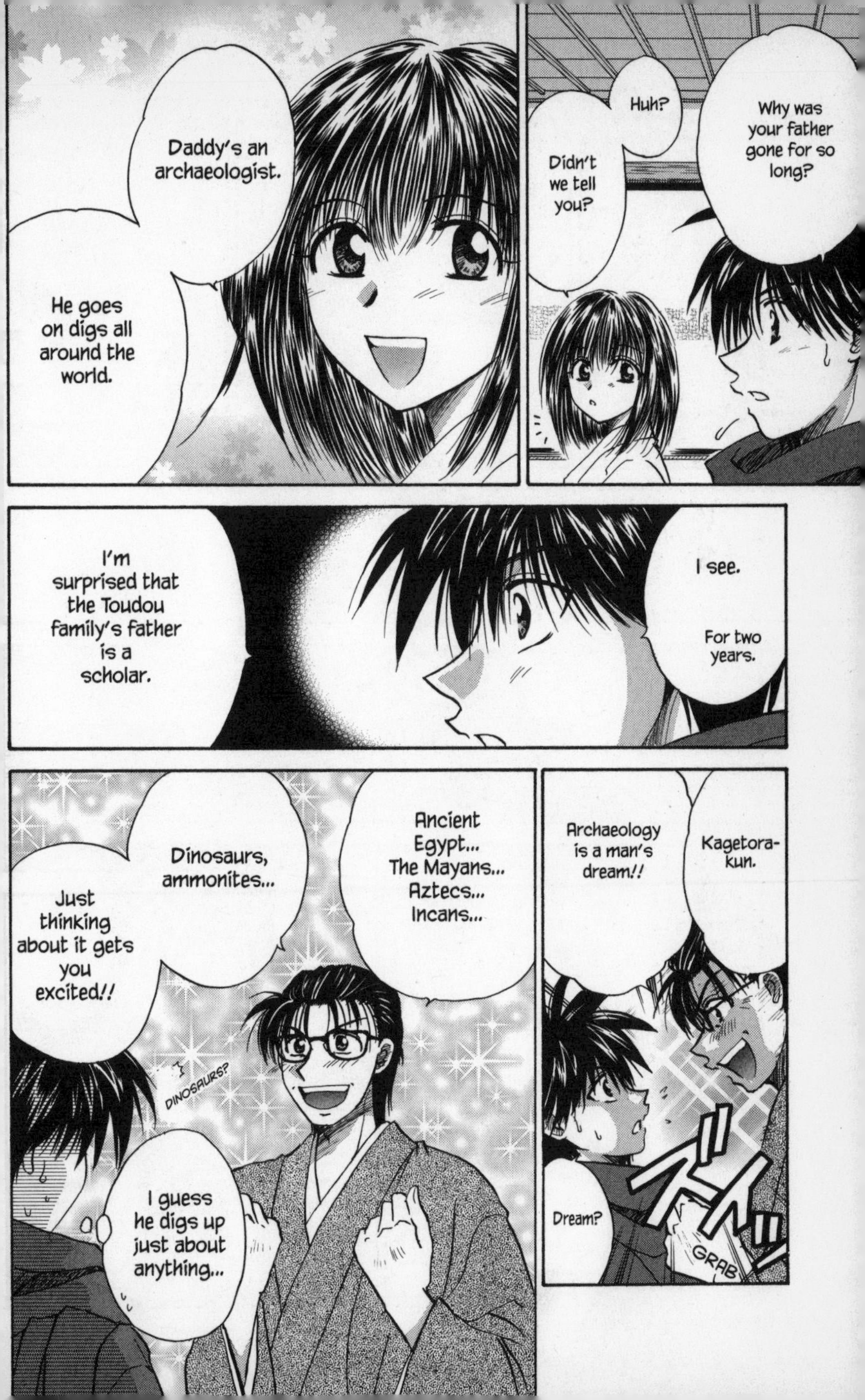
Why was your father gone for so long?
Huh?
Didn't we tell you?
Daddy's an archaeologist.
He goes on digs all around the world.
I see.
For two years.
I'm surprised that the Toudou family's father is a scholar.
Kagetora-kun.
Archaeology is a man's dream!!
Dream?
GRAB
Ancient Egypt... The Mayans... Aztecs... Incans...
Dinosaurs, ammonites...
Just thinking about it gets you excited!!
DINOSAURS?
I guess he digs up just about anything...

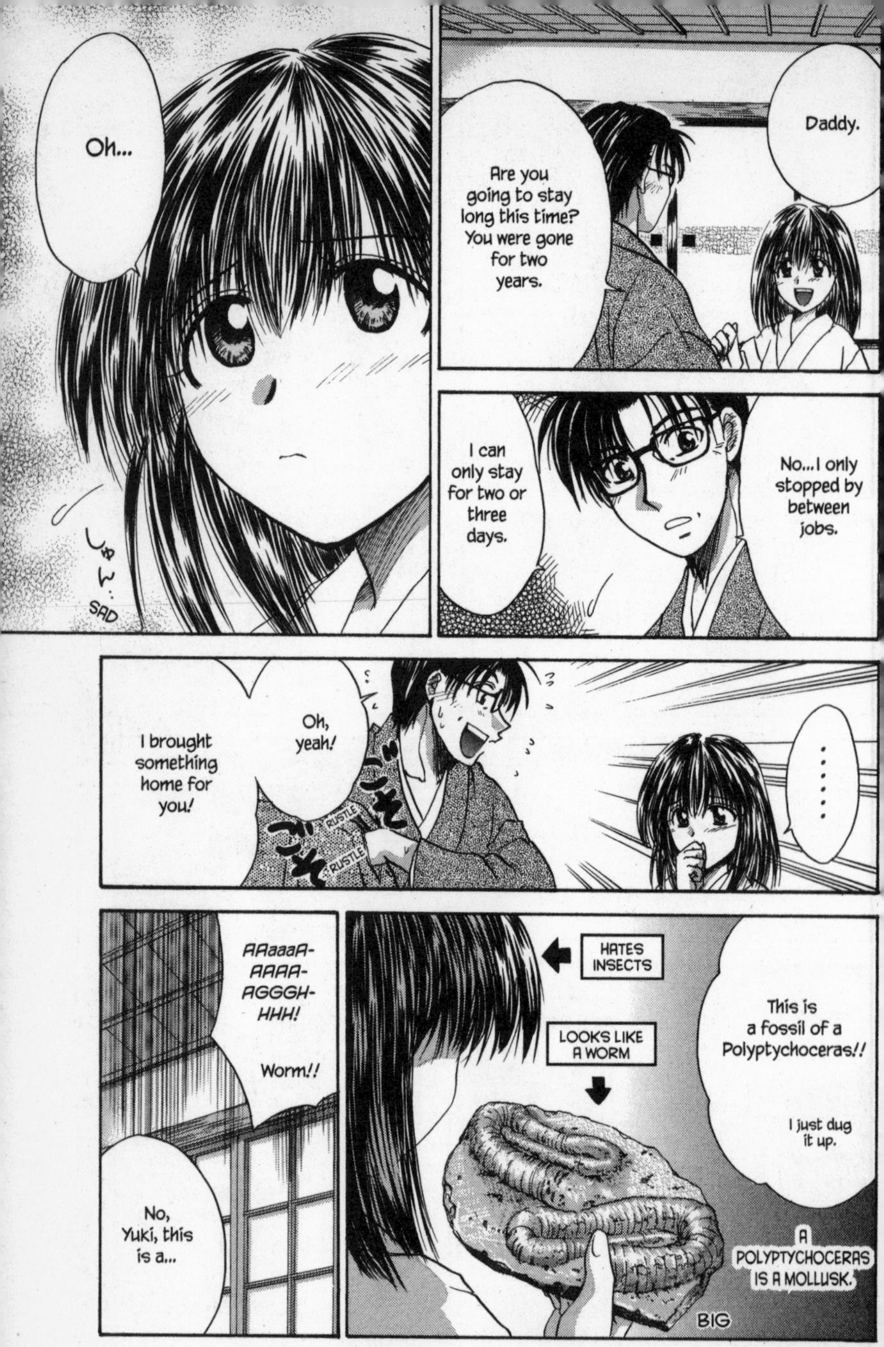
Daddy.
Are you going to stay long this time? You were gone for two years.
No...I only stopped by between jobs.
I can only stay for two or three days.
Oh...
SAD
......
Oh, yeah!
I brought something home for you!
RUSTLE
RUSTLE
This is a fossil of a Polyptychoceras!!
I just dug it up.
HATES INSECTS
LOOKS LIKE A WORM
A POLYPTYCHOCERAS IS A MOLLUSK.
BIG
AAaaaA-AAAA-AGGGH-HHH!
Worm!!
No, Yuki, this is a...

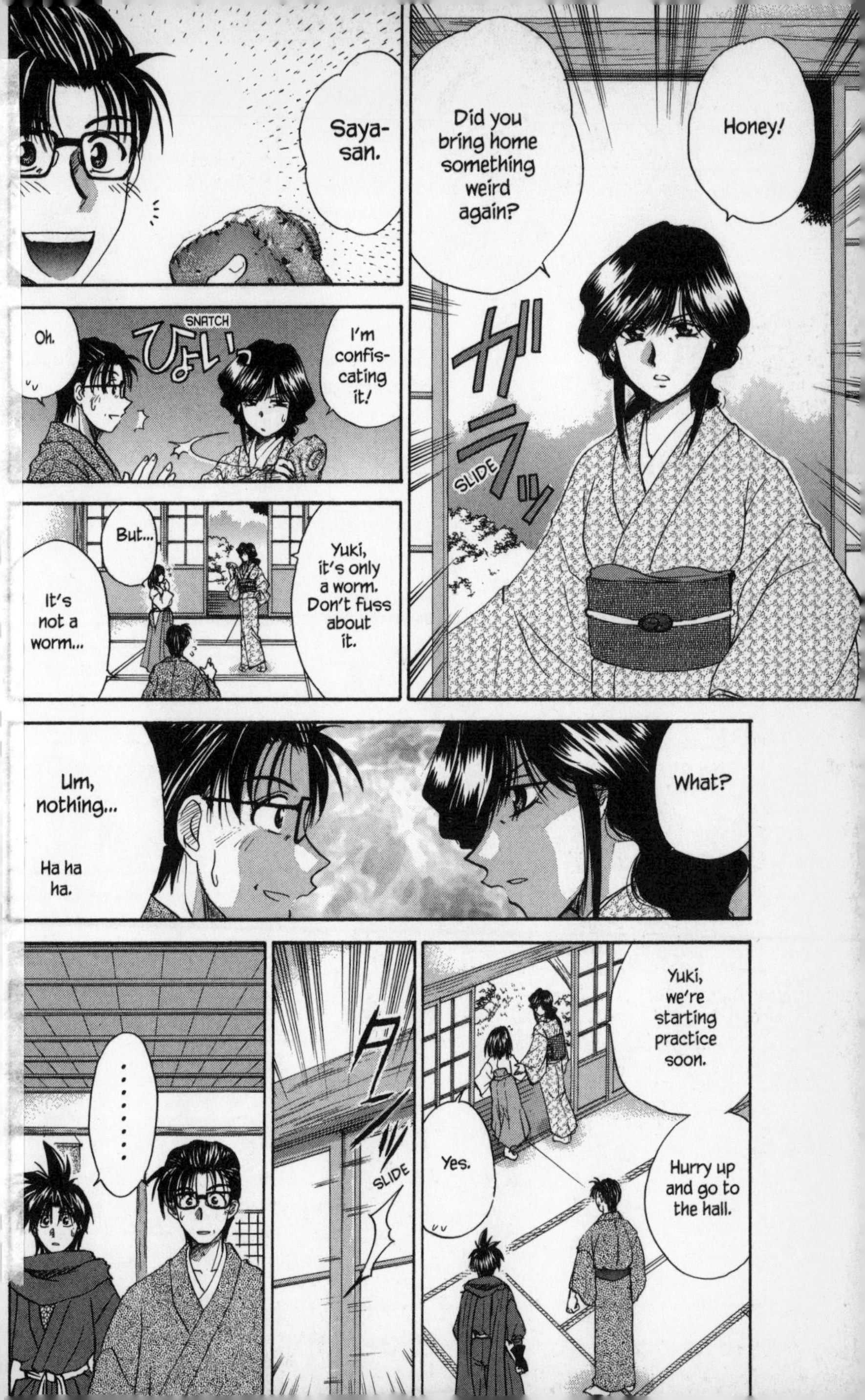

Honey!
Did you bring home something weird again?
ガラッ
SLIDE
Saya-san.
I'm confis-cating it!
ひょいっ
SNATCH
Oh.
Yuki, it's only a worm. Don't fuss about it.
But...
It's not a worm...
What?
Um, nothing...
Ha ha ha.
Yuki, we're starting practice soon.
Hurry up and go to the hall.
Yes.
タンッ
SLIDE
......

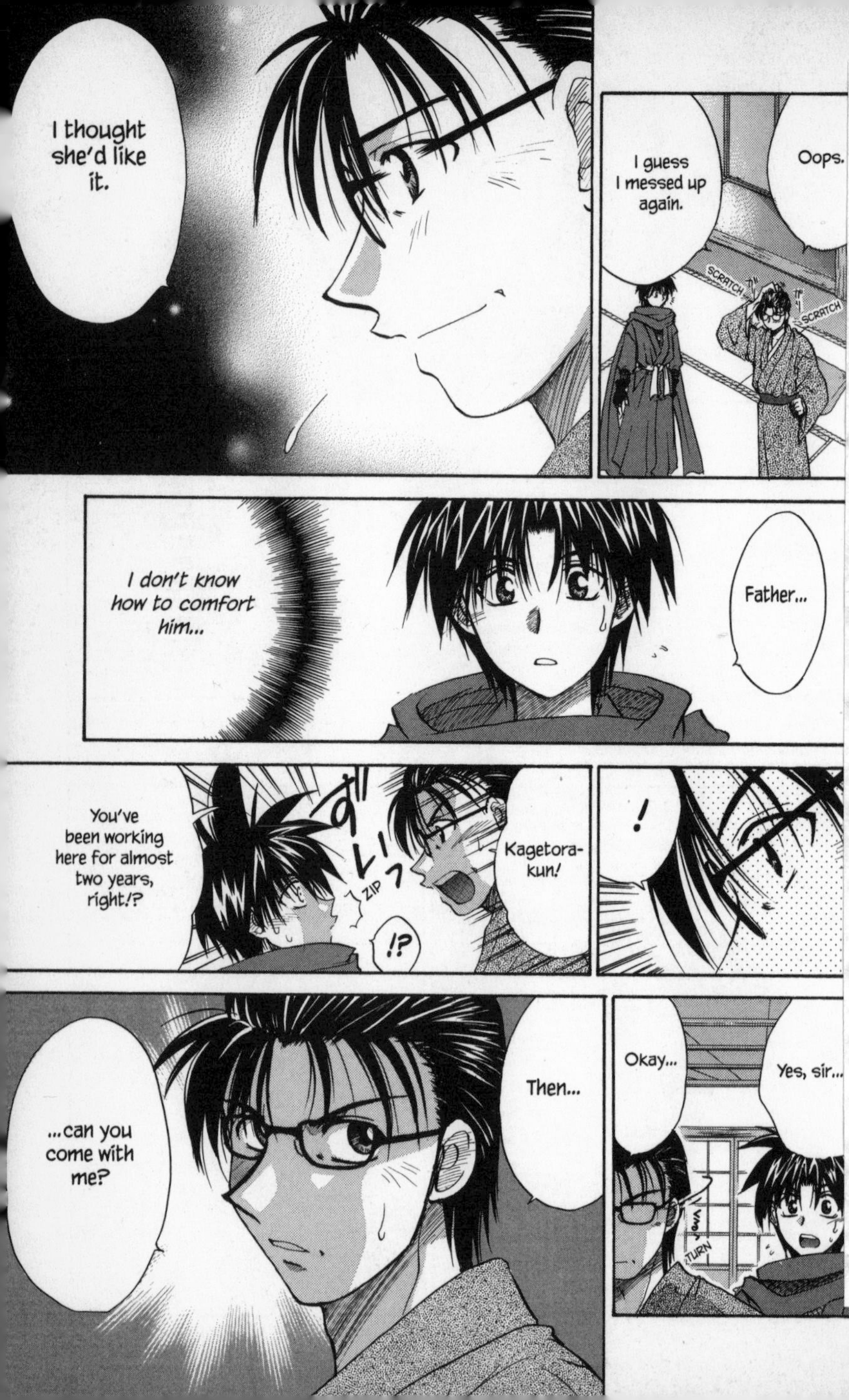
Oops.
I guess I messed up again.
SCRATCH
SCRATCH
I thought she'd like it.
Father...
I don't know how to comfort him...
!
Kagetora-kun!
You've been working here for almost two years, right!?
ZIP
!?
Yes, sir...
Okay...
TURN
Then...
...can you come with me?

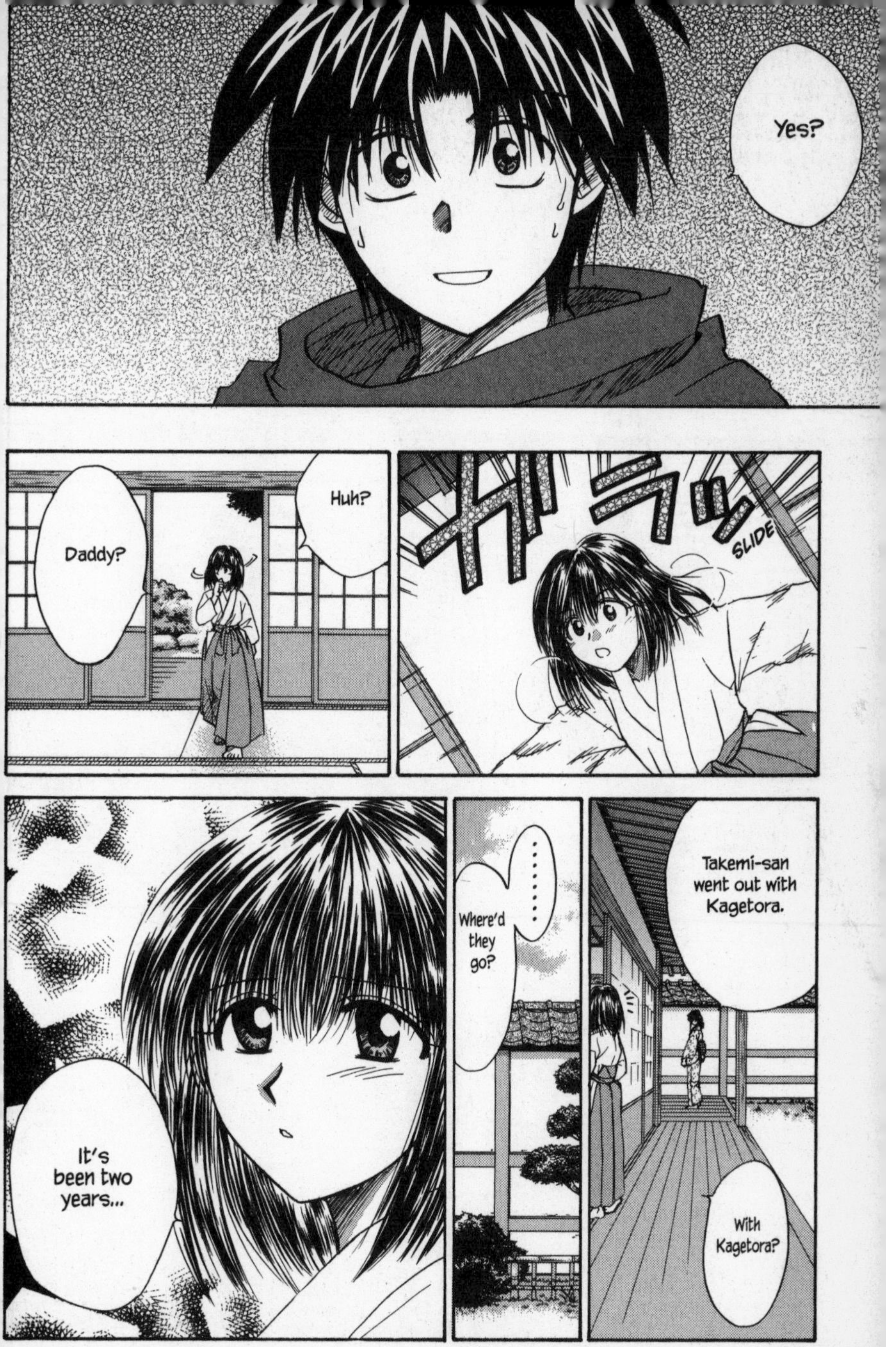
Yes?
ガラッ
SLIDE
Huh?
Daddy?
Takemi-san went out with Kagetora.
With Kagetora?
......
Where'd they go?
It's been two years...

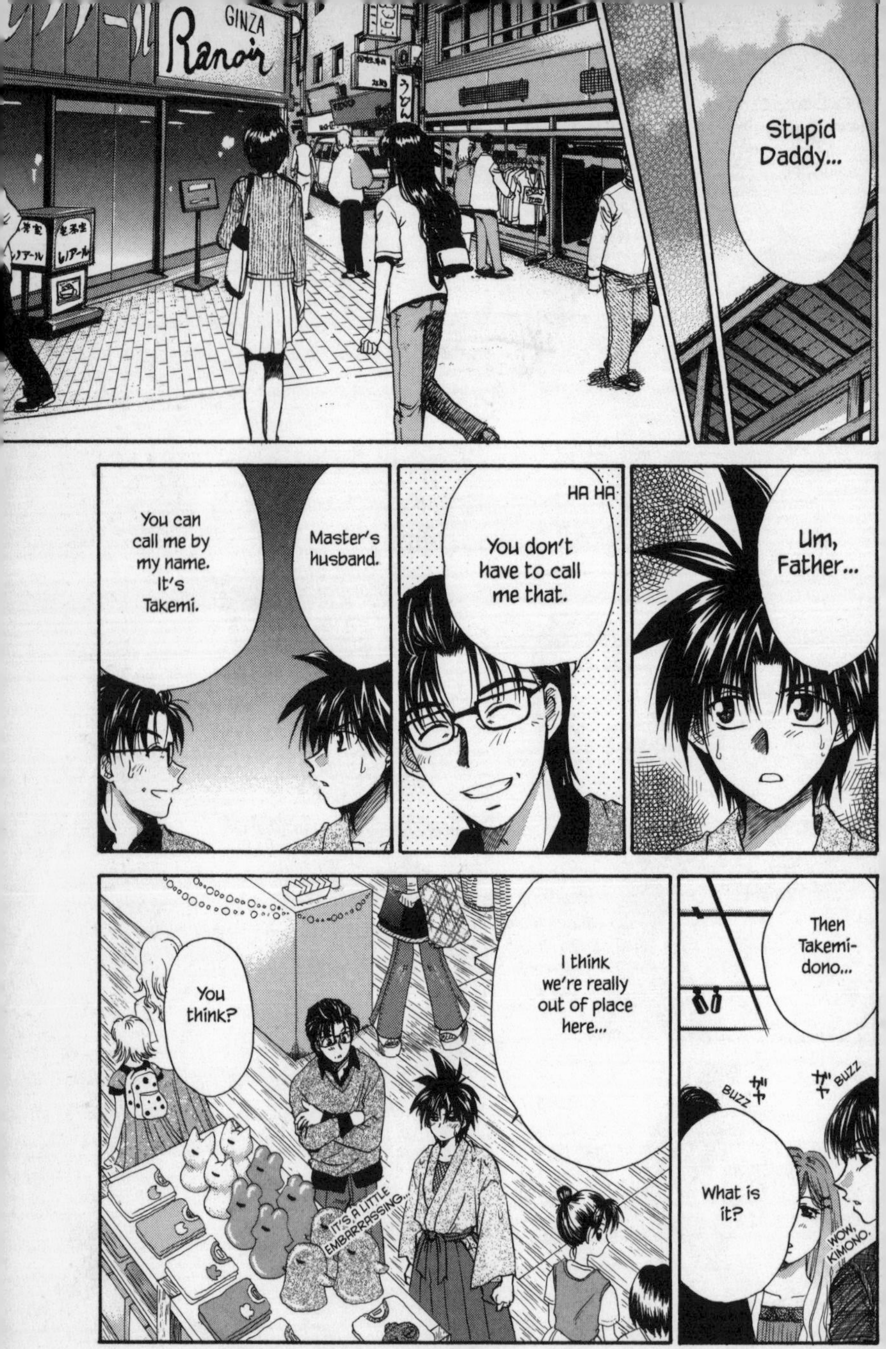
GINZA
Ranoir
Stupid Daddy...
Um, Father...
HA HA
You don't have to call me that.
Master's husband.
You can call me by my name. It's Takemi.
Then Takemi-dono...
BUZZ
BUZZ
WOW, KIMONO.
What is it?
I think we're really out of place here...
IT'S A LITTLE EMBARRASSING...
You think?

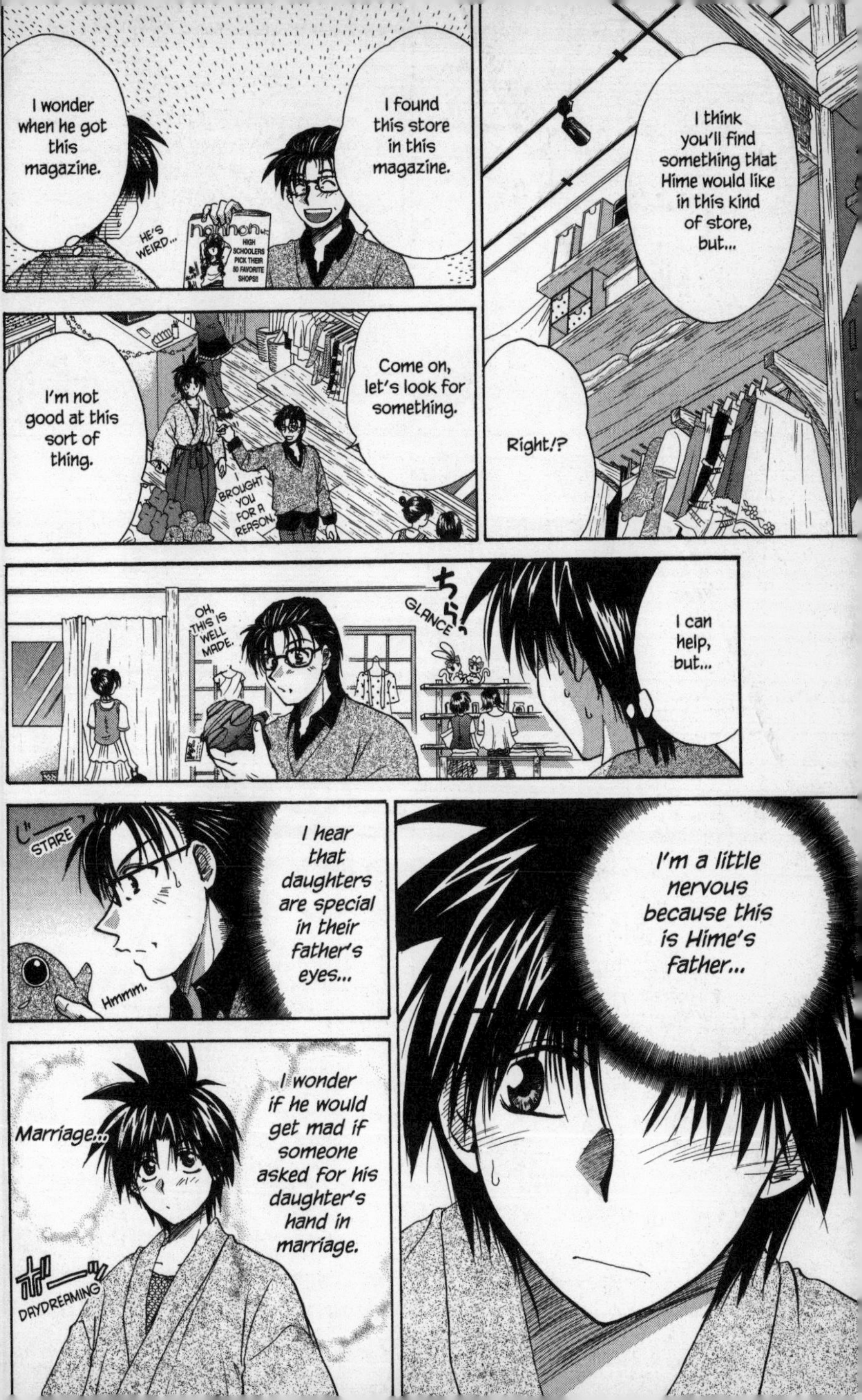

I think you'll find something that Hime would like in this kind of store, but...
Right!?
I found this store in this magazine.
non-no
HIGH SCHOOLERS PICK THEIR 50 FAVORITE SHOPS!!
HE'S WEIRD...
I wonder when he got this magazine.
Come on, let's look for something.
I BROUGHT YOU FOR A REASON.
I'm not good at this sort of thing.
I can help, but...
GLANCE
OH, THIS IS WELL MADE.
I'm a little nervous because this is Hime's father...
I hear that daughters are special in their father's eyes...
STARE
Hmmm.
I wonder if he would get mad if someone asked for his daughter's hand in marriage.
Marriage...
DAYDREAMING

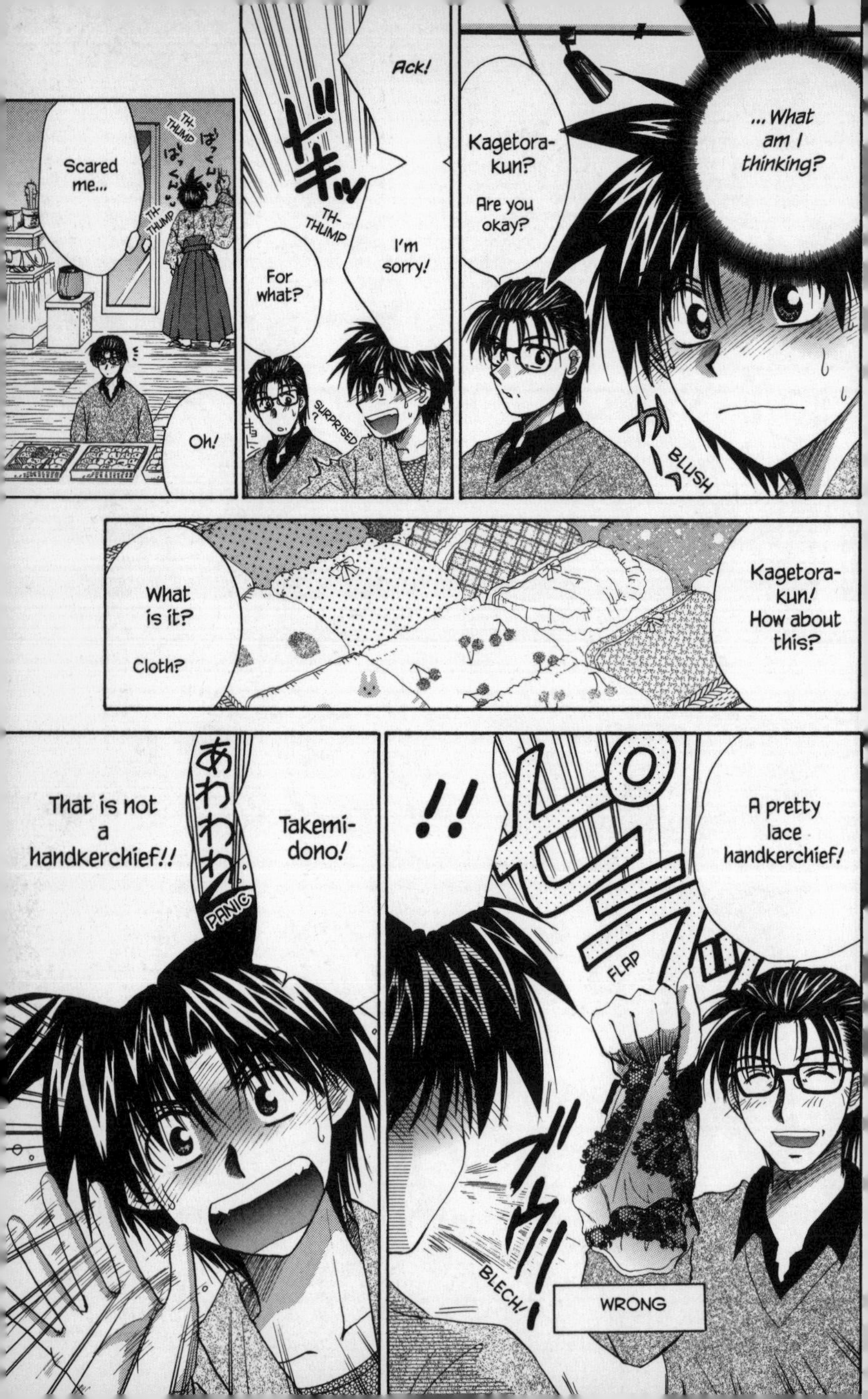
...What am I thinking?
BLUSH
Kagetora-kun?
Are you okay?
Ack!
TH-THUMP
I'm sorry!
For what?
SURPRISED
Scared me...
TH-THUMP
TH-THUMP
Oh!
Kagetora-kun! How about this?
What is it?
Cloth?
A pretty lace handkerchief!
!!
FLAP
BLECH!
WRONG
Takemi-dono!
あわわわ
PANIC
That is not a handkerchief!!

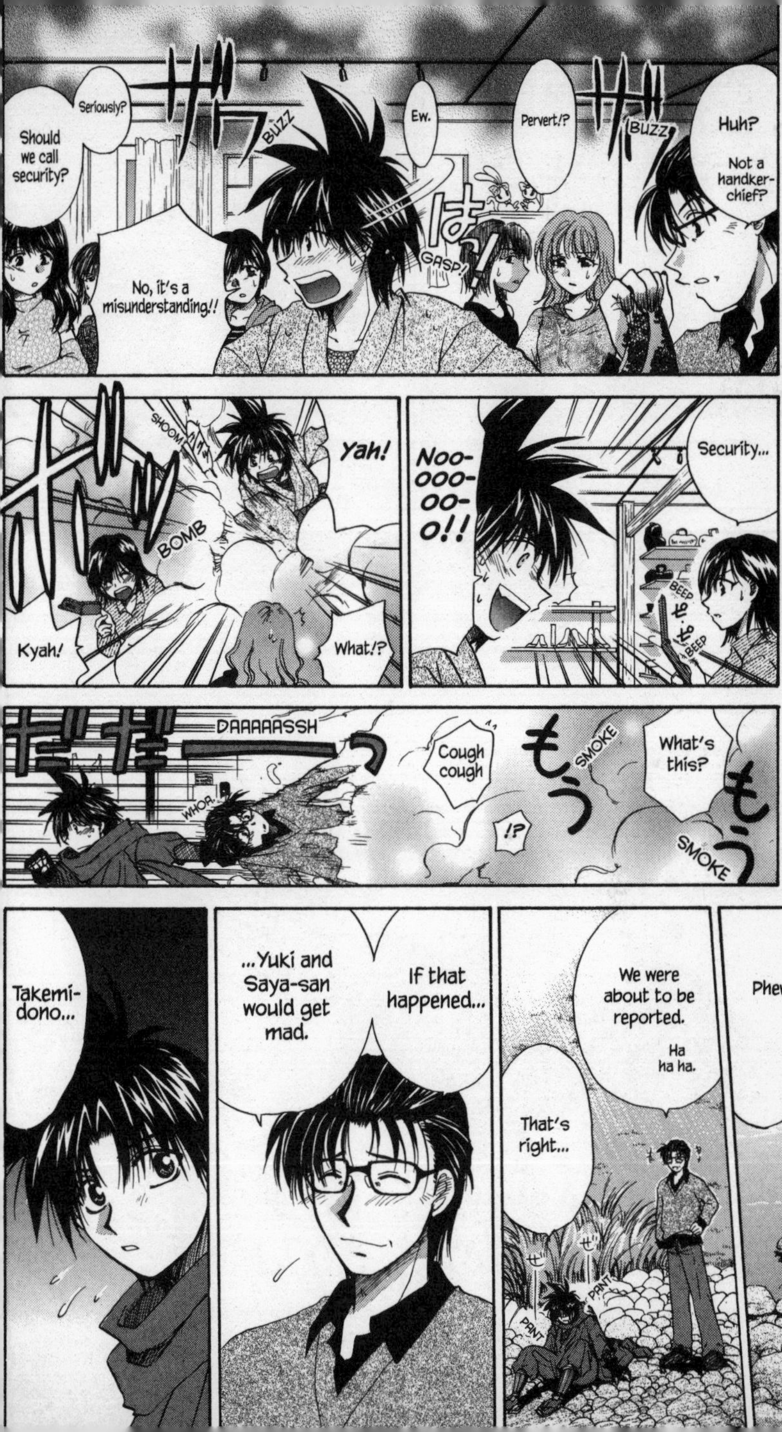
Huh?
Not a handker-chief?
BUZZ
Pervert!?
Ew.
GASP!
BUZZ
Seriously?
Should we call security?
No, it's a misunderstanding!!
Security...
BEEP
BEEP
Noo-ooo-oo-o!!
Yah!
SHOOM
BOMB
What!?
Kyah!
What's this?
SMOKE
SMOKE
!?
Cough cough
DAAAAASSH
Phew.
We were about to be reported.
Ha ha ha.
That's right...
PANT
PANT
If that happened...
...Yuki and Saya-san would get mad.
Takemi-dono...

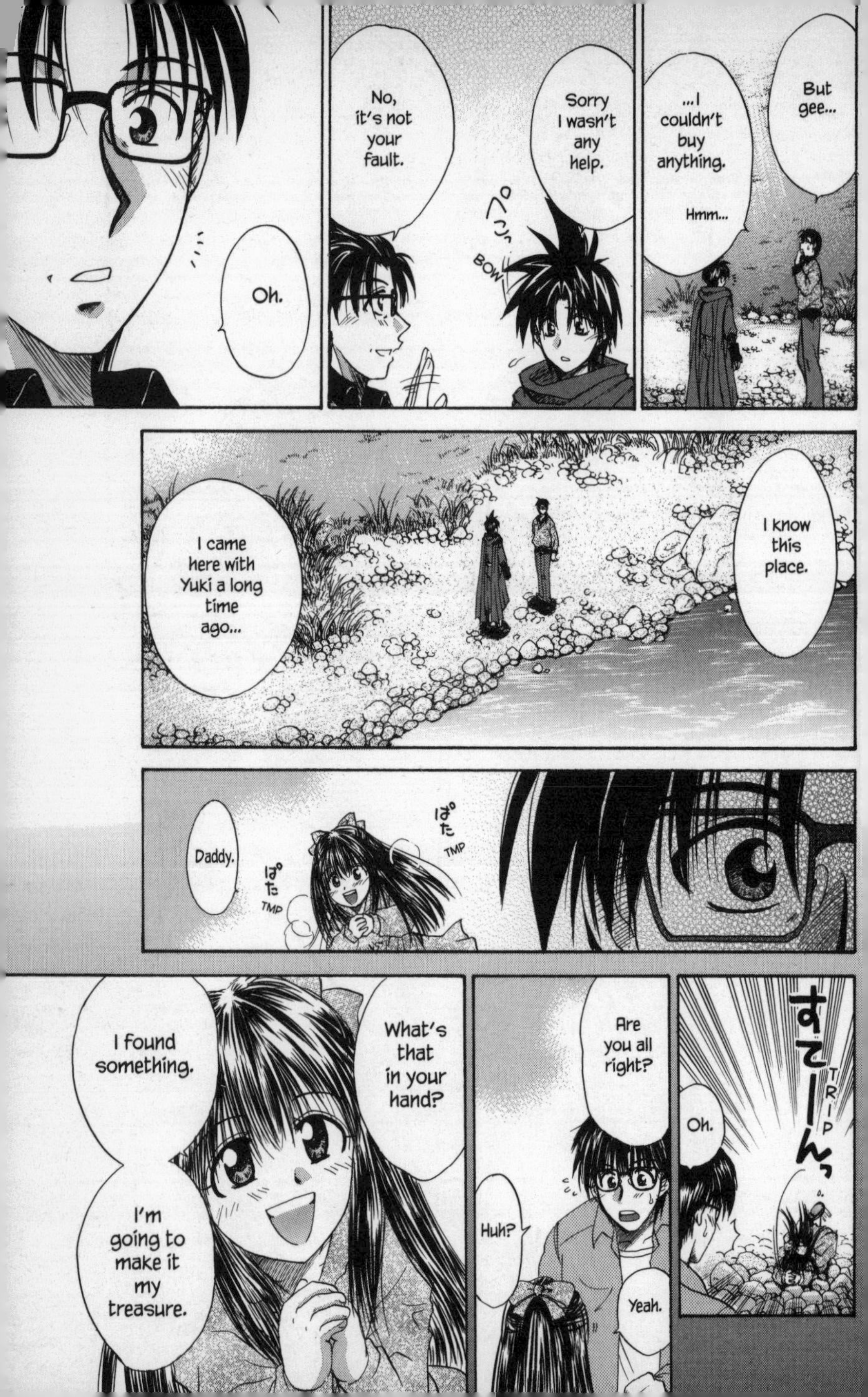
But gee...
...I couldn't buy anything.
Hmm...
Sorry I wasn't any help.
ぺこっ
BOW
No, it's not your fault.
Oh.
I know this place.
I came here with Yuki a long time ago...
ぱた
TMP
Daddy.
ぱた
TMP
すてーん
TRIP
Oh.
Are you all right?
Huh?
Yeah.
What's that in your hand?
I found something.
I'm going to make it my treasure.

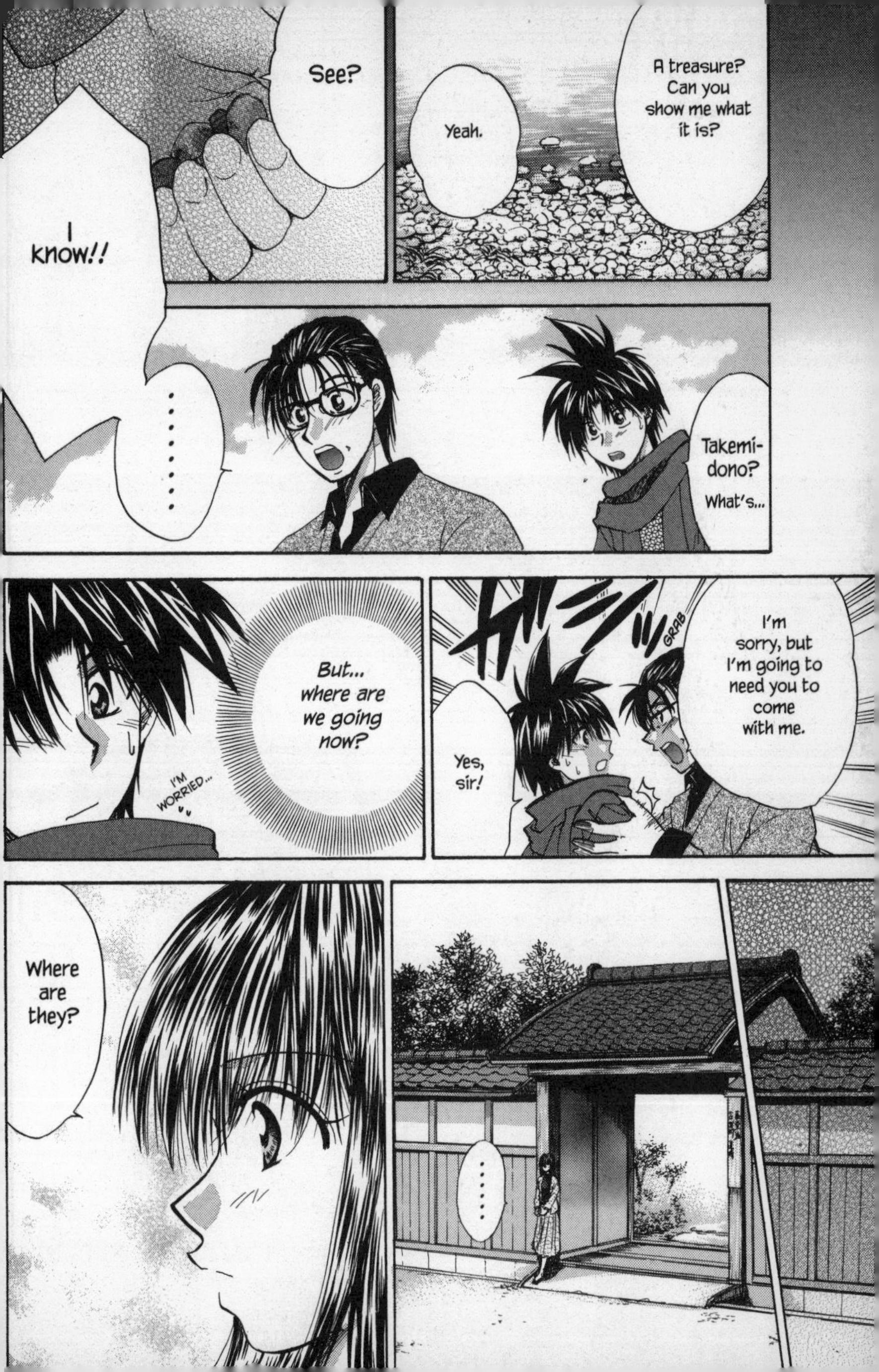
A treasure? Can you show me what it is?
Yeah.
See?
I know!!
Takemi-dono? What's...
......
GRAB
I'm sorry, but I'm going to need you to come with me.
Yes, sir!
But... where are we going now?
I'M WORRIED...
......
Where are they?

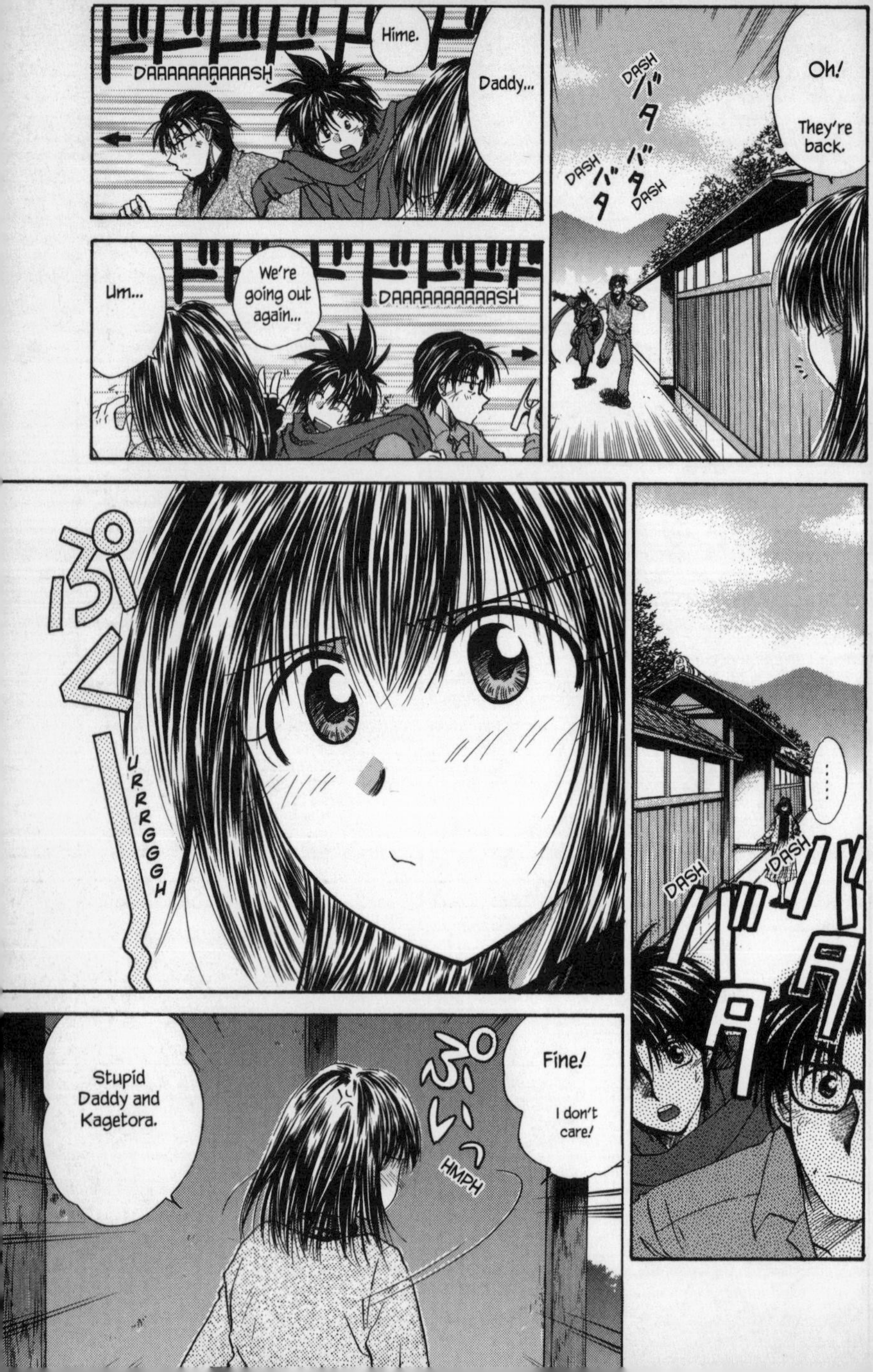
Oh!
They're back.
DASH
DASH
DASH
Daddy...
Hime.
DAAAAAAAAAAASH
We're going out again...
Um...
DAAAAAAAAAAASH
......
DASH
DASH
URRRGGGH
Fine!
I don't care!
HMPH
Stupid Daddy and Kagetora.

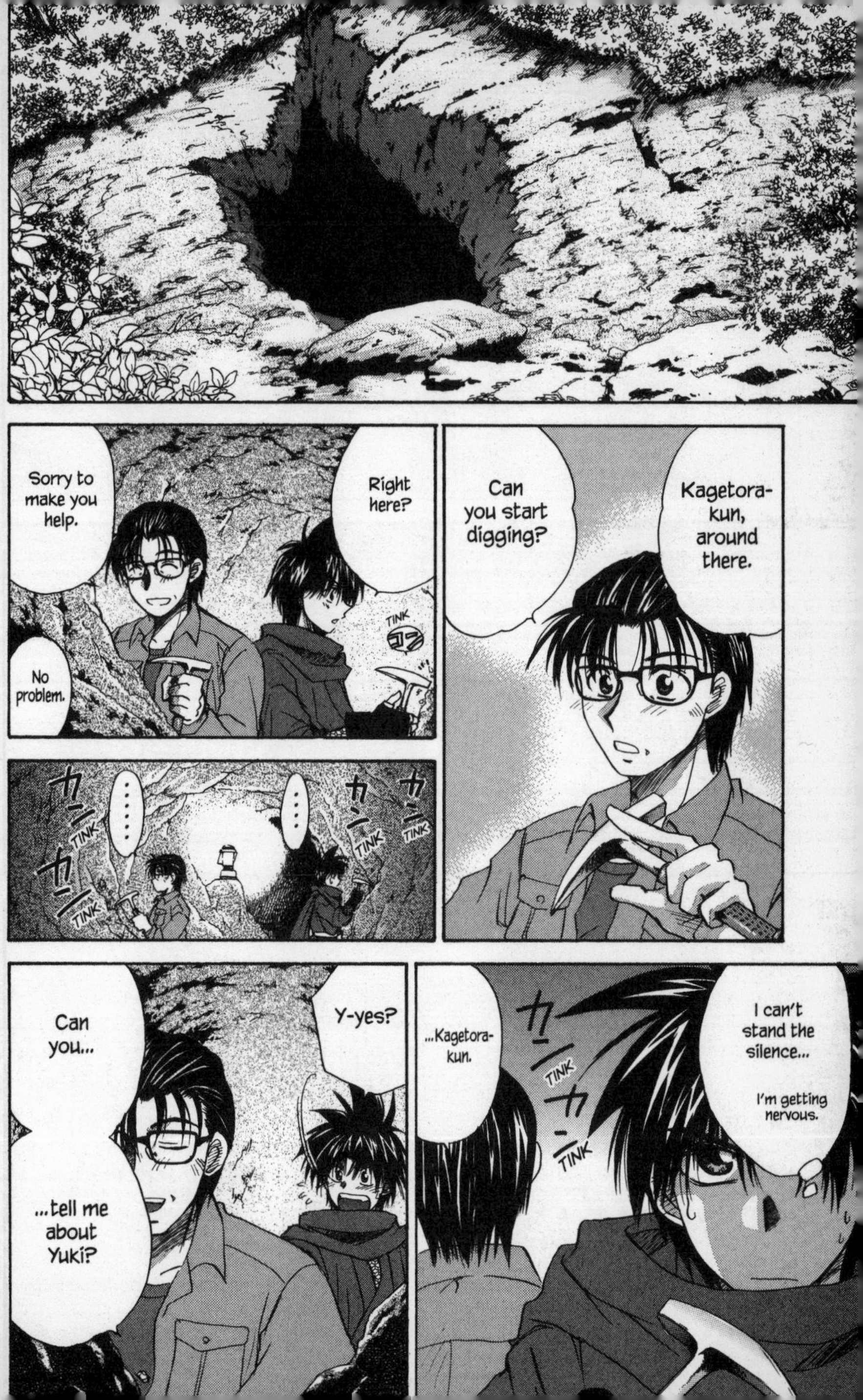
Kagetora-kun, around there.
Can you start digging?
Right here?
TINK
Sorry to make you help.
No problem.
TINK
.....
TINK
.....
TINK
I can't stand the silence...
I'm getting nervous.
...Kagetora-kun.
TINK
TINK
Y-yes?
Can you...
...tell me about Yuki?

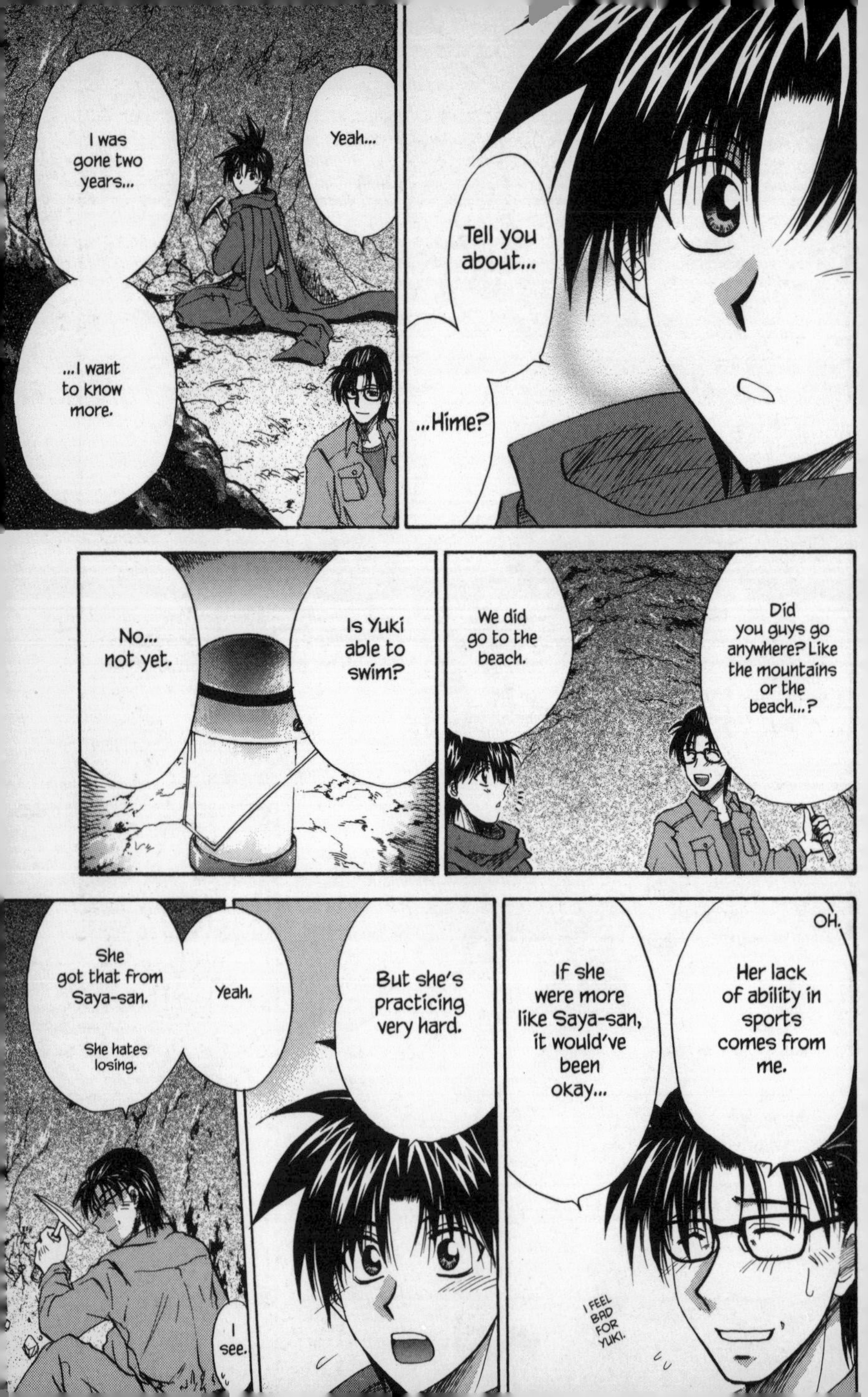
Tell you about...
...Hime?
Yeah...
I was gone two years...
...I want to know more.
Did you guys go anywhere? Like the mountains or the beach...?
We did go to the beach.
Is Yuki able to swim?
No... not yet.
OH.
Her lack of ability in sports comes from me.
If she were more like Saya-san, it would've been okay...
I FEEL BAD FOR YUKI.
But she's practicing very hard.
Yeah.
She got that from Saya-san.
She hates losing.
I see.

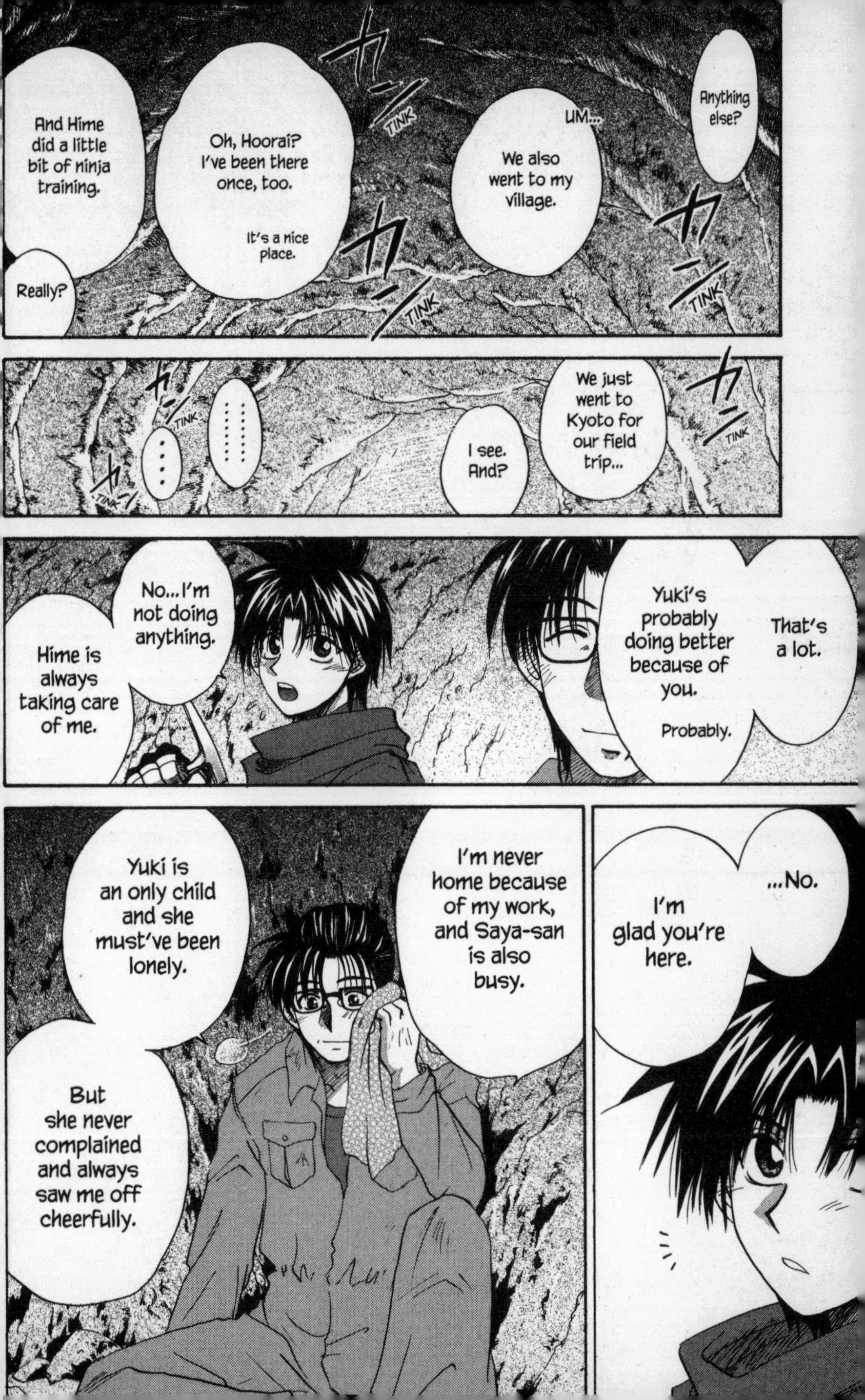
Anything else?
TINK
UM...
We also went to my village.
TINK
Oh, Hoorai? I've been there once, too.
It's a nice place.
TINK
And Hime did a little bit of ninja training.
Really?
TINK
We just went to Kyoto for our field trip...
I see. And?
......
TINK
...
TINK
That's a lot.
Yuki's probably doing better because of you.
Probably.
No...I'm not doing anything.
Hime is always taking care of me.
...No.
I'm glad you're here.
I'm never home because of my work, and Saya-san is also busy.
Yuki is an only child and she must've been lonely.
But she never complained and always saw me off cheerfully.

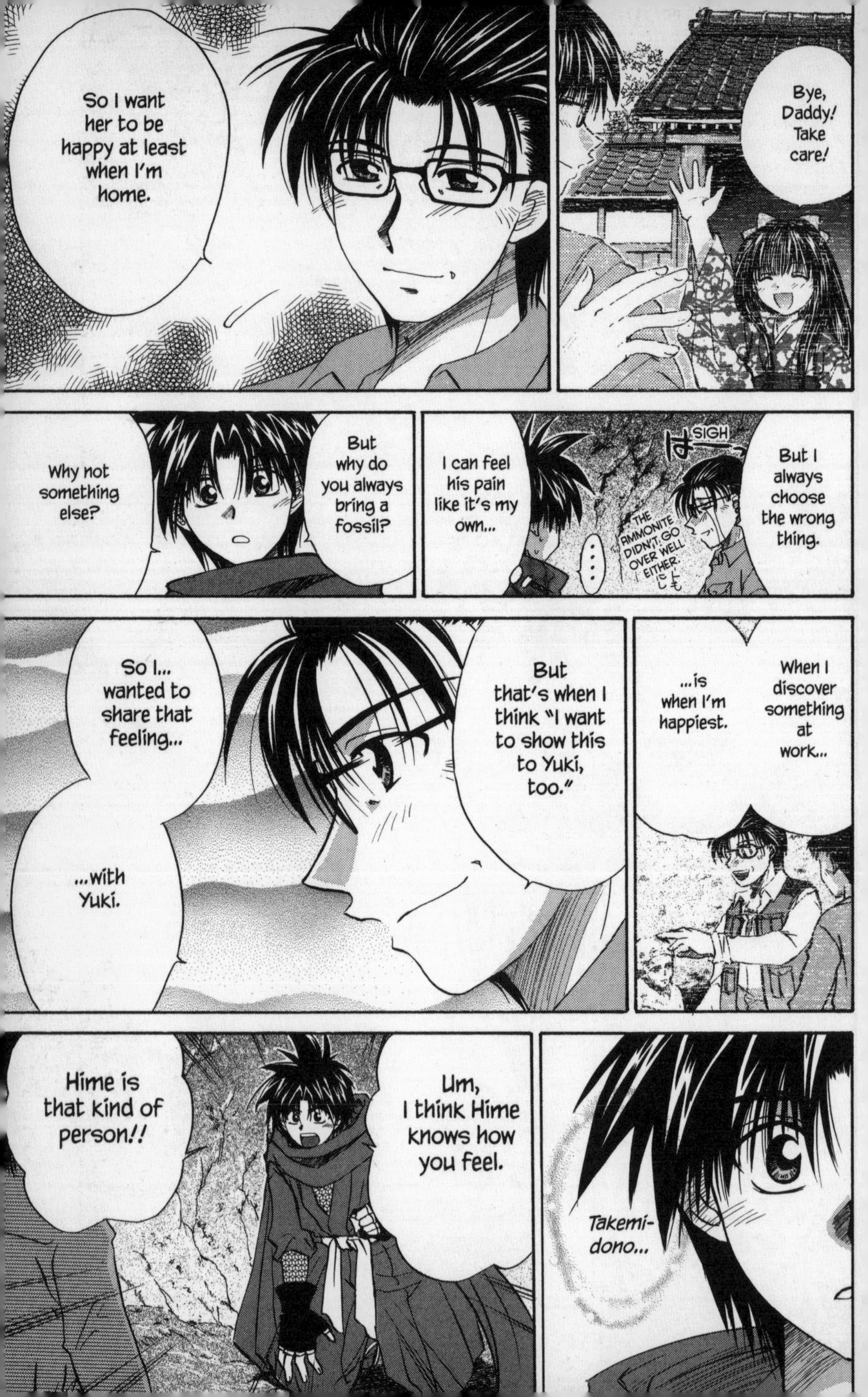
Bye, Daddy! Take care!
So I want her to be happy at least when I'm home.
SIGH
But I always choose the wrong thing.
THE AMMONITE DIDN'T GO OVER WELL EITHER.
...
I can feel his pain like it's my own...
But why do you always bring a fossil?
Why not something else?
When I discover something at work...
...is when I'm happiest.
But that's when I think "I want to show this to Yuki, too."
So I... wanted to share that feeling...
...with Yuki.
Takemi-dono...
Um, I think Hime knows how you feel.
Hime is that kind of person!!

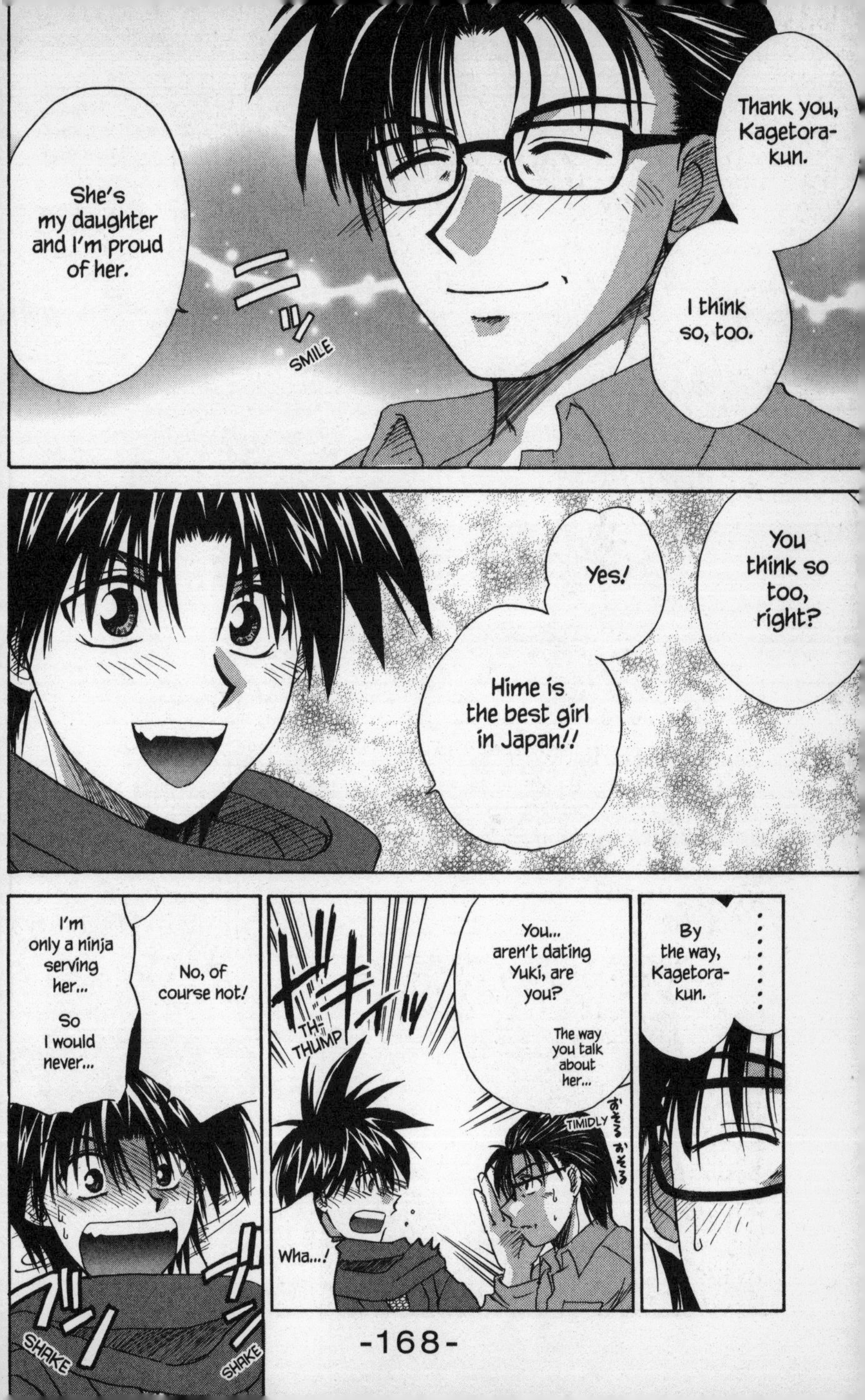
Thank you, Kagetora-kun.
I think so, too.
SMILE
She's my daughter and I'm proud of her.
You think so too, right?
Yes!
Hime is the best girl in Japan!!
By the way, Kagetora-kun.
......
You... aren't dating Yuki, are you?
The way you talk about her...
TIMIDLY
TH-THUMP
Wha...!
No, of course not!
I'm only a ninja serving her...
So I would never...
SHAKE
SHAKE

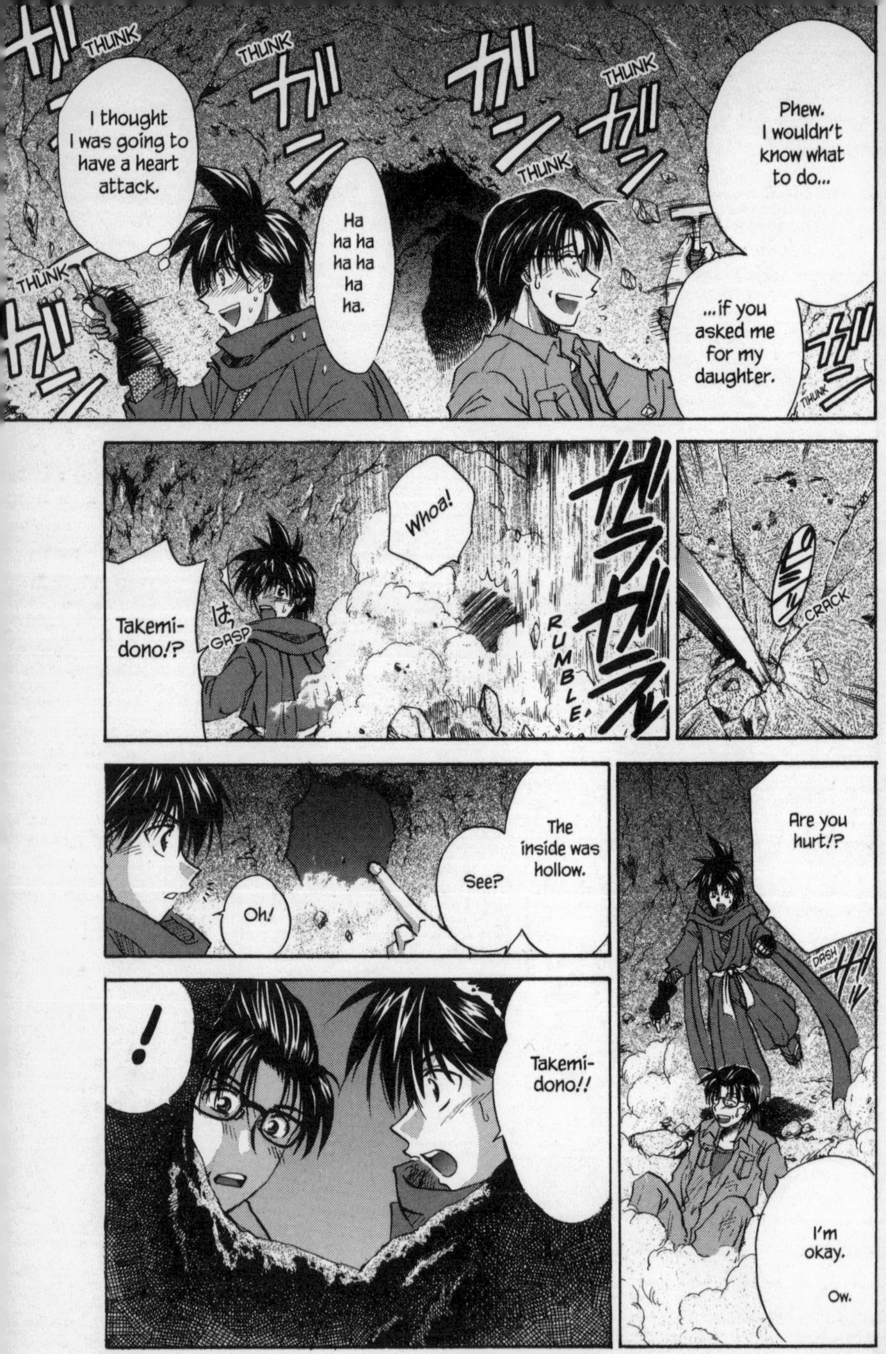
THUNK
THUNK
Phew. I wouldn't know what to do...
...if you asked me for my daughter.
THUNK
THUNK
Ha ha ha ha ha ha ha.
THUNK
I thought I was going to have a heart attack.
THUNK
CRACK
RUMBLE
Whoa!
GASP
Takemi-dono!?
Are you hurt!?
DASH
I'm okay.
Ow.
The inside was hollow.
See?
Oh!
Takemi-dono!!
!

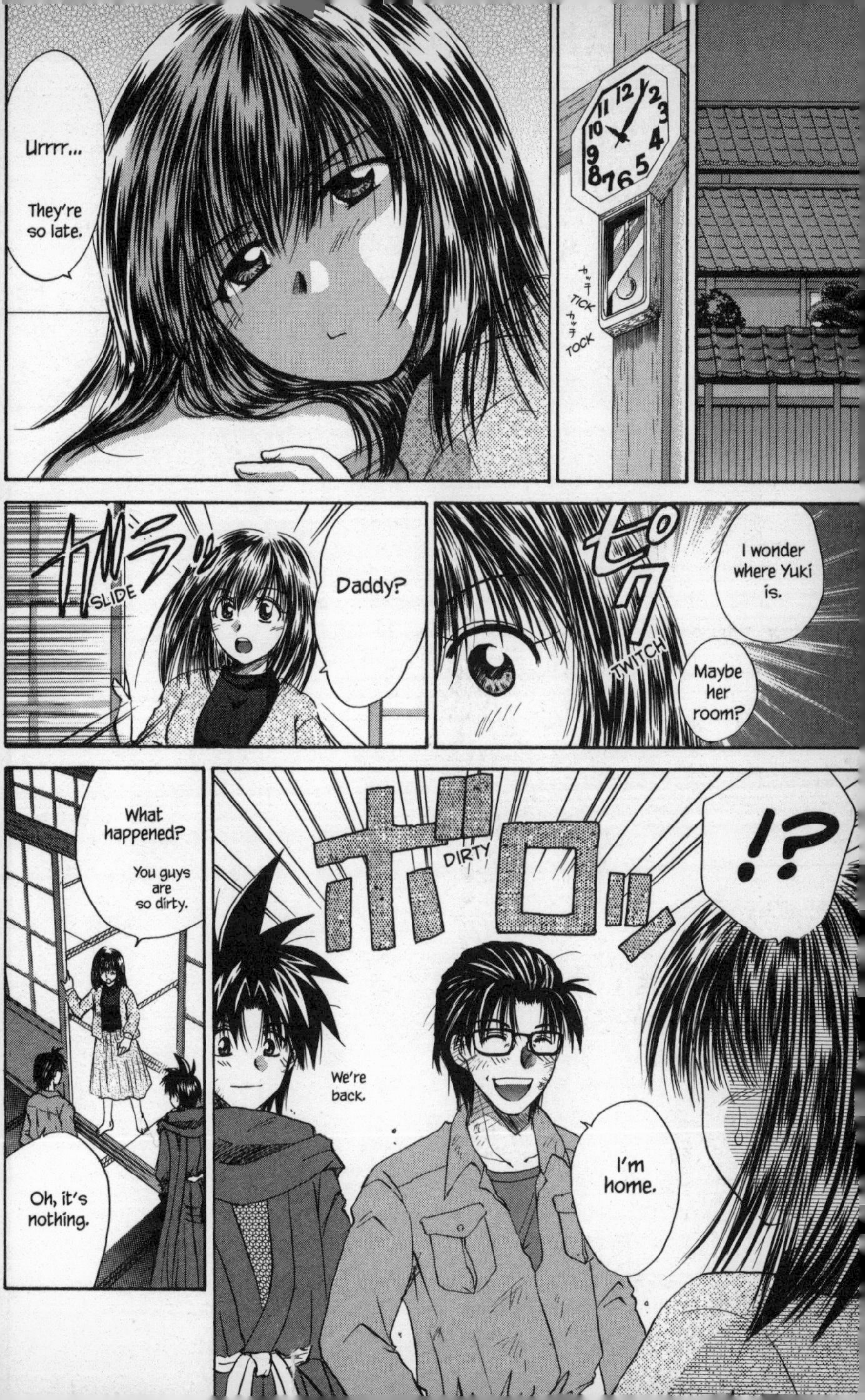
TICK
TOCK
Urrrr...
They're so late.
TWITCH
I wonder where Yuki is.
Maybe her room?
SLIDE
Daddy?
!?
DIRTY
I'm home.
We're back.
What happened?
You guys are so dirty.
Oh, it's nothing.

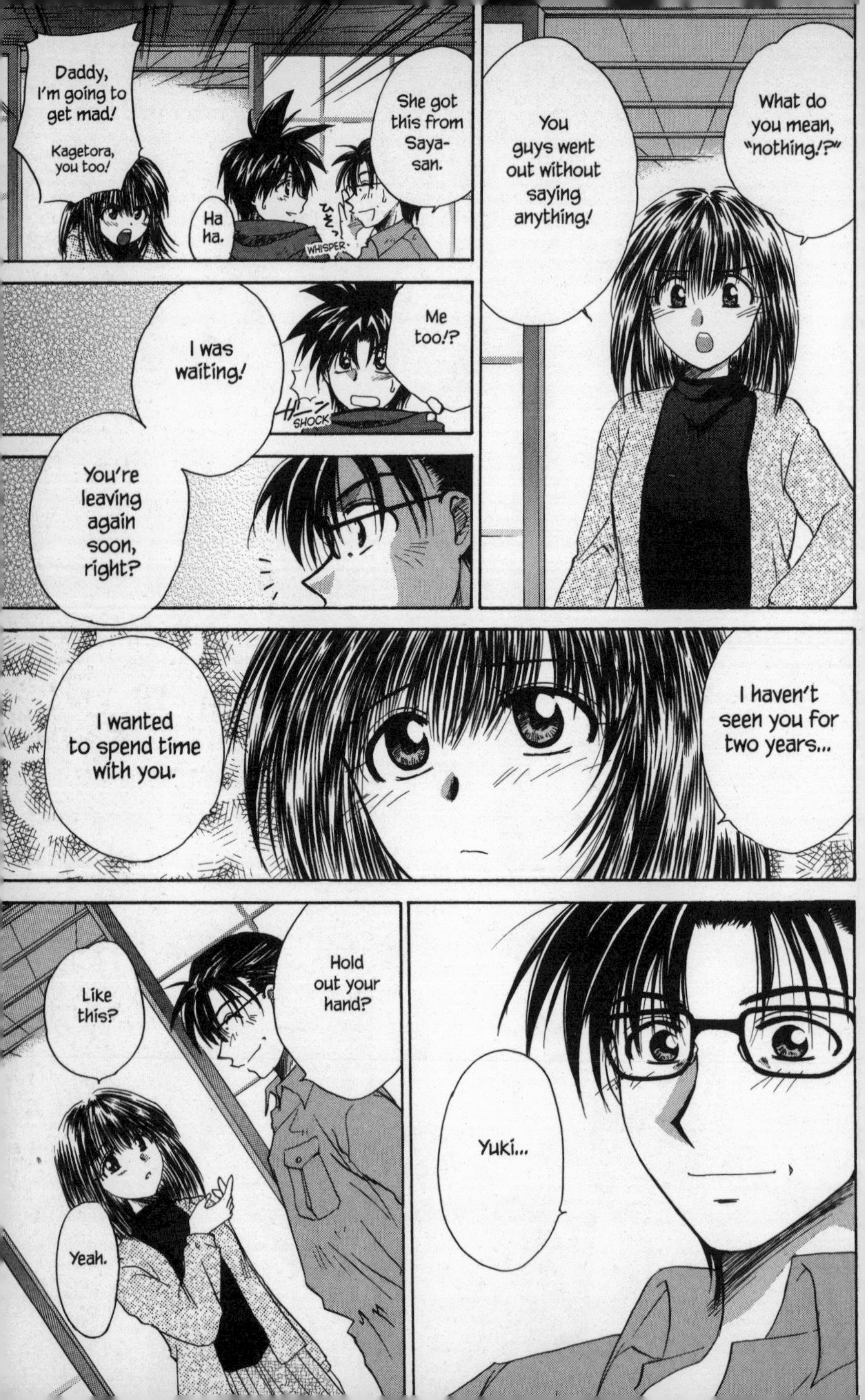
What do you mean, "nothing!?"
You guys went out without saying anything!
She got this from Saya-san.
WHISPER
Ha ha.
Daddy, I'm going to get mad!
Kagetora, you too!
Me too!?
SHOCK
I was waiting!
You're leaving again soon, right?
I haven't seen you for two years...
I wanted to spend time with you.
Yuki...
Hold out your hand?
Like this?
Yeah.

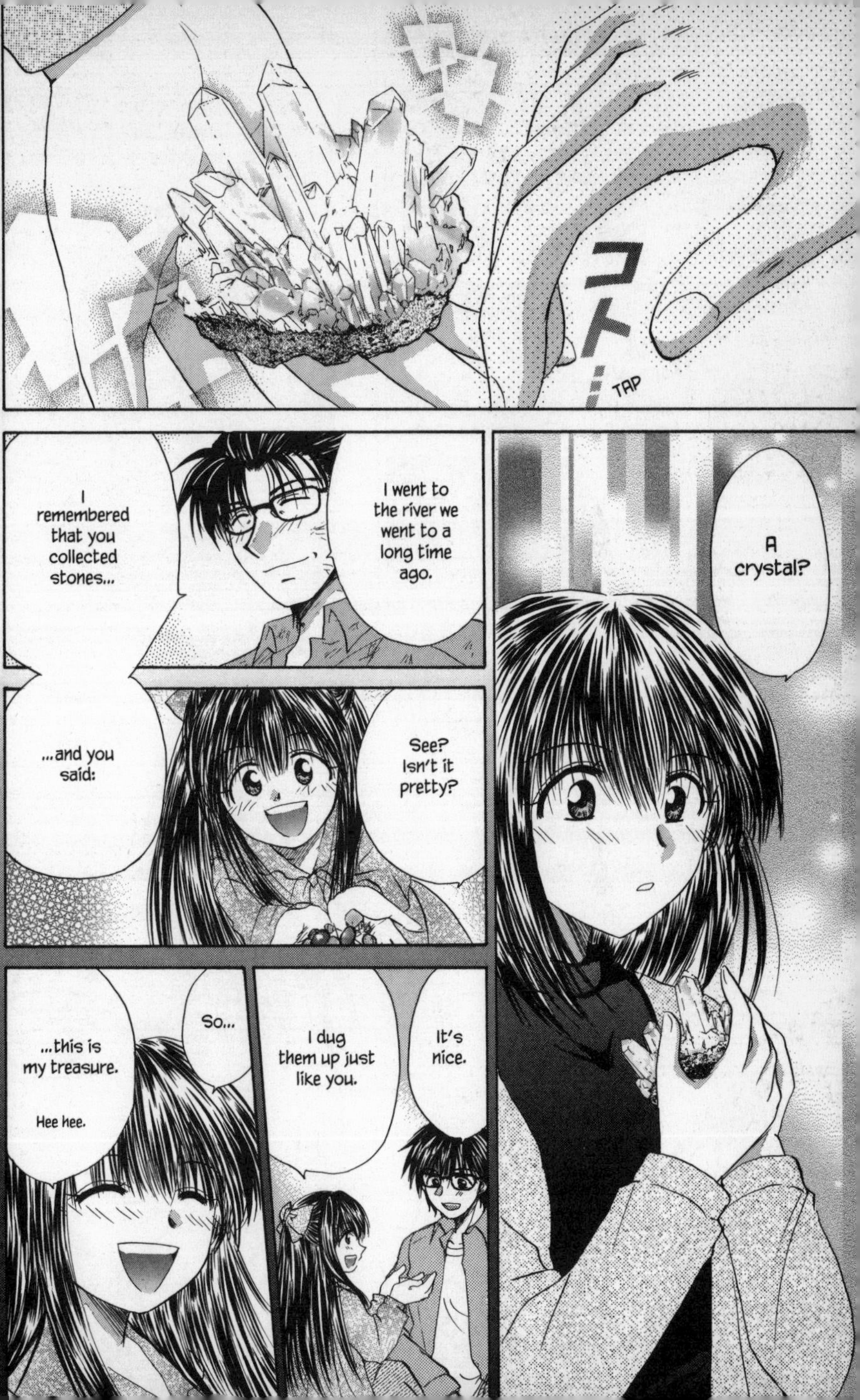
コト…
TAP
A crystal?
I went to the river we went to a long time ago.
I remembered that you collected stones...
See? Isn't it pretty?
...and you said:
It's nice.
I dug them up just like you.
So...
...this is my treasure.
Hee hee.

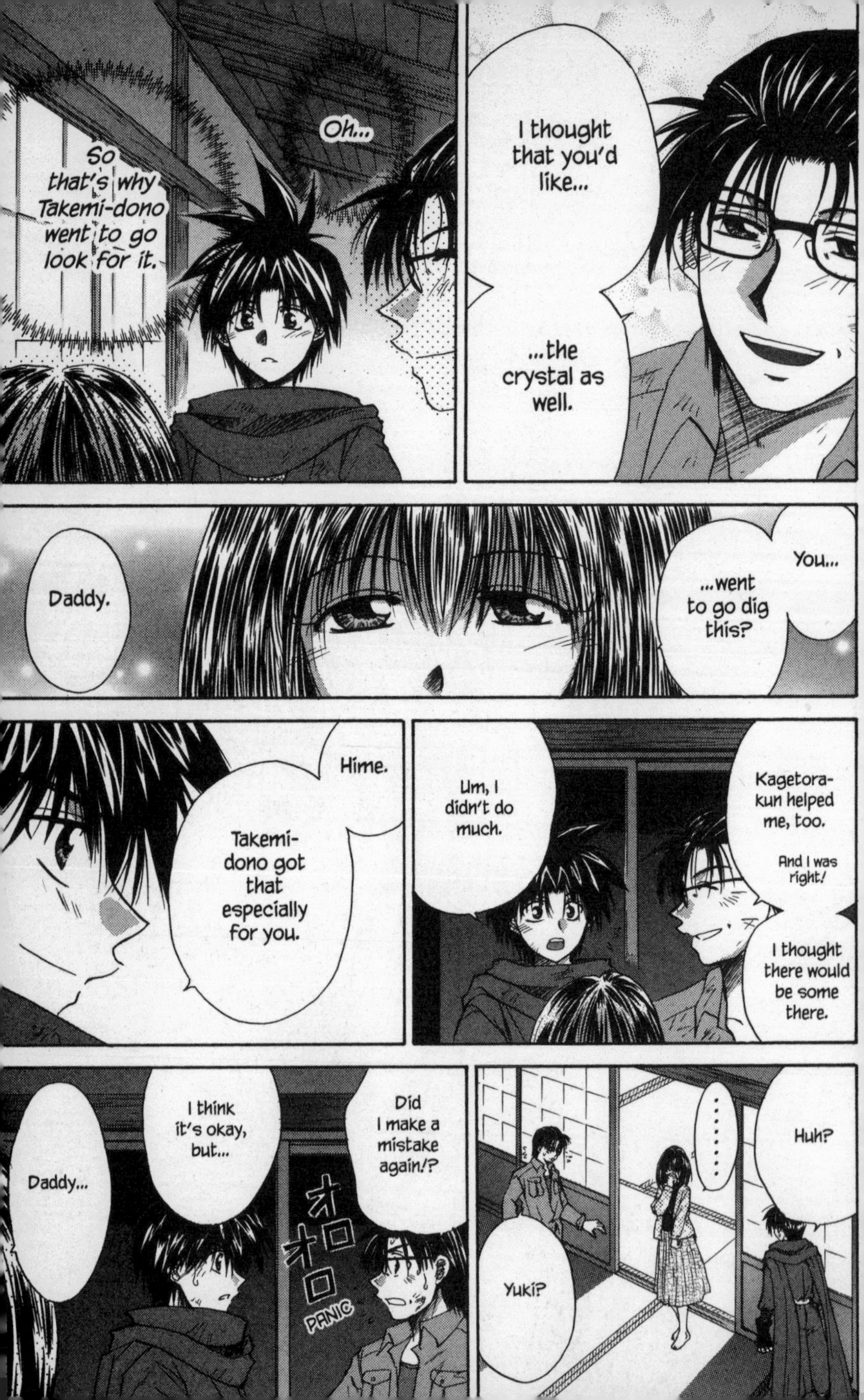
I thought that you'd like...
...the crystal as well.
Oh...
So that's why Takemi-dono went to go look for it.
You...
...went to go dig this?
Daddy.
Kagetora-kun helped me, too.
And I was right!
I thought there would be some there.
Um, I didn't do much.
Hime.
Takemi-dono got that especially for you.
Huh?
......
Yuki?
Did I make a mistake again!?
オロオロ
PANIC
I think it's okay, but...
Daddy...

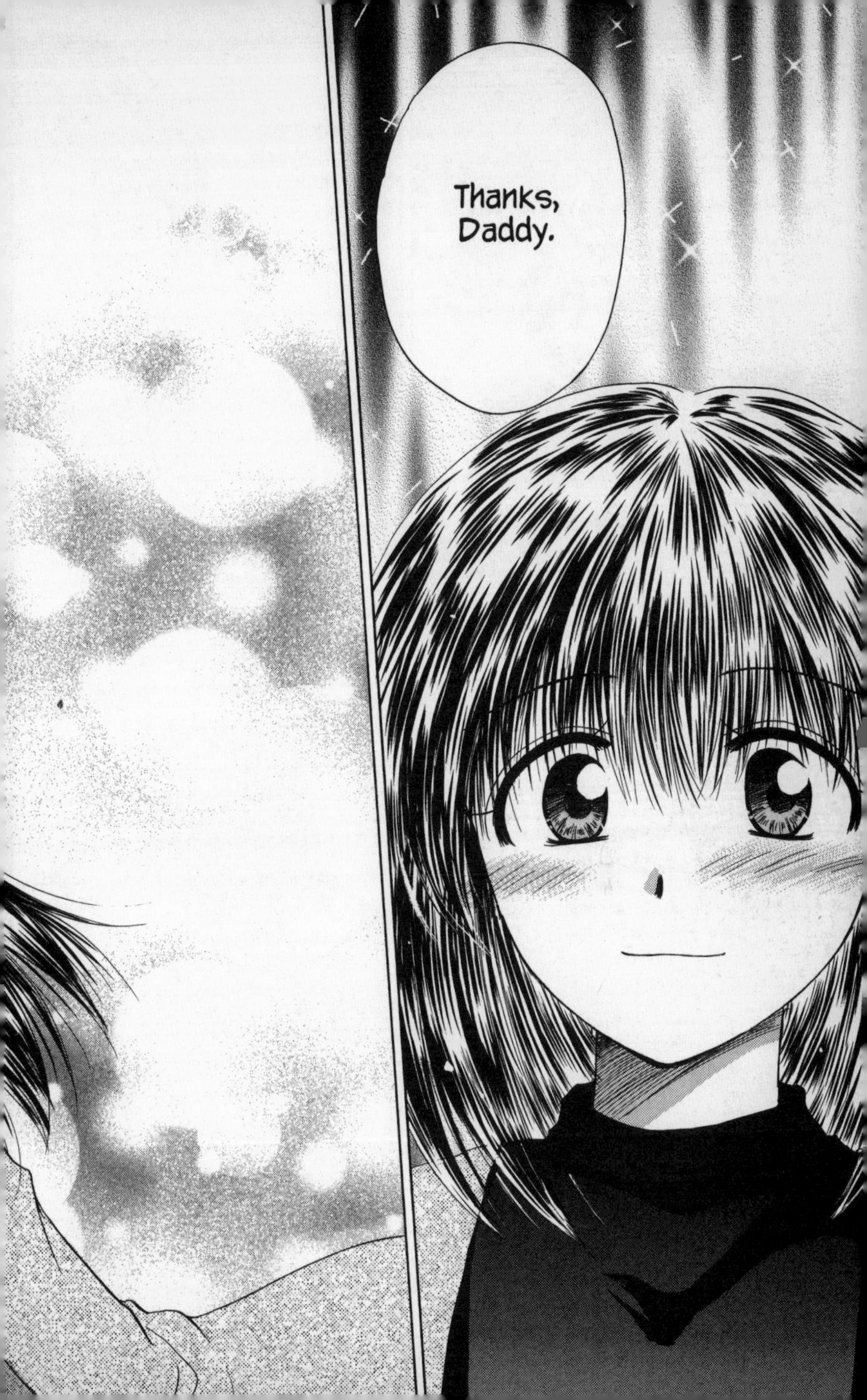
Thanks, Daddy.

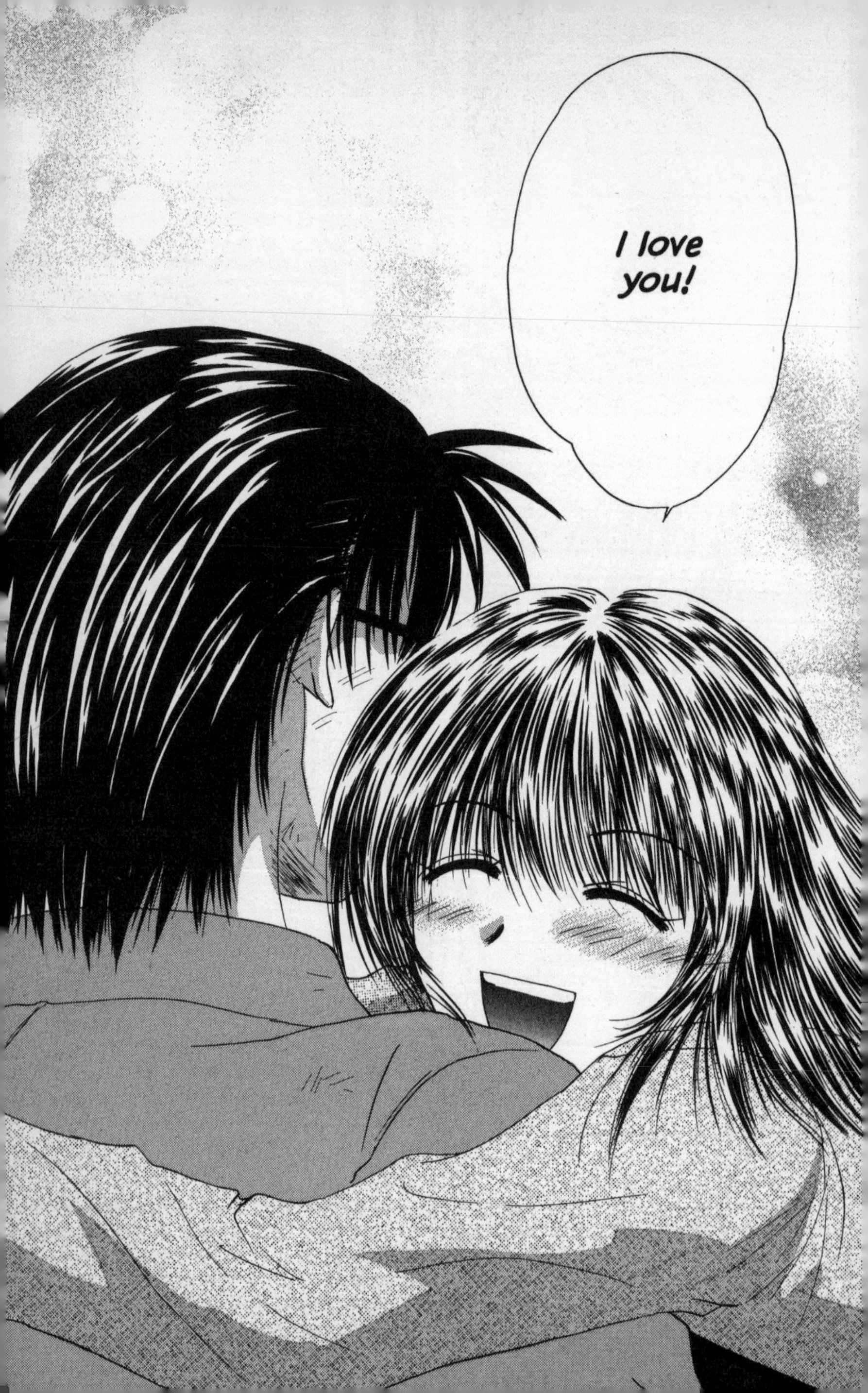
I love you!

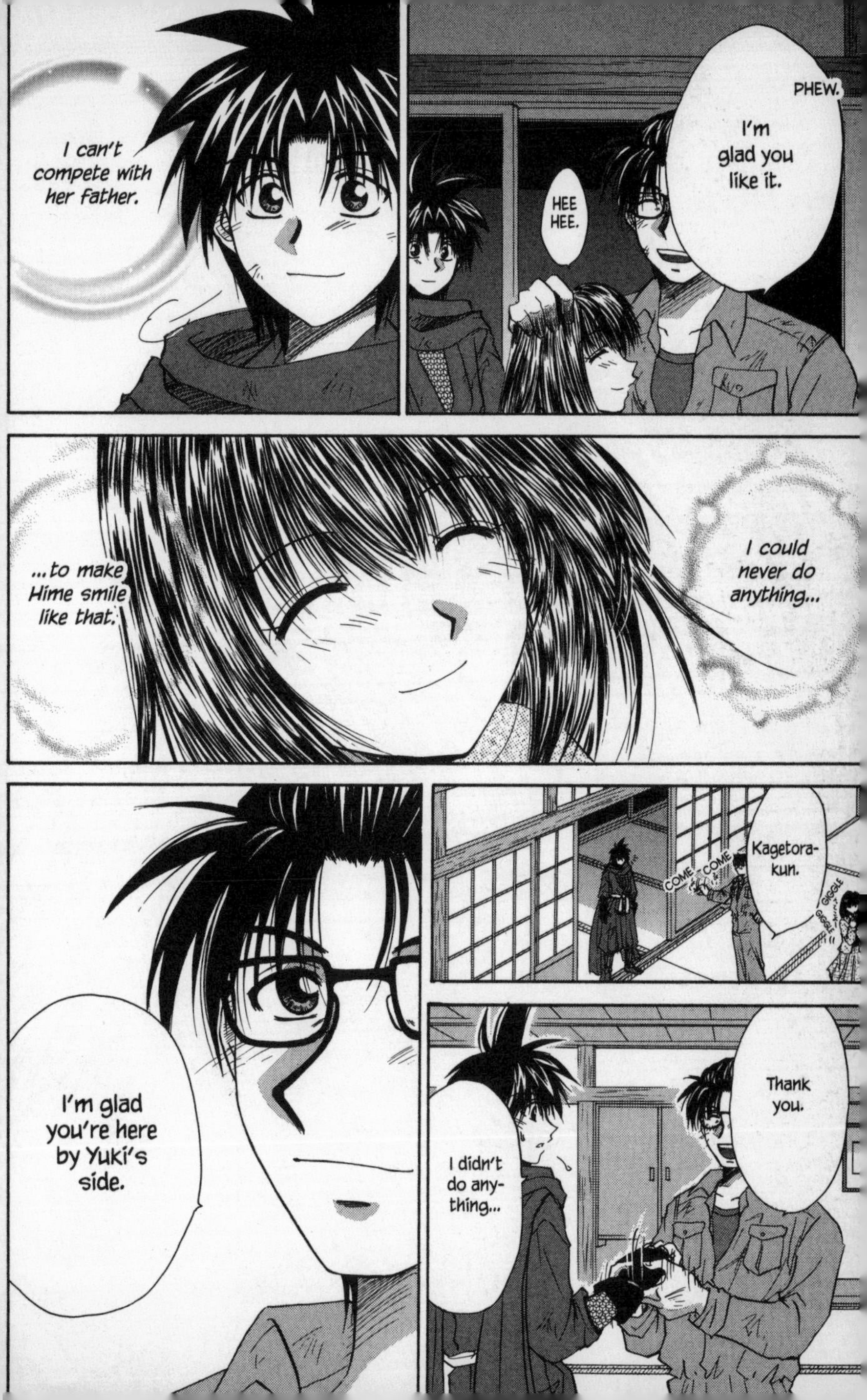
PHEW.
I'm glad you like it.
HEE HEE.
I can't compete with her father.
I could never do anything...
...to make Hime smile like that.
Kagetora-kun.
COME COME
GIGGLE GIGGLE
Thank you.
I didn't do anything...
I'm glad you're here by Yuki's side.

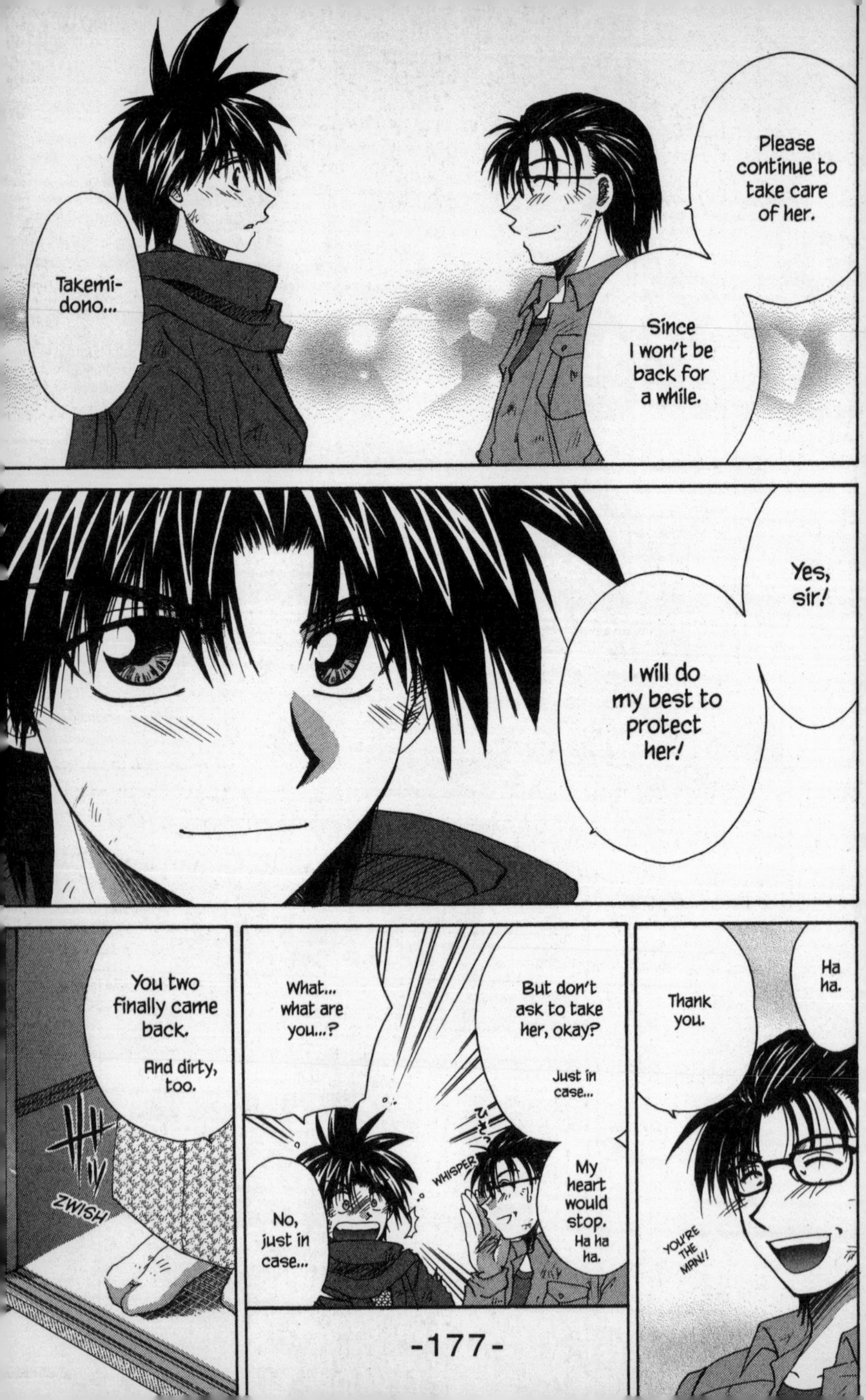
Please continue to take care of her.
Since I won't be back for a while.
Takemi-dono...
Yes, sir!
I will do my best to protect her!
Ha ha.
Thank you.
YOU'RE THE MAN!!
But don't ask to take her, okay?
Just in case...
WHISPER
What... what are you...?
No, just in case...
My heart would stop.
Ha ha ha.
You two finally came back.
And dirty, too.
ZWISH

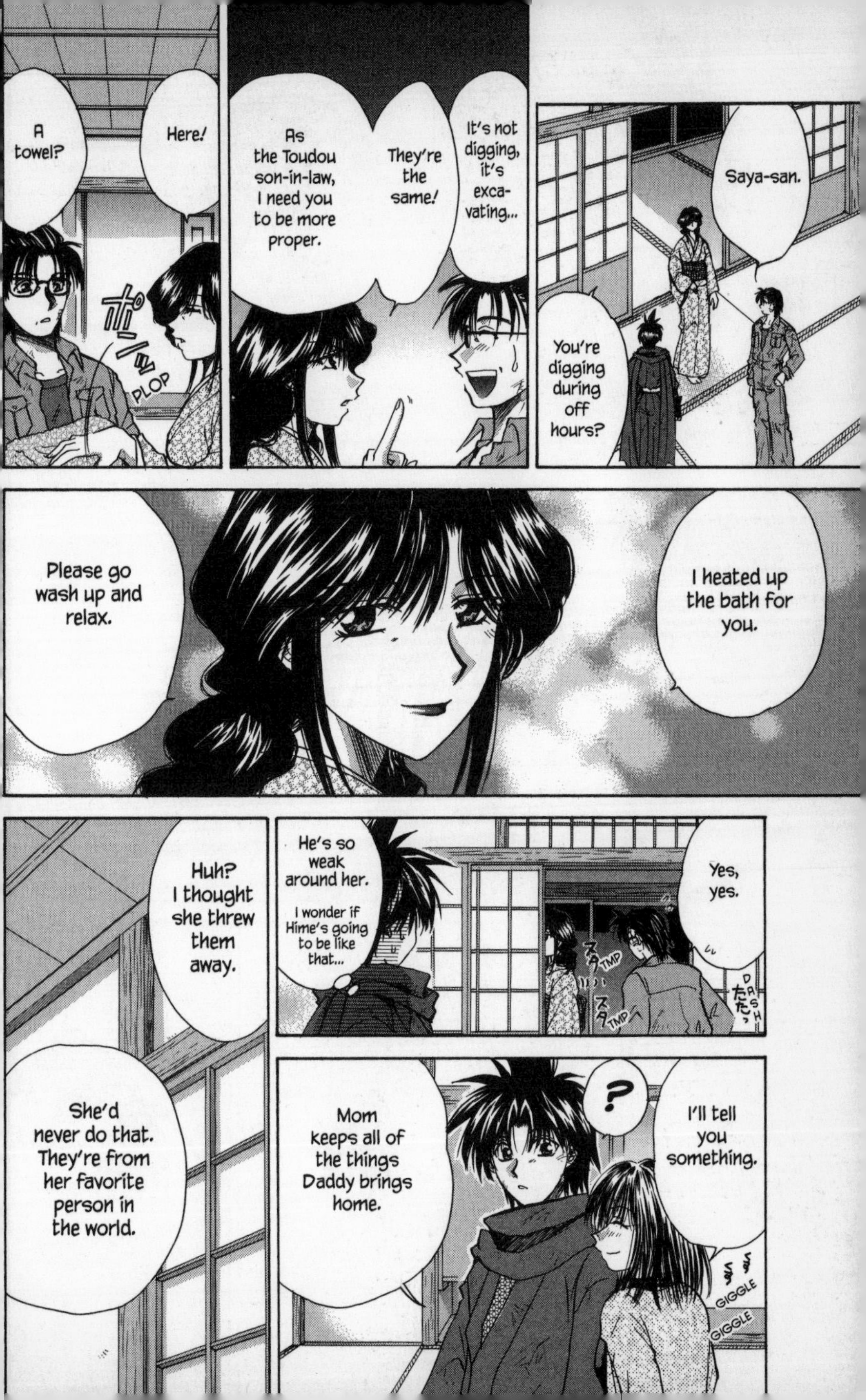
Saya-san.
You're digging during off hours?
It's not digging, it's excavating...
They're the same!
As the Toudou son-in-law, I need you to be more proper.
Here!
A towel?
PLOP
I heated up the bath for you.
Please go wash up and relax.
Yes, yes.
TMP
TMP
DASH
He's so weak around her.
I wonder if Hime's going to be like that...
I'll tell you something.
?
Mom keeps all of the things Daddy brings home.
GIGGLE
GIGGLE
Huh? I thought she threw them away.
She'd never do that. They're from her favorite person in the world.

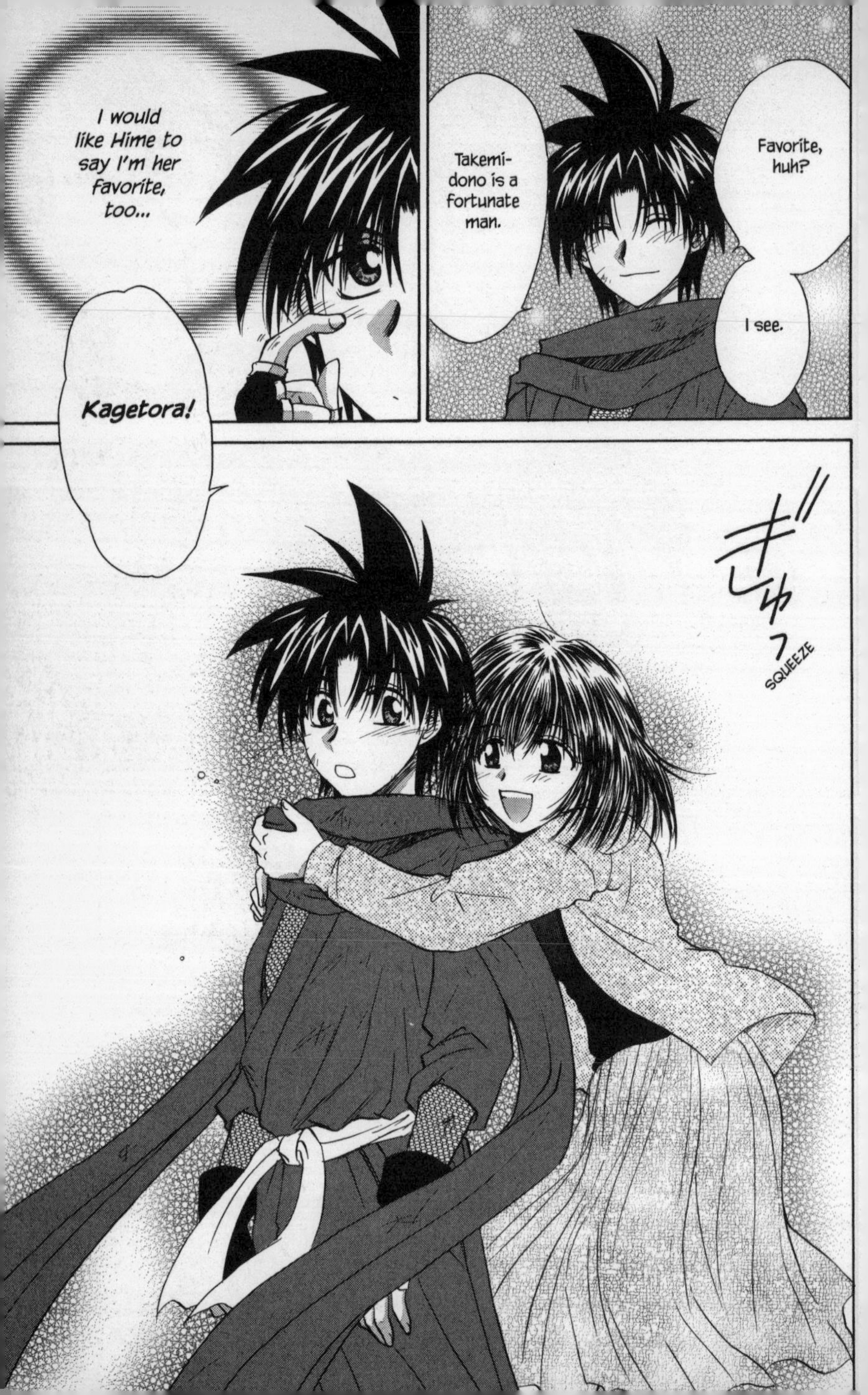
Favorite, huh?
I see.
Takemi-dono is a fortunate man.
I would like Hime to say I'm her favorite, too...
Kagetora!
ぎしゅっ
SQUEEZE

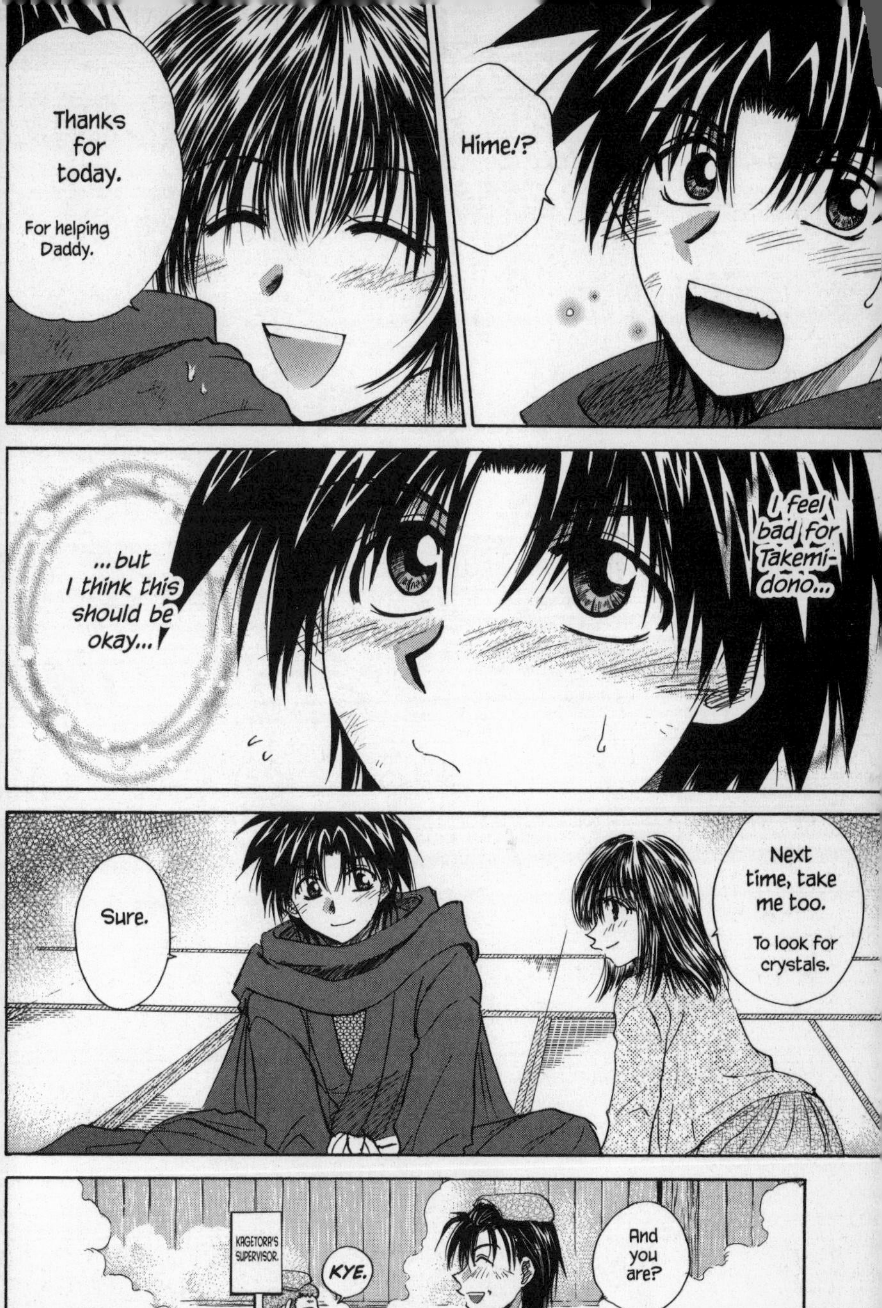
Hime!?
Thanks for today.
For helping Daddy.
I feel bad for Takemi-dono...
...but I think this should be okay...
Next time, take me too.
To look for crystals.
Sure.
And you are?
KAGETORA'S SUPERVISOR.
KYE.

To be continued in volume six.

Bonus Page

This is **Segami**. It's already volume 5. This is to thank all of you readers. To express my gratitude, I will work hard to include more bonus pages. This time there are 4-panel comics, too.

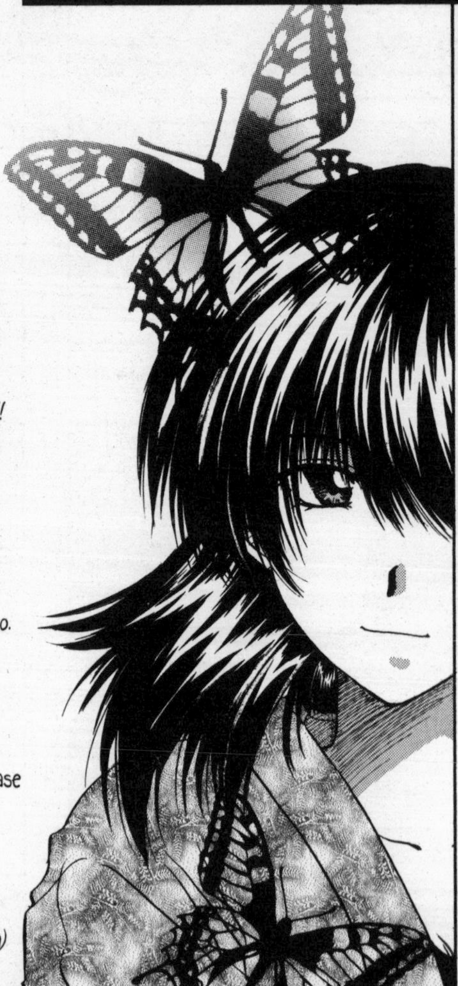

o About Ninjas- Part 5
Actually, I haven't been going anywhere ninja related. I would like to go to Nikkou Edo Village...When I'm taking pictures, the ninjas just pop in within the frame there... And that's part of the fun. *(laugh)*

o About Traveling
I talk about it in the 4 panel comic too, but I went to Hida! This time my main purpose was not Sarubobo... This time I went to eat Hida beef! It was really good. Lately I have a feeling that I'm traveling only to eat. Oh no... But I took my work!! I took many pictures that don't have me in them, too... which is sad, really.

o About Weapons - Part 3
There's more. I won't make any excuses... this is my hobby!! Of course, I use them as reference, too.

o Thanks
Thank you for all the letters. There are some with illustrations in them and I enjoy reading them. Please wait for a reply. (I always say this) I will reply!

o About Motorcycles
I want to buy one, but my editor stopped me. *(laugh)*

← He thinks I'll definitely get into an accident. There's no trust...But I feel the same way

条件反射
Reflex

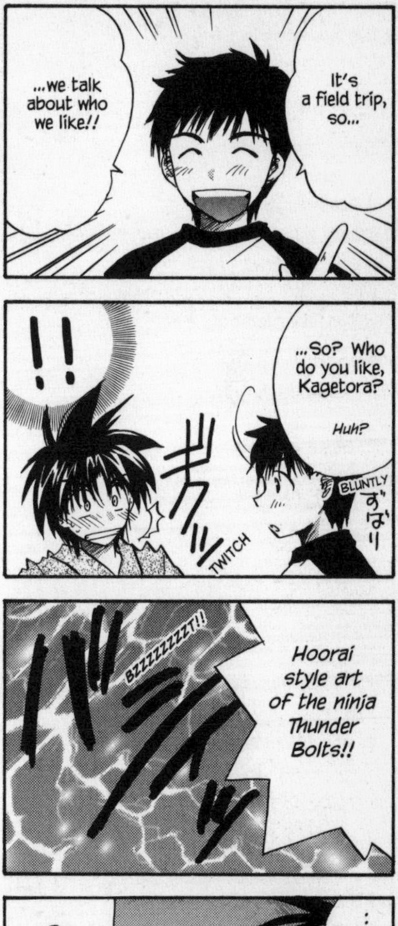
It's a field trip, so...
...we talk about who we like!!
...So? Who do you like, Kagetora?
Huh?
BLUNTLY
ずばり
!!
TWITCH
Hoorai style art of the ninja Thunder Bolts!!
BZZZZZZZZT!!
An incident on the last night of the field trip.
......
Shoot
SIZZLE
SIZZLE
SIZZLE

大同小異
Lost and Found

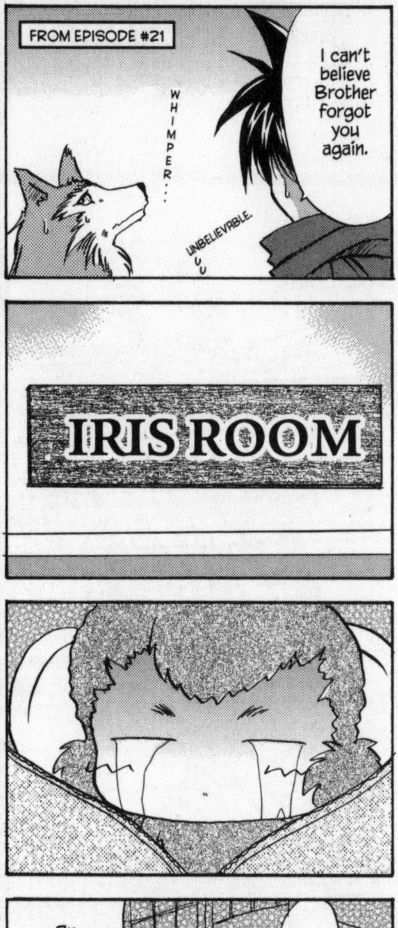
FROM EPISODE #21
I can't believe Brother forgot you again.
WHIMPER...
UNBELIEVABLE.
IRIS ROOM
An incident on the last night of the field trip.
....
ぽつ— ん
SILENCE

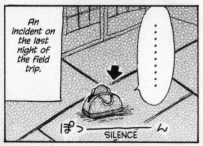

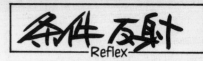

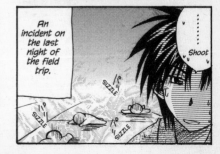

近況報告
Recently

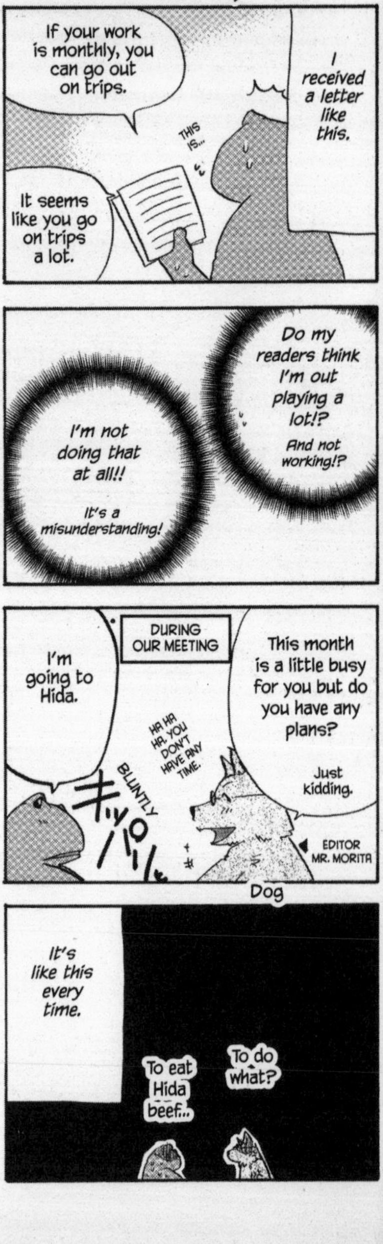
I received a letter like this.
If your work is monthly, you can go out on trips.
This is...
It seems like you go on trips a lot.
Do my readers think I'm out playing a lot!?
And not working!?
I'm not doing that at all!!
It's a misunderstanding!
DURING OUR MEETING
This month is a little busy for you but do you have any plans?
Just kidding.
EDITOR MR. MORITA
Dog
HA HA HA. YOU DON'T HAVE ANY TIME.
BLUNTLY
キッパリ
I'm going to Hida.
It's like this every time.
To do what?
To eat Hida beef...

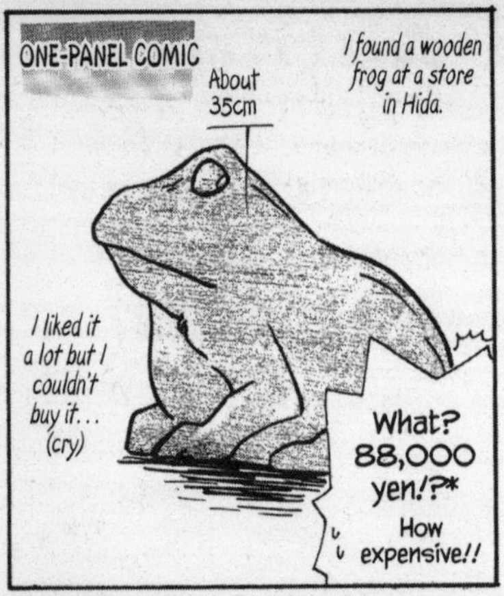
ONE-PANEL COMIC
I found a wooden frog at a store in Hida.
About 35cm
What? 88,000 yen!?*
How expensive!!
I liked it a lot but I couldn't buy it... (cry)

Why was it so expensive? I didn't get it...

*$880.00

Special Thanks

アシスタント‥田中くん・大島ちゃん
Assistants: Tanaka-kun, Oshima-chan

担当‥森田氏
Editor: Mr. Morita

コミックス担当‥法土さん
Comic Editor: Houdou-san

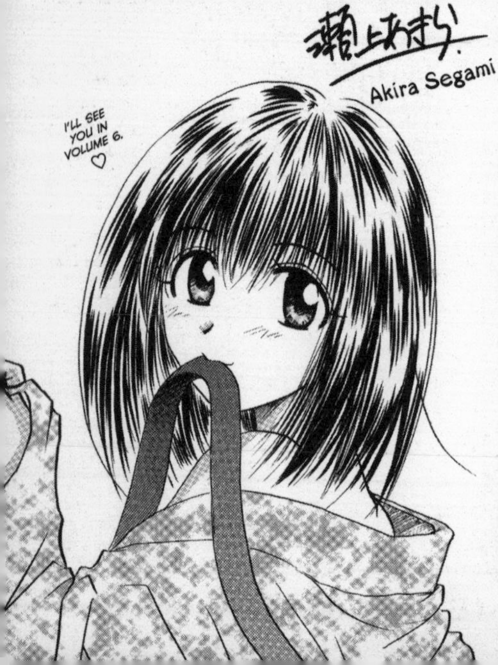
瀬上あきら
Akira Segami
I'LL SEE YOU IN VOLUME 6. ♡

About the Author

Akira Segami's first manga was published by Shogakukan in 1996. He went on to do a few other small projects, including two short stories entitled "Kagetora" in 2001 and 2002. The character proved to be popular with fans, so Segami began his first ongoing series, Kagetora, with Kodansha in 2003. The series continues to run today.

Translation Notes

Japanese is a tricky language for most Westerners, and translation is often more art than science. For your edification and reading pleasure, here are notes on some of the places where we could have gone in a different direction in our translation of the work, or where a Japanese cultural reference is used.

Hakkouda, page 16

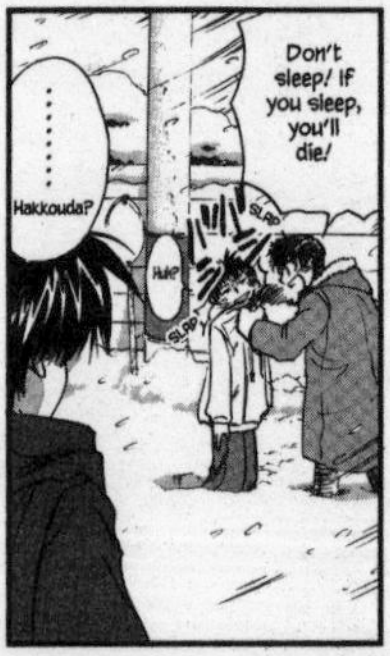
Don't sleep! If you sleep, you'll die!
SLAP
SLAP
Huh?
......
Hakkouda?

"Hakkouda Mountain" is a famous movie from 1977. It is about 199 soldiers dying in a snow storm. It is based on a true story from 1902. In the movie, there is a famous scene where the captain slaps his soldiers saying these exact words.

Sneezing, page 31

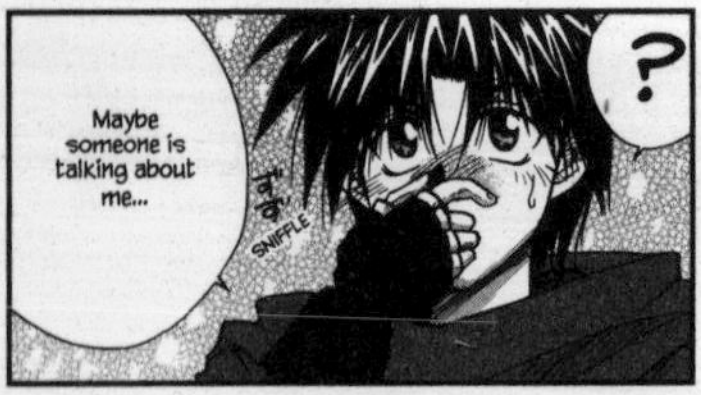
?
SNIFFLE
Maybe someone is talking about me...

The Japanese have an idea that when you sneeze, someone is saying something about you. If you sneeze once, someone is saying something good; if you sneeze twice, someone is saying something bad. If you sneeze three times or more, it is just a cold.

Yamato Nadeshiko, page 39

Yamato Nadeshiko means a true or ideal Japanese woman, according to Japanese culture. Some of the desired characteristics include feminine, chaste, devoted, and willing to do anything for her husband.

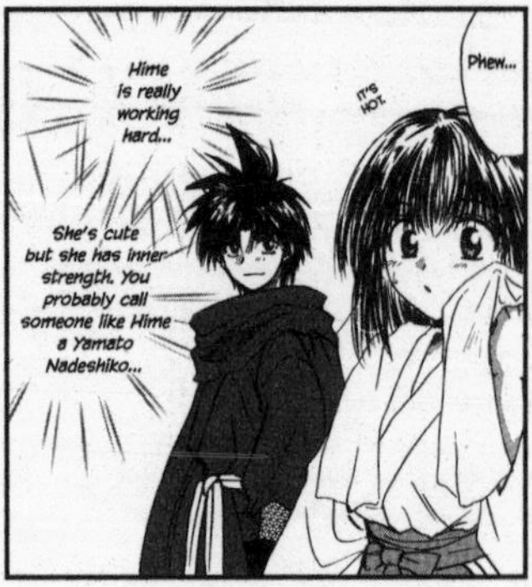
Phew...
IT'S HOT
Hime is really working hard...
She's cute but she has inner strength. You probably call someone like Hime a Yamato Nadeshiko...

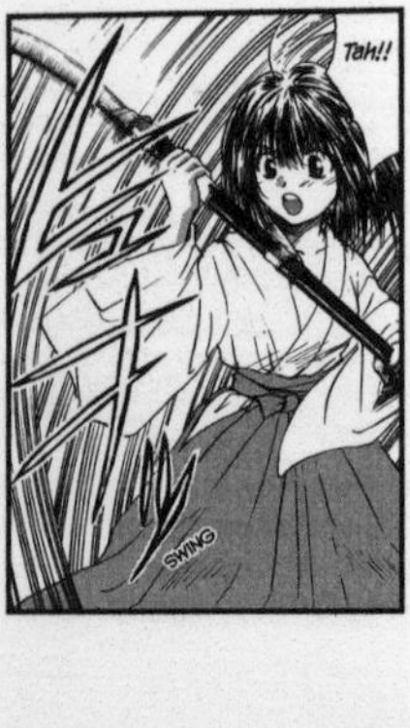
Tah!!
SWING

Naginata, page 39

A *naginata* is a long-handled sword. It looks like a spear with a short sword at the tip of it. In modern Japan, it is usually a martial art for women.

-han, page 46

Adding "-han" instead of "-san" is a convention of those speaking with a Kansai (western region) accent. Not only would one add it to someone's name (i.e. Kagetora-han), they would replace it for onee-han (older sister) or okaa-san (mother) as well.

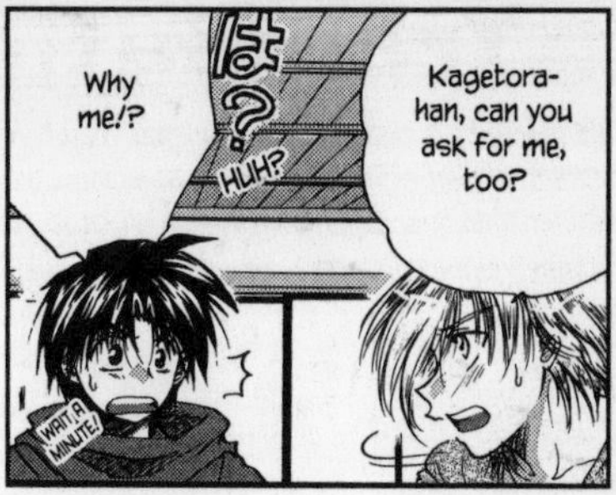
Kagetora-han, can you ask for me, too?
は？
HUH?
Why me!?
WAIT A MINUTE!

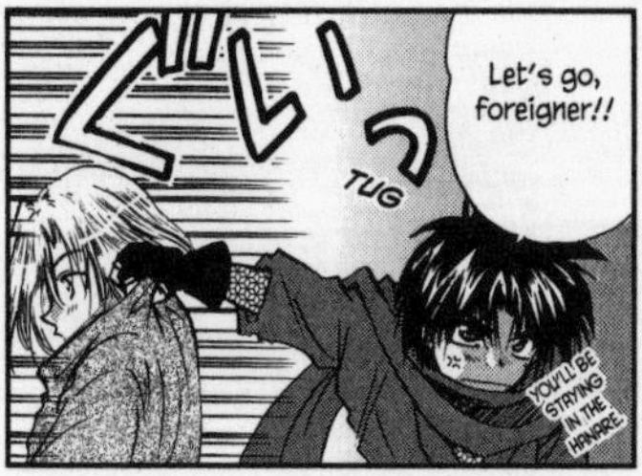
Let's go, foreigner!!
ぐいっ
TUG
YOU'LL BE STAYING IN THE HANARE.

Hanare, page 48

Hanare is a detached building, separate from the main building in classical Japanese homes. Usually farm machines and implements are kept inside of the *Hanare.* The Toudou family *Hanare* is where Kagetora lives.

Keith's accent, page 49

In the original Japanese, Keith's Japanese dialogue was written to have a western region accent, similar to how they speak in Kyoto. When translated into English, the nuances of this particular accent cannot be captured or replicated. A Kyoto accent is a little gentler than the more common Osaka accent. Geisha typically have a Kyoto accent.

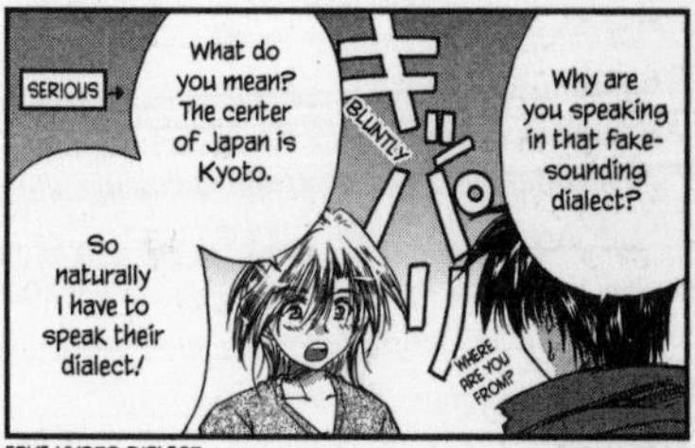
Why are you speaking in that fake-sounding dialect?
キッパリ
BLUNTLY
What do you mean? The center of Japan is Kyoto.
SERIOUS →
WHERE ARE YOU FROM?
So naturally I have to speak their dialect!

FAKE KYOTO DIALECT

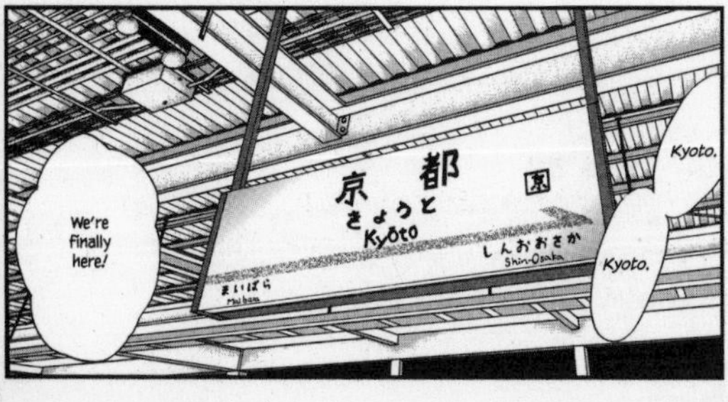
Kyoto.
Kyoto.
京都
きょうと
Kyoto
しんおおさか
Shin-Osaka
まいばら
Maibara
We're finally here!

Kyoto, page 73

Kyoto is the former capital of Japan, located in the western region. It is a popular spot for field trips, mainly because of the many historical sites. There are many temples and shrines to visit.

I'm going to work hard!!
Whoa.
Nice view. ♡
Kiyomizu Temple

Kiyomizu Temple, page 76

The Kiyomizu Temple is one of the most famous temples in Japan. There is a veranda called the Kiyomizu Stage, and there is a saying in Japanese, "Do it like you're jumping off the Kiyomizu Stage." This came from the fact that many people jumped off the Kiyomizu Stage hoping their wish would come true.

Oh, we can see the Otowa Falls.
See?
Hime...

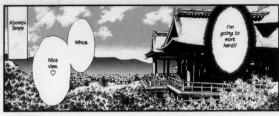

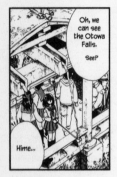

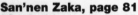

Otowa Falls, page 76

The Otowa Falls is a waterfall where three channels of water fall, and visitors can drink the water. This water is said to be very pure and the Japanese believed that it brought you good health and longevity.

OH!
Speaking of life expectancy...
San'nen Zaka (San'nei Zaka)
...they say that if you fall here, you're going to die within three years.
Yeah.
But it's probably just an urban legend.

San'nen Zaka, page 81

San'nen Zaka, also known as San'nei Zaka, literally translates to "three-year hill." Among the children in Kyoto, it is said that if you fall here, you will die within three years. Therefore, you hardly see children running around in this area. San'nen Zaka is very steep, and it is tiring to walk up this hill, especially in the summer.

Look, Kagetora.
MONKEY DHARMA
This looks just like Kosuke.

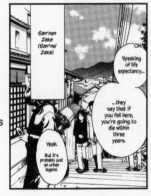

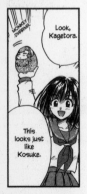

Dharmas, page 81

Yuki is holding a dharma that is shaped like a monkey. Usually dharmas are round and red with blank eyes. You fill in one eye to make a wish, and when that wish is fulfilled, you fill in the other eye. Other than the original red, round dharma, there are other shapes. One of the most famous ones is the "fortune-telling cats" typically found in a Japanese restaurant. These various dharmas are sold at all tourist spots, not just in Kyoto.

Uzumasa Movie Village, page 85

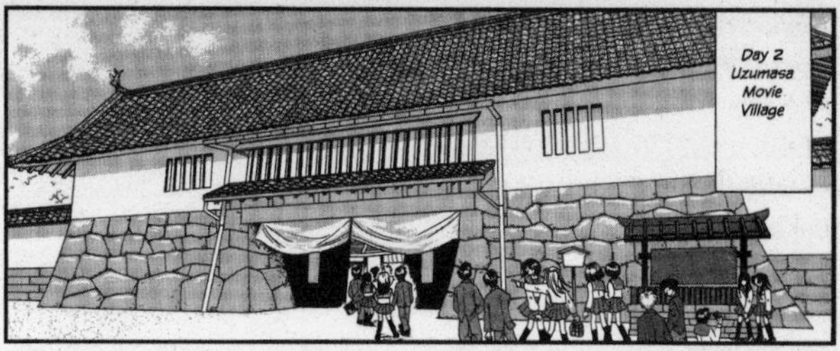

Day 2 Uzumasa Movie Village

The Uzumasa Movie Village is a movie set open to the public. They usually film period dramas where people are slain with swords. Along with the cosplaying house Kagetora and Yuki visit, there is a haunted house and other events. Toei Studio, one of the biggest movie production studios in Japan, runs it.

Shinsengumi, page 86

The Shinsengumi are a band of warriors formed in the late shogunate period to protect the shogunate. Their uniform was an easily identifiable outfit with a jacket that had light blue and white zig zags.

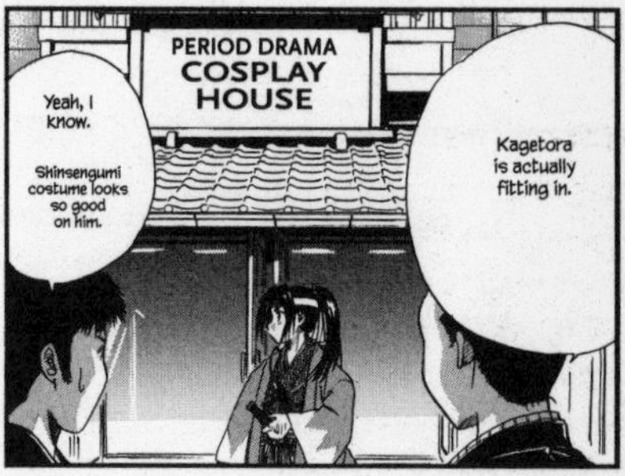

PERIOD DRAMA COSPLAY HOUSE
Kagetora is actually fitting in.
Yeah, I know.
Shinsengumi costume looks so good on him.

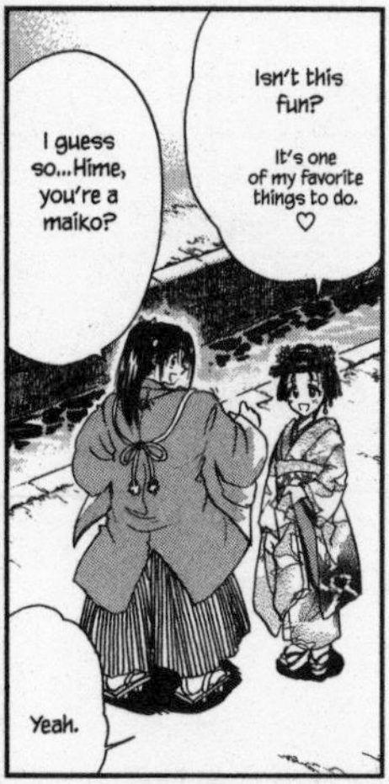

Isn't this fun?
It's one of my favorite things to do. ♡
I guess so...Hime, you're a maiko?
Yeah.

Maiko, page 87

A maiko is an apprentice to a geisha. They are usually easy to distinguish by their tall shoes and ornate kimono. Only girls under the age of twenty can become a maiko, so usually they start their training in junior high or after they graduate junior high school.

Hara-kiri, page 89

Hara-kiri literally translates to "stomach cutting." It is a form of suicide in which men slashed their abdomen. A detailed ritual of a hara-kiri involved dressing ceremonially, sitting properly, and stabbing the short knife into the stomach. Usually a close friend then decapitated him.

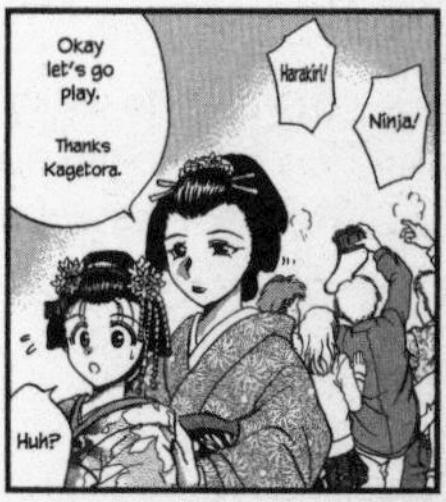

Harakiri!
Ninja!
Okay let's go play.
Thanks Kagetora.
Huh?

Yasaka Shrine, page 99

Yasaka Shrine is also known as the Gion Shrine. The Gion Festival, one of the most famous festivals in Japan, is held there.

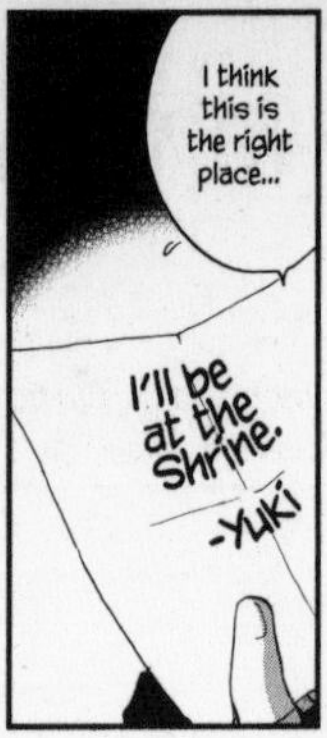
I think this is the right place...
I'll be at the Shrine. -Yuki

Hotaru-nee, page 112

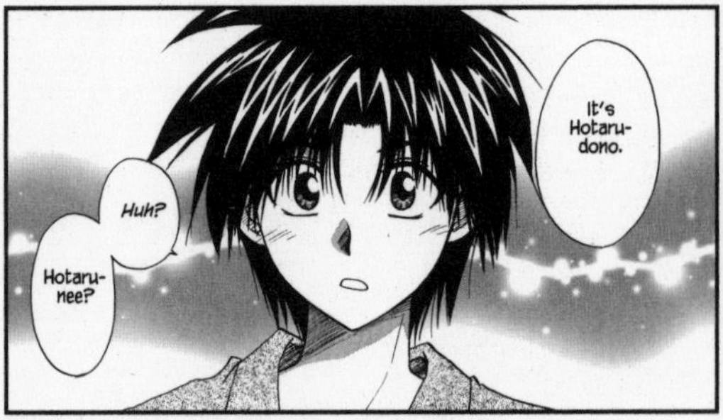
It's Hotaru-dono.
Huh?
Hotaru-nee?

Kagetora refers to Hotaru with the suffix of "-nee." This is a shortened version of "onee-chan," which means "older sister." Hotaru and Kagetora are not siblings, but Japanese kids tend to call the older people around them "older sis" or "older bro." It shows how close Kagetora and Hotaru were when he was in training When Kagetora and Hotaru meet each other again, Kagetora calls her "Hotaru-dono," indicating respect, but then toward the end returns to calling her "Hotaru-nee" to indicate affection.

Nikkou Edo Village, page 181

Located in Tochigi prefecture, the Nikkou Edo Village is an amusement park with samurai houses and ninja displays. There are performances by actors dressed up as ninjas in a house with trap doors and special effects.

Hida, page 181

Hida is located in the Gifu prefecture, north of Nagoya prefecture. The sarubobo Segami talks about is a charm famous in Hida. They are meant to bring good luck in marriage and childbirth. Hida is also famous for their Hida beef, which is equal in quality to Kobe beef.

Preview of Volume 6

We are pleased to present you a preview from volume 6.
This volume is available now.

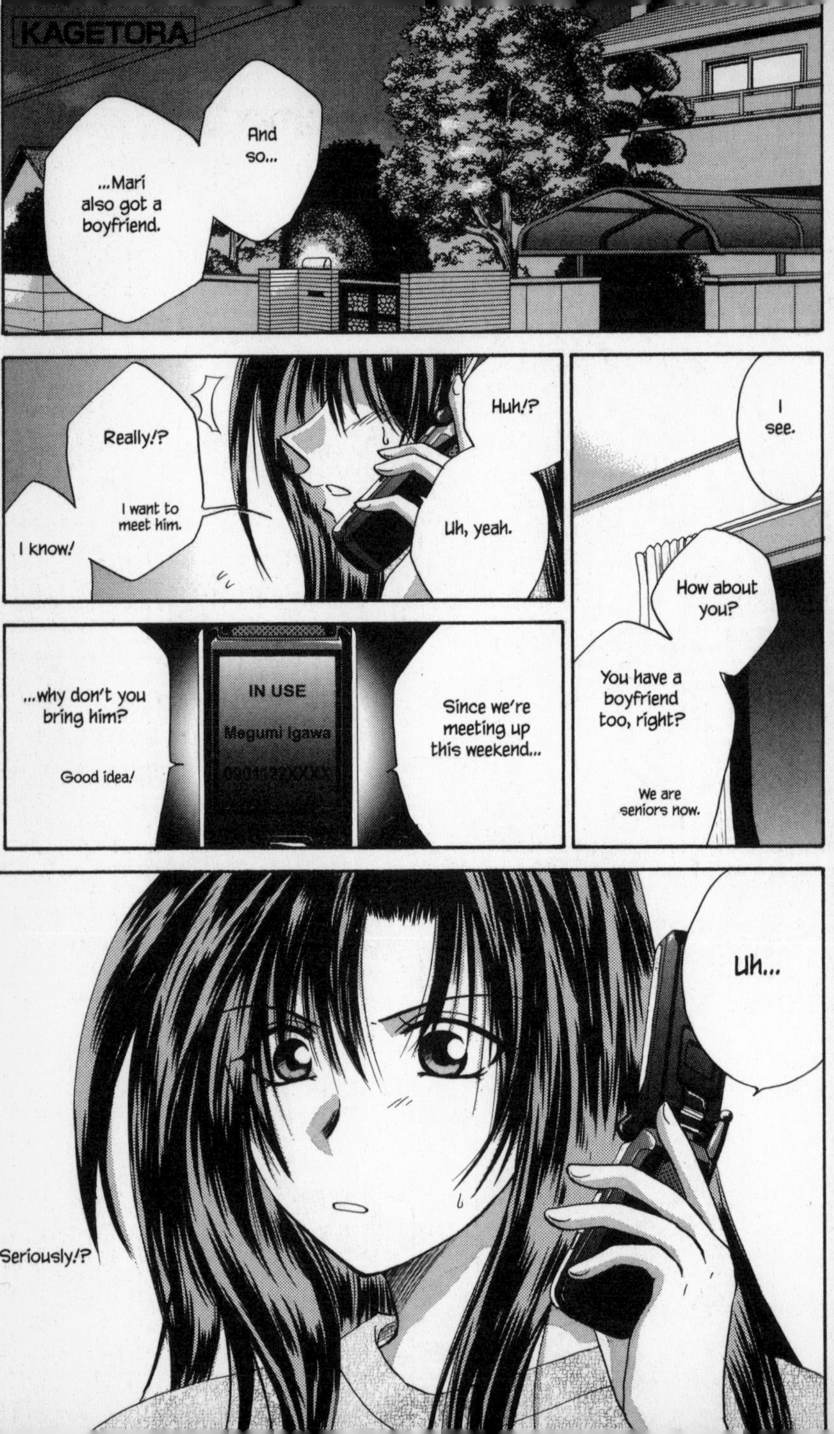
And so...
...Mari also got a boyfriend.
I see.
How about you?
You have a boyfriend too, right?
We are seniors now.
Huh!?
Uh, yeah.
Really!?
I want to meet him.
I know!
Since we're meeting up this weekend...
IN USE
Megumi Igawa
...why don't you bring him?
Good idea!
Uh...
Seriously!?

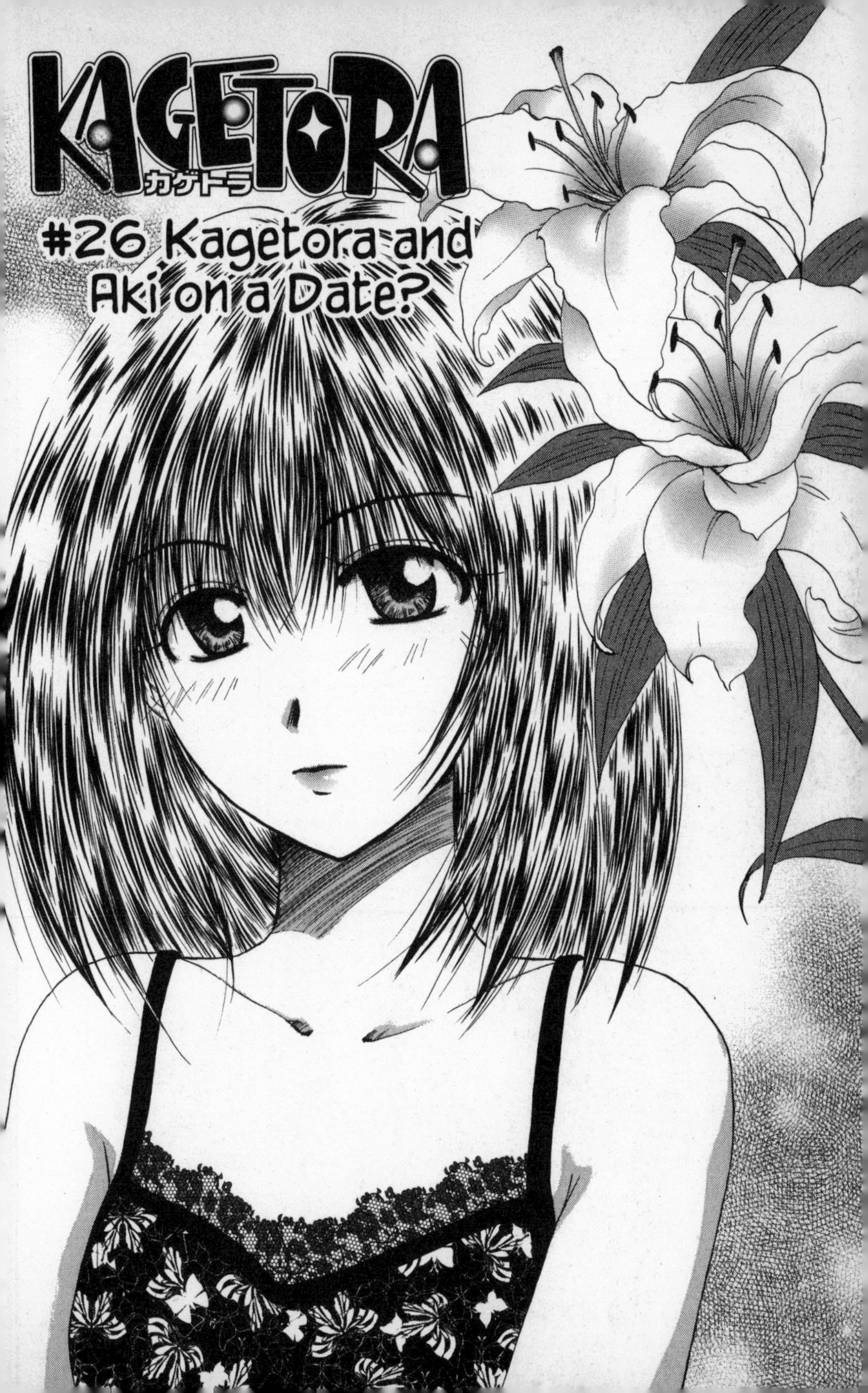
KAGETORA
カゲトラ
#26 Kagetora and Aki on a Date?

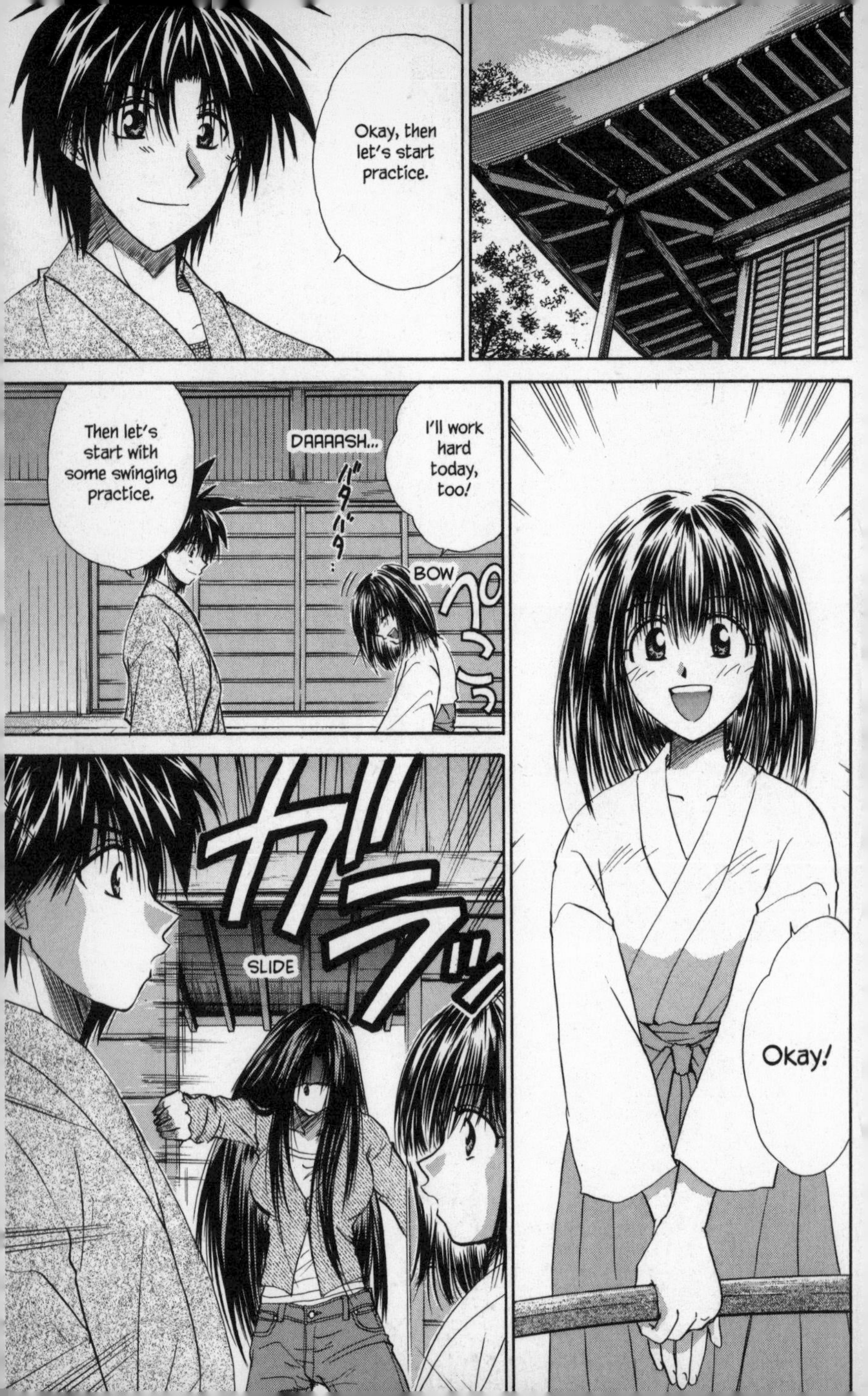
Okay, then let's start practice.
Okay!
I'll work hard today, too!
DAAAASH...
バタバタ…
BOW
ぺこっ
Then let's start with some swinging practice.
ガラッ
SLIDE

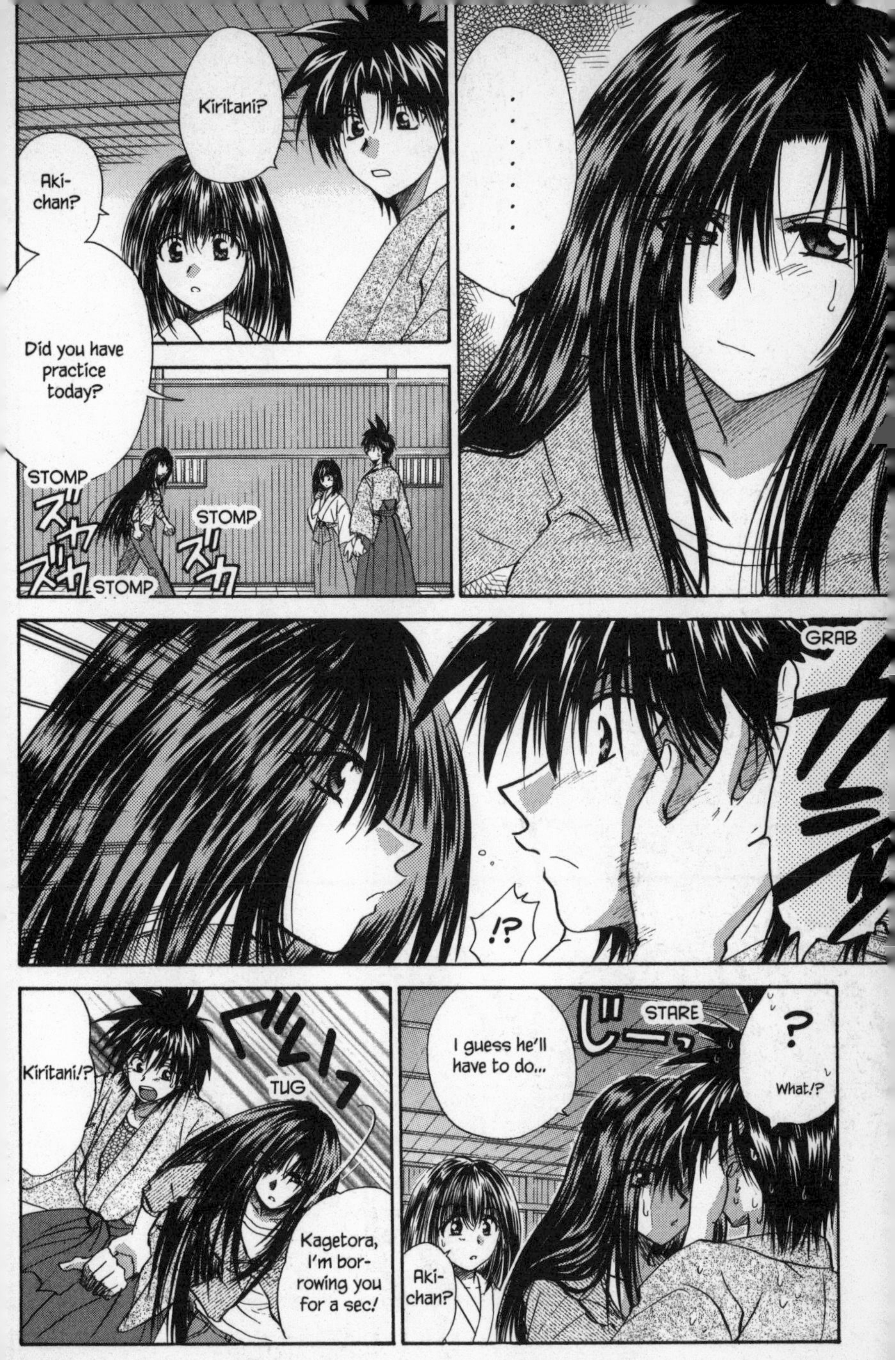
. . . .
Kiritani?
Aki-chan?
Did you have practice today?
STOMP
STOMP
STOMP
GRAB
!?
?
What!?
STARE
I guess he'll have to do...
Aki-chan?
TUG
Kiritani!?
Kagetora, I'm bor-rowing you for a sec!

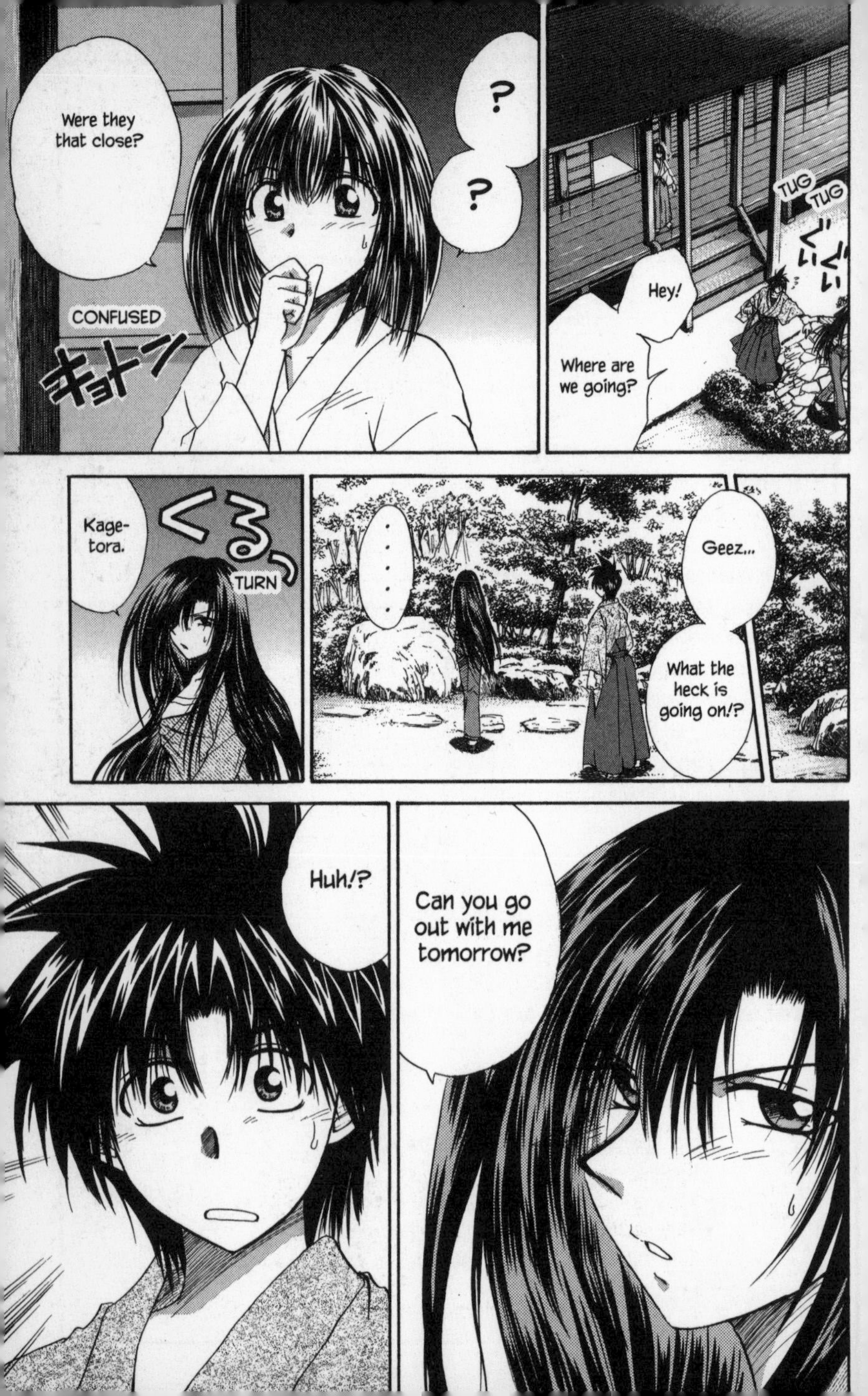
TUG TUG
ぐいぐい
Hey!
Where are we going?
?
?
Were they that close?
CONFUSED
キョトン
Geez...
What the heck is going on!?
......
Kage-tora.
くるっ
TURN
Can you go out with me tomorrow?
Huh!?

BY Oh!great

Itsuki Minami needs no introduction—everybody's heard of the "Babyface" of the Eastside. He's the strongest kid at Higashi Junior High School, easy on the eyes but dangerously tough when he needs to be. Plus, Itsuki lives with the mysterious and sexy Noyamano sisters. Life's never dull, but it becomes downright dangerous when Itsuki leads his school to victory over vindictive Westside punks with gangster connections. Now he stands to lose his school, his friends, and everything he cares about. But in his darkest hour, the Noyamano girls give him an amazing gift, one that just might help him save his school: a pair of Air Trecks. These high-tech skates are more than just supercool. They'll enable Itsuki to execute the wildest, most aggressive moves ever seen—and introduce him to a thrilling and terrifying new world.

Ages: 16 +

Special extras in each volume! Read them all!

VISIT WWW.DELREYMANGA.COM TO:
- Read sample pages
- View release date calendars for upcoming volumes
- Sign up for Del Rey's free manga e-newsletter
- Find out the latest about new Del Rey Manga series

BY JIN KOBAYASHI

SUBTLETY IS FOR WIMPS!

She . . . is a second-year high school student with a single all-consuming question: Will the boy she likes ever really notice her?

He . . . is the school's most notorious juvenile delinquent, and he's suddenly come to a shocking realization: He's got a huge crush, and now he must tell her how he feels.

Life-changing obsessions, colossal foul-ups, grand schemes, deep-seated anxieties, and raging hormones—School Rumble portrays high school as it really is: over-the-top comedy!

Ages: 16 +

Special extras in each volume! Read them all!

VISIT WWW.DELREYMANGA.COM TO:
• Read sample pages
• View release date calendars for upcoming volumes
• Sign up for Del Rey's free manga e-newsletter
• Find out the latest about new Del Rey Manga series

Pastel

by Toshihiko Kobayashi

I LOVE YUU

Poor 16-year-old Mugi Tadano is left heartbroken after his girl-friend moves away. A summer job at his friend Kazuki's beachside snack bar/hotel seems like the perfect way to get his mind off the breakup. Soon Kazuki sets Mugi up on a date with a girl named Yuu, who's supposed to be...well...a little less than perfect. But when Yuu arrives, she's not the monster that either of the boys had imagined. In fact, Yuu is about the cutest girl that Mugi has ever seen. But after Mugi accidentally walks in on Yuu while she's in the bath, Yuu is furious. When Mugi goes to apologize the next day, he learns that Yuu has left the island. Mugi vows to search high and low for her, but will he ever see the beautiful Yuu again?

Ages: 16+

Special extras in each volume! Read them all!

VISIT WWW.DELREYMANGA.COM TO:
- View release date calendars for upcoming volumes
- Sign up for Del Rey's free manga e-newsletter
- Find out the latest about new Del Rey Manga series

Nodame Cantabile

BY TOMOKO NINOMIYA

WINNER OF THE 2003 MANGA OF THE YEAR AWARD FROM KODANSHA

The son of a famous pianist, music student Shinichi Chiaki has always wanted to study abroad and become a conductor like his mentor. However, his fear of planes and water make it impossible for him to follow his dream. As he watches other young students achieve what he has always wanted, Shinichi ponders whether to quit music altogether.

Then one day he meets a fellow music student named Megumi Noda, also known as Nodame. This oddball girl cannot cook, clean, or even read her own score, but she can play the piano in incomparable Cantabile style. And she teaches Shinichi something that he has forgotten: to enjoy his music no matter where he is.

Ages: 16 +

Special extras in each volume! Read them all!

VISIT WWW.DELREYMANGA.COM TO:
• Read sample pages
• View release date calendars for upcoming volumes
• Sign up for Del Rey's free manga e-newsletter
• Find out the latest about new Del Rey Manga series

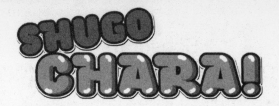

SHUGO CHARA!

PEACH-PIT

Creators of *Dears* and *Rozen Maiden*

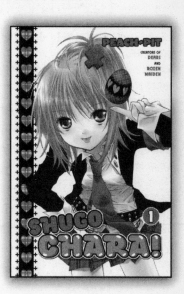

Everybody at Seiyo Elementary thinks that stylish and super-cool Amu has it all. But nobody knows the *real* Amu, a shy girl who wishes she had the courage to truly be herself. Changing Amu's life is going to take more than wishes and dreams—it's going to take a little magic! One morning, Amu finds a surprise in her bed: three strange little eggs. Each egg contains a Guardian Character, an angel-like being who can give her the power to be someone new. With the help of her Guardian Characters, Amu is about to discover that her true self is even more amazing than she ever dreamed.

PEACH-PIT
CREATORS OF DEARS AND ROZEN MAIDEN
SHUGO CHARA!
1

Special extras in each volume! Read them all!

VISIT WWW.DELREYMANGA.COM TO:
- Read sample pages
- View release date calendars for upcoming volumes
- Sign up for Del Rey's free manga e-newsletter
- Find out the latest about new Del Rey Manga series

RATING T AGES 13+

DEL REY MANGA デルレイ

The Otaku's Choice

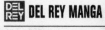

TOMARE!

[STOP!]

You are going the wrong way!

Manga is a completely different
type of reading experience.

To start at the *beginning*, go to the *end*!

That's right! Authentic manga is read the traditional Japanese
way—from right to left. Exactly the opposite of how American
books are read. So flip to the other end of
the book, and read each page—and each panel—from right side
to left side, starting at the top right. Now you're experiencing
manga as it was meant to be.